THE ENGLISH COURT IN EXILE

JAMES II. AT SAINT-GERMAIN

BY

EDWIN AND MARION SHARPE GREW
AUTHORS OF "THE COURT OF WILLIAM III"

ILLUSTRATED

MILLS & BOON, LIMITED
49 RUPERT, STREET
LONDON, W.

Printing Statement:

Due to the very old age and scarcity of this book, many of the pages may be hard to read due to the blurring of the original text, possible missing pages, missing text, dark backgrounds and other issues beyond our control.

Because this is such an important and rare work, we believe it is best to reproduce this book regardless of its original condition.

Thank you for your understanding.

JAMES II.
From the Painting by Largillière.

Published 1911

PREFACE

In "The English Court in Exile" the authors have sought to reconstruct the life of James II. and his family at the Château of Saint-Germain-en-Laye, and their relations with the French Court after their precipitate flight from London in 1688. The history of the exiles has been written nearly chronologically, and in the order in which it naturally groups itself about the successive attempts and corresponding failures of James and his supporters to recover the throne of England. The most notable and important of these attempts was James's expedition to Ireland, which accordingly occupies a distinct portion of the book.

The authors have drawn their materials from contemporary diaries, memoirs, histories, pamphlets, and manuscripts. Among the last-named, special interest attaches to one which furnishes a list of items of expenditure by Louis XIV. on behalf of his guests at Saint-Germain, for which grateful acknowledgment must be made to M. Dunoyer, of the "Archives de France" in Paris; and the list of residents at the Château of Saint-Germain, for which they have to thank Mr Richard W. Goulding, the Librarian at Welbeck Abbey. To Mr Goulding the authors are again indebted, as in a previous volume, for his kindness in reading the proofs and for many useful suggestions. Miss Constance Lingen gave them much valuable help in copying MSS., both in Paris and at the British Museum. They desire further to acknowledge their indebtedness to the Duke of Portland, who granted them permission to make extracts from the Welbeck archives; and to Mr D. A. Chart, of the State Record Office, Dublin, for contemporary references.

The courtesy titles in use at the French Court, though frequently recurring, are very confusing, and the following list may be found useful for reference:—

"Monsieur": brother of Louis XIV., Philippe, Duc d'Orléans.

"Monseigneur": the Dauphin, son of Louis XIV.

"Madame": second wife of "Monsieur," a Bavarian Princess.

"Mademoiselle": Anne Marie de Montpensier, granddaughter of Henri IV.

Duc de Chartres: son of "Monsieur" and "Madame."

La Princesse de Conti,
Madame la Duchesse,
Mademoiselle de Blois, afterwards Duchess de Chartres.
} The three illegitimate daughters of Louis XIV., sometimes called "The Princesses."

CONTENTS

	PAGE
INTRODUCTORY	1

PART I.—THE RECEPTION IN FRANCE

CHAP.
1. CLOSING EVENTS OF JAMES II.'S REIGN—FLIGHT OF THE QUEEN AND PRINCE OF WALES TO FRANCE . 5
2. FLIGHT OF JAMES . 23
3. ARRIVAL OF THE FUGITIVES IN FRANCE . 44
4. SAINT-GERMAIN-EN-LAYE . 58
5. FIRST IMPRESSIONS AT SAINT-GERMAIN . 77
6. GAIETIES AT THE FRENCH COURT . 98
7. MARIA IN JAMES'S ABSENCE — THE CONVENT OF CHAILLOT . 114

PART II.—IRELAND

8. THE EXPEDITION TO IRELAND . 143
9. JAMES'S IRISH ARMY . 167
10. DUBLIN . 188
11. THE FAILURE OF THE IRISH CAMPAIGN . 212

PART III.—THE JACOBITE COURT

CHAP.		PAGE
12.	REVIVAL OF JACOBITE HOPES	243
13.	THE HOUSEHOLD AT SAINT-GERMAIN	262
14.	FRESH SCHEMES FOR AN INVASION OF ENGLAND	288
15.	BIRTH OF A PRINCESS—THE ENGLISH JACOBITES	312
16.	JAMES AT LA TRAPPE	331
17.	FURTHER JACOBITE NEGOTIATIONS—THE ASSASSINATION PLOT	347
18.	TREATY OF RYSWICK—END OF JAMES'S HOPES	366
19.	JAMES II.'S FORLORN HOPES FROM THE PAPACY AND SCOTLAND—PORTLAND'S MISSION	383
20.	JAMES'S LAST DAYS AND DEATH	408

LIST OF ILLUSTRATIONS

James II. . . . . *Frontispiece*	
From the painting by Largillière.	
	FACING PAGE
Le Duc de Lauzun	17
By Rigaud.	
"Mademoiselle"	48
An Apartment of the English Royal Family at Saint-Germain	64
Reproduced by permission of M. Salomon Reinach.	
"Monsieur"	74
Maria, Wife of James II.	115
Reproduced from the portrait in the Museum of Saint-Germain by permission of M. Salomon Reinach.	
Louis XIV.	118
By Rigaud.	
Richard Talbot, Duke of Tyrconnel	156
From a portrait in the National Portrait Gallery.	
Fanny Jennings, Lady Tyrconnel	194
John Drummond, Lord Melfort	222
John Caryll	272
From "West Grinstead et les Caryll," by M. de Trenqualéon.	
James Drummond, Earl of Perth	274

	FACING PAGE
"Madame"	282
James II., his wife Maria, and their two children . .	365
Prince James Stuart (the Old Pretender) and his sister Princess Louise	371

From a picture in the National Portrait Gallery.

The Monument to James II. in the Parish Church of Saint-Germain-en-Laye	430

The English Court in Exile

INTRODUCTORY

NOTHING in the history of the Stuarts at Saint-Germain-en-Laye is more impressive than the obliteration which overtook, not only their mortal remains, and the places associated with them, but nearly all the most treasured archives of their House—memoirs, correspondence, State papers, and family records. The pious Jacobite of to-day, searching for some traces of the last Stuart King of England in the home of his exile, will search in vain. Only a modest marble monument in the modern parish church recalls the association of James II. with Saint-Germain-en-Laye. Of those Stuart papers which safely reached the hands of James II.'s son, James III., as he was known to his faithful followers, all but a remnant perished through the ignorance or negligence of their custodians; and of the priceless records of his House that were preserved in France, few indeed escaped the fury of the Revolution.

But though much is taken, much remains—enough to reconstruct the scenes and characters of James II.'s closing years: years of failure and disappointment, of frustrated hopes and abortive projects, but years sweetened to the melancholy old man by the consolations of religion, and the belief that the pious exercises of his latter days expiated the sins of his youth. It was his oft-repeated reflection that in losing his crown he had gained his soul. For in the obstinate perversity of the last acts of his reign, the violation of constitutional liberties, which drove his distracted people into the arms of William of Orange, James II. was actuated by but one motive. The Revolution of 1688 was brought about by the King's efforts to impose Roman Catholicism on his unwilling people; and it should always be remembered to his credit, that he sacrificed his crown to his convictions. If James II. would have declared himself a Protestant, or even consented before it was too late to safeguard the religious independence of his Protestant subjects, then, in the opinion of the men best able to judge at the time, William of Orange would have had little chance of retaining the throne. James II. remained steadfast in his loyalty to Rome, clinging to his convictions with the enthusiasm of a convert and the tenacity of a narrow understanding, and in consequence he was destined to continue a pensioner on the French King's bounty till the end of his life.

Part I

The Reception in France

CHAPTER I

CLOSING EVENTS OF JAMES II.'S REIGN—FLIGHT OF THE QUEEN AND PRINCE OF WALES TO FRANCE

No one is more ignorant of what is going on about him than an unpopular man. The happy, instinctive comprehension of what is passing in other people's minds that we call tact, enables its possessor to gauge the current of public opinion and to steer clear among the shoals of prejudice. James might have been deaf and blind for all he realised the passion of indignation and religious fervour that he had roused among his people by his persecution of the Seven Bishops for refusing to read his illegal Declaration of Indulgence.[1]

Safeguarded though he was by the doctrines of the divine right of kings and the duty of passive obedience, James's attack on the Church had undermined the loyalty of the clergy. "We honour you, but we fear God," Bishop Ken had exclaimed in self-defence to the King, when refusing to read his Declaration. Unfortunately for James, it was while the enthusiasm for the persecuted Bishops was at its height that his Queen, Maria d'Este, Mary of Modena, as she

---

[1] Suspending the Penal Statutes against Roman Catholics and Protestant dissenters.

was called, gave him an heir to the throne, the Prince afterwards to be recognised by Louis XIV. as James III., and known in history as the Old Pretender.

The child, whom the people believed to be supposititious, and foisted on them by Jesuit fraud to secure a Roman Catholic heir to the throne, was born on June 10th. On the 30th the Seven Bishops were acquitted, and on the same day another "immortal Seven" sent to the nearest Protestant heir to the throne, James's son-in-law, William of Orange, that authoritative invitation for which he had long been waiting and preparing. In six months from the birth of his son James was a fugitive and a refugee. But, strange as it seems now, it was impossible to convince him at the time of the critical character of the situation or of his own danger.[1] His adviser, Sunderland, who had already urged lenity in the case of the Bishops' prosecution, again counselled pacific measures in vain, and put himself so much out of favour by doing so that he was obliged to buy back his master's good graces by an apostasy that he afterwards declared to have been simulated.

James refused to give credence to the rumours of his son-in-law's designs, and was content to remain in ignorance of them. In September the Comte de Gramont, arriving in Paris from England, reported that all was quiet in that country, notwithstanding the apparent intention of the Prince of Orange to invade it. As late as the 19th of the month it was noted with

[1] When Adda, the Papal nuncio, counselled moderation, James cited the example of his father and brother, whose authority had been weakened by a too great indulgence—an indulgence that had finally caused the "lamented death" of his father (Vatican Transcripts, British Museum).

surprise at Versailles that though there was no longer any doubt about the intention of the Prince of Orange to make a descent upon England, and he was embarking six thousand saddles and all the necessary accoutrements for a large body of cavalry, the King of England was quite unconcerned, and in London all went on as usual.[1]

James had, in fact, been lulled into a false security. Albeville, his envoy at The Hague, an unscrupulous man, who was in the pay both of France and of Holland, had, when on a recent visit to England, expressed it as his opinion that the intentions of Holland to his master were friendly, and, though well aware that the Dutch were preparing an expedition against England, "took pains to infuse into all people that they designed no such thing."[2]

But though James was ignorant of his son-in-law's intentions, Louis XIV. took care to keep himself well informed of them through the Comte d'Avaux, his envoy at The Hague. When news had come in August that the Dutch were raising levies, Louis immediately made preparations for war on his own account. D'Avaux had informed both his master and Barillon, the French ambassador at St James's, of the designs of William of Orange in a manner that left no room for doubt, and the French King took steps to save James in his own despite. The English envoy at Versailles, Colonel Bevil Skelton, had in vain besought James to look into the reports from The Hague. With Skelton's approval, Louis now sent a special envoy, Bonrepaux, to England to assure the King of the danger he was in,

[1] Dangeau, ii.
[2] Burnet, *History of His Own Time.*

and to offer him immediate support. At the same time D'Avaux received orders to announce to the States General that France had taken the King of England under her protection. But these well-meant offers from his all-powerful neighbour, and the suggestion that he needed protection, only served to fire James's vanity. With ill-timed dignity, he asserted his ability to stand alone. He knew he was the King of England, and would show himself to be so when the necessity occurred, he said proudly to the Imperial ambassador.[1] In this attitude he was encouraged by Sunderland, who had now made overtures to William on his own behalf. James finally accepted the assurances of the Dutch ambassador, Van Citters, that the States General had no hostile intentions against him, and Bonrepaux, after an audience in which he was coldly received, returned to France, having accomplished nothing. James declared indignantly to the Papal Nuncio that " adulation and vanity had turned the French King's head." In after years he threw all the blame of his self-deception on Sunderland :—

"My Lord Sunderland found means to work the King rather into a displeasure at the proposal; they remonstrated how ungratefull a thing such troops will be to the people, and that the French King's magnifying the Dutch preparations was but a contrivance to fright his Majesty into an allyance with him. So Mons. Bonrepos finding his master's kindness so ill accepted, returned home again, no less astonished than the Court of France itself, at his Majesty's surprizing security."[2]

[1] Hoffman, ambassador to the Emperor Leopold.
[2] Clarke, *Memoirs of James II.*, vol. ii. 177.

But a time came when even James could no longer deceive himself. The palpable defection of "so many men of quality" who went to join the Prince of Orange, the repeated intelligence from abroad, the visible desertions at home, at last convinced the King that the Dutch preparations for war were intended against himself, "tho' he never gave any real credit to it till about the middle of September; . . . The Earl of Sunderland, whom he trusted most, turned anyone to ridicule that did but seem to believe it."

Meanwhile Louis XIV. had, with strange want of judgment, recalled his armies from Flanders and directed their attack on Germany, leaving the coast clear for William of Orange. The Dutch States General gave their long-delayed consent to William's expedition.[1] At last James understood, and as he fully realised his danger was unnerved by it. The days that follow present a pathetic spectacle of bewildered indiscretions and terrified vacillation. By tardy and wholesale concessions, which deceived nobody, he sought to undo the work of the last five years and propitiate his people. He attempted to make preparations against invasion with an army that he could no longer trust. "Every hour teaches him that his soldiers are his most dangerous enemies," wrote the Imperial ambassador; and "He has still less reason to depend upon the sailors . . . who with even less shame than the army declare they will not serve against Holland. We may therefore say that the whole of the clergy, the whole of the

---

[1] Formal Declaration of States General, October $\frac{18}{28}$; Declaration of William, September 30, enumerating James's illegal acts and asserting that as Mary's husband he was coming with an army to secure a free Parliament.

nobility, the whole of the people, the whole of the military and naval forces are with a few exceptions hostile to the King, which must necessarily keep him apprehensive on every side."[1] In another letter he adds that "the sailors are running away and hiding themselves so as not to be used against their friends the Dutch as they give out";[2] and after enumerating James's attempts at conciliation he comments: "God grant he may not take these steps in vain, in which he proceeds from one extreme to the other, thereby losing credit with his people, who attribute such a change not to genuine repentance but to sheer necessity."[3] Meanwhile all the great nobles, except those whose official positions enforced their attendance at Court, had absented themselves, and retired to their country estates.

But James had at least one loyal friend in his wife, Maria d'Este, a princess of the House of Modena, whom he had married out of a convent when she was little more than a child, and who exhibited at this crisis of their fortunes a high courage and dignified self-control.

Maria d'Este, at fourteen, was already famous for her beauty and accomplishments, when Henry Mordaunt, Earl of Peterborough, came to Modena in 1673 to arrange a second marriage for James, then Duke of York. The marriage negotiations were not at once concluded, though the ambassador wrote enthusiastically to Charles II. of the charm, beauty, and accomplishments of Maria d'Este:—"Sir, I think

---

[1] Hoffman to Emperor Leopold II., October 1, 1688, from the original German, published by Cavelli.
[2] *Ibid.*, October 8.
[3] See also Burnet.

you will find this young Princess to have beauty in her person and her mind, to be faire, tall, well shap'd and very healthful."[1] The reluctance was on the side of Maria herself. Penetrated by the example of her devout mother, the Duchess Laura, and deeply influenced by continual association with the Nuns of the Visitation, whose convent adjoined the palace at Modena, she had set her mind upon the religious life, and resisted and resented all efforts to turn her from it. But in the Church of Rome political and religious interests are always inextricably interwoven. It was important to the Papal schemes that James Duke of York, the future King of England, should marry a wife whose religious principles were of such a firmness as to withstand the pernicious contact with a heretical and light-minded Court. The Pope, Clement X., himself condescended to write a letter to Maria d'Este, in which he exhorted her to: "Keep in view such an advancement of the Catholic Religion as may accrue to this kingdom from your nuptials, and so to enter there upon a wider field of merit than is possible to the cloistered rule of virginity."[2] He adds that facilities for her worshipping according to the Romish ritual should be specially provided for and safeguarded.

On the receipt of this letter the Duchess of Modena and her daughter consented to the marriage, which was concluded in Italy with all haste (lest the English Parliament should learn what was taking place), Peterborough standing proxy. From the first James's second wife was to pay heavily for the sacrifice she had made

[1] Peterborough to Charles II. Record Office.
[2] From the original Latin, published by Cavelli, vol. i. p. 66.

of her own inclinations in consenting to the marriage. On her arrival in England she was met at Dover by her husband, a man of forty, whose eldest daughter was only a few years younger than herself. She had come from the warm, familiar atmosphere of home and friends, and the radiant sun of Italy, to a land whose cold gray skies were typical of the hostility of the strangers among whom she was to live; to a land where the faith for which she had sacrificed all was so detested that her prudent brother-in-law, Charles II., thought it inexpedient to allow her to have any but a private chapel. But at all events James was charmed by his wife's youth and beauty, and this and his genuine devotion to their common faith was some consolation in her loneliness. In a letter to the Mother Superior of the convent at Modena she wrote at this time: "I cry very often and grieve, not being able to free myself from melancholy, but blessed be God this is my cross. May this be a consolation to you, dear my mother,—I say it to the glory of God, that the Lord Duke is a very good man, he has the holy fear of God, and is very well disposed towards me, and would do anything to show it to me; he is so firm and steady in our holy religion, which as a good Catholic he professes, that he would not leave it for anything in the world, and in my griefs, to which is added the departure of my dear mama, this serves as a comfort to me."[1]

In the fifteen years that followed her arrival in England, Mary of Modena was to know every heavy cross that could fall to the lot of woman—last and least, the loss of her crown. With her husband's infidelities

[1] *Secret Archives of the Monastery of the Visitation at Modena.* Published in the original by Cavelli.

we are fortunately unconcerned. But they were flagrant and notorious, and his young wife was deeply wounded by them, not only in her womanly pride and self-respect, but on the grounds of religion and morality. She was herself frequently ailing in health, and her life in England had been still further embittered by the death of her children in infancy. Indeed, the life of the little Prince of Wales who survived was only saved by the intervention of his father, who insisted on his having a wet-nurse, instead of a continuance of the diet of a kind of paste made out of barley flour mixed with water with which his doctors were feeding him.[1] "C'est ainsi qu'on élève à Londres beaucoup d'enfants de qualité," comments a contemporary French diarist.[2] The Prince of Wales's nurse, says Ellis in his "Correspondence," "hath that good effect which is natural and usual to children. . . . The nurse is the wife of a tilemaker, and seems a healthy woman; she came in her cloth petticoat and waistcoat, and old shoes and no stockings, but now she is rigged out by degrees (that the surprise may not alter her in her duty and care) and £100 per annum is already settled upon her, and two or three hundred guineas already given, which she saith that she knows not what to do with."

In all their married life James had done nothing to earn the loyalty and support from his wife which he received abundantly in this supreme crisis of his fortunes.[3] The Queen's courageous dignity and self-

[1] Terriesi, the Tuscan envoy, describes him at the point of death from colic.

[2] Dangeau, ii. 149.

[3] Self-abandonment of James and courage of his wife: *Medici Archives*, Cavelli, ii. 368. Abbé Melani, an Attaché at the Tuscan legation in France, writing to the Grand-Ducal Secretary (L'Abbé

control animated her frightened attendants. All went on at the Court as usual. On October 5th her birthday was celebrated with a Court ball in the evening, at which she and James both appeared with such a show of cheerfulness as they could muster; but by the time the King's birthday, October 24th, came round, things were too serious for even a show of festivity, for the westerly wind which had detained William on his own shores now changed, and a "Protestant wind," as the Prince's supporters called it, blew from the East. William's armaments were, however, delayed by a storm. The Haarlem and Amsterdam Gazettes were ordered to give a dismal relation of the great damage his fleet had sustained, in order to quiet James's apprehensions.[1] It was not till November 2nd that the Prince actually set sail.

Meanwhile James had been preparing to receive him. The Italian Abbé Rizzini[2] had from the first urged that the Queen and the Prince of Wales should be sent to a place of safety, but James had decided that they should not leave England till he saw what measure of success attended the invader, a decision in which Maria gallantly concurred. She gave orders through her secretary, Mr Caryll, that some of the landed property bequeathed to her by her mother should be sold to raise funds for her husband's defence of his

Gondi), December 16th, says that the King, on coming into the Queen's room, almost entirely abandoned himself to despair, notwithstanding his great courage, telling her Majesty that all was lost, while he saw himself betrayed and deserted by his dearest and most trusted servants. . . . The Queen encouraged him.

[1] Oldmixon.

[2] Gaspard Rizzini, a Venetian by birth, but attached to the House of Modena, was for many years one of its most devoted servants, and Modenese Envoy in Paris.

CLOSING EVENTS OF JAMES II.'S REIGN 15

throne and kingdom.[1] A still stronger proof of devotion was her consenting to part with her son, who was despatched to Portsmouth for greater safety. Here his illegitimate brother, the Duke of Berwick, was governor, and the fleet, under the command of Lord Dartmouth, was in readiness to convey him to France.[2]

James's departure for Salisbury to meet the Prince of Orange took place the same day. He arrived there on the 19th November, but the physical weakness resulting from a violent and continued bleeding at the nose which there overtook him, and his despair and bewilderment at the continued defections to the enemy, not merely of his troops but of the members of his own family, completely unhinged him.[3] He hurriedly returned to town. To gain time a council was hastily summoned, a free Parliament was convoked; the Catholic governor of the Tower was dismissed from his post, and that Colonel Skelton who had been instrumental in procuring Bonrepaux's mission to warn James of his danger, and had been summoned home and confined in the Tower for his impertinent zeal, was now created its governor. Messengers were sent to treat with William. All these measures were dictated by the cunning of desperation, for James,[4] "being delivered over to all the contradictions that malice or ingratitude could throw in his way, . . . saw

[1] Adda, Add. MSS., 15,397, f. 432.
[2] Hoffman comments on the folly of this plan, in a letter to the Emperor of October 29th (Cavelli), 3; see also Dartmouth's letter to James, Clarke, ii. 220.
[3] Sir John Reresby: "So terribly possessed of his danger and so deeply afflicted when the Princess Anne went away, that it disordered him in his understanding."
[4] Clarke's *Life*, ii. 227.

no hopes of redress, so turned his whole attention how to save the Queen and Prince his son, and cast about which way to do it, with most security and secrecy."

Here too the King was doomed to disappointment. Lord Dartmouth, who was in correspondence with William, refused his aid; and there was nothing for it but to risk bringing the Prince back to London, which was safely accomplished, though with some danger and difficulty, by Lord and Lady Powis. James's letter and instructions about his son have been preserved.[1] He writes:—

"I think my sonne is not safe (as things are now) where he is, and therefore thinke it necessary to have him removed thence as soon as may be. I have written to Lady Powis to that purpose, if the way be open by land, he shall come that way, and I have sent troops to meet him, and ordered Lord Dover to command them and come up with him. If the Prince of Orange's men gett between this and Portsmouth, then he must come by sea or in a yacht, and you must send what number of ships you judge sufficient to see him as far as Margate, after which he may come o'er the flats, and so up the river without danger."

On the day that James's representatives reached the Prince of Orange at Hungerford, the Prince of Wales arrived at Westminster. An escort had already been decided upon for him and for the Queen in the person of the Comte de Lauzun, who had arrived in England in October on purpose to offer his services to James.

Of the Comte de Lauzun, who at this juncture steps into the history of the Stuarts, his countryman,

---

[1] For full account see Clarke, ii. 235-7, and correspondence of James and Dartmouth, B.M. Ad. MSS., 18,447.

LE DUC DE LAUZUN
By Rigaud.

La Bruyère, remarked that others were not allowed to dream what he had lived. He was, says his friend and relative Saint-Simon, "a little fair man, of good figure, with a noble and an imperious face, but one which was ever without charm, as I have heard people say who knew him when he was young. He was full of ambition and caprice, of fancies, jealous of all, wishing always to go too far; never content with anything; proud in his dealings, disagreeable and malicious by nature, still more so by jealousy and ambition; nevertheless a good friend, when a friend at all (which was rare); a good relative. . . . Extremely brave, as dangerously bold. As a courtier he was equally insolent and satirical, and as cringing as a valet; full of foresight, perseverance, intrigue, and meanness in order to come at his ends; with all this dangerous to the ministers at the Court: feared by all, and of a biting wit which spared nobody."

Saint-Simon shared a pavilion with Lauzun when the Court was at Marly, and in Paris they dined together every other day, so that this curious medley of attributes was applied to the diarist's brother-in-law from the closest personal observation. The intrigues, the adventures, the amours of Lauzun, are an entertaining by-path of history into which we cannot stray far. He had come early to Court, won high favour with the King, to whom he had on one occasion been so insolent, that Louis, turning his back upon him, threw his cane out of the window, and, saying that he should be sorry to strike a man of quality, left the room. Lauzun was sent to the Bastille, from which he soon emerged to secure higher favour than ever. The King consented to his marriage with "Mademoiselle," as she was called, the granddaughter of Henri IV.,[1] and a woman of enormous wealth. But Court intrigues, in which the King's mistress, De Montespan, whom Lauzun had called a hussy to her face, took an active part, resulted in the withdrawal of the royal consent; and not long afterwards Lauzun was sent to a dungeon in the fortress of Pignerol, where he remained for years. Mademoiselle at length succeeded in buying his liberty at the price of immense bequests to Madame de Montespan's illegitimate son, the Duc de Maine. Such in outline was the career of this new friend of the Stuarts.

Before James sent his wife and child with Lauzun to a place of safety, he took the precaution to secure another possession which was rated by him almost as highly—the Memoirs of his Life. These he had kept punctiliously and in great detail. He bethought himself of the Tuscan envoy Terriesi as a trustworthy custodian. Terriesi readily consented to undertake the charge of a box. "So the King having just time to thrust them all confusedly into it, sent it to him, which he, imagining it to be jewels of great value, was exceeding careful of it; tho' that imagination had like to have occasioned its miscarriage. . . . An Italian servant of the envoy's conveyed it safe to Leghorn, as directed; from whence the Grand Duke sent two galleys on purpose to convoy it into France, through which kingdom it was brought likewise guarded up to St Germains, all persons supposing it to be some great treasure: which tho' it was

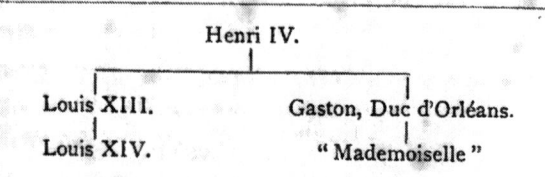

---

[1]
```
              Henri IV.
                 |
        ---------------------
        |                   |
   Louis XIII.      Gaston, Duc d'Orléans.
        |                   |
   Louis XIV.         "Mademoiselle"
```

not of that nature which people imagined it, contained what in itself was much more valuable . . . nine tomes, writ in his own hand, and which . . . he appointed to be lodged in the Scotch College at Paris, where they will remain, not only an eternal, glorious monument of his actions, but a standing model both to his own Royal Posterity and to all Christian Princes of the most perfect resignation while a subject, and the most generous moderation while a king." This aspiration was doomed, like all other hopes of James, to frustration, and the Memoirs perished in the flames of the French Revolution.[1]

Terriesi gave an account of these papers to his master.[2] He describes how James had sent one of

---

[1] Ranke, in repeating the story of the destruction of the original Memoirs, remarks that there is no evidence that Innes, Principal of the Scotch College, had the largest share in their composition, as had been supposed. An abridged work in four volumes was compiled on the life of James II.: the Chevalier de St George underlined it, and after the death of the wife of the last Pretender it passed into the hands of the Benedictines at Rome, and was ultimately purchased by the British Government. On these materials Clarke's *Life of James II.* is founded. It is likely that the original was written in a fragmentary manner—the most detailed portions by James, others compiled by secretaries. Ranke had not access to the Caryll Papers, which show that Maria's secretary, John Caryll, was engaged upon the Memoirs, presumably on the abridged edition. At Welbeck there is a MS. (folio), "Memoires de Jacques Second, Roy de la Grande Bretagne, etc. De glorieuse Memoire. Contenant l'histoire des quatre Campagnes que sa Majesté fit, estant Duc de York, sous Henry de la Tour D'Auvergne, Vicomte de Turenne, dans les Années 1652, 1653, 1654 et 1655. . . . Traduits sur l'Original Anglois écrit de la propre main de sa dite Majesté, conservé par son ordre dans les Archives du Collége des Ecossois à Paris. Le tout certifié et attesté par Reyne Mère et Regente de la Grande Bretagne, etc., MDCCIV."

The volume once belonged to Henri-Oswald de La Tour d'Auvergne, Archbishop of Vienna, afterwards to Augustus Frederic, Duke of Sussex; then to Sir Thomas Phillipps, then to the Duke of Portland.

[2] Archives of Medici at Florence, quoted by Cavelli.

his most confidential servants to him at midnight with important papers and writings, earnestly begging him to take charge of them, as "he knew not where to place them in more honest hands." He added that the previous night, December 9th, the King had also confided to his charge the sum of £3500 guineas, and had requested that his carriage should be sent to convey the Queen and the Prince of Wales from Whitehall. Maria consented unwillingly to this parting, declaring that she could bear with patience the separation from her son, but that she would rather endure "all hardships, hazards, and imprisonment itself" with her husband.

James confided his plans to as few persons as possible. He took into his confidence, besides Lauzun, an Italian gentleman called Francesco Riva, of whose loyalty he was assured, and who held the office of Keeper of the Royal Wardrobe. He was to share with Lauzun the perilous charge of conveying the Queen and Prince to France. About an hour after midnight on the 9th, Riva, disguised as a seaman, went to the King's room by a secret staircase, provided with a disguise for the Queen, who even at that moment clung in tears to the King, protesting that she would die with him. Informing his master that all was ready, Riva withdrew into an adjoining room, where he found Lauzun, and they waited there while the Queen dressed herself. They then started, with the Prince and his two nurses, going by way of the private gardens to an outer door at which Terriesi's carriage was in waiting. The little party entered it hastily, Riva mounting the box with the coachman, so as to be prepared for all emergencies.

Arriving at the Horse Ferry near Westminster, where a little boat equipped as if for a shooting expedition had been ordered by Riva to be in readiness, they crossed the river to Lambeth : the baby happily sleeping through the wind and rain. At Lambeth a page, Dufour, was waiting for them ; but the coach and six that should have been also there had to be fetched from a neighbouring inn, where Riva found the coachman chatting with his friends. The Queen had taken shelter from the biting wind behind the wall of a church, while a man from the inn came out with a lantern, to see who was calling for a carriage on such a night, and in such haste, a suspicious circumstance in those disordered times. But the resourceful Riva lunging, as if by accident, against him, they fell together in the mud, and the inquisitive stranger returned ruefully to the inn to brush his clothes. The carriage with the fugitives left London safely behind them, though some soldiers called out as they passed, " Let's see if that's not a carriage full of papists." At Gravesend a little boat was concealed at some distance from the road, to take them to the yacht. Here were anxiously waiting for the Queen some of the faithful friends who were to share her exile—Lady Powis, the Prince's governess, and her husband ; the assistant governess, Lady Strickland.

With them was one of Maria d'Este's oldest and closest friends, the Countess Vittoria Davia, a Bolognese lady, who had recently come to England on the Queen's invitation. The yacht had been taken in her name, and now, to avert the suspicion of the captain, she came forward and, greeting the Queen as a sister, loudly reproached her for having kept her waiting. The Queen, who was dressed in the common clothes that Riva had provided, came on board with the Prince tucked under her arm like a bundle of dirty linen,[1] and bestowed herself in the hold, where she remained during the voyage. The child never betrayed his presence by a sound. Directly the embarkation was safely accomplished, a French gentleman called Saint-Victor, who had followed the carriage on horseback, hastened to London to reassure James. Lauzun, who was the first to board the yacht, drew the captain aside, gave him a large sum of money, and begged him to allow some French Catholic friends of his, with their wives, to be included among his passengers. Lauzun was prepared to poniard him if he did not obey orders, but the captain had recognised the Queen, though he did not appear to do so, and slipped past the fleet with a favourable wind. After having had to cast anchor for some hours off the French coast, owing to the violence of the waves, the yacht landed them safely at Calais on December 11th (old style) at nine o'clock in the morning, "where they landed gladly."[2]

[1] Dangeau, ii. 235.
[2] A detailed account of the Queen's flight was written by Riva and preserved in the Archives of Modena. It is confirmed by other contemporary French accounts published in the original by Cavelli.

CHAPTER II

FLIGHT OF JAMES

MEANWHILE James, who had designed to follow his wife and son in twenty-four hours, had fared less successfully. He had kept up the farce of negotiations and appeared to be acting vigorously. He summoned the Lord Mayor and Sheriffs, and explaining that he had thought it advisable to send the Queen and Prince to France for safety, assured them that he had no intention of following. He ordered the writs for the new Parliament, together with the Great Seal, to be brought to his own room. Macaulay, with unnecessary severity, describes James's conduct at this conjuncture as unkingly and unmanly. But James was not a strong man morally or intellectually. His nearest relations, they of his own household, his friends and servants, the men his favour had made, all were deserting him; turn which way he would, the ground was insecure beneath his feet. His nerves were shattered as by an earthquake, and he was suffering from sleeplessness, which, added to all his other miseries, might well have unstrung the nerves of a stronger man. Besides all this, he had always in his mind the fate of his father, whose life a timely flight would have saved. The dread of personal violence hovered over him. A man does not stop to be dignified and kingly when he is horribly frightened. James retained of his mental powers only a sort of childish cunning, which he pathetically extols in his biography. He was anxious to paralyse the forces he was leaving behind, so that they should not be used against him. To this end he burnt the writs for the new Parliament, and wrote the following letter to Lewis Duras, Earl of Feversham, the Commander-in-chief :—

"Things being come to that extremity that I have been forced to send away the Queen and my son, the Prince of Wales, that they might not fall into my enemy's hands, which they must have done had they stayed; I am obliged to do the same thing, and endeavour to secure myself the best I can, in hopes it will pleas God, out of his infinite mercy to this unhappy nation, to touch their hearts again with true loyalty and honour: if I could have relyd upon all my troops, I might not have been put to this extremity I am in, and would at least have had one blow for it; but . . . you yourself . . . tould me it was no ways advisable to venter myself at their head: there remains nothing more for me to doe, but to thank you and all those officers and soldiers who have stuck to me and been truly loyal; I hope you will still have the same fidelity to me, . . . tho' I do not expect you should expose yourselves by resisting a foreign army and poisoned nation."

Feversham took the closing words in the sense in which the writer intended that he should. He disbanded the troops under his command. Thus had James taken such measures as he could to cover his retreat; or, as he himself says with a sort of chuckle, had " thus prudently lessened, as much as he could, the force that was like to be turned against him, . . . which he knew would disconcert the measures and malice of those who sought his ruin, and retard at least the injuries they designed him."

On the night of December 10th, which fell on a Monday, James went to bed as usual. The Lord of the Bedchamber on duty was George Fitzroy, Duke of Northumberland, a son of Charles II. and the Duchess of Cleveland. To him the King gave orders that his bedroom door was to remain closed till the ordinary time. He then took the Great Seal with him, and in the early hours of the morning of December 11th he stole away by a secret staircase. A man who had every reason for being faithful to James was waiting for him with a hackney-coach. This was Sir Edward Hales, one of the most hated men in England. He was a Catholic, whose tenure of a commission in the army had been made a test case, when James claimed the right of dispensing with the penal disabilities in individual cases. He had been Lieutenant of the Tower, where he had incurred additional odium from his conduct to the Seven Bishops, when they were imprisoned there, and his removal from that post had been one of James's tardy efforts to placate his subjects. Altogether, Sir Edward Hales had nothing to hope from staying behind. The two went to Milbank, where the King took a pair-oar boat and crossed over to Vauxhall, dropping the Great Seal overboard as he went.

On the opposite shore a carriage was waiting to convey them to Sheerness. Relays of horses were in charge of an equerry, Ralph Sheldon, and the King safely accomplished his journey to Emley Ferry, near Feversham, where he arrived at ten o'clock on Wednesday morning, the 12th. But here the first hitch in the arrangements occurred. Sir Edward Hales had neither the force of character to act in an emergency nor the ability and foresight of Lauzun in making his arrangements. He had engaged a Custom-House hoy, which should have been waiting on the spot, to start immediately for France. The King had to lose precious time in waiting about for it, and when at last it arrived and they embarked with a favourable wind, blowing a fresh gale, it was found that the boat lacked sufficient ballast to venture on the crossing. They were obliged to run ashore at half ebb at the "west end of Sheepway" (Sheppey). It was nearly eleven o'clock at night before the hoy could be got off again, since they had to wait for the tide, and in the meantime the news had got about that some Papists were escaping to France.

Just as the hoy had at last got under way, three boat-loads of rough Feversham fishermen boarded her, and their leader, a sword in one hand and a pistol in the other, jumped down into the cabin where the King was seated with his companions, and declared that they must go before the Mayor of Feversham to be examined as suspected persons. They had not recognised James, and he, hoping that he still might get safely away, did not make himself known. Sir Edward Hales, "as the Captain, whose name was Amis sat examining them in the cabine, took a time, when none of his men looked that way to clap fifty guineas into his hand, and tould him in his ear, he should have a hundred more, if he would get him and his two friends off before they were carried to Feversham." Captain Amis took the money and promised all that was asked of him, and the vessel being now afloat, she was anchored at the mouth of Feversham water, as they were obliged to wait for high tide for going ashore here. Meanwhile the captain left them, assuring them that he would find means to get them away. Before he went he took the precaution of taking charge of such valuables as they had about them lest his men, "who," he said, "were unruly fellows, might plunder them in his absence." They consented to this proposal, giving him their watches and what money they had; but the King "kept the great diamond bodkin, which he had of the Queen's, and the Coronation ring, which for more security he put within his drawers."[1] The captain had promised to return in three hours, but the long December night had passed and day broke before his return; and in the meantime his predictions were verified, for when it was light several of the fishermen, leaping down into the cabin, insisted on searching the King and his companions, who assented at once, "immagining by that readiness, to persuade them they had nothing more."

But the fishermen were not to be so easily put off, and searched them narrowly; and "at last one of them feeling about the King's knees, got hould of the diamond bodkin, and cry'd out he had found a prize, but the King faced him down he was in a mistake, that he had several things in his pockets, as sizers, a toothpick case, and little keys—and that perhaps it was one of these things he felt; at which the man thrusting his hand suddenly lost hould of the diamond, and finding those things there the King had mentioned, remained satisfy'd it was so; by which means the bodkin and the ring were preserved"[2]—a small enough

---
[1] Clarke's *Life of James II.*, ii. 252.
[2] Sir John Knatchbull, Add. MSS., B.M.

consolation to a man who had lost his crown. The sailors had now turned the boat up the river towards Feversham. "Setting themselves down between the prisoners, whilst the rest sat on the deck making a fire, the smoake of which gave great offence to the King, whereupon Sir Edward Hales, telling them the smoake was very troublesome, they brutishly answered, 'Damn you, if you cannot endure smoake, how will you endure hell fire?'" "As if his destiny designed to be severe upon him, the seamen treated the King very roughly above the rest, though incognito. One cried out 'twas Father Petre, they knew it to be so by his lean jaws. A second called him old hatchet-faced Jesuit, a third swore he was a cunning old rogue they would warrant him, and all night long they welcomed him with these rough salutations, and perfuming the room with tobacco, a smell that the King hates."[1] It was broad daylight before the captain returned and told Sir Edward Hales, who had by this time been recognised, for he had an estate in the neighbourhood, that he must appear before the Mayor, and that a coach had been ordered to carry them up. They therefore landed in a small boat, and were taken up to Feversham, accompanied by a crowd of the rabble to an inn.

Here James was willing by all arts at first to conceal himself; and "at his first coming in he called for bacon and eggs, as if he were some ordinary man in his diet, whereas he tastes no meat that is in the least salted, as it afterwards appeared." But the King was soon recognised, notwithstanding his disguise of a black periwig. Further deception was useless, and learning that Lord

[1] Harleian MSS.: printed in Tindal's *Continuation of Rapin.*

Winchelsea and other country gentlemen were then at Canterbury, he sent for them to come to his aid. At the same time James despatched the equerry Sheldon to the master of the hoy, with orders to be on the watch for him, and to have horses in readiness to convey him to the shore. But here again the King's confederate blundered, and allowed one Edwards, who had jealously watched their progress to the inn, to guess what was intended ; so that, collecting a mob of his roughs together, he set so close a guard upon the King's lodging that escape was out of the question.

The King seemed bewildered by "the noise of the rabble," and at first, when ink and paper were brought him to write to the Earl of Winchelsea, he "was so discomposed, that he wrote, and tore, and begun again, as if he were overcome with disorder or fears." He talked freely to the writer.[1] " He told me that the rage of the people was up, and quoted the words, 'I who still the raging of the sea, must still the rage and madness of the people.' . . . He insisted on his integrity, said he had a good conscience and could suffer and die. He told me he read Scripture much and found great comfort in it. He declared he never designed to oppress conscience, alter the government, or destroy the subjects' liberties ; and at last asked me plainly, ' What have I done, what are the errors of my reign ? Tell me freely ?'" To such questions a respectful and compassionate silence could be the only reply. In the disordered state of the King's mind tags of Scripture ran in his head, and he "sermonised half an hour" on the text, "He that is not with me is against me." Imploring each of his captors in turn to get him

[1] Of the Harleian MS. mentioned above.

a boat that he might escape—"The Prince of Orange sought his crown and life," he said, "and if he were delivered up his blood would lie at our doors,"— he insisted on going off, begging, praying, tempting, arguing, persuading, reproving, "till at length, fearing that some might listen to him, and be prevailed on to aid his escape, so that they would lose their prize, the rage of the seamen took fire and thereupon arose some contemptuous words and no small insolencies offered." At times James further provoked his captors by a fitful assertion of his dignity, telling them to stand further back, or "go down and keep your distance," which so enraged them that some of them forgot all decency and reverence to him, till Sir Edward Hales was begged to "take the King off from that discourse which made him cheap."

The same evening, however, Lord Winchelsea arrived. He was a royalist, though a Protestant, and a relation of that Daniel Finch, Earl of Nottingham, who became Secretary of State to William III. Winchelsea could do little more than remove the King to a private house. As he made his way out of the house he was rudely hustled by the mob, in spite of the efforts of Winchelsea and one or two other gentlemen to protect him. They feared that Hales would make his escape, "whom they had a mighty spleen against for haveing changed his Religion, and at that very time the people of the country were plundering his house and killing his deer; and he, being sencible how odious he was to them, prudently stayd in the Inne, that he might not draw a greater inconvenience upon him."[1]

As the fugitive King made his way to his new

[1] Of the Harl. MS. 6852 before referred to.

lodging, a crowd of sailors and others of the common people pressed round him, narrowly watching lest he should slip away, and assuring him that "a hair of his head should not be touched." A number of them followed him into the house and kept watch at his door. After his removal to a private house, James's spirits rose. He "was full of discourse which was chiefly in his own vindication." He "pleasantly entertained us with a long discourse about St Winifred and her well, and the whole legend of it. He grievously lamented his loss of Edward the Confessor's cross, which contained a piece of the true Cross. At other times he appeared overcome with melancholy and often shed tears." Meanwhile "his guards were so severe upon him, and pursued him from one room to another, and pressed upon him so that he had scarce leisure to be devout."

It was not only at Feversham that the "mobile," as contemporary writers call them, had broken bounds. The news of James's flight and the disbanding of the troops was the signal for a wild outburst of disorder, such as London has seldom seen. The Lords Spiritual and Temporal who remained in London, assembled at the Guildhall, declared for the Prince of Orange, and took such measures as they could for the preservation of order. They dismissed Colonel Skelton from his governorship of the Tower, and summoned James's two Secretaries of State, the Earl of Middleton and Viscount Preston. The first declined to recognise their authority; Preston, more timorous, complied with their request. But their action was ineffectual in checking the outbreak of disorder in London. "On such occasions," says Macaulay, in one of his noble oratorical passages, "it will ever be found that the human vermin, which neglected by ministers of State and ministers of religion, barbarous in the midst of civilisation, heathen in the midst of Christianity, burrows among all physical and all moral pollution, in the cellars and garrets of great cities, will at once rise into a terrible importance." So under the cover of the popular cry of "No Popery" all the idle and vicious population of the slums overflowed into an orgy of riot and destruction. Roman Catholic chapels were destroyed and their contents burnt, the houses of Papists were ransacked, even those of foreign ambassadors plundered. The horrors of those days culminated in what was long remembered as the "Irish night."

"On Thursday morning the 13th December about 3 of the clock there was a dreadful alarm, that the Irish in a desperate rage were approaching the City, putting men, women, and children to the sword as they came along, whereupon the citizens all rose, placing lights in their windows from top to bottom, and guarded every man his own doors with his musquet charg'd with bullets. All the Trainbands in the City were assembled, and there was nothing but shouting and beating of drums all night."[1] Luttrell in his Diary notes: "The mobile got together, and went to the Popish Chapel in Lincoln's Inn Fields and perfectly gutted the same, pulling down all the wainscott, pictures, books, etc., and part of the house and burnt them, and then proceeded to Wild House, the Spanish Ambassador's, and did the same, and continued in a great body several thousands all night." And writes another contemporary: "This night I was

[1] Edmund Bohun's *History of the Desertion.*

frightened with the wonderful light in the sky, and it was the rabble, had gotten the wainscoat and seats at a Popish Chapel, in Lincoln's Inn Fields, and set it on fire in the middle of it. Till we knew what it was we guessed it to be a great fire."[1]

The origin of this baseless alarm has never been fully explained. James believed that it was intended to provoke a massacre of the Catholics all over the country, for the rumour had been industriously circulated elsewhere besides London, "while this handfull of Irish, who were thus imagined to be burning and destroying all over England at once, were disarmed and dispersed, not generally knowing where to get a meal's meat or a night's lodging, and lyable themselves to be knocked in the head, in every town they came to."[2] If so, the design was frustrated, for not a Catholic lost his life.

On the morning of the 13th the news of James's arrest at Feversham began to be spread abroad in London. Among the common people it produced a curious revulsion of feeling that surprised even James himself; to the Lords in Council it caused profound consternation. Some of the King's faithful friends hastened to join him, Middleton among them; for though he had refused to abjure his religion at the King's bidding, Middleton never wavered in his allegiance. He found the King in charge of two militia troops, whose captains, under pretence of protecting him from the rabble, were subjecting him to a harsh and rigorous confinement, hoping to suck thereout no small advantage with the Prince of Orange;

[1] Ellis Correspondence.
[2] *Memoirs of James II.*

and the King's friends were obliged to deliver up their swords before they were allowed access to him. But the worst of James's troubles were now over, for on Saturday morning the Earl of Feversham arrived with authority from the Lords to bring the King back to London.

Accompanied once more by respectful and sympathetic friends, the unfortunate James was removed to Rochester—a journey which he bore with some return of dignity and self-control, in spite of his exhausted condition of body and mind. At Rochester[1] he stopped to rest, despatching Feversham to the Prince of Orange with a letter in which he told his nephew, with a rather pathetic resumption of authority, that he "would be glad to see him at London on Monday, to endeavour by a personal conference to settle the distracted nation, and that he had ordered St James's Palace to be prepared for him." That wise Prince had not forgotten that Feversham had added to the dangers and disorders of the moment by letting loose his disbanded troops upon the country. The King's messenger was promptly put under arrest, and Zulestein, the Prince's intimate friend and relative, was himself sent off to prevent James from leaving Rochester.

James, meanwhile, had made a triumphal re-entry into London.[2] He had arrived in some apprehension, especially as he heard that the guards at Whitehall had declared for William. He entered London by way of

---

[1] Mulgrave's account of the Revolution, Clarke, ii. 261.

[2] December 19th: "On Sunday about four in the afternoon came through the city preceded by a great many gentlemen bare headed and followed by a numerous company with loud huzzas. . . . The evening concluded with ringing of bells and bonfires" (Ellis Correspondence).

the City, but "as soon as he arrived there he was hugely surprised with the unexpected testimonys of the people's affection to him ; it is not to be imagined what acclamations were made and what joy the people expressed at his Majesty's return ; such bonfires, such ringing of bells, and all imaginable marks of love and esteem, as made it look liker a day of triumph than humiliation ; and this was universall amongst all ranks of people that none that were with him had ever seen the like before, the same crowds of people and crys of joy accompanying him to Whitehall, and even to his bed chamber door itself." [1]

Deceived by this delusive enthusiasm on the part of the mob and a few time-servers, James instantly resumed a course of action which showed that the events of the last few days had made no impression on his understanding. In spite of himself, he was back at Whitehall ; his people, shocked by his misfortunes, had made some show of loyalty. He knew how violent was the feeling against Popery ; it was but two or three days since the houses and chapels of Catholics had been plundered and burnt all over London, as well as elsewhere. But his first action on returning to Whitehall was to offend popular prejudice. "The King," says Evelyn, "is persuaded to come back ; comes on the Sunday ; goes to masse, and dines in public, a Jesuit saying grace (I was present)." "During the time the King staid at Whitehall it was crowded with Irishmen, priests, Jesuits, and Roman Catholics, after the old wont, and one of the priests sent an imperious message

[1] "The shouts of joy and shew of welcome which attended his coach through London both startled his enemies and inclined him a little to slight his friends" (Mulgrave).

to the Earl of Mulgrave the Lord Chamberlain to furnish his lodgings with new furniture, for he meant to continue in them. So that all things were returning apparently into the old channel, and we were to expect nothing, but what we had already seen and felt, and some that wished well to the King, said, he was cunningly invited back to Whitehall, with a design to ruin him the more effectually and without any pity from his Protestant subjects."[1]

William of Orange, however, was not a man to wait on the facile sentiment of the populace. If James's presence in London roused their fickle enthusiasm, the sooner James went the better. Zulestein, with the Prince's letter, arrived at Whitehall almost as soon as James himself, and told the King that William would not come to London while James's guards were there, and followed up this message by sending three battalions of his own foot-guards, under the Count de Solmes, to take up their position at Whitehall. This unpleasant news was brought to James just as he was getting into bed at eleven o'clock on this eventful Sunday, by Lord Craven, who stoutly declared that he would rather be cut in pieces than resign his post at Whitehall to the Dutch guards. But the King "prevented that unnecessary bloodshed, with a great deal of care and kindness, and directed my Lord Craven to draw out his men and let Count de Solmes take the postes."[2]

James philosophically observed, when it was objected that it might not be safe for him to sleep in the middle

---

[1] *History of the Desertion.*
[2] Mulgrave. John Sheffield, Earl of Mulgrave, afterwards Duke of Buckingham, a man of considerable ability, who wrote mediocre verse and was in love with the Princess Anne.

FLIGHT OF JAMES

of the Dutch guard, that "he knew not whether those or his own were worse."[1] He then went to bed and fell sound asleep. But that night was not destined to be a tranquil one for him. After midnight there arrived from William, Lords Halifax, Shrewsbury, and Delamere, with orders for James. Lord Middleton, who seems to have been the King's best friend at this time, begged them to let his master have his sleep out, and when they insisted that their mission was of the utmost moment, went himself to wake the King, and, drawing aside the curtains of his bed, found him in a deep sleep, from which he could not rouse him, till he knelt down and spoke into his ear. James awoke, startled, and on learning of the arrival of the Prince's messengers ordered them to be shown into his bedroom, as, indeed, he had no choice but to do, surrounded as he now was by William's Dutch guards. The messengers had come with orders that James should at once repair to Ham. The message signed by the Prince was concise and to the point. William intended to be in London himself by noon the next day, and to avoid disorders James must be gone before he arrived. Ham House was named as the place to which he should retire; he was to be attended by a suitable guard to secure him from molestation. James objected that Ham was "a very ill winter house and unfurnished," but Halifax replied curtly that that could easily be remedied. Shrewsbury, always sweet-mannered and compliant, with the gentle courtesy that afterwards endeared him to William, listened to what James had to say, and when he earnestly pleaded to be allowed to retire to Rochester, the three Lords consented to refer

[1] Clarke's *Life*.

the matter to William, and obtained this concession for him, together with a blank pass from the Prince, that he might send a messenger to the Queen in France.

The letter which James wrote to Louis XIV., who was to afford him and his family the most generous of asylums, runs as follows :—

"MONSIEUR MON FRÈRE, — As I hope that the Queen my wife, and my son, have since last week set foot in some one of your ports, I hope that you will do me the kindness of giving them your protection ; and if I had not been unfortunately arrested on my way, I should have been there also, to ask it on my own behalf as well as theirs. Your ambassador will give you an account of the evil condition of my affairs, and will assure you that I shall never do anything contrary to the friendship that exists between us. Being very sincerely your good brother,

JAMES R.[1]

So to Rochester James went, on a windy Monday morning,[2] in the royal barge, preceded and followed by a hundred Dutch guards in rowing-boats. Many tears were shed by the lords and gentlemen about him when he took leave of them.[3] His daughter Anne, while her poor old father was making his windy progress, not without danger, down the river, went with her friend, Lady Churchill, to the play, covered with orange ribbons, in her father's coach, and attended by his guards.[4]

[1] Translated from Cavelli : original in the Ministère des Affaires Etrangères.
[2] The King objected that it blew so hard they could not well pass Lambeth Bridge.
[3] Clarendon writes : "I stirred not out. I thought it the most melancholy day I had ever seen in my whole life."
[4] Basil Higgons, *Short View of English History*.

The best thing that could happen for William and his supporters, was that James should make his escape to France. His detention and return were nothing short of a catastrophe, that was only averted by the prompt and vigorous action of the Prince in freeing London from his presence. Indeed, Burnet thinks that the ill-timed arrest at Feversham *created* the Jacobite party. James had no following before that except Papists ; "What followed gave them colour to say he was forced away."[1]

Halifax has been credited with frightening his late master away by the bogey of personal violence. Halifax had this grudge against James, that he had been made a fool of by him. He had been loyal to James. He had refused to sign the Invitation to William. He had advised concessions while there was yet time. But he had been sent by James as his commissioner in the sham negotiations at Hungerford, and while these were proceeding James had run away. Halifax was much too astute not to see that nothing was to be hoped for from James. For the sake of the country's good, he was better out of it. William's feeling in the matter was no secret.

James himself soon saw that the back door was left ajar for him, so to speak. For at Rochester he observed that "sentinels were only set at the fore door towards the street, and none at the back door, which went towards the river; by this the King was still further convinced the Prince of Orange had a mind he should be gone, which hinder'd him not from continuing in the same mind himself, being persuaded, that should he neglect that opportunity and disappoint

[1] Burnet's *History of His Own Time.*

the Prince of Orange by not going out of the kingdom, he would probably find means to send him out of it, *and the world* too, by another way." And when James heard how volatile London had received the Prince of Orange, the "universal running in to the invader," as he described it, and his welcome by almost all the nobility and gentry, he was more than ever determined to escape to France. While at Rochester his friends had free access to him. He was urged by them to remain. "Severall of the Bishops, and others who wished him well, advised him not to go out of England."[1] He discussed the whole question with Lord Middleton, who shrank from the responsibility of giving definite advice. "He owned it was a hard point to give council in, that to advise him to stay was extream hazardous, considering how his father had been used." But he added very pertinently, that if James deserted his kingdom the door would be immediately shut upon him. James tried, but unsuccessfully, to open negotiations with the City and with the Bishops,[2] and finally he made all arrangements for his departure. What finally determined him may have been his promise to the Queen.

Tindal says "a vehement letter from the Queen (which was intercepted and afterwards conveyed to the King), claiming his promise to go over to her, determined him contrary to the solicitations of his friends; so he left Rochester very secretly on the last day of that memorable year." But first note that passion for writing (and publication) which characterised him, and which more than once betrayed his interests.

[1] Clarke's *Life*, ii. 271.
[2] Tindal's *Continuation of Rapin*.

James wrote out a vindication of his conduct. It is lengthy and rambling, with—considering the magnitude of the occasion—a curious peevishness of tone. "The world," he said,[1] "cannot wonder at my withdrawing myself now this second time: I might have expected somewhat better usage after what I had writt to the Prince of Orange by My Lord Feversham and the Instructions I gave him, but instead of an answer such as I might have hoped for, what was I not to expect, after the usadge I receaved? by his making the said Earl a prisoner against the practice and Law of Nations,[2] the sending his own guards at eleven at night, to take possession of the posts at Whitehall, without advertising me in the least manner of it, the sending to me at one o'clock when I was in bed a kind of an order by three lords to be gon out of my own Palace before twelve that same morning; after all this how could I hope to be safe soe long as I was in the power of one, who had not only done this to me, and invaded my kingdoms, without any just occasion given him for it, but that did by his First Declaration lay the greatest aspersion upon me that malice could invent, in that claus of it which concerns my son."[3] . . . He goes on to say that he will "be within a call whensoever the Nation's eyes shall be opened, so as to see how they have been abused and imposed upon, by the specious pretences of Religion

[1] From an original MS. at Welbeck signed James, countersigned Melfort, dated $\frac{26}{5}$ of January $168\frac{8}{9}$, incorporating what he had written at Rochester.

[2] Feversham had gone into a hostile camp without providing himself with a safe-conduct.

[3] William alluded to the general belief that the Prince of Wales was a supposititious heir.

and property. I hope it will pleas God to touch their hearts out of his infinitt mercy and to make them sensible of the ill condition they are in."

The Declaration concludes with some belated but excellent sentiments concerning liberty of conscience, which accorded ill with James's previous conduct of the government. After supper the King showed what he had written to Lord Middleton, left orders that it was to be printed, and went to bed at his usual time on December 22nd.

Rising again later, he went out by way of some back stairs, through the garden, guided by one Captain Macdonnel to the river, where another trusted servant, Captain Trevanion, was waiting with a small boat. Into it James clambered, accompanied only by his son, the Duke of Berwick, the two captains, and a Mr Biddulph. It was now twelve o'clock, and they rowed out to the smack that was lying in readiness to sail for France. But a strong wind and a contrary tide prevented their reaching it, and as it was now six in the morning, James proposed that they should go on board Captain Trevanion's ship, the *Harwich*, which was near at hand. Trevanion, however, feared to trust his men, though he could answer for his officers' loyalty. So they boarded the *Eagle* fireship, whose captain was of tried fidelity, and waited there till daybreak, when they saw the smack lying at anchor in the Swale. They at once went on board her, taking Captain Trevanion's boat's crew with them, so that they were about twenty men all told; and the smack's captain, a Lieutenant Gardiner, served out arms, so that this time they should be well prepared for boats of men "a-priest codding."

The north-easterly gale blew so strong that they were obliged to put in under the Essex shore, and lie at anchor on Sunday ; but at dusk the wind sank, and the next morning they got under sail before sunrise, and went away with a light easterly breeze, and snow showers towards evening. At eleven o'clock they sighted the French cliffs, and standing in-shore they anchored at Ambleteuse, and landed about three o'clock on Tuesday, which was Christmas Day (old style). The whole of this long voyage James was penned up "in a small cabin, where was just room for him and the Duke of Berwick to sit, in continual aprehensions of being attacked and recaptured." "However, it was some cause of mirth to him, when growing very hungry and dry, Captain Trevanion went to fry his Majesty some bacon, but by misfortune the frying pan having a hole in it, he was forced to stop it with a pitched rag, and to ty an old furred can about with a cord and make it hould the drink they put in it; however, the King never eat or drank more heartely in his life." So ended, not without danger and difficulty, James's flight from the ship of state, that he was never again to steer.

CHAPTER III

ARRIVAL OF THE FUGITIVES IN FRANCE

On her arrival at Calais the Queen retired to a private house, where she wished to remain incognito till her husband joined her. But the governor of the town, the Duc de Charost, immediately sent tidings of her landing to Louis XIV. through the War Minister, Louvois. "I despatch a gentleman to you," he wrote, "in order to inform the King that the Queen of England and the Prince of Wales have just disembarked at Calais. The King of England confided them to the Comte de Lauzun, who has fortunately saved them. She wishes to remain unknown here. I am going to offer her on his Majesty's behalf everything proper for her, not doubting that my action will be approved. I have had her lodged in the best house in the town, mine being exposed to all the inclemencies of the weather. I am having her waited on by my officers. I have no further details to send."[1]

Another account of the Queen's landing explains that the Duke's house was unfit to receive her, as it was all in disorder, and in the hands of builders, so that she

[1] Published by Cavelli in original French from a MSS. in the Bibliothèque Nationale.

THE FUGITIVES IN FRANCE

was obliged to lodge at the house of M. Ponton, Procureur du Roy. On her arrival there, she exclaimed, seating herself in an armchair, that she had not felt so safe and peaceful for three months. Her first act was to hear mass at the Church of the Capucins. She also wrote to Louis XIV., throwing herself on his protection [1] :—

"SIR,—A poor Queen, a fugitive and bathed in tears, has not hesitated to expose herself to the gravest perils of the sea, in order to seek consolation and shelter, near the greatest and most generous monarch on earth. Her ill fortune procures her a happiness that more distant nations have desired. Necessity does not diminish it, since she has chosen it, and that it is from a *singulier estime* that she wishes to confide to him her most precious possession, in the person of her son the Prince of Wales. He is still too young to share her proper gratitude; her heart is full of it, and I take a special pleasure, in the midst of all my troubles, in living at present under your protection.—I am, with deep feeling, Sir, your very affectionate servant and sister, THE QUEEN OF ENGLAND."

In spite of Maria's wish to remain incognito, it was not long before the news of her arrival spread abroad, and the nobles of the district assembled to meet her. Her departure from Calais, after two days' stay, was very different from her unceremonious arrival there. As she left the town the guns of the fort fired a salute. She was attended on her journey by fifty dragoons and a detachment of cavalry. The little Prince's carriage went first, followed by three others for the Queen and her friends. It was Maria's wish to retire to an

[1] Copied from Bib. Nat., trans. Has been held to be of doubtful authenticity.

Ursuline convent in Boulogne, but as the Duc d'Aumont had placed his house there at her service, and had his wife's and his own rooms prepared for her and the Prince, she could not refuse his hospitality.

Maria remained eight days at Boulogne. She appeared as little as possible in public, but when she did so, she was always outwardly calm and collected, in spite of the poignant anxiety which consumed her as to her husband's fate. The sadness of her expression was tempered with dignity,[1] says an anonymous writer whose narrative is full of little touches bearing the marks of the observation of an eye-witness. The Queen's meals were served to her alone, in accordance with her desire for privacy; but M. d'Aumont, "magnifique en toutes choses," kept several large tables for the English and French in her suite. Four and five times a day Maria d'Este visited her child's temporary nursery, where in her absence he had many visitors. But, as always throughout a life of disappointment, Maria in these anxious days sought consolation in religion. On Christmas Eve she heard midnight mass in the castle chapel, on Christmas Day three masses. On the feast of S. Etienne she went, accompanied by Lauzun and D'Aumont, to hear the sermon in the cathedral church; and on St John's Day she heard mass at the Capucins. But except for these occasions she remained in seclusion. Meanwhile, it may be easily imagined that the arrival of the Queen of England, a fugitive in disguise, and her little son, at Calais, occasioned no small interest; in fact, nothing else was talked of, especially as she owed her escape to Lauzun. That

[1] "Parut toujours calme sur son visage, et si l'on y vit regner la tristesse, elle étoit melée avec la grandeur" (Cavelli).

diminutive knight-errant[1] lost no time in improving the occasion in his own interest. Immediately on his arrival at Calais he wrote to Louis XIV. that the King of England had given him orders to confide the Queen into no hands but his,[2] and that he was indeed unfortunate to be unable to execute this order, not having permission to present himself before his Majesty. It was impossible for Louis to avoid making some concessions to his former favourite ; and with the graceful tact in which he was a past master, he wrote to Lauzun with his own hand "a very obliging letter," giving him permission to return to Court. "He will be very surprised, and very glad to see my handwriting," said the King to his ministers, "he was well accustomed to it once upon a time."[3] But if Lauzun was rejoiced at this long-despaired-of restoration to Court favour, his former mistress was passionately annoyed at his reinstatement. Louis had indeed attempted to placate her. He wrote to Mademoiselle de Montpensier, who had returned to Paris some few days earlier, acquainting her with the unwelcome fact of Lauzun's prospective return to Court. She ought not to be vexed about it, the King added, as he could not avoid giving permission to see him to a man who had just successfully accomplished so important an action. This consideration of the King for Lauzun gave food for reflection to his ministers, and "made them desperately apprehensive lest the King's fancy for M. de Lauzun might revive."[4]

[1] His figure was very diminutive (Berwick's *Memoirs*).
[2] "De ne remettre la reine qu'entre ses mains."
[3] "Il sera bien surprise, et bien aise de voir mon écriture ; autrefois il y étoit bien accoutumé" (Dangeau).
[4] Madame de Lafayette, *Histoire de la Cour de France.*

Mademoiselle, who was in a position to express her feelings more frankly than the ministers, was transported with anger on reading the King's letter, and exclaimed bitterly to Louis XIV.'s emissary, M. de Seignelay, "This, then, is the gratitude I receive for what I have done for the King's children!"[1]

The intrepid Lauzun attempted to soften Mademoiselle's heart on his own account. He sent one of his friends to her with a letter. Taking it from him, she immediately threw it into the fire; but he, snatching it from the flames, implored her at least to read it. Mademoiselle then took it out of the room with her, but, returning immediately, told him that she had burnt it without reading it—a statement which posterity may take leave to doubt.

Another phase of Lauzun's conduct caused almost as much gossip in Paris as his rescue of the Queen of England and his adroit recovery of his King's good graces. This was his quarrel with Charost, a man reputed to be his friend. Apparently Lauzun, who wished the Queen to remain incognito, was annoyed that Charost had, on his own account, sent word to Paris of her arrival, taking care that his letter should come into the King's hands before that of Lauzun. In revenge Lauzun spread about Paris mendacious reports of Charost's want of proper attention to the Queen, and his neglect to give her a sufficient guard.

This was sufficiently paltry, seeing that Lauzun had done his best to prevent Charost from giving her a guard at all; and at last Charost, not content with

[1] Lafayette.

"Mademoiselle."

sending his own version of the affair by letter,[1] and hearing that he was being vilified at Court, came to Paris himself, in January, and was very well received by the King,[2] so that, as Madame de Sévigné says, "cela ne fait point honneur à ce dernier [Lauzun], dont il semble que la colère de Mademoiselle arrête l'étoile. Il n'a ni logement, ni entrées, il est simplement à Versailles." But if this squabble between two old friends caused "beaucoup de bruit," it was after all a matter of secondary interest. Nothing was talked of but the arrival of the Queen of England and the probable fate of her husband. A very few days after her landing, another message[3] from Charost brought to Paris the news of James's first flight to Feversham. Louis had lost no time in sending a messenger to congratulate Maria on her safe arrival, and at once despatched carriages for her use, with guards and officers to attend on her. It was determined to prepare Vincennes for her reception. "On ne parle, ma chère bonne, que de la reine d'Angleterre," says Madame de Sévigné, writing from Paris to her daughter. "The King has sent three carriages with ten horses to this Queen, litters, pages, footmen, guards, a lieutenant and officers." As to James's fate all sorts of rumours were current in Paris: he was at Calais, at Boulogne, he was still in England, he had landed

[1] Charost wrote to Louvois, Minister of War: "Pendant le séjour qu'elle a fait ici je luy ay rendu tout les respects que luy sont deubs, elle n'a pas vouler que je luy donne de gardes devant son logis, mais seulement mes gardes, qui ont toujours esté auprès d'elle . . . j'ai tasché de faire ensorte que sa majesté, M. le Prince de Galles, et pas un de sa suite n'ayent manqué de rien" (Archives du Ministère de la Guerre: Cavelli).
[2] Lafayette, "fort bien traité."
[3] By M. de Pointis, officer of marine, who reached Paris on Christmas Day.

4

at Brest, he was lost at sea. Feeling was strongly Jacobite. When rumours of the destruction of William's fleet had reached Paris, it was held that it was the hand of God, a miracle performed by a special Divine intervention.[1] Mary of Orange was compared with Tullia, the wife of Tarquin the Superb, who had her chariot driven over the bleeding corpse of her father.

In these days of suspense, while Maria concealed her intolerable anxiety under an outwardly calm and dignified bearing, she found some relief from the strain of continued uncertainty as to her husband's fate by pouring out her distress of mind to the young brother whom she had always tenderly loved, and who was now the reigning Duke of Modena. She writes[2]:—

"You will be astonished, and with reason, to hear that I am in this country and the manner in which I have come here. Having fled by night with my son, and having had a strong but favourable wind, we came from London to Calais in a little more than twenty-four hours. From there we came to this place, where I am in an indescribable anxiety, having had no news of the King since my departure eight days ago. He said that he would leave the day after me, but all the seaports are closed, and I can neither see him, nor have news of him, while they do not allow letters to pass. You can imagine in what a state I am. I am sure that if you could see me, you would be filled with compassion for me. My sole consolation is that my son is well, and that he flourishes in misfortune; he alone is happy in that he is ignorant of what has befallen him, and of the condition to which he and his parents are reduced. Pray God for me, dear brother, that He may give me patience and resignation, for without His special aid, I believe that I should lose my

[1] De Sévigné, November 8. [2] Cavelli.

reason." After telling him something of her future plans she concludes: "Dear brother, pity me, advise me, and console with your affection your poor distressed sister, who, in whatever state she may be, will always love you from her heart, and will be with all sincerity and affection wholly yours,— M. R."

The Duc de Modena, on hearing of his sister's arrival at Calais, decided to set out immediately incognito, with the smallest possible following, "on the impulse of his tenderest love" for his sister. He was dissuaded from doing so on account of his unsatisfactory state of health.

At last came the disquieting news that James's flight had been arrested. The Queen learned of it two days after she had written to her brother, on December 29th. The news was brought her by a Benedictine monk, a Capucin, and an officer. On being urged by her to say where they had left the King, they were forced sorrowfully to confess, "Your sacred Majesty, the King is arrested." "I was present," says the faithful Riva, "and I do not know how to say which touched me most, to hear such desolating news or to see the Queen my mistress in such extreme affliction. She sighed deeply a thousand times, raised her eyes to Heaven, and hung her head." The Duc d'Aumont, in writing to apprise Louvois of the arrival of this report, says: "She is in a pitiable state of grief: however, she bears it with great virtue and infinite fortitude."[1] He adds that she is very anxious about the King, and awaits news of him here.

Maria had always declared her intention of return-

[1] D'Aumont, Governor of Boulogne: "Elle est dans une douleur a faire pitie cependant elle soutient cela avec une grande vertu et une constance infinie. . . . J'ai logi sa M. dans le logis du roi où je suis."

ing to England if her husband were taken, to suffer martyrdom with him. But Louis XIV. was much too shrewd and experienced a diplomatist to permit her to complicate the political situation by any such useless act of sacrifice. Hasty orders were sent through Louvois to M. Beringhen,[1] Louis XIV.'s envoy to the Queen, that she was to proceed immediately to Vincennes. If the Queen should show any inclination to return to England with her son, he was to conduct her to Vincennes, explaining that it was the King's order, and that she was neither to stop on the road nor to take any other. He was to have no doubt that she would be glad enough to come to see Louis and to take measures with him for her husband's aid. One of the princes of the blood would meet her at Beaumont. Lauzun was given orders to the same effect: he was to persuade the Queen to come to Vincennes by all "les prétextes les plus honestes que vous pourrez vous imaginer." In accordance with these directions the Queen left Boulogne next day, the Duc d'Aumont and a great number of gentlemen accompanying her three leagues from the town. On her arrival at Montreuil she found the household that Louis had appointed to attend her in waiting for her. Here too the news reached her that James was back at Whitehall: the intelligence was brought by Vice-Admiral Strickland, who had arrived by way of Calais. The royal party of exiles and courtiers went on to Abbeville, where the Queen spent New Year's Day, hearing mass at the

---

[1] "M. Beringhen, M. le Premier, premier écuyer de la petite écurie du roi." Beringhen was Louis XIV.'s first equerry, and there was a peculiar appropriateness in his being deputed to attend on Maria, as his father had been sent as envoy on a like occasion to Henrietta Maria, the wife of Charles I., who had found a refuge in France.

Church of the Carmelites; and on the next day (Sunday), when they reached Poix, she learnt that her destination was not to be Vincennes, but Saint-Germain-en-Laye.

On that day, too, further appointments were made to the exiled royal household. Louis despatched the "grand écuyer," M. Le Grand, as he was called by virtue of this office, Louis de Lorraine, Comte d'Armagnac, as he was by birth. Yet another appointment was that of the diarist Dangeau, who chronicles much of the King and Queen of England's subsequent history, and who was despatched by the Dauphine as her representative to greet Maria. Dangeau had "owed his success at Court to his good looks, to the court he paid to the King's mistresses, and to his skilfulness at play."[1] He also owed much to the friendship of Madame de Maintenon. La Bruyère gives a merciless dissection of his character: "In a word, he wishes to be great and believes himself to be so, but is not. If occasionally he should chance to smile upon a man of low rank, upon a man of wit, he chooses his time so carefully that he is never caught in the act, for he would blush if he were unluckily surprised in the least familiarity with anyone neither rich nor powerful, neither the friend of a minister, nor his supporter, nor his servant. He is inexorably distant towards anyone who has not made his fortune. He may observe you one day in a gallery and avoid you, and the next day, if he finds you in a less public place, or in the company of some important person, he comes up to you and says, 'You did not seem to see me yesterday.' Presently he quits you abruptly to

[1] Saint-Simon.

join some nobleman, and presently again, should he find you in conversation with such an one, he will cut in, and carry them off from you."

On January 3rd the Queen arrived at Beauvais. Here the bishop and all the townspeople came out to meet her, and she was taken to the cathedral to worship its precious relic, a piece of the true Cross.

A letter of this date from the Abbé Melani, an Italian, attached to the Tuscan legation in Paris, describes Maria as "having up till now done nothing but weep, and although various clothes have been sent her from the King suitable to her condition, she was unwilling to wear any but the simple black dress in which she came from London. All those who have been to compliment her on behalf of the King, have hardly been able to refrain from tears themselves at the deplorable condition of so great a princess." But at last the news reached the Queen that her husband had left London. It was probably brought by Labadie, the valet who was in the secret of the Queen's first flight from Whitehall, for he arrived in Paris the next day. This hopeful intelligence "marvellously consoled the Queen and all the Court." On the 5th, when she was arrived at Beaumont, came the glad news that James had landed at Ambleteuse. D'Aumont wrote to Louvois on January 4th that James had landed at Ambleteuse at 1.30 a.m., and had retired to bed. He himself was on the point of starting with carriages to bring the King to Boulogne. He had not sent to tell the Queen, because he thought it would give the King, his master, pleasure to send her this good news himself. M. FitzJames was also there. Louis immediately sent off an equerry to Beaumont to the Queen.

She was praying when the King of France's messenger arrived, and in this glad tidings all her misfortunes were forgotten. Raising her hands and eyes to Heaven, she repeatedly exclaimed, "How happy I am! How happy I am!" Dangeau had presented the compliments of Madame la Dauphine only an hour before, and now "he returned to her, and found her transported with joy. It would be impossible to appreciate more highly than she does, all the kindness that she receives from the King, and she is more pleased than she can say with her reception on her route." Not Maria alone, but all her little court were beside themselves with joy (says the faithful Riva), though 'twas short-lived, "for the Queen was seized with violent pains which lasted some hours."

The courtiers [1] who had been deputed by Louis XIV. to greet the Queen at Beaumont were ordered to proceed at once to greet James; and the equerry Leyburn, who had accompanied the Queen on her flight, took a letter from her to her husband. Meanwhile she continued her journey with a mind at rest. The worst of her misfortunes were over—what were the loss of two kingdoms and all her temporal possessions now that the tension of anxiety as to her husband's fate was relieved?

On January 8th Louis went to meet his royal guest in person. Modern writers have stripped the great monarch of the halo that surrounded him. But in the

[1] Among the components of the household sent by Louis to meet the Queen were:—"Three royal carriages, each with 8 horses, without including that of M. le Premier, 2 equerries, 8 pages, 12 footmen; M. de Saint-Viance, lieutenant of the bodyguard, at the head of 50 guards with an exempt" (a term formerly used for an officer commanding in the absence of the Captain-lieutenants); "2 royal *valets de chambre* and 8 ushers, a chaplain and 2 clerks of the chapel, a *maître d'hôtel* and many inferior officials" (quoted by Cavelli).

accounts of the Most Christian King's daily life which were penned by the many writers of his time, something of the glamour which surrounded him in their eyes radiates from their pages. Saint-Simon alone watched the King with a merciless scrutiny that condoned no weakness, in sharp contrast to Dangeau, in whose adulatory chronicle any criticism of the King or the Court would appear impious. But in one respect Louis XIV.'s conduct stands out as that of a great king and a great gentleman. His relation to his fugitive and ruined guests is without reproach. It was dictated by the most delicate courtesy, by the most boundless generosity ; all that he had was placed at their disposal, no pains were spared to treat James and Maria as a great King and Queen, whose prestige had undergone no diminution. And just because they were discredited and shamed in the eyes of all Europe, the more punctilious care was taken to exceed what etiquette demanded on the occasion of royal visits. It is easy to say that Louis XIV.'s conduct on this occasion was dictated solely by a magnificent kind of vanity, but if so, it was a vanity that did not weary in well-doing, for it must be remembered to his honour that Louis abated no jot of his hospitality when he realised that his guests were to be his pensioners for life.

On January 6th, the day on which Maria was to arrive at Saint-Germain, Louis went to receive her on her way. "The King, after his dinner, left here [Versailles] with Monseigneur [the Dauphin] and Monsieur [the Duc d'Orléans] in his carriage, and went to Chatou, where he waited for the Queen of England, who arrived a quarter of an hour later. As soon as her carriages were seen approaching, the King,

THE FUGITIVES IN FRANCE

Monseigneur, and Monsieur alighted. The King stopped the carriage which preceded that of the Queen, where was the Prince of Wales, and embraced him. Meanwhile the Queen of England got out of her carriage, and expressed her gratitude to Louis on behalf of herself and her husband. The King replied that it was but a melancholy service he rendered her on this occasion, but he hoped to be in a position to help her more effectually in the future. To do honour to the Queen were assembled the King's guards and other troops, as well as the whole court. Louis and his son and brother, Monseigneur and Monsieur, took their seats with the Queen of England in her carriage. The proceedings had been arranged the day before, with that order and ceremony so dear to Louis's heart. The Queen was accompanied only by Lady Powis and Donna Vittoria Montecuccoli Davia: even so they must have been fairly crowded with three each side. The carriages then proceeded to the Château of Saint-Germain-en-Laye.

CHAPTER IV

SAINT-GERMAIN-EN-LAYE

THE Jacobite pilgrim of to-day, seeking to sentimentalise over the haunts of the last of the Stuarts, will meet with nothing but disappointment. Fate, that swept away this hapless family, has passed an obliterating hand over nearly everything on earth that was sacred to their memory, and scattered their very ashes to the winds. Whitehall, the London home of the Stuarts, that centre of irresponsible gaiety and intrigue, where Charles and James kept Court, was totally destroyed by fire soon after James II.'s flight; there remained only the banqueting hall, from the window of which their father had stepped on to the scaffold. In the two hundred years that have passed away since the Queen of England, worn out with fatigue and anxiety, alighted at the hospitable doors of the ancient Château of Saint-Germain-en-Laye, it has been so completely restored and renovated that the first sight of the brand new pink brick dispels any historical associations, and all images from the past that the imagination has conjured up fade into the light of common day. Perhaps the persevering traveller crosses the bridge and enters the building, hoping that he may at least stand beneath the roof that sheltered James II. in his exile, and that, walking through the empty rooms where the King held his meagre court of penniless followers, he may people them in imagination with the faded liveries of the past. But here too, alas! further disillusionment is in store for him. The uniformed custodian (all unwitting that the walls beneath which he is standing are weighted with august memories), puzzled but indulgent, waves him towards an open door beyond which he finds only neat galleries laden with Franco-Roman antiquities. The Musée des Antiquités, with its defaced stones and worn inscriptions, carries a message only from a past far more remote; and its bare pavements echo, for those that have ears to hear, with the words of the Preacher: "There is no end of all the people, even of all that have been before them: they also that come after shall not rejoice in him. Surely this also is vanity and vexation of spirit."[1]

One thing time has had little power to change. The face of the countryside must still show something of the features on which the Stuarts looked out over Paris to the distant hills beyond. The woods in which Monseigneur was for ever hunting with the hounds of M. de Maine are replaced by trim avenues of chestnut precisely lopped in the Gallic manner, and interspersed by gay flower-beds and subtropical borders, among which Sunday Paris comes out by train to walk. But below the noble terrace stretching a mile and a half along the brow of the hill which the Château dominates, is spread the same matchless view whereon the eyes of the exiles must have so often rested. The broadly winding Seine was at their feet, and beyond

[1] Eccles. iv. 16.

the fertile spreading countryside, girdled with hills, sprinkled with villages and spires among its trees, broods distant Paris and the rising ground of Montmartre. The exiles too must have felt the sense of light and space, and the great sweet wash of air from the distant hills.

Where the Château of Saint-Germain now stands was originally a convent. In the twelfth century a fortress was built close to the monastery, and Saint Louis added the now melancholy dismantled chapel. Francis I., struck by the beauty of the site, had the ancient buildings of his predecessors rased to the ground, and erected the Château in the form in which it has been restored and reconstituted to-day. Henri IV. added the Pavillon which still bears his name, and the gardens of which descended to the Seine by a series of terraces. Saint-Germain was a favourite residence of Louis XIII., who passed much time there, leading the life of a private gentleman, and occupying himself with painting, hunting, music, even cooking, and wearying of them all. Here too he parted from the virtuous Mademoiselle de Lafayette, who entered a convent to escape the ardour of her royal lover. "Alas, I shall never see him again," she wept,[1] as his carriage drove out of the Château court-yard; but happily, in those days, religious zeal was tempered by worldly prudence, and the King could hold converse with his lost love through the convent grating. At Saint-Germain Louis XIV. was born, and here his father died. After his death his mother, Anne of Austria, deserted the Château; it fell into neglect and, almost dismantled, was uninhabited till

[1] Madame de Motteville, vol. i. ch. iii.

it became a refuge for Henrietta Maria, who fled to France during the Civil War, and occupied here a very modest apartment hardly furnished with necessaries. When the Fronde broke out, during the mock civil war that agitated Paris in 1648, Anne of Austria and the Court fled to Saint-Germain. They found the Château without beds, furniture, linen, servants, or any necessaries—so much so that most of the Court had to sleep on straw, which in a few hours rose to so high a price in Saint-Germain that money could not buy it.[1]

Here Henrietta Maria learned that her husband, Charles I., had died upon the scaffold, and here she kept her melancholy shadow of a Court. When Charles II. was restored to the throne of England, Louis XIV. set up his Court at Saint-Germain in his old Château, since the new Château, the Pavillon of Henri IV., had already become very dilapidated. Here Mademoiselle de la Vallière and Madame de Montespan saw the zenith of their favour, and here took place the disgrace and arrest of Lauzun. But suddenly Louis XIV. took a dislike to Saint-Germain; once more the Château was dismantled and the Court removed to Versailles. It was said that the view of the steeple of St Denis, the last resting-place of the Kings of France, which he could not avoid seeing from the terrace, irked the King.

The Château of Saint-Germain had now been hastily prepared for the reception of the King and Queen of England. Its rooms had been magnificently furnished in readiness for their reception, every detail necessary for the proper appointment of the royal nursery had been specially considered, and, to complete his generous

[1] Madame de Motteville.

care of his guests' comfort, Louis had ordered his upholsterer to present to the Queen a little casket containing 6000 pistoles, which was to be placed on her dressing-table—so that she should have money for her immediate use.

Meanwhile James was sleeping at Breteuil, and the Duke of Berwick had come on to bring tidings of him to the Queen. In the relief of finding himself among friends and in a place of safety, treated once more with the deference due to his rank, James was seized with a kind of senile garrulity. He seems to have talked very freely to D'Aumont during the day he spent at Boulogne. "He spoke much of the infidelity of his subjects, and especially of Lord Churchill, whose treason he exaggerated to us with such extraordinary circumstances, that they are almost incredible. He did not forget that of the Earl of Sunderland, and several other lords, whom he had loaded with honours and benefits." James was very gratified by his reception in France, and contrasted it bitterly with the conduct of his own subjects.[1] He was now sufficiently recovered to talk hopefully of the future. He looked forward with entire confidence to his meeting with Louis, and expressed his belief that he would soon return. When D'Aumont courteously declined any recompense on the plea that in his hurried flight the King of England could hardly have more than he would himself want for his present expenses, James told him with childish pleasure how he had concealed and saved his diamond buckles. James was not wholly without resources, for Terriesi, writing to the Grand Duke of Tuscany,[2]

[1] Le Duc d'Aumont to Louvois (Cavelli).
[2] Archives di Medici ; Terriesi (Dec. 27th, 1689).

describes his rescue of the royal casket:—"That which put me in great peril of destruction in my flight, were the writings and money of the King, and more than that a great heavy casket full of gold and jewels, which his Majesty gave to me just in the act of leaving, which I agreed to save secretly, without the servants' knowledge, as I finally did, dragging it with me, with the writings, over the wall." He adds that this was the cause of his having to abandon to destruction not only all his own property, but some of his master's, as the box was of such a weight, it could hardly be moved by one man. He had already apprised his master of the destruction of the ambassador's house.[1]

On January 7th, the day that James was expected to arrive at Saint-Germain, Louis set out from Versailles between five and six o'clock to receive and welcome him. He took with him "Monseigneur" (the Dauphin) and his nephew, the young Duc de Chartres, the son of "Monsieur," Louis's brother, the Duc d'Orléans. The circumstances of the visit and the reception have been scrupulously chronicled. When they arrived at Saint-Germain, the Queen was in bed. Louis spent half an hour chatting with her in her room, while he was waiting for James's arrival. At last a messenger hastened in with the news that he was approaching the court of the Château. Louis went to the door of the Salle-des-Gardes to receive him. James, as though oppressed with a sense of his humiliating misfortune, bowed down to Louis's knees, but Louis embraced him most tenderly, while the King of England expressed himself as greatly touched by the

[1] For subsequent fate of the casket see Clarke's *Life of James II*.

marks of affection he had received from the French people on his journey. To which their King gallantly responded: "I am indeed glad to learn from your Majesty that my people have so entered into my feelings; they could not find a better means of paying court to me."[1] Then, holding him by the hand, Louis led James to his wife's apartments and presented him to her, saying: "I bring you a man, that you will be very glad to see." The husband and wife embraced tenderly, not without tears, so that the bystanders had difficulty in restraining their own. James "remained long in the arms of his wife," according to Dangeau; but Madame de Lafayette says that "le roi d'Angleterre n'embrassa pas sa femme, apparemment par respect."

The King of France afterwards presented to James Monseigneur his son and M. de Chartres, the Princes of the Blood, and some of the courtiers, with whom the King of England was already acquainted. He then led him away to the nursery to see the Prince of Wales. "I have taken great care of him; you will find him in good health," said his host. "Unhappy Prince!" exclaimed his father sententiously, "to be unwitting of the tenderness of the greatest king of kings in the world." As they left the room Louis said: "I give a number of orders, but I have not foreseen everything. You will give me great pleasure if you let me know all that you want. You are the master of my kingdom." Louis then escorted James back to the Queen's room, and soon after left his guests, saying as he left the room—and one can see him waving back his

---

[1] "J'ai beaucoup de joy d'apprendre de voltre Majesté que mon peuple ay si bien entré dans mes sentiments; ils ne peuvent mieux me faire la cour" (Affaires Etrangères, Anon. Relation (Cavelli)).

An Apartment of the English Royal Family at St. Germain.
(Reproduced by permission of M. Salomon Reinach.)

nervous guest at the same moment,—" Je ne veux pas que vous me reconduisez ; vous êtes encore aujourd'hui chez moi. Demain vous viendrez me voir à Versailles comme nous en sommes convenus ; je vous en ferai les honneurs, comme vous me les ferez de Saint-Germain, la prochaine fois que je viendrai, et nous vivrons en suite sans façon." This aspiration was not yet to be fulfilled ; the question of etiquette, and the precise amount of deference to be paid the exiled Court by the French nobility, who were as anxious to stand upon their dignity as the King was to forgo his, was for long a vexed question.

Time only deepened the first impressions made by James II. and his wife on Louis XIV. and his Court. For her there is a chorus of praise, with hardly a dissentient voice. A contemporary writes that Louis XIV. " trouva beaucoup d'esprit et de grandeur d'âme dans cette princesse. Elle a l'air noble ; tout pénétré qu'elle est de sa douleur elle m'en parait point embarrassée "—and here her sense of queenly dignity is beautifully indicated—" Elle sent bien ce qu'elle est, et quoiqu'elle soit fort honnête, elle sçait placer ses honnêtés selon les gens, et est tout-à-fait maîtresse d'elle-même." But James was a surprise and a disappointment to everyone. Madame de Lafayette says that " the appearance of the King of England has not at all impressed the Court, and still less his conversation. He related to the King in the Prince of Wales's room, where there were several courtiers, the principal events that had happened to him, and he told them so badly that the courtiers had to remind themselves that he was English, and consequently spoke French imperfectly. Besides this, he stammered a little, he was fatigued, and it is not extraordinary that so great a misfortune as that which has befallen him should diminish a much more perfect eloquence than his."

Madame de Sévigné says much the same thing. "This Queen gives general satisfaction, and has much *esprit*. She said to the King, seeing him caressing the Prince of Wales, who is a beautiful child: 'I was envious of the happiness of my child, who does not know his misfortunes, but now I pity him for not being sensible of the caresses and goodness of your Majesty.' All she says shows judgment and good sense. . . . One cannot say the same of her husband: he has much courage, but a common mind, and he recounts all that happened in England with an insensibility which makes him look a fool."

For some time after the King and Queen of England were installed at Saint-Germain, visits of ceremony continued. One of the earliest would-be visitors to the Queen was Louise de Querouaille, the Duchess of Portsmouth, but she was warned off by Lauzun. With the indiscretion of her class, the mistress of Charles II. had indulged in speculations about the origin of the Prince of Wales, and this gossip had reached the Queen's ears. Her son, the Duke of Richmond, complained to Louis about the "ill that had been done to himself and his mother, by spreading false reports that she had held ill-natured talk about the birth of the Prince of Wales, and that he himself had said he would join the Prince of Orange if he were in England, which was false." A woman of the type of Maria d'Este does not readily consent to receive highly placed hussies like the Duchess of Portsmouth.

SAINT-GERMAIN-EN-LAYE

But the Duchess was not the only person to receive a snub. French etiquette soon found other victims. Lord Powis was put in his place when he went on the Queen's behalf to make complimentary inquiries for the Dauphine. He thought his rank entitled him to salute her, "but he did not see her." "As he has only the title of Marquis and not of Duke, the Dauphine will not salute him, and did not even wish to consent to the expedient that he proposed, which was to see her in her bed, for she did not desire that he should be able to say that a compromise had been sought for."[1] On January 8th took place the important ceremony of James's first visit to Versailles. M. de Trémouille was punctiliously despatched by Louis in the morning to inquire after the health of the English royal family, and later in the day James returned the King of France's visit of the day before. The King's guards were drawn up under arms to receive him, and the King himself made a point of coming outside the Salle-des-Gardes to meet him. Ceremonial required that he should receive a brother sovereign inside it, but, as he himself said, on such an occasion it was necessary to exceed ordinary custom to mark the respect due to royalty, and the tender compassion with which he entered into the misfortunes of the exiled monarch. First of all Louis took James into his cabinet, where they remained together alone for a long time. James was then conducted to the Dauphine's apartments. She received them standing at the door with her ladies, and they all remained standing while they talked. After this Monsieur's apartments were visited. Here James examined all

[1] Dangeau.

the works of art the rooms contained with particular attention, and commented on them with the knowledge of a connoisseur. He was delighted with everything, pictures, porcelain, crystals, enamels. Finally he was presented to "Monsieur," who was ill in bed, and to his wife "Madame," Duchesse d'Orléans. He returned home about six o'clock. Dangeau was present, but only records the fact that James told them he always paid his army eight days in advance, and that the men were paid up to the day he left.

The King and Queen of England kept up a continual interchange of visits with the French royal family in after years, and among their most frequent callers was Monsieur of Orléans, the father of the Duc d'Orléans (then Duc de Chartres), who ruled over France as Regent during the minority of Louis XV. Saint-Simon describes him as "a little round-bellied man, who wore such high-heeled shoes that he always seemed mounted upon stilts; was always decked out like a woman, covered everywhere with rings, bracelets, jewels; with a long black wig, powdered and curled in front, with ribbons wherever he could put them; steeped in perfumes, and in fine a model of cleanliness" —in itself a virtue, and an unusual one at that time. He had a natural dignity, and a profound knowledge of social etiquette, which Saint-Simon, to whom there was nothing more important, noted approvingly. He was the life and soul of all Court gaieties — pleasure-loving and greedy.[1] The drawers of his cabinets were

---

[1] "Le gros de la cour perdit en Monsieur: c'était lui qui y jetait les amusements, l'âme, les plaisirs, et quand il la quittait tout y semblait sans vie et sans action."

crammed with sweetstuffs, and his pockets bulged with them, for he was continually eating between his heavy meals. He was, besides, weak, vain, and vicious. His wife, "Madame," appeared to Saint-Simon as an austere German lady, who made herself feared by her husband's favourites and dependants by her harsh and surly temper, and spent the greater part of her time writing and copying letters in a small private sitting-room hung with portraits of her countrymen. But these letters of hers reveal "Madame" as the most human and warm-hearted member of Louis XIV.'s family or court. Monsieur, who was notoriously indifferent to her, was careful to observe conventions. His first wife was the beautiful Henrietta, the sister of James II., whom everybody believed to have been poisoned.

The day after James returned the visit of the French King was Sunday, and in the morning everyone went to mass. But after dinner Monseigneur called. The Dauphin, grandfather of Louis XV., was described by Saint-Simon — a hostile witness, however — as being above middle height, very fat, but without being bloated, with a very lofty and noble aspect unmixed with any harshness. He had a beautiful fair complexion with a healthy colour, but a broken nose and an entire lack of expression spoiled his appearance. Although he had "the most beautiful legs in the world" and very small and delicate feet, he was uncertain in his gait, and felt his way with his feet; he was afraid of falling, and if the path was not perfectly straight and even, he called for assistance. "As for his character, he had none; he was without enlightenment or knowledge of any kind, radically incapable of acquiring any; very idle, without imagination or constructiveness; without taste, without discrimination, without discernment; neither seeing the weariness he caused, nor that he was as a ball moving at haphazard by the impulsion of others; obstinate to excess in everything; amazingly credulous and accessible to prejudice, keeping himself always in the worst hands; ... absorbed in his fat and ignorance." Such was one of James and Maria's most frequent visitors.[1]

On this the first occasion James received him at the end of the room, but did not go outside it, as it was important to mark the difference in rank between the Dauphin and his father. Host and visitor stood while talking, and afterwards visited the Queen, who gave the guest an arm-chair, but below her own. She told him that she was only waiting for an appropriate costume in which to go and pay her return visit to his father and his wife. The Dauphin was careful to visit the royal nursery before he returned to Versailles. Visits of ceremony continued during these days because Louis insisted on it, but there was great agitation among the courtiers on the question of procedure. "Il y eut grandes contestations pour les cérémonies," says Madame de Lafayette. Louis XIV. wished James to treat his son, Monseigneur, as an equal, and he consented on condition that Louis paid the same attention to the Prince of Wales. Finally it was decided that the Dauphin was to have a folding chair, only, in the presence of the King of England, but that he had the right to an arm-chair when in the presence of the

[1] Saint-Simon: Bayle St John's translation.

Queen—a nice distinction, and one on which much stress was laid at the French Court, but one which, reciprocally applied, was not without its absurdity in the case of a baby in arms, the Prince of Wales, whose claims to a throne were never likely to be realised.

The French Princes of the Blood also had their pretensions. They claimed that, as they were not subjects of the King of England, their relations should be regulated by a special etiquette. Finally everything was settled to their satisfaction. "But when it came to the women it was not so easy,"[1] says Madame de Lafayette,[2] whose sly and mordant pen illuminates the early days of the English Court at Saint-Germain. The Princesses of the Blood were three or four days without going to visit the Queen of England, and when they at last went, the duchesses would not follow their example. In England they stood in the presence of their sovereign, but the Queen kissed them. In France it was not the custom for the Queen to kiss them, but they had the right to sit. They now claimed the right to both. However, a domineering autocrat like Louis XIV. was not likely to permit any airs on the part of his Court or his family, when he himself had waived all his rights in favour of his guests. Besides, Maria, "who, though

[1] *Mémoires de la Cour*, Madame de Lafayette.
[2] Madame de Lafayette, author of *La Princesse de Clèves* (1634–1693), was the daughter of a field-marshal and governor of Havre. She was distinguished for her wit and learning, and was the friend of many of the most celebrated men of her time, as well as of Madame de Sévigné. She was intimately acquainted with all the social events of her day, and was always in favour at Court. Her husband, Comte de Lafayette, left her early a widow, and does not appear to have counted for very much in her career.

very proud, was not without plenty of common sense,"[1] begged him to arrange the ceremonial to be observed as he chose, and she would do whatever he thought best. It was then decided that the etiquette in vogue in France was to be observed with regard to the duchesses.

At the same time Louis settled 50,000 crowns on James for his establishment, and 50,000 francs a month for current expenses. Though James was unwilling to accept more than half, his expenses were afterwards regulated on that footing. The Court was touched by Louis's generosity to his guests, and Madame de Sévigné's appreciation reflects the general opinion : " Le Roi fait pour ces Majestés angloises des choses toutes divines ; car n'est-ce point être l'image du Tout-Puissant que de soutenir un roi chassé, trahi, abandonné comme il est."

This question and the far more imposing one of etiquette having been put on a firm basis, "Madame" paid her visit of ceremony to Saint-Germain. There was no more notable personage at the Court of Versailles than Louis's sister-in-law, the Duchesse d'Orléans.[2] Her letters show her to have been a woman of keen intelligence, strong affection, and virulent animosities. Her life was by no means a happy one. A woman of high principles and strong character, she could not feel anything but contempt for her husband. She was not dazzled by " the great man," as she calls Louis with a covert sneer. Her detestation for his mistress, Madame de Maintenon, was un-

[1] De Lafayette.
[2] She was the daughter of Charles Louis, Elector Palatine, and thus related both to William III. and George I.

SAINT-GERMAIN-EN-LAYE

measured. For the Dauphin she had a contemptuous pity, and for his poor little ailing wife, a compassionate affection. In her letters home she pours out all her most intimate thoughts with the utmost frankness, in vigorous and effective terms, although Louis XIV. had a regular system of opening them—as she knew.[1] The letters are written principally to her aunt, the Electress Sophia of Hanover, mother of George I. of England. Writing them was her one escape from a life full of mortification, that her strong sense of humour and high courage alone enabled her to support. She had the humiliation[2] of seeing her son, the Duc de Chartres, married perforce to Louis's illegitimate daughter, Mademoiselle de Blois, who, she says, gets as drunk as a courier two or three times a week.[3] She knew or believed that De Maintenon was intriguing to get her daughter married to "this limping Duc du Maine"[4] with the aid of Mademoiselle, who, "because she has been such a fool as to give her possessions to the bastard to save

[1] "I know beyond all doubt that they open our letters; the post does us the honour to close our letters up again very subtly. Madame la Dauphine often gets hers in a singular state, torn at the top." She adds a story of Mademoiselle, who, seeing that the letters she received from her men of business had been opened, put a postscript in her replies: "As M. Louvois has excellent judgment, and as he will see this letter before most of you, I beg him in opening my packet to add a word of advice about my affairs—they will be all the better for it."

[2] "If you knew," she writes, "the position of affairs here, you would not be surprised that I am not gayer. Anyone else in my place, if she had not had my fundamentally jovial humour, would have died of vexation long ago; as for me, I grow fat on it. I have few intimacies here. I lead a life apart like a little free town. I cannot say that I have more than four friends in all France."

[3] For the "rejoicings by command" at this most unpopular wedding, and Madame's impotent but unconcealed rage, see Saint-Simon.

[4] Louis XIV.'s illegitimate son, and the nurse-child and favourite of de Maintenon.

that little toad Lauzun from prison, she wishes us all to be as mad as herself."

With the Duchesse d'Orléans came all the Princesses of the Blood. The Queen kissed them all, and gave an arm-chair to Madame and folding chairs (*sièges pliantes*) to the Princesses. The next day the recalcitrant duchesses paid their visit, and were given stools to sit upon (*tabourets*). All had been sent by Louis, says Dangeau, who assured them they would be treated by the Queen as if she were Queen of France, and the same etiquette was to be observed. The same writer notes that the Princes of the Blood were to keep on their hats when James had on his, and that the Queen was to give them folding seats and to kiss them. She had omitted this civility in the case of Monsieur, who was sulky about it;[1] though, bearing in mind Saint-Simon's description of this bedizened and painted person, one sympathises with Maria's aversion for kissing him.

No one in Paris was talking of anything but the new Court and the ceremonial to be observed at it. "It is so extraordinary a thing to have this Court there, that we never stop talking about it," writes Madame de Sévigné.[2] "They are trying to regulate ranks (*régler les rangs*) and to arrange life on a permanent footing with people who appear to be so far from being re-established. The King said the other day that this King was the best fellow in the world, that he should hunt with him, that he should come to Marly and Trianon, and that the courtiers would have to get used to it." She concludes: "One is greatly occupied with this new Court." She adds

[1] "Qui en boude" (De Sévigné).   [2] January 12.

PHILIPPE DE FRANCE
DUC DE ORLEANS. &c.

"MONSIEUR."

later that "Madame la Dauphine will not go to see this Queen."

The Dauphine was a Bavarian princess. Mademoiselle describes her arrival in France in her memoirs. She was not beautiful, but had a good figure. Her husband was kept much in the background, being besides rather a poor thing, and she herself was continually ailing. Medicine and morals were the two worst points about the age of Louis XIV. Medical remedies were few but violent, and a sick person did considerably better by avoiding them altogether. "Madame" d'Orléans, who was sincerely attached to this princess, writes that "Madame la Dauphine grows weaker, and her illness has become so chronic that I am much afraid that there is no longer any remedy. Now that she is obliged to keep her bed, they are forced to own that she is really ill, but they are extremely ignorant, and only know how to purge, bleed, and blister; now, none of all that will do Mme. la Dauphine's business."

This was the infirm lady whose pretensions, none the less, exceeded those of anyone else. She wished to sit on the Queen's right and to have an arm-chair. That was not according to precedent. Even "Madame" was only accorded an arm-chair on the Queen's *left*. The difficulty was ultimately solved by her remaining in bed—officially as well as actually indisposed—where Maria visited her.

There remain only two other incidents connected with these ceremonial visits which call for notice. One was that the pertinacious Duchess of Portsmouth contrived to find her way in on one of the visiting days. The other was that, on the day when Madame came, and the Princesses of the Blood were given *sièges pliantes*, the same accommodation was offered to Queen Maria's friend and lady-in-waiting, Donna Vittoria Montecuccoli Davia. This was regarded as most extraordinary, and it was determined to ask for an explanation. To overcome the difficulties of the etiquette, the Queen had had her old friend created Comtesse d'Almond. Donna Vittoria had left her people, her country, even her husband, to share the exile of Maria d'Este.

Visits had been paid by everyone of importance. There only remained the return visit of Maria Beatrice to Versailles, which, as she had explained to Monsieur, she was only waiting to pay till her Court dress arrived. After that, life at Saint-Germain settled down into some sort of routine, though the household of James and Mary was not placed on its regular footing till after the return of James from his abortive visit to Ireland, for which he soon began to make ready.

CHAPTER V

FIRST IMPRESSIONS AT SAINT-GERMAIN

WHILE everyone was discussing the King and Queen of England, the charm and tact of Maria of Modena, the probable duration of their stay, and the magnanimity of Louis in his reception of them, two letters from Saint-Germain show how the refugees regarded their new environment. The first is from Donna Vittoria Montecuccoli to the Duke of Modena.[1] She tells the Duke that she can now give him better news of the Queen his sister than she was able to do from Boulogne. She is in the best of health. After Louis XIV. had restored James to her, he returned to Versailles, leaving her quite happy again (*tutta consolata*). They only want the Duke's presence there to fully satisfy her (*per maggior suo contento*). She describes the joy of great and small at the arrival of the Queen, who has been everywhere received as a sovereign. It is marvellous how well the Prince of Wales is, in spite of all he has been through. The Queen has never shown distress at having left the kingdom and all the rest; she lamented greatly the separation from the King, " but now I believe that she will think a little of

[1] Archives d'Este at Modena, quoted by Cavelli.

the rest. In every way her virtue is indeed great, and I hope that God will deign to assist their Majesties and restore them very soon to their kingdom."

On January 12th, Maria Beatrice found time to write to her brother herself:—

"DEAR BROTHER,[1]—If I wished to undertake the relation of all the things that have happened to me and the King after our leaving London, it would make a volume rather than a letter. Be content, then, that by this post, which Marchese Rangoni[2] will forward to you, I will only tell you the most important part of it, our happy arrival at this place. My son and I reached it on the 6th, the King on the 7th, after having caused me many sighs and tears, and not without reason. But God be praised, we are in safety, and receive many favours from the King." She adds: "I don't know what has become of poor Abbé Rizzini."

On January 13th, the day after writing this letter, Maria paid her state visit to Versailles. Madame la Dauphine had persisted in saying that she was too ill to go and pay the first visit, as Louis XIV. had wished, and, to prevent any infringement of her rights, kept her bed. The Queen of England was in her new Court dress "habillée en perfection; une robe de velours noir, une belle jupe, bien coiffée, une taille comme la Princesse de Conti,[3] beaucoup de majesté."[4]

---

[1] Arch. Este at Modena, from original Italian, quoted by Cavelli.

[2] Rangoni had been sent by the Court of Modena with congratulations on the Prince of Wales's birth.

[3] "On n'a vu aucune personne de grande taille danser parfaitement, si ce n'est la grande Princesse de Conti, mais personne au monde ne dansait aussi bien qu'elle."—*Correspondance de Madame.*

[4] De Sévigné.

FIRST IMPRESSIONS AT SAINT-GERMAIN

Louis went to meet her at her carriage door.[1] He conducted her first to his dressing-room, where they chatted for half an hour. Louis always enjoyed talking to her ; her readiness and easy self-possession pleased him. They next went to visit the Dauphine. Louis XIV. left the Queen at the door, as etiquette forbade his daughter-in-law to sit in an arm-chair in his presence. The Dauphine, after all, was up and dressed: perhaps she too had a new dress for the occasion, and felt impelled to wear it. "Madame, I thought you were in bed!" said Maria, very much surprised. "Madame," replied the Dauphine, "I wished to get up to receive the honour that your Majesty does me." By this little artifice, however, Madame la Dauphine had gained her point. The Queen of England was given an arm-chair on the *left* of Madame's own.

Even Louis himself always seated Maria on his right. Three other arm-chairs were provided for the three little Princes, the Dauphine's sons, the Ducs de Bourgogne, de Berry, and d'Anjou. The Court was very full ; a crowd of duchesses were present. The talk was brisk and unconstrained, and the visit lasted half an hour. Maria only brought with her Lady Powis and Lady d'Almond (Montecuccoli Davia). On leaving the Dauphine, she visited Monsieur and Monseigneur. She was filled with admiration for the beauties of Versailles, and astonished at its magnificence, especially that of the great gallery. Her discreetly expressed but sincere admiration greatly gratified Louis.[2] At the conclusion of her visit, after he had seen her to her

[1] Outside the guard-room, Dangeau says.
[2] De Lafayette.

carriage,[1] he returned upstairs and loudly expressed his approbation of the Queen of England to his Court. "That is what a Queen ought to be physically and mentally, holding her Court with dignity."[2] He admired her courage in her misfortunes, and her passionate affection for her husband. Madame de Sévigné adds other details of Maria's first visit to the French Court. "Those of our ladies, who wanted to play the princess, did not kiss her robe; some of the duchesses followed their example. The King was very annoyed about it; presently they will kiss her feet."

The first impression made by James and his wife on the French was enhanced by closer acquaintance. "Plus les Français voyaient le roi d'Angleterre, moins on lui plaignait de la perte de son royaume. Ce Prince n'était obsédé que de jésuites : . . . la conversation finit par dire qu'il était de leur société : cela parut d'un très mauvais gout." It is curious to find Catholic France reproaching James with the very same weakness that had outraged Protestant England. Even the French clergy seem to have regarded him with something of contempt. The Archbishop of Rheims, Louvois's brother, watching him come out of Church, said ironically: "There is a very good man; he has left three kingdoms for a mass." "Belle réflexion dans la bouche d'un archevêque!" comments Madame de Lafayette. There could be no two opinions on James's piety, but that is not quite the same thing as virtue. The Abbé Mélani, who was attached to the Tuscan legation in Paris, wrote

---

[1] According to Mme. de Sévigné.
[2] "Voila comme il faut que soit une reine, et de corps, et d'esprit, tenant sa cour avec dignité."

to the Grand Duke of Tuscany's secretary, the Abbé Gondi : " The King of England passes for a very good Prince in the opinion of those who have come in contact with him, but not of that elevation that Fame has hitherto credited him with."

James, unconscious of the criticism that he was exciting, seems to have had the happy faculty of living in the present; and Louis XIV. was as good as his word about making him a participator in all his amusements. Meanwhile that needy stream of emigrants, to feed whom Maria had later on to sell her diamond buttons, had already begun. As early as January 11th, M. Colbert Maulevrier, probably a nephew of the great Colbert, had written to Louvois[1] apprising him of the arrival of some of these refugees, the Countess of Sussex, Anne Palmer, natural daughter of Charles II., and the Duchess of Cleveland ; with her was her niece, Miss O'Brien, daughter of the Lord Clare, who was to die at the Battle of the Boyne. With them was Charles Skelton, who afterwards became a lieutenant-general in France, and married the Earl of Sussex's daughter Barbara.

" I believe," says Madame de Sévigné at this time, " that the King and Queen of England are very much better off at Saint-Germain than in their own perfidious kingdom. The King of England calls M. de Lauzun his governor ; but he does not govern anyone else, for he is not in high favour elsewhere." Lauzun's reinstatement was slow. Mademoiselle de Montpensier remained obdurate, and the King's former favourite had no lack of enemies at Court. As for Mademoiselle, the romantic attachment of a middle-aged woman

[1] Archives of the French War Office (Cavelli).

for a young man, who dared not respond to advances from his master's cousin otherwise than by respectful homage, had changed into bitter and obstinate resentment. When Lauzun lost the King's favour, he had not troubled about conserving that of Mademoiselle, and after she had bought his enlargement he repaid her with ill-humour, insolence, and ingratitude, which culminated in his telling her that he would have been much better off if she had not interfered. Goaded beyond the endurance even of her long-standing adoration, Mademoiselle had ordered him out of her sight and out of her house. She had too much dignity ever to forgive him, and Lauzun had a lodging at the Château of Saint-Germain.

With regard to the household there, Madame de Sévigné says that "their Majesties have only accepted 50,000 francs a month of all that the King wished to give them, and do not wish to live like kings. Many English have joined them; without that they would be content with still less; they have, in fact, resolved to begin as they mean to go on (*de faire vie qui dure*)."

The French Court would have been quite content to continue paying ceremonious calls on Saint-Germain for ever, but James soon tired of it. When next Louis and his son Monseigneur [1] visited the King and Queen of England, two days after Maria had been to Versailles, James, who did not want to sit in a row in arm-chairs, remained standing talking by the chimney to Monseigneur. "We agreed that we would not

---

[1] The title of Monseigneur was given to the Dauphin by Louis XIV., and must not be confused with "Monsieur," the title of the King's brother.

FIRST IMPRESSIONS AT SAINT-GERMAIN 83

stand on ceremony after this visit," he said. "I am going to begin from this evening." The next day James went over to Versailles after dinner. Louis was with Madame de Maintenon. He set himself, however, to entertain his visitor, showed him all his cabinets in his small private room, took him to Salut,[1] and afterwards to visit the Dauphine. Monseigneur wanted to accompany him out, when he took leave, saying, "I am going to do the honours of the house," but James again, with his characteristic dislike of ceremony, insisted on his leaving him at the door of his wife's apartments.

The day after, on January 17th, James paid that visit to Paris on which Madame de Lafayette comments adversely. He went first to the Carmelite Convent, to visit the Mother Agnes, who had been the first person to influence him in his conversion to Roman Catholicism. He then attended service at the Jesuits', and dined with Lauzun. It was on this occasion that James is reported to have said that Father Petre had never given him any but good counsels — another instance of his extraordinary blindness to the true state of his affairs, since Petre's presence on the Council had so much contributed to his ruin. It was a blindness not shared by his wife.[2] Subsequently he drove about Paris incognito in a carriage of Lauzun's, with only a brigadier of guards mounted behind him; but he was nevertheless recognised, and so inconveniently large a crowd collected that he relinquished his inten-

[1] Term applied to afternoon or evening service in the Roman Catholic Church.
[2] It appears from a letter of Rizzini in the Archives d'Este at Modena that the Queen had used her influence to get him sent away from Court.

tion of going to Val-de-Grâce.[1] Excursions in other people's carriages seem to have suggested to James that there was no reason why he should not have his own. Accordingly he wrote the following letter to Lord Dartmouth, requesting that they might be sent to him :—

"SAINT-GERMAIN, *January* 19.

"Howsoever the Prince of Orange uses me in other things, sure he will not refuse me the common civility of letting all my coaches and horses come over to me ; 'tis but what I did to Prince George, when he went away from me. I send this bearer Ral. Sheldon to you to bring them away, so soon as a pass can be got from the Prince of Orange. Speak for the pass yourself or to Lord Middleton to have it solicited, and give directions to De la Tree to bring it over himself, or if he be not yet ready to come, to send the best of my guns and pistols over with Sheldon,[2] this bearer, to whom I refer what else I have to say.

"JAMES R."

That want of high-mindedness observed by James's critics at the French Court is sufficiently exemplified by his consenting to ask small favours of the man who had supplanted him. William at once acceded to this request of James, but countermanded the order on hearing that James was going to head the troops against him in Ireland. The carriages of the Queen had, however, already gone, and her own coachman,

---

[1] In the Chapel of the Hearts at Val-de-Grâce the hearts of Louis XIV.'s mother and wife were preserved.

[2] The Ralph Sheldon here mentioned was an equerry who had followed James into France and died there at ninety in 1723. His brother Dominic was deputy governor to the Prince of Wales, and afterwards became a general in the French army. Edward, the youngest brother, was also an equerry at the exiled Court.

who, curiously enough, had formerly been in the service of Cromwell, followed her to France.

It was about mid-January that James paid his first visit to Marly, at which Louis had so enthusiastically declared his intention of entertaining him, and an invitation to which was the highest mark of the Most Christian King's favour. Marly was the refuge which Louis had built for himself as the antithesis of the bustle, the crowds, the courtiers of Versailles. The thought which he had in his mind was that of a place to which he might repair with a dozen courtiers at most, which should betray him into no expenses, and which should enable him to escape for a little from the magnificence and display by which he was surrounded. To an ordinary mind Marly, when it was first discovered, would not have seemed promising. After examining the neighbourhood of Versailles, Louis found a deep, narrow valley, completely shut in, inaccessible from its swamps, and with a wretched village called Marly upon the slope of one of its hills. He was overjoyed at his discovery. It was a great work, that of draining this sewer of all the environs, which threw there their garbage, and of bringing soil thither. The hermitage was made, but Louis could not resist his passion for building and altering the face of nature.[1] Buildings, gardens, water, aqueducts, costly furniture and statues were added. Then a park was made. Full-grown trees were transplanted there from Compiègne, and replaced as soon as they died. Woods were changed into ornamental waters, and then reconverted into forest: so that from first to last Marly was estimated to have cost even more than Versailles.

[1] Saint-Simon.

Going over soon after five o'clock, James found Louis just returned from shooting. They spent some time shut up together, discussing political matters (Dangeau asserts that it was on this occasion that the expedition of James to Ireland was first mooted), and before he left Marly, James was taken over the house and was received by Madame de Maintenon. The career and character of Madame de Maintenon are too well known to make it necessary to give more than a few words to either here. Françoise d'Aubigny was an orphan dependent on the charity of a hard old woman who employed her in menial offices. From this servitude she was rescued by the poet Scarron. No longer young, a hopeless cripple reduced to live by his wits, Scarron did all he could for so friendless a creature—he gave her the protection of his name. The society of the brilliant invalid was sought after by all classes, so that Madame Scarron had made many influential acquaintances when her husband's death threw her on her own resources. She passed from one house to another in a subordinate capacity. In those days there were no bells. It was useful to have a complaisant and subservient dependent to send on small errands to the servants. At last Madame Scarron attracted the notice of Madame de Montespan, the mistress of Louis XIV., and was by her engaged as governess to her children, one of whom, M. du Maine, later owed so much to the affection of his old governess.

So it happened that, when the children came to be acknowledged, the governess was brought into contact with their father. From that time her fortune was made. Madame de Montespan was a most generous patroness. It was she who extracted from Louis the gift of an estate (of Maintenon) for the governess, whom Louis began by greatly disliking. Gradually the gentle, supple, insinuating dependent vanquished the King's dislike, won his favour, and finally ousted the imperious mistress of whose temper and caprices Louis had grown weary. For more than thirty years Madame de Maintenon governed Louis through his ministers with a subtly concealed art, playing not on his passions but on his piety. She had an admirable wit, incomparable grace, a gentle, easy, respectful manner, and in later years cultivated studiously an air of devotion.[1]

James's formal visit to Marly was not at once returned, for the next day was so wet that Louis stayed at home and played "trou-madame," a popular game that consisted in throwing balls into a kind of bagatelle board. Monseigneur went over to Saint-Germain for wolf-hunting in spite of the weather. "They had persuaded him that he liked hunting," says Saint-Simon ; but he was not happy unless a man rode in front of him always to make a way for him, and if this advance guard of his got out of sight, he would dismount and wait by a tree till the arrival of some of his people. On this occasion no wolves were found, so Monseigneur went stag-hunting instead with the hounds of M. du Maine.

M. du Maine, the son of De Montespan and Louis XIV., had been confided to the care of De Maintenon in his childhood. He was crippled, and she took him into the country to see a doctor who was reputed to have skill in curing lameness. The letters of the

[1] See Saint-Simon.

governess to the mistress during this journey are models of consummate adroitness : devoted, respectful, zealous, intended also for the eye of the King. Sometimes she encloses a letter from the Prince, which in its unchildlike and discreet homage suggests the guiding hand of his governess, and is far from being, as she describes it, " un barbouillage du mignon."[1] Du Maine owed much in after-life to Madame de Maintenon's real affection for him. Faint echoes of the storm of impotent rage produced by his being declared a Prince of the Blood still vibrate from the pages of Saint-Simon. But though he and Madame de Maintenon had left the King no peace till they had attained this end, its achievement was by no means an unmixed joy, for, as Du Maine pleasantly expressed it to his familiars, what with the legitimate Princes of the Blood and the Peers, he felt " like a louse between two finger-nails." His wife's folly and extravagance, which he did not venture to control, were still further stimulated by this new honour.

James went hunting too, and it was noticed with approval by the onlookers that he kept up well with the hounds ; but the weather continued atrocious, and they lost the stag. "His Britannic Majesty did not give up going boldly to the hunt with Monseigneur, in spite of his vexatious circumstances," says Madame de Lafayette, and she adds with the little sting of contempt characteristic of her—" and hunted as a man of twenty years might have done, who has no other care than that of amusing himself." The implied reproach was, however, unjust on this occasion. As noted by Dangeau, James had discussed with Louis the situation

[1] "A rigmarole from the darling."

that had arisen in England from the offer of the Government which the Lords had made to William; and on the day of the hunting he had so far occupied himself with his own affairs as to direct Melfort to write to Louvois, the Minister of War, asking for an audience.

A few words must be said of Louvois, who ministered military affairs in France for a period of more than twenty-five years. He had directed the military operations which had covered French arms with glory. A great historian has declared him to be "the greatest adjutant-general, the greatest quartermaster-general, the greatest commissary-general that Europe had seen. He may be said to have made a revolution in the art of disciplining, distributing, equipping, and provisioning armies." But despite the splendour of his ability and his services, he was not beyond the hurt of intrigue. He was one of the two witnesses to the secret marriage of Louis and Madame de Maintenon,[1] and he had extracted a solemn promise from his master, that she should never be publicly acknowledged. Later on, when Madame de Maintenon was sufficiently secure of her position to insist on having the marriage made public, Louvois became aware of the King's intentions, and going to him flung himself on the ground before him and clasped his knees, and implored Louis to kill him on the spot with the sword he was wearing, rather than cover himself with infamy in the eyes of Europe. This loyal servant's entreaties were successful, but henceforward Madame de Maintenon set herself to

[1] They were married by Père de la Chaise at Versailles by night, in the presence of Bontems, governor of Versailles, Harlay, Archbishop of Paris, Louvois, and Montchevreuil, a friend of Madame de Maintenon when she was Madame Scarron.

work his ruin, to make him odious to the King. It was an evil day for France when she achieved her purpose.

It was to this great minister that James applied through Melfort, in order to enlist his sympathies in schemes for recovering the throne and kingdom that had been lost. News was already coming from England that there was much discontent in influential quarters. Admiral Herbert and the young Duke of Grafton were among the malcontents. James was informed of the position of affairs by vague and illusive rumours of a kind which became increasingly frequent, and on which the exiles were always too ready to build hopes. The reports, however, must have been conflicting. There were many to bring them. Among recent arrivals from England was the Papal Nuncio Adda. The relations between Louis XIV. and the Pope being what they were, he was not well received, and it was hoped he would go on at once to Italy. The faithful Rizzini arrived about the same time in France, and hastened to write an account of all he had been through to the Duke of Modena. His perils had not been inconsiderable, owing to the disturbed state of the county, and to his having been mistaken for the detested Father Petre. He had been to Saint-Germain as soon as he arrived, when James and Maria showed "extraordinary pleasure" at his escape from so many dangers. They recommended him to seek an audience of the French King. He did so, and was graciously received in private.

Louis told him he had been in great anxiety for him. Before he left England Rizzini had been entrusted by the French King with a considerable sum of money to be devoted to James's interests. He had saved part

FIRST IMPRESSIONS AT SAINT-GERMAIN 91

of it, although he had lost his own property. After kind congratulations on his safe arrival, Louis went on to praise the Queen of England in compliments which the gratified Italian hastened to convey to her brother. Even if she had not been born a Princess, and were not Queen of England, Louis said, she possessed so elevated a nature, such straightforward, dignified manners, that together with her piety and virtue laid one under the strictest obligation to serve her, and to desire above all things to be able to do more for her. After commenting on the universal admiration for the Queen, Rizzini goes on to say : "Meanwhile the dispossessed King enjoys tranquil repose in this kingdom, the asylum of safety given to him with true brotherly love by this ever-glorious and unvanquished monarch ; and it appears to him to be infinitely less unhappy to be an exile and a fugitive in the arms of friendship than to reign, although peacefully, over perfidious and ungrateful subjects. So that the indifference or insensibility that he appears to show to his misfortunes is noted with varying reflection, but whoever understands his always imperturbable nature is well aware that, however inured he is grown to suffering, so that he is never accustomed to show pain, he is not on that account exempt from severest inward wounds, which are so much the more painful as they are concealed and deep."

This testimony from one who knew the Royal family well is interesting compared with the impression of light-mindedness that James left upon his new French acquaintances. There does not, however, appear to be corroborative testimony to James's deep sense of his position. At this time he probably did not realise it :

he was always optimistic about the future, and he appears to have confidently expected to recover his throne by way of Ireland. This subject perhaps formed the topic of another long private talk James had with Louis at Versailles on the 27th, after which he visited the Dauphine, who was, as usual, poor lady, in bed. These days must have been the least unhappy, in a worldly sense, of the Stuarts' exile. They were welcome and honoured guests, they were enjoying peace and tranquillity after all they had undergone of alarm and anxiety, they were not without reasonable hopes of their restoration in the near future.

Writing to the Duc de Modena at this time, Donna Vittoria Montecuccoli-Davia says that the Queen "wins the hearts of all, and is esteemed and honoured with special distinction by everyone. She now enjoys the best of health and bears everything else courageously, only regretting her inability to recompense those who serve her, as she formerly did." She adds that the Queen has been hitherto served by French officials, but expects that they will soon leave, as there are already many English to take their place, and their numbers are added to every day, including even Protestants.

"The Royal Prince," says this good creature, "is in the best of health and grows more beautiful every day. I am therefore perhaps the only person, who when I have the honour to see him, feel regret at seeing the manner of his bringing up so different from ours. . . . The thing that troubles me most is seeing him bounced up and down on pretence that it is necessary to do so to cure an ailment, which we call rickets, which attacks babies. Then again he is only bandaged (in swaddling bands after the fashion still in use abroad) in the evening, while all day he remains dressed,—sleeps so dressed as if he were seven years of age." In conclusion, she informs the Duke that she has received the patent of her new title, Comtesse d'Almond. Madame de Sévigné's remarks on the dress of the Prince are interesting also: "Mme. de Chaulnes a vu la reine d'Angleterre : elle en est fort contente ; le petit prince, habillé comme un godenot,[1] mais beau, gai, qu'on élève en dansant. Voilà le vrai temps du bonheur des enfants."

James was not idle at this time in his own interest. He sought to enlist support among other European Powers—among them the Grand Duke of Tuscany, to whom he wrote :—

"MY BROTHER,—As you always take much interest in all which concerns me, I do not doubt that you have been sincerely affected by the misfortunes which have befallen me. You and all Christendom see that without the pretext of Religion, the Prince of Orange would never have been able to chase me from my kingdom, as he has done. It is by this means that he has corrupted my troops and the greater part of my Protestant subjects, and that he has persuaded the Princes of this same religion to assist him. I hope that the Catholic Princes will follow this example, and will think of making peace among themselves, in order to be more in a condition to help me to regain my throne, and to establish then the Catholic religion, without, however, doing wrong to anybody. Not doubting that you will lend a hand as a good Catholic and near relation. For the rest, I beg you to believe that I shall have for you all the esteem and affection that you have reason to expect from your affect. brother,
"J. R."[2]

[1] *Godenot*, "figure de petit homme ridicule" (mannikin).
[2] Published by Cavelli from Medici Archives in original Italian.

To all of which the Duke replied in a highly complimentary style, condoling with James on the sacrifices he had made for Holy Religion, and adding ardent expressions of his desire to see so much royal merit speedily recompensed. It is evident from this letter of James's, as from many others written by himself and Maria, that they confidently regarded their cause as that of all Roman Catholic rulers : it is in the name of Holy Religion that they call upon the principalities and powers of Europe to come to their aid. Alas for them ! the day of religious wars was over. Commerce and not creed was to be henceforward the motive power of war. With the rise of nationalities and the need of national expansion, new causes controlled political action ; and while the master-mind of Europe, William III., welded together Protestant and Roman Catholic, Emperor and Pope, against the aggression of France, Louis XIV., his rival, jeopardised his own life's work and that of his predecessors on the throne of France in a spirit of mediæval chivalry.

Meanwhile the interchange of visits went on briskly between Versailles and Saint-Germain. Dangeau describes at length one such visit that took place on January 30th. Louis received James and Maria in his dressing-room ; Monseigneur was present with Madame la Duchesse, and the Princesse de Conti, and Mademoiselle de Blois. With Mademoiselle de Blois, sister of the Duc du Maine, and daughter of Louis's mistress De Montespan, the exiles had already met. Saint-Simon remarks that she and her sister, Madame la Duchesse, were bound together in their aversion for their half-sister, the Princesse de Conti. Madame la Duchesse was the wife of a son of the great Condé.

The Princesse de Conti, the daughter of Louis and the gentle Mademoiselle de la Vallière, the mistress of his youth, had married Louis Armand, Prince de Conti, who had died three years before.

James and Maria went into King Louis's cabinet with these ladies and a few courtiers, and sat down in the medal room—Maria in an arm-chair near the fire, the others on folding chairs: the Countess of Almond sat behind the Queen. They went to Salut, and returning repaired to the Dauphine's room. She received them in bed, and Maria sat with her, while the two Kings shut themselves up in her little cabinet to talk of affairs. It is to Maria that henceforward must be traced most of the initiative in any steps that were taken to secure their restoration. Now and later on, when James was content to resign himself to the consolations of religion and had sunk into a kind of pious lethargy, Maria still had her son's interests at heart. "The Queen of England," says Madame de Sévigné, "has every appearance, if God willed it, of preferring to reign in the fair kingdom of England, where the Court is large and beautiful, than to remain at Saint-Germain, although overwhelmed with the kindness of the King (Louis), which is quite on a heroic scale. As for the King of England, he appears content here, and it is for that reason that he is where he is."

At this moment, James and Maria having decided to appeal to the Pope to unite the Catholic Princes of Europe, Maria writes on February 1st to her uncle, Cardinal Rinaldo d'Este[1] at Rome, in order that their

[1] Published in the original Italian by Cavelli from Archives d'Este at Modena.

messenger may be guided by the advice of a trusted friend who is on the spot, and in a position to judge of the most auspicious moment for presenting their appeal to his Holiness. She excuses herself for delay in writing because for the first fifteen days after her arrival she suffered the pains of death from the uncertainty in which she was about her husband. She is sending her letter by James's messenger Mr Porter, a truly honourable man (*de grande spirito*) and a zealous Catholic, who has orders to show his instructions to her uncle and act only on his advice. She fondly hopes that this may be a means of putting an end to the differences between Roman Catholic Princes "and that all may unite together to defend our Holy Faith," and naïvely continues: "because in truth it would be a shame that while all the Protestant Princes are unwearying and of one accord in the advancement of their faith and religion, the Catholics, instead of uniting to defend it, continue to contend with one another. I am certain that when his Holiness is fully informed of the miserable condition in which we and all the Catholics of our kingdom find ourselves, he will be moved with compassion, and that he will do everything to alleviate it."

James wrote himself to his wife's uncle, telling him that he proposed to inform his Holiness of the present state of his affairs by his Vice-Chamberlain, Mr Porter,[1] "since I have not anyone about me more capable of doing it." His letter is to the same effect as that of his wife. He hopes that the Pope will put an end to the strife between the Roman Catholic Princes of Europe, in order that the Most Christian King may

[1] Colonel James Porter, an Irishman from Wexford.

be free to replace him on his throne, and by so doing to avert the extirpation of the true Religion in the three kingdoms. So important did they consider this mission to the Pope that Melfort wrote some days later, on February 5th, to the same effect to Cardinal d'Este. After describing the existing position of the King and Queen of England's affairs, he continued: "But as there is an almost universal war among the Catholics, the King cannot hope that the Catholic Princes can give him the assistance necessary to his re-establishment and the welfare of Religion."[1] He adds that the interests of Louis XIV. and James are so bound up, that D'Este would do well to consult with the French ambassador on the steps to be taken, but without the Pope's suspecting that he had done so.

The change in the internal economy of the household at Saint-Germain, which Lady d'Almond foreshadowed in writing to the Duke of Modena, was made on the 1st of this month, February. There remained all the stable officials (James, it will be remembered, had not succeeded in recovering his own horses and carriages); but the chaplains, the *maîtres d'hôtel*, "and all that regards the table," as Dangeau puts it, returned to Versailles. James was now served by his own officials, and had "a very mediocre table." Already the rising tide of refugees was making economy a necessity.

[1] Archives at Modena (Cavelli).

CHAPTER VI

GAIETIES AT THE FRENCH COURT

From the enforced economies of Saint-Germain, James and Maria often escaped at this time to share the gaieties of Louis XIV.'s splendid Court. Later on Maria sought a refuge from all her anxieties and disappointments in the neighbouring nunnery of Chaillot, between whose walls she found once more the conventual peace that she had learned to value in her girlhood. But at this time she entered with zest into all the entertainments that Louis XIV.'s Court afforded. Perhaps even in her pious breast may have arisen the thought that the more she deepened the favourable impression she had made on the susceptible French King, the more likely he would be to follow up his "heroic kindness" by practical and substantial aid in re-seating her husband on his throne.

On February 5th Maria, whose searchings of heart on the spiritual danger of witnessing the performance of stage plays were subsequently recorded by her friends and admirers the nuns of Chaillot, accompanied James to a performance of *Esther* at Saint-Cyr.

Madame de Montespan had founded at Paris an institution in which young girls were instructed in the art of fine needlework. Madame de Maintenon wished to outdo this, and founded Saint-Cyr for the education of the daughters of poor nobility. She hoped to win adulation for herself in influential quarters by this good work, and at the same time provide amusement for the King, and an asylum for herself if ever she wanted one. Saint-Cyr was within reach of the Court, though at the same time not too near to unsettle the minds of its occupants. These were to be limited at first to two hundred and fifty young girls, thirty-six nuns, and twenty-four lay sisters. Madame de Maintenon attended personally to every minutest detail. She had not forgotten the economies which Madame Scarron had been forced to practise.

Louis XIV. endowed the institution and gave Madame de Maintenon *carte blanche* for furniture, on which she spent 50,000 florins. She was anxious to avoid equally all that savoured of luxury or of indigence for her little protégées. Neither Louis nor Madame de Maintenon had any liking for the cloister; they wanted to found a community in which the virtues of the convent should be combined with the graces of the world. The King was even averse to the nuns in charge wearing a habit. Madame de Maintenon devised a modification of it, in which she arrayed one of her women for his inspection. "What devil of a nun's bonnet have you given them?" he asked; and the pupils wore a uniform of brown cloth with a white piqué bonnet decked with knots of ribbon denoting the form the pupil was in.

Saint-Cyr was at this time "worthy of the greatness of the King, and of the mind of her who had conceived it, and who conducted it," says Madame de Lafayette;

but she goes on, with her usual sly sneer: "This place, now that we are *dévots*, is the abode of virtue and piety." She foresees frightful rocks ahead, and continues: "To suppose that three hundred young girls, who remain there up to twenty years old, and who have at their door a Court full of lively young men[1]— above all, when the authority of the King will be no longer exercised there; to believe, I say, that young men and girls will be so near each other without climbing over the walls is hardly reasonable." The character of Saint-Cyr was, however, so far irreproachable.

Madame de Maintenon was always seeking some fresh means of amusing Louis,[2] and at the same time liked to provide entertainment for her young protégées; and it was she who had commissioned Racine to write a comedy to be performed by them before the King, choosing, of course, an improving subject — for, as Madame de Lafayette observes, "As things stand now there is no salvation at Court without piety, any more than in the other world." Racine selected the history of Esther and Ahasuerus, and the dramatist not only wrote the play, but coached the little actresses in their parts. The music was pleasing; a pretty little theatre was constructed, with changes of scene. The position of its promoter ensured the success of the performance.

Everyone said that the comedy of *Esther* was superior to anything of the kind that had ever been written. The little girls came in for their share of praise, and Madame de Maintenon was highly flattered by the success of poet and performers; both alike

[1] "Gens éveillés."
[2] "Toujours occupé de dessein d'amuser le roi" (Lafayette).

reflected credit upon herself. For the spectators were not slow to draw a parallel between the fall of Madame de Montespan and of Vashti, and to hail Esther as the prototype of Madame de Maintenon. "Only," adds the irrepressible Lafayette, "all the difference was that Esther was a little younger, and less nice in the matter of piety (*moins précieuse en fait de piété*)." Madame de Maintenon was not a little gratified by the comparison; she wished to extend her triumph. The King had come away from the first performance delighted with it, and so everyone was anxious to see *Esther*, great and small; and what had been originally intended as a convent school entertainment created an incredible amount of excitement, and became the most talked-of affair at Court. The King's ministers sought to ingratiate themselves by leaving the most urgent affairs of State to go and see *Esther*. A second performance was given for such people as Père de la Chaise,[1] the King's confessor, accompanied by a bevy of Jesuits and other pious persons. Then the courtiers were admitted, and finally Louis bethought himself that it was just such an entertainment as would be to the taste of his guests at Saint-Germain.

Accordingly, on February 5th James and his wife arrived at Saint-Cyr at three o'clock in the afternoon, where Louis received them in the chapter-house. Three arm-chairs had been arranged in the little theatre. Louis sat in the middle, with the Queen on his right hand and James on his left. La Beaumelle describes

[1] Père de la Chaise, a Jesuit father, was appointed confessor of Louis in 1675, a post which he occupied for more than thirty years—even after his physical powers had decayed and his memory had failed.

Madame de Maintenon at *Esther*, seated near the King on a *tabouret*, exposed to all regards, meeting them with a majestic modesty, dissimulating, by an openly expressed delight at the success of her pupils, that which she secretly felt at the flattering application of the principal character to herself. Madame de Caylus took the part of Esther, and the actresses surpassed themselves.

Madame de Caylus was a niece of Madame de Maintenon. "Her mind is still more beautiful than her face," writes a contemporary enthusiast, the Abbé de Choisy, "and no Champmêle in the world could have had such ravishing tones as escaped her in declamation; perfect if her carriage had been freer, and if her gaiety had not given her little airs of coquetry which her aunt and advancing age will correct later on." The King did not at first like Madame de Caylus; he found her "précieuse" and a coquette, and she was twice exiled from Versailles to Paris. Her second disgrace ended in her retreating to the Carmelites, whence Madame de Maintenon fetched her back to Court "toute dévote, toute sainte," and the King gradually came to view her with less disfavour.

A day or two earlier an event had taken place which, though insignificant to posterity, divided polite attention with *Esther* and the affairs of the King and Queen of England. The chroniclers of the day, with that lack of a sense of proportion proper to the courtier, record it solemnly. It was that Lauzun had recovered "les grandes entrées."[1] It was thought that he owed this privilege to the intercession of James. At any rate, so important an affair surprised everybody,

[1] The *entrées* of the first gentleman of the chamber.

and infuriated Mademoiselle. The Comte de Bussy-Rabutin had written of Lauzun only the day before this announcement: "He is one of the smallest men in mind as well as body that God has ever made"; and he continues, that such extraordinary reversals of fortune recall that game in which one says: "I have seen him alive: I have seen him dead: I have seen him alive after death—" . . . "'Tis he to the life! I do not think that the King has much regard for the anger of Mademoiselle." . . . "I believe," he concludes, "that she is now thoroughly ashamed of an attachment for such a poor thing."

On February 6th James and Maria visited Louis at Trianon, with which they expressed themselves charmed. Louis and James retired for some private conversation. The proposed visit to Ireland was now under constant discussion. The Queen played at "moitié" with Monsieur against Madame de Ventadour and Madame d'Epinay. Madame la Duchesse de Ventadour was Charlotte-Eléanore-Magdaleine de la Mothe-Houdancourt, daughter of a Duke and Marshal of France. She married the Duc de Ventadour, and was made "gouvernante des enfants de France," a post that had been held by her mother before her. She had attached herself to Madame de Maintenon, and was in receipt of a pension. Besides Lady d'Almond, several English ladies had accompanied the Queen—Lady Sussex, and a sister of the Duchess of Richmond. The latter two had arrived at Saint-Germain on January 15th.

It was at this time that the Queen, who never lost sight of the serious business of life, began the attempt to enlist in the interest of herself and James the support and sympathy of the General of the Jesuits. Neither Emperor nor Pope was in a position actively to espouse the cause of the exiled King and Queen, and this was a bitter and bewildering blow to Maria, though the reason was not far to seek. Both Leopold and Innocent XI. were bound by every instinct of self-preservation to resist the aggression of France.

It is impossible to understand the fruitlessness of the persevering attempts of James II. and his wife to elicit support from the Pope and the Emperor without some general acquaintance with the events which had led up to the then existing position of European politics, and had induced the two Catholic heads of Christendom, the Emperor and the Pope, to throw in their lot with the Protestant Powers of Europe, against the interests of a true son of the Church—the dispossessed King of England. France was in the seventeenth century the preponderating power in Europe. The events of the period group themselves round the commanding figure of Louis XIV. The first half of his reign had marked the building up of his power. He was the arbiter of Europe. But after 1688 he had to deal with the combination of European Powers against him formed by William III. With the latter years of this period we are not concerned, since long before the conclusion of Louis XIV.'s reign James II.'s melancholy and ineffective life had come to an end. But throughout his reign the French King never lost sight of the twofold aim of his foreign policy. He wanted to make the Rhine the frontier of France, and to unite France and Spain under one monarchy. By war, by treaty, by aggression he had striven to realise these aims; but by 1688 he was beginning, by the operation of various causes, to decline from the zenith of his power. The disastrous Revocation of the Edict of Nantes, the persecution of the Protestants, and the consequent loss to France of the enterprising and industrious Protestant population, had been a contributory incident. But earlier, in 1686, Louis's territorial aggressions had so alarmed Europe that the League of Augsburg was formed (through the influence of William of Orange) by the Emperor, the Electors of Saxony and Bavaria among others—and was secretly joined by the Pope, Innocent XI. It is then easy to see that James and Maria had little to hope from Imperial or Papal support.

Thus Maria turned to the heads of the Jesuit Order, to whom she addressed an eloquent and bitter appeal.[1] "Has not Religion," she asks, "been the cause of the treason and revolt of our subjects? And have we not lost our own kingdom through having tried to advance that of Jesus Christ? For this reason I cannot enough wonder at the strange politics of those Princes, even professing Catholics, who have fallen a prey to such false and unchristian ideas, as to say that Religion had no part in our misfortunes, and who have subsequently not ceased to treat us as enemies from the moment that the heretic usurper possessed himself of our throne." "En vérité c'en estoit un peu trop que d'ajouter des calomnies et des injures aux malheurs dont il a plu à la Divine Providence de nous éprouver." She entreats the prayers of the Order for their cause, and herself prays "que Dieu me donne la grâce d'une entière résignation à la sainte volonté."

[1] Saint-Germain, Feb. 1689. Stuart Papers at Windsor. Published by Cavelli.

106 THE ENGLISH COURT IN EXILE

Meanwhile James wrote to the Emperor Leopold early in February, hoping, as he says himself, that "when his Imperial Maty saw the Prince of Orange make use of his friendship and assistance, to pursue his own unnatural ambition, and dethrone a Catholic King, he might relent in some measure on account of Religion at least, and be inclined to redress so crying an injustice, when he found his honour and conscience engaged beyond what 'tis probable his intention was in the beginning."

But "to His Majesty's great surprise he found that interest had blinded the Austrian zeal and had over-balanced all thought of repairing injuries, which, if they are profitable, easily pass upon Princes as necessary for self-preservation. . . . Accordingly his Imperial Majesty writ the following harsh and provoking answer."[1] Leopold took two months to reply, so that his letter did not reach James till he was in Ireland. It is noteworthy that he addresses James as "your most Serene Highness," not as "your Majesty."

The tenor of James's letter may be deduced from the Emperor's reply :—"Leopold, etc. The letter of the 6th of February which your Serenity writ to us, from the Castle of St Germains, we receiv'd from the Earl of Carlinford your ambassador in our Court, in which you gave us an account into what circumstances your Serenity was reduced by the desertion not only of your army, on the Prince of Orange's coming, but even of your servants, and those you put most confidence in, which forced you to seek refuge in France, and there-

[1] James's original letter, which is in Latin, is preserved in the Vienna Archives. Leopold's reply, likewise in Latin, is translated in Clarke's *Life.*

fore request our assistance for the regaining of your kingdoms. We do assure your Serenity, that we no sooner heard that deplorable instance of the instability of human affairs, but we were sencibly touched and truly afflicted, not only out of the common motives of humanity, but for our sincere affection to you, to see that happen, which (tho' we hoped the contrary) we had too much reason to aprehend; for had your Serenity given more attention to the kind representations we made you by our ambassador the Count of Kaunits, instead of harkening to the fraudelent suggestions of France, who by fomenting division betwixt your Serenity and your people, thought to have had a better opertunity of insulting the rest of Europe; and had you thought fit to use your power . . . to put an end to their continual breaches of faith . . . and for that end had entered into the same measures with us, and those who had a right notion how things stood; we doubt not, but your Serenity would by that means have extreamly mollifyd and repress'd the odium, which your people have of our Religion, and have settled peace and tranquility not only in your own kingdom, but in the whole Roman Empire."

The Emperor, continuing, leaves it, he says, to James's own judgment whether he is in a position to give him any support, when he had not only a war with the Turks on hand, but was engaged in "repressing a cruel and unjust one, which the French thinking themselves secure of England, have (against their solemn faith and engagement) lately brought upon us." Then follows a long indictment of France and French policy, which has forced the Emperor to act in self-defence; and he concludes: "Your Serenity is too reasonable to think us worthy of blame, if we endeavour by the force of armes to gain that security, to which hithertoo so many treatys has proved so inefectual, and that we enter into such measures with those that have the same interest with us, as seems necessary for our common security and defence; beseeching Almighty God to direct all for his glory, and that he will grant your Serenity true comforth in your afflictions; whom we embrace with a lasting, tender and brotherly affection.—Vienna, Aprill 9, 1689."

While these vain negotiations were maturing the gaieties of the English and French Courts were undiminished. On February 8th Monseigneur came over to Saint-Germain to hunt with James, and two days later the English royal family went to Marly. James and Louis went off together to talk business, while Maria played at "bête," a game of cards, with the Princesse d'Harcourt and Madame de Croissy. Afterwards they played at "portique," a kind of billiards, greatly in vogue at the French Court. Heavy stakes were sometimes laid at this game, for Dangeau mentions that on one occasion, making a bank with Lauzun and others, he won 2000 pistoles. For the first time James and his wife dined with Louis. Lady Powis and the Countess d'Almond sat at the same table. It was a lovely day, and all the English who were present declared themselves delighted with Marly. The Abbé Rizzini, writing to the Duke of Modena of the entertainments at the French Court at which the King and Queen of England had been present, adds that they receive there from everyone "demonstrations of the most cordial friendship, the opinion of the Queen being ever heightened. The eagerness and the joy shown by the Most Christian King at seeing her consoled are indescribable." It is curious that he here employs almost the same words that Burnet uses of Mary in England.[1] No one comes in contact with her "que non ne parte piena di contento e d' ammiratione"—who does not leave her filled with contentment and admiration.

Through the early part of this month detachments of men and horses kept arriving from England at Saint-Germain to take service with James, "all of them the finest men," says an Italian correspondent of the Grand Ducal secretary at Paris.[2] This writer thinks James was not unpopular with the men, whatever may have been the attitude of their officers, and is of opinion that if he had put himself at the head of his army he might have achieved something. He continues: "He always lives surrounded by priests, and speaks of his misfortune with such indifference, as if he was not concerned in it and had never been King, so that the French themselves have quite lost the opinion they had of him, and those that knew him when he was in Flanders, when he was only Duke of York, assert that he is no longer the same man. Such and so great is the change which is found in his Majesty, who for the rest, is so affable and courteous to all, that in this respect he leaves nothing to be desired."

Meanwhile James, unconscious of these strictures, was hunting again with Monseigneur at Saint-Germain, and two days later, on February 18th, he was again a visitor at Versailles—a visit of some importance,

---

[1] "She gave a wonderful content to all that came near her."

[2] Abbé Melani, Medici Archives, February 7, writing to the secretary of the Grand Duke of Tuscany (Cavelli).

evidently, since he arrived at two o'clock, and he and the King spent a long afternoon together, walking in the gardens, orangeries, and among the famous fountains till half-past five, talking of James's departure for Ireland, which was now drawing near, and of all that depended upon it.

A day or two after James's visit to Louis XIV. and their long afternoon walk together, he wrote once more to Rome, to Cardinal d'Este,[1] telling him of all he hoped from the Irish expedition: "The Most Christian King furnishes me with a good enough fleet to ensure my safety, and also with some munitions, and some experienced officers; with as much money as I could expect from him, in the condition in which he is himself, having so many enemies on his hands, but not as much by a great deal as is necessary to achieve the enterprise in which I am engaging, and on which depends the success of my entire re-establishment in all my kingdoms. For you must know that I have at present in that country an army of 20,000 men all Catholics, under the conduct of Lord Tyrconnel; . . . and besides there are in Ireland a great abundance of provisions and men, the loyalest in the world, who are all ready to shed the last drop of their blood in my defence, provided that there is the wherewithal to arm and pay them. Besides this it is well known that from Ireland to Scotland is an easy crossing, convenient for the transport of an army."

Once there, James thinks all the Catholics will rally round him, and together they will descend upon England. And after begging the Cardinal to use all his influence with the Holy See, he concludes: "I hope

[1] Written from Paris, February 16 (Cavelli).

that his Holiness will believe that the present opportunity of destroying Heresy with a Catholic army is not one that must be lost, and that he will not spare the treasures of the Church, when I am freely risking my own life."

James's wife added a few words on the same subject herself two days later. She laments sadly enough the want of a good understanding between the Pope and Louis XIV., and continues:[1] "To speak as in a confessional and with an open heart, they (this Court) do not appear to me to have the wish to do right (*di far bene*). They say, replying in general terms, that the Pope does not wish for a reconciliation. . . . I pray God that He will inspire these two great men to unite together for the greater glory and the good of our Holy Religion, and that they will co-operate in restoring us to our kingdom. This King has indeed given us much aid, and I hope his Holiness will do the same, because without money we can hope for nothing good." Maria was always strictly practical, but in the concluding sentences of her letter her carefully guarded feelings break through the cloak of reserve: "I, for my part, am in the greatest distress, tormented in mind and body. I have had for many days the cruellest pains from the stone, that have left me so cast down that it is not without fatigue that I write this letter." The King, she adds, has formed the praiseworthy resolution of going to Ireland, . . . "while I stay here desolate, and abandoned by all." Meanwhile Bevil Skelton, who had been sent as envoy to the Emperor to plead his master's cause, succeeded in eliciting no more practical aid than fair words and

[1] Archives of Modena.

expressions of sympathy. There was obviously no hope of rousing the Catholic Powers of Europe to engage in a crusade for the restoration of the King of England. Louis XIV. was the exiles' only friend, and James's one hope lay in the recovery of his throne by force of arms furnished by the Most Christian King.

It may be recorded that the Papal Nuncio, Adda, whom James declared to have betrayed him, returning from England at this time, expressed a great desire to see the glories of Versailles, and received a grudging permission to visit them in the King's absence. Of these glories, one of Louis's courtiers has left a scathing indictment. "Saint-Germain," wrote Saint-Simon, "a lovely spot with a marvellous view, rich forest, terraces, gardens, Louis abandoned for Versailles, the dullest and most ungrateful of all places, without prospect, without wood, without water, without soil: for the ground is all shifting sand or swamp, the air accordingly bad. But he liked to subjugate nature by art and treasure. He built at Versailles on and on, without any general design, the beautiful, the ugly, the vast, the mean all jumbled together. His own apartments and those of the Queen are inconvenient to the last degree, dull, close, stinking. . . ." (One may note in respect of the palaces of kings at this time, that Evelyn says the apartments of Charles II. were always "nasty and stinking.")

But Saint-Simon is not at the end of his indictment. ". . . The gardens wearied, the vast reservoirs for the fountains, defective as was their supply, disseminated unhealthy damps and odours; . . . and the vast enterprise was no less costly in men than in millions, for the soldiers drafted in to carry out the vast designs sickened and died like flies." However, the bitter critic stood almost alone among his contemporaries in this clear-eyed condemnation. Though La Bruyère and Bussy-Rabutin, who like him kept their opinions secret, would have endorsed his views, the new royal residence roused a practically unanimous enthusiasm, while the King's insensate vanity and love of display engendered an extravagance and taste for luxury which permeated all ranks of society with mischievous results.[1]

[1] See La Beaumelle.

CHAPTER VII

MARIA IN JAMES'S ABSENCE—THE CONVENT OF CHAILLOT

OF all Maria d'Este's melancholy life, probably the months of James's absence in Ireland were the most trying. The inexorableness of death brings its own consolation; to her devout imagination James's entry into another world could only mean for him the possession of an incorruptible crown instead of the earthly one he had sacrificed in this life. But the most burning faith, the most pious trust, are hardly proof against the grinding pain of uncertainty, the long-drawn-out, gnawing anxiety of the slow days passing without news; and Maria's piety was never of an ardent, ecstatic type: it seems always something attenuated, wan and cloistered.

It is difficult to realise to-day, when a few hours can bring news of the absent from the farthest ends of the earth, how great must have been the suspense of those who remained at home two hundred years ago. Then news was slow and uncertain; roads were so bad that the journey from Brest to Paris could take six days; ships were at the mercy of the winds.

MARIA, WIFE OF JAMES II.
Reproduced from the Portrait in the Museum of St. Germain.
(By permission of M. Salomon Reinach.)

The departure and absence of the King, wrote the faithful Lady d'Almond to the Duke of Modena,[1] "was the only thing which had power really to pain his wife, who shows an indescribable courage, and a total indifference to all her other losses—so much so that she declared she rather liked having her ease, and fewer personal possessions, that she is only pained for the sake of those who suffer through her. As for the King, he accommodates himself very contentedly to a private life." Even the news of the election of William and Mary to the throne "has not affected their Majesties at all, at which all marvel."

In these sad months, while James was staking all his hopes on his unsuccessful venture in Ireland, his incompetence pitted against the youth and genius of his son-in-law, and while James's daughter Mary, struggling with disaffected nobles in England, and torn with anxiety for the husband she so passionately loved, found a vent in her diary for all her pent-up feelings,—James's wife, Maria, sought a refuge for her soul among the nuns of Chaillot.

The Convent of the Visitation at Chaillot stood on a hill overlooking the Seine. All traces of this cherished sanctuary of the exiled Queen have long since disappeared; but here in days still more remote than hers the Maréchal de Bassompierre had built himself a lordly pleasure-house, and the gay world had strolled on those lovely banks of the Seine where sober nuns demurely bent over their breviaries. The contrast inspired the author of the *Mémoires de Gramont* with verse that we

[1] Archives d'Este, February 16 (Cavelli).

have ventured to translate into still more halting English :—

> By what strange irony of fate
> Sees Bassompierre's mansion, late
> The abode of gallantry and grace,
> A convent risen in its place?
> But still within its sober wall
> Gathers of worth and greatness all
> That earth can show. And first that Queen
> Whose charming son bears like a king,
> Calm and unmoved, the battle's din :
> He whose sweet sister, rising star,
> Softens with radiance from afar
> England with rebel strife still torn,
> And shall that Court once more adorn.[1]

By a curious coincidence, the monastery of Chaillot had been founded by Henrietta Maria, the daughter of Henri IV., mother of James II., who likewise had found a refuge at Saint-Germain when "la rebelle Angleterre" had executed her husband. According to the strange and repulsive sentiment of the time, she had bequeathed her heart as a legacy to the convent, and it was piously guarded there among their most sacred relics. The royal family

---

[1] Par quel bizarre enchantement
La maison du feu Bassompierre,
Cet homme jadis si galant,
Est-elle aujourd'hui le couvent
Qui reçoit tout ce que la tems
A de plus digne et de plus grand?
La mère de ce roi charmant
Que dans les dangers de la guerre,
J'ai vu tranquille, indifférent,
Et sa sœur cet astre naissant,
Qui de la rebelle Angleterre,
Sera quelque jour l'ornement.

and the nobility often visited this convent, many of whose nuns bore the names of the most ancient and most honoured families of France. It was here that Mademoiselle de la Vallière had sought a refuge from the ardent pursuit of Louis XIV. The charms of Chaillot were by no means wholly of an ascetic kind. Externally its surroundings were pleasant to the eye; it commanded a lovely view; while within the convent's walls were many rich legacies, and the Queen's apartments had been luxuriously furnished for her by the French King's command. At the time of the suppression of the convent during the French Revolution, an official record was made of the "Tableaux et objets précieux du monastère de Sainte-Marie de Chaillot," and lists of their treasures had been also made by the nuns themselves.[1] "The Queen," says one such record of 1716, "never lets pass any opportunity of testifying her royal affection to us. She has done us the honour of giving us last year two grand and magnificent pictures in gold frames, seven feet high by five, to put in our 'grande tribune.' One of these pictures represents to the life her august husband, the late King James II., who leads to eternal glory (represented in the clouds) the Princess Louise-Marie, his incomparable daughter, painted also to the life. The other picture represents our Queen (Maria) as a Saint Helena, holding in her hand the Cross of our Lord, which she presents to the King as to another Constan-

[1] Such of these records as survived were discovered by the industry of Cavelli and published by her in the original French. The original letters of Maria to the nuns of Chaillot are in the Archives de France Two volumes of them have also been published by the Roxburghe Club.

tine. These pictures are very beautiful and greatly admired. . . ."

Rigaud[1] is mentioned as the artist who painted them; and Rigaud was one of the most celebrated portrait-painters of Louis XIV.'s reign, regarded, indeed, by his contemporaries as without a rival in Europe. His portrait of Louis XIV. in the Louvre is typical of his grandiose style; but the mean and sensual old face of the Grande Monarque, emerging from an enormous wig, discloses a strong sense of character. Among other pictures on the walls of Chaillot was one painted by a better artist, Mignard. It also was a picture of James and his daughter, the Princess Louise Marie, who held in her hand an open book in which could be read the words from Psalm xlv.: "Hearken, oh daughter, and consider: incline thine ear. Forget thine own people and thy father's house." The picture must have been commissioned by the Queen before 1695, because Mignard, who painted the heads, died in that year. This painter had been regarded as the rival of Le Brun in the fashionable world of his time. Louis XIV. frequently sat to him for his portrait, and he was entrusted with extensive decorations at Versailles. So that James and Maria had employed the best portrait-painters of the day. The picture was subsequently completed by the painter Gobert after James's death in 1701. Another portrait of Maria by Mignard hung in the gallery, as well as portraits of Henrietta Maria, Catharine, wife of Charles II., the Princess Louise and her brother, and portraits of the French royal family, distinguished members of the Order, and saints in

[1] Hyacinthe François Honorat Pierre André Jean Rigaud, born at Perpignan, July 1659, influenced by Le Brun.

LOUIS XIV.
By Rigaud.

the costume of the time. Among them the Prince of Wales figured as Moses in the bulrushes.

In the church were precious marbles and bronzes, and all sorts of medals and curiosities of the Stuarts. They are all scattered and gone; and of the fine library there survives only some of the correspondence of Maria with her loved Sisters of the Visitation, especially with La Mère Claire Angélique de Beauvais. This correspondence, says Cavelli, must be read in order to appreciate this "âme d'élite, et sa piété si vraie." The Queen could write to the nuns at Chaillot when her hopes seemed at their lowest :—

"Our affairs are in a more pitiable state than ever, almost desperate, but what consoles me is that they are in good hands—in the hands of God! I am sure that all which happens to us will only be for the salvation of my soul. What are all the kingdoms of the earth, and even this miserable and uncertain life, compared with God and Eternity? God is my all! That is the refrain that my heart is unwearied in repeating, and which elevates and gladdens me."

James's departure for Ireland took place on Sunday, February 27th, and Maria was left alone at Saint-Germain, "abandoned by all," as she said bitterly. But in these first days of her solitude Louis XIV. did everything possible to cheer and console her. Dangeau's journal records a visit to Saint-Germain of one or other of the royal family almost every day. On March 4th, for instance, Monsieur went to Saint-Germain to see the Queen, "qui est toujours fort triste et assez incommodée." The day after, Louis XIV. paid her a visit in person, and a few days later Monseigneur, accompanied by the Princesse de Conti, paid her a visit. Apart from the natural depression of spirits consequent on the anxiety about her husband, the Queen was suffering in health, and alternating between hopes that she might be going to have another child, and fears that these hopes were delusive. Early in March she instructed Lady d'Almond to write to Cardinal d'Este as follows: "I must ask pardon of your most serene Highness for having been too eager to inform you of the hopes that I had of the pregnancy of her Majesty the Queen. She had no doubt about it, and already the King of France was a party to the secret. . . . She finds that she has made a mistake, and distresses herself about it, especially from the consideration that the King will be upset by it, since he went away hoping, with good ground, to see himself shortly presented with another son. . . . The Queen passes her time writing and reading, and spends much time at her prayers. . . . She is always the same, and her virtue is incomparable. . . . This evening the Queen has received letters from Brest, where the King arrived at five o'clock, and was waiting for a favourable wind. He writes that he is not at all tired."

The birth of another child meant much both to James and Maria; it would dispose for all time of the shameful insinuations as to the origin of the Prince of Wales, and confound those who had made them. A few days after her lady-in-waiting had written, Maria followed up her letter with one from herself to the Cardinal.[1] She begins by reiterating her entreaties to him to use his influence to reconcile the Pope and Louis XIV.: "I have nothing so much at heart as these differences between Rome and the King of

[1] Archives d'Este (Cavelli).

France. . . . I pray you not to be wearied—labouring not only in the King's service and mine, but for God Himself and His Holy Church." She continues in a quite businesslike strain to ask what the first steps should be. She wants it clearly explained. She knows that here it would be desired that the excommunications should be withdrawn, and the ambassador received, but her knowledge is too superficial; and she adds that it is said that if the Pope would take the smallest steps, here much would be done—but no one wishes to begin —how then can it be hoped to finish ?

In the following month of March Maria was so unwell that Monseigneur came over to Saint-Germain to inquire for her. But she seems soon to have recovered, aided perhaps by good news of James's safe arrival in Ireland which was brought to Marly. On April 3rd came a letter from James himself, one of his optimistic letters. The Irish received him as well as he could wish. He has found 50,000 men ready to serve him. Not all armed, it is true, but he will provide them with arms. They show an indescribable joy at seeing him, and have sent fifty oxen and four hundred sheep for the sailors.

About the same time Maria wrote to the nuns of Chaillot, who had paid her the compliment of proposing to elect her as their head, declining the honour, and at the same time congratulating them on "the marks of kindness and consideration that our great King shows you, and to me in the first place, since you indeed wish to put me at your head, although I can truthfully say that my greatest ambition, and the strongest desire I have ever had in my life, has been to be one of the least among the daughters of the

Visitation. But God not having wished to grant me this grace, which would have been a good for myself alone, gives me now that of being able to procure good for the whole Order. . . . I shall not fail to express to the King my gratitude and the true pleasure that I take in all the kindness that he does you . . . and I shall never omit to show to all the world that part that I take in all concerning your Holy Order, and our dear Chaillot in particular. . . ."

This letter, which was addressed to the Mother Superior while she was at Saint-Cyr, continues: "We are all in good health here, thank God. I will send my son to see you whenever you like. Let me know if you think that M. de M.[1] would be worried by him, for in that case I will send him while she is away; if not, I will send him one day next week. I am in doubt whether I shall go to bid farewell to M. de M. and take leave of you at Saint-Cyr before her journey; or whether I shall wait to go to see you till after her departure, which I should like much better, provided that I can see her here before she goes away; but if that is inconvenient to her, I will go to Saint-Cyr." There is more than a suggestion here that it behoved the most favoured to walk warily with Madame de Maintenon, and avoid giving her any ground of offence. The Queen of England was obviously most anxious not to do so.

The letter concludes: " I propose to go to Chaillot and sleep there for one night. I expect that you will return there on the 2nd or 3rd of April, and that I shall see and embrace you there with all my heart in Holy Week. Here is a long enough letter, and yet

[1] Evidently Madame de Maintenon.

I have said nothing, but we must wait for all the rest till I have the pleasure of talking with you.—M."

There is a familiar charm about these letters of the Queen's. They recall her early childish letters to the Superior of the Convent of the Visitation at Modena. Behind the convent doors class distinctions fell away, the Queen could talk freely and intimately to the sympathetic nuns. No tiresome etiquette, no questions of fauteuils and tabourets disturbed the peace of their relationship; her own words show how much she valued the simplicity of their lives : " Thank you, my very dear Mother, for the offer you have made me of giving me dinner in your assembly room. But I don't care about that. I wish to eat in the refectory with all of you. I beg you to expect me on Tuesday till eleven o'clock, remembering that it is a fast day. . . . I have already ordered, before seeing Riva, that they bring you food for Tuesday's dinner, which I am persuaded my sister Marie Francis will gladly prepare when she knows that a portion of it will be for me. I charge her to make it just like yours without any ceremony. Adieu, my very dear Mother ; adieu to all our dear sisters. I please myself with thinking I shall soon be for some hours at Chaillot. I am in great need of such a solace, for since I left you I have had no repose of mind or body."

Other sources of contemporary information throw light on the Queen of England's relations with the French Court, especially during James's absence. A coolness arose at one time between Louis and the Queen of England, through James's enemies at the French Court having told Louis that the King of England was discontented at his treatment of him ; that he complained that the Court had mocked at his misfortune; and that he was quite unappreciative of all that had been done for him. Louis was piqued at these reports. His civilities to the Queen temporarily ceased, together with invitations to Versailles; and worse still, the reinforcements for Ireland hung fire. Madame de Maintenon was generally accused of having made mischief. On learning the cause of Louis's annoyance, Maria confided her trouble to Madame de Maintenon, who consoled her and promised to undeceive the King. La Beaumelle, who tells the story, adds that De Maintenon alone remained the friend of the Queen of England when all hope of her restoration was abandoned. Madame de Lafayette gives an entirely different view of their relations: "However the Queen of England was at Saint-Germain in a condition of terrible melancholy and depression. Her tears never dried. The King, who has a good heart, and an extraordinary tenderness, especially for women, was touched with the misfortunes of this Princess, and softened them in every way he could imagine. He had all the kindness for her that she deserved. . . . In fact, his manner towards her was so agreeable and engaging that the world believed he was in love with her. The thing appeared probable enough. People who did not look at things very closely gave out that Madame de Maintenon, although she only passed for a friend, regarded the manners of the King towards the Queen of England with the liveliest inquietude." She adds that there was nothing in it except gossip.

In later years the Queen's own letters show that it was to Madame de Maintenon that she applied as a go-between to make appeals to Louis XIV. for money,

MARIA IN JAMES'S ABSENCE

both for the Convent and for her own necessities. She gave the nuns an account of one of these applications, which were not always cordially received by the all-powerful lady. It was on the occasion of a visit of Maria's to Marly at a time when her affairs were extraordinarily embarrassed by the influx of Irish refugee priests. She spent some time alone with Madame de Maintenon, who was ill in bed, and took this opportunity of telling her that her pension was eight months overdue. She added that she had partly come to speak to the King about it, but that courage failed her, though her heart was pierced at the sight of the sufferings of so many people. Madame de Maintenon appeared greatly touched, and said she would speak of it to the King without fail, and he would be concerned to hear of it. She added that the news surprised her, for she had heard that 50,000 francs had been recently paid. The Queen said that that was the case, but this sum was for arrears of the seven months before. Maria added with a deep sigh that all knew well what she received was not for herself but for these poor Irish. "Do they think much is over for us of this 50,000 francs when they are divided? Perhaps, 2000 florins to put in our pockets."

To preserve, however, the narrative in proper sequence — it was on April 6th that Maria retired to Chaillot, occupying the rooms which Louis had had furnished there for her; though he had no idea of allowing her to mope for long in a convent. After four days spent after her own heart among the nuns, in prayer and self-communings, she was present at a supper party at Marly. Arriving there at seven o'clock, she played "portique" till nine. Then there was music and a grand supper, at which Maria sat apart with Louis XIV. Meanwhile James had written from Waterford in good spirits. Three days later, on April 13th, the Queen went to visit the Dauphine at Versailles. The Dauphine was up, but received her visitor in her bed-room, where three fauteuils were provided for Maria, the Dauphine, and her husband, Monseigneur. As the Queen was getting into her carriage, Louis, who had just come in from hunting, saw her from a window and hurried down to talk to her at the door. A few days later, April 25th, saw Maria again at Versailles. The Dauphine was in bed, where a terribly large proportion of her short life must have been spent. Madame, who had much liking and affection for her, declares in one of her letters that Madame de Maintenon had amiably persuaded Louis that his unfortunate daughter-in-law was malingering. At any rate, none of the physicians of the day—"all very ignorant," as even Madame could see—were able to diagnose her malady. It must have been a cheerless visit on this occasion in any case, for Monseigneur had just been bled. After visiting these two invalids, the Queen spent some time walking with Louis in the garden, discussing the news from Ireland, no doubt, and putting in a judicious word of encouragement to the Most Christian King to continue the reinforcements on which depended their restoration.

The next day Maria returned to Chaillot, and from thence visited Paris, and received the Holy Communion at Notre Dame, where she was welcomed by the Archbishop at the doors. Let us hope the holy rites of her religion fortified her to bear the mortifying news of the coronation of William and Mary, which reached her on the 25th. Louis evidently felt this was a moment for offering his sympathy to his guest, for he paid her a visit at Saint-Germain the next day, finding her just returned there from Chaillot. The Queen's thoughts turned to her friends at Chaillot even when she could not be with them. She now writes (April 20th) :—

"The too-great respect you have for me, my dear Mother, keeps you from writing to me, and the true friendship that I have for you obliges me to do it, for I take pleasure in telling you that as soon as I am out of your holy cloisters I wish to re-enter them. I believe, however, that this is self-love, for to speak truth I have not found true repose since the King has left me except at Chaillot. It is seventeen days since I have heard any news of him. I ask in charity your good prayers, and those of all your community that I greet from my heart, and especially my dear sisters 'la Déposée' [the ex-Mother Superior; the office was elective] and 'l'Assistante,' whom I pray to offer for me some of their acts of simplicity and humility ; and you, my dear Mother, offer also some part of the many acts of virtue that you perform each day, for me who am from the bottom of my heart your good friend,   MARIA R."

It is curious to find the young Queen Mary in England, occupant of the throne from which her stepmother had been deposed, expressing the same feelings in much the same way, though she had no confidant but her diary: ". . . My heart is not made for a kingdom, and my inclination leads me to a retired quiet life, so that I have need of all the resignation and self-denial in the world."[1] Mary of Orange had no such refuge as Chaillot, though she needed it even

[1] *Memoirs of Mary Queen of England.* Ed. by Dr Doebner.

more, for Maria was at least among friends, while Mary was constrained to live in a hostile atmosphere. But if Mary of Orange was not made for a throne, Maria was certainly made for a cloister. She had more than all the requisite piety, and that love of little ceremonies and details which would have made her an excellent mother superior. She was a nun by nature and inclination. "I am dying to be among you—meanwhile, I will strive to unite my sinful prayers to your holy ones in order to offer them to God."

One day, at the end of April, the three young Princes came to visit the Queen at Saint-Germain, the Dukes of Burgundy, Anjou, and Berry, "and were given fauteuils." Louis was not incapable of occasional endearing acts of small kindness, and about this time he gave Maria an elaborate present which he had had constructed for her, and which was entirely after her own heart. It was one day early in May when she was paying him a visit at Marly, and after walking with her for some time on the terrace, Louis took her into his room and showed her a small cabinet, which on being opened was metamorphosed into a prie-dieu. It could, moreover, be converted into an altar, and was fitted with every accessory of a chapel in miniature. What more appropriate present could have been devised for a pious, depressed gentlewoman! Maria was charmed with it, and "astonished and delighted to see so many pretty things shut up in so small a space." After this presentation followed a game of "portique" and supper. The Queen's next visit was to Saint-Cyr to see Madame de Maintenon, who had evidently not paid the hoped-for visit to Saint-Germain. The two ladies—the Queen in name and the Queen in power—

MARIA IN JAMES'S ABSENCE

spent a long time together, Maria returning, on the authority of Dangeau, "well pleased with her day." A few days afterwards the Prince of Wales went to see the Dauphine's children at Marly.

Meanwhile frequent rumours arrived from Ireland, which came sometimes by way of England, and were generally unfounded. It was said that the fleet was deserting to James, and that he had already landed in Scotland. On the 23rd, however, a courier arrived from him with authentic news, though of no great importance. It was perhaps at this time that Maria wrote from Saint-Germain to the Mother Superior at Chaillot, that she had received, "just as I was finishing my dinner, a very long letter from the King, of a quite recent date, which assured me that he was in quite perfect health. . . . God be for ever praised that He has hearkened to your prayers and those of your dear daughters."

On June 17th she went to Chaillot, returning in time for poor little Prince James's first birthday on the 20th. A fête was held for him at Saint-Germain, a rather forlorn merry-making.

Nothing of importance seems to have occurred during the month of June. Porter, who had been the bearer of letters to Rome, returned, and had an audience with Louis, who afterwards provided him with a frigate that he might report himself to James in Ireland. During July came a rumour of the fall of Londonderry, though as it came through England its truth was doubted. At least once this month Maria dined at Marly to see the hunt, "which was very fine."

In August she was again at Chaillot. Lord Dover found her there when he at last arrived from Ireland with trustworthy news of James. Londonderry was still holding out, but Dover told the Queen the inhabitants were living on horse-flesh, and in great distress. Henry Jermyn, Lord Dover, was a man who had been more notorious than famous. He had been a friend of the ignominious Castlemaine, and a favoured lover of Castlemaine's infamous wife. Unscrupulous in intrigue, he was noted as a duellist; but the fact of his being also a Roman Catholic was a sufficient passport to promotion. He was made Lord Dover, and was one of the Roman Catholics who became Privy Councillors by virtue of James's Dispensing Power. Afterwards he was given a seat at the Treasury Board, a position for which his principal qualification appeared to be that he had lost all his own money at cards. "Though he was brave and certainly a gentleman," says Anthony Hamilton, "yet he had neither brilliant actions nor distinguished rank to set him off, and as for his figure there was nothing advantageous in it. He was little, his head was large and his legs small, his features were not disagreeable, but he was affected in his carriage and behaviour. This was the whole foundation of the merit of a man so successful in amours." He had been entrusted with the secret of the Prince of Wales's escape to France, and had gone to bring him back when Dartmouth had refused to carry him over to France. He had accompanied James to Ireland, whither he returned again on September 14th, when he had delivered his messages.

About a week later Melfort arrived at Brest, sent by James to solicit reinforcements. He was so far successful that on the last day of the month Louis went to Saint-Germain to acquaint Maria with the welcome news of his decision to send 7000 men to Ireland, with Lauzun at their head. For a very long time after this the weather was so bad that no news at all reached Saint-Germain of the war in Ireland. Maria's life must have been uneventful, except for such business as came through her hands connected with the household. But on November 26th she entertained a large party at Saint-Germain. Monseigneur and Monsieur came over to see her, accompanied by Mademoiselle and other ladies. The Princesses, according to Dangeau, would not go to see the Queen of England except in the presence of Monsieur or Madame, because she only gave them stools to sit on. In the presence of Louis XIV.'s brother and sister-in-law they were not entitled to anything else, but elsewhere they had other pretensions. . . . The quarrels of the Princesses among themselves were so violent and so ill-concealed as to be disturbing to the peace of an elderly dyspeptic gentleman, and the King threatened them with banishment from the Court altogether, a warning of such enormity that they were reduced at least to outward decorum.

November was uneventful. Dangeau comments on the very generous allowance made to Lauzun for his Irish command. He was given 10,000 florins for his outfit, and a salary of 50,000 francs a year, while the generals commanding in France were only paid at the rate of 2000 écus every forty-five days.

Early in December there was authentic news from Ireland, for Porter returned. James had wished him to go on to Rome, but Louis thought it better to send Melfort, while Porter remained with the Queen at Saint-Germain. Melfort's mission to Versailles to ask for reinforcements had, as a matter of fact, been sanctioned unwillingly by James; he was only forced to consent to it by Melfort's extreme unpopularity with the French and Irish. John Drummond, Lord Melfort, was brother to the Earl of Perth. He had been Secretary of State for Scotland, and both he and his brother had become Catholics. At Rome such a man was safely occupied and out of the way. Porter meanwhile had an audience of the King on December 9th, and reported, with an echo of the extraordinary optimism by which James was always blinded, that all was going well in Ireland. In the spring, James would, he said, be able to cross into Scotland, and thence descend upon England with a good army.

There was a special reason for the despatch by James of an ambassador to Rome at this time. The great Innocent XI. had lately died, and had been succeeded by Alexander VIII. James hoped that this new accession to the Papacy might be beneficial to himself, and lost no time in sending his congratulations. From Ireland, James wrote at once to Alexander, as follows, in November 1689 :—

"The letter written in your Holiness's own hand demonstrating your sincere and paternal love and compassion for our sufferings have so much increased the joy which we had conceived at the exaltation of your Holiness to St Peter's Chair that they have lessened the sense of our own misfortunes. The only cause of the troubles raised against us is that we have embraced the Catholick Faith: and we do not deny that we had resolved to restore it to three kingdoms and to the several colonies of our subjects of very considerable extent in America. What we have done in this kingdom doth prove the same. We have obtained frequent though small victories over the rebels; they avoided a great one by obstinately declining the same. We improved these for the advantage of Religion, which will I hope be soon established here, intending to doe the like in our other Dominions as soon as we are restored to them. This doth not seem so difficult provided we have some releif [sic] granted, so uneasy are our subjects under the Usurpers yoke and so general is the desire of our return—which a Peace among the Catholick Princes will promote; and if the shortness of time doth not permit it, (the peace), a Truce which will put an end to the tragedy begun in Germany where the Hereticks gnaw the very bowells of the Church. These need no words where things themselves speak and soe clearly call for help. The Apostolick zeal of your Holiness will provide a remedy equal to the disease, and in this confidence we pray God to give your Beatitude a long and happy reign, and being prostrate at your feet, with all filial love and observances we beg your Apostolick Benediction.

"Given in Dublin, 26 Nov. 1689."

The letter is written in Latin in James's own hand, and is translated by a contemporary.[1] It was a letter to which the Pope replied with guarded expressions of paternal benevolence and nothing more. Melfort, however, on arriving in Rome was obliged to present a memorial from the Queen merely, because James's letter had not yet crossed the seas. Melfort assured his Holiness "there never was a King of England so beloved and so obeyed by his people as his Majesty, until it appeared by his actions, that he was more zealous to gain a heavenly crown for his subjects than careful to preserve an earthly one for himself. This, and the extirpation of heresy in France, gave such

[1] Letters written by King James II. to Pope Alexander VIII., contemporary manuscript (Phillips Collection).

alarm to the Protestants throughout all Europe, and even in hell itself, that they put in practice every means however detestable to ruin the King, and with him all those who had the same sentiments of piety and religion." "This mystery of iniquity" must have disastrous consequences to the Catholic Religion. "His Most Christian Majesty has so generously assisted the King that he has been able to quell almost entirely the Irish Rebellion," and it now only remains for his Holiness to give an immediate supply of money and to bring about a peace among Catholic princes, who might then be persuaded to reinstate James. "As for myself," Melfort concludes, "I reckon it a happiness to be at the feet of your Holiness. Having nothing to solicit, but the concerns of the King my master, which are at present those of your Holiness; and after having endeavoured to discharge my duty towards God and my King, although in a more weak and defective manner than another would have done, I have an opportunity of soliciting for myself your Holiness's apostolical benediction."

Some of the statements both in James's appeal and in Melfort's memorial were, we need hardly say, a good deal removed from fact. In reply both to them and to the appeal to which they were joined, Alexander wrote an affectionate letter to James, recommending Melfort to his good graces (a rather unnecessary testimonial) and exhorting the King to patience and perseverance. He promised him the assistance of prayers—even of money—for his restoration; but he never sent more effectual aid than apostolic blessings and indulgences.

Meanwhile the year sped to its close. News of her husband came seldom and uncertainly to the waiting, anxious Queen at Saint-Germain. Let us hope that she found some amusement and distraction in the day's gossip. . . . That the Duchess of Portsmouth, for instance, had asked and obtained an increase of pension on behalf of her son, the Duke of Richmond. It was indeed a golden age for highly-placed hussies: Louise de Querouaille now had an income of 2000 livres from a country whose resources were rapidly becoming exhausted.

Maria spent this sad Christmas quietly at Chaillot, but on the last day of the year came a courier from James who reported that Schomberg (William's general) was dead or dying and had only 5000 men left—news which later intelligence proved to be untrue, but which seemed to Maria like an answer to the prayers she had said with tears before the altar on Christmas Day at Chaillot, from Him who gives "light to them that sit in darkness and in the shadow of death." Overwhelmed with relief and gladness, she hastened to send the glad news to the Sisters who had shared her anxiety.

"*December* 31, 1689.

"It is always on a Saturday, my very dear Mother, that I have news of the King. Thus after the mercy of God I owe all to His Holy Mother, who constantly intercedes for me her wretched and unworthy daughter. I believe that my dear daughters of Sion may already begin to sing canticles of praise to the Most High, whose powerful arm without making use of human means has almost entirely destroyed our enemies. They are almost all dead miserably; a small party with Mr de Schomberg, who was dying himself, have returned into England; and a very small number has remained, of which I believe the King entirely master, and in a position to think of going further. May God be for ever praised, both by me and by my dear sisters, who take part in all which concerns me, and to whose prayers I attribute all our good success. I have just received your letters as I was sending this one. I have only time to read yours, and to thank you with all my heart for your good wishes, which are assuredly prophetic; and a thousand times I thank you for the pretty St John the Baptist, which I love. This is all that I have time to tell you, being overwhelmed with business, to the last point. Only I beg for your continued prayers, and those of your daughters. M. R."

But that was the highest moment of hope that the Queen ever touched. No other confirmatory piece of good news ever came—till James returned in the autumn of the next year with the climax of his own disaster—and the intervening months were spent by the Queen in such business as her little Court necessitated; in prayer; in gaieties at the French Court. During January Louis had an attack of gout, and Maria went over to sit with him, paying him a long visit. On the 19th she drove over to Saint-Cyr to see another performance of *Esther*.

Towards the end of the month a death occurred at Saint-Germain. Lord Waldegrave died there on the 24th. He had married a daughter of James and Arabella Churchill, and James regarded him with so much consideration that he left him in charge of his affairs in his absence. He had continued to fill the now superfluous office of ambassador of James at Versailles. He had a high reputation for honesty and ability, and the Court, which had few faithful and able servants, could ill afford his loss. Perhaps it was as a relief from the gloom it occasioned that

Louis specially arranged a party for Maria two days later. She arrived at four o'clock in the afternoon, and Louis, who had hurried back from hunting on purpose, was waiting to receive her on the steps, with Monseigneur, Madame, the Princesses, and all the principal Court ladies, who joined in games of "portique" and "lansquenet."

In February 1690 the Queen was again at Chaillot, in spite of such severe floods that she had to go home *via* Montmartre and Versailles to reach Saint-Germain. In April occurred the death of the Dauphine. She had been ailing for some time, and had gradually become worse. "The poor Dauphine," writes Madame on February 8th, 1690, "is again very ill. She is now in the hands of a Capucin called Brother Ange. They pretend that he has cured Duke Max of Bavaria and his wife of very dangerous maladies. God grant that the thing may succeed here; but unfortunately it does not look much like it. They kill her by dint of mortifications. They do all they can to reduce me to the same condition, but I am a harder nut to crack than Madame la Dauphine, and before they make an end of me the old women will be sure to break some teeth." Poor Marie-Anne Christine of Bavaria! Few people troubled themselves about this Princess, "because she neither contributed to the fortunes of individuals nor the gaieties of the Court."[1] But Madame at least sincerely regretted her. "At the funeral of the Dauphine," she writes, "I cried so horribly for six whole hours, that I could not see for two days afterwards. Besides that I was very sad to lose Madame la Dauphine, of whom I was very fond, the sight of

[1] Lafayette.

our arms, which were everywhere on the coffin and the black hangings of the Church, recalled to me so vividly the death of the Elector my father, and of Madame my mother, and my dead brother, that I thought I should burst with crying. The Wednesday which followed this terrible ceremony, we went to Marly and stayed there till Saturday. My grief ought certainly to have been dissipated, for they led the ordinary life there. In the afternoon they hunted; in the evening there was music; but that only increased my melancholy."

We have said that after James's letter foolishly describing Schomberg as destroyed no news of a reassuring kind came for months. As a matter of fact, other letters which reached Maria from Tyrconnel, the Irish Viceroy, were the reverse of reassuring, and, as we read them now, promised no hope of ultimate triumph. But at the end of July 1690 came news of a great victory in which Schomberg had been killed, William of Orange had been wounded, and had died of his wounds two days later. No greater good-fortune could have befallen France. Paris went wild with joy. Bonfires were lighted in the streets, and tables erected at which passers-by were forced to stop and drink. Even the carriages of the great were stopped and their occupants "forced to submit to this folly." The Prince of Orange was burnt in effigy; it was impossible to control the wild excitement of the mob. A curious contemporary pamphlet called "The Follies of France, or the Relation of the Extraordinary Rejoicings in Paris, August 8th, 1690," gives a full account of these revellings :—" One could hear nothing but Trumpets, Drums, Hautboys, Fifes, Flutes and

Sackbutts; one could see nothing but tables furnished in every street, where wine was not spared in the least; ... the Religious Fraternities distinguished themselves, and especially the good Fathers of the Cordeliers, who spent all night long a prodigious quantity of Petards and other fireworks in their garden, and distributed their wine about in abundance. All ... as they passed in their coaches through the city were stopped on their way and forced to drink a health to King James and the Prince of Wales, and to cry out the Prince of Orange is dead. They burnt the effigies of the Prince and his Royal Spouse the Princess in several places. ... They dragged them through the city, where they made a solemn procession, and there was neither man nor woman who did not throw dirt and stones at them." A few days later it was known that James's hopes had ended in failure and defeat, that he was coming back to France, while William was entering Dublin in triumph.

Part II
Ireland

CHAPTER VIII

THE EXPEDITION TO IRELAND

IN the declining fortunes of the Stuarts, the expedition of James to Ireland seems to mark a distinct step downwards. After its failure every succeeding attempt to regain the throne that had been lost resembles a forlorn hope. The effort which was to have given James access to England through the side door of Ireland was neither ill conceived nor impracticable. It seems less so now than when defeat and mismanagement obscured the strategical value of the attempt, and when the failure was bitterly ascribed to the incompetence of its leader. Its failure, as we read it now, was due chiefly to the fact that the one person who perceived its true importance was the leader who thwarted it, William of Orange. James, who commanded it, was so preoccupied with the superior advantages which to his mind would have been offered by an expedition against England, that he regarded it rather as a makeshift than as a means, the only means, to an end. To Louis XIV., who financed and equipped it, the expedition seemed a promising way of diverting the attention of William, but scarcely a flank attack into which the whole weight of French resources should be thrown. To Louvois, whose clearness of vision was obscured by his dislike, from economical and personal reasons, of the Court of Saint-Germain, it seemed merely an expedition on which too much should not be spent. In short, the expedition to Ireland was a raid; and it suffered, as more than one raid has suffered since, from being under-financed.

The way in which ministers of State regarded the prospects and probabilities of James's expedition to Ireland is reflected in the gossip of the Court. Madame de Sévigné writes apprehensively of the ill-fortune of the English royal family. Even when she is speaking of the departure of the royal Ulysses, " Was ever family so unfortunate ?" she exclaims ; and she goes on to opine that the difference of religion between James and his English subjects must ever be a hindrance to his restoration. Her correspondent, the Comte de Bussy-Rabutin, responds that there is nothing impossible to a nation which on occasion cuts off the head of its King ; perhaps James's children may succeed where their father has failed ; but for his part he expects to be paying his respects to James at Saint-Germain again within the year. Madame de Lafayette is even more sceptical and more plain-spoken. The departure of the King of England for Ireland, she writes, does not fill the King (Louis XIV.) with any great hope of seeing him re-established on his throne. King James was not long in France, she continues contemptuously, before he was perceived for what he was—a priest-ridden fanatic. But that was not his greatest failing in the eyes of the Court of Versailles. He was feeble ; if he bore his misfortunes well, it was not from fortitude but from insensibility—though he might be physically brave, for "like most of the English he despises death." Poor James! even that merit was not long to be allowed him.

In short, the more one considers the outset of the expedition, the more it seems to resemble a diversion which was royally gilded to appear important rather than an attempt in force to change the history of a nation. It was fairly well but not brilliantly officered; it was not well equipped either in men or munitions of war. Of General Rosen, a bluff German who had shouldered his way up to the rank of a major-general in Flanders, who was to command it, and of Maumont, of the Guards, Pusignan, Lery-Girardin, and Boisseleau and L'Estrade, who took subordinate rank, Madame de Lafayette observes that they were good honest men, no doubt, but they were among the more mediocre of the King's officers. Possibly they might shine when compared with the Irish. James would have preferred to take M. de Lauzun—a choice dictated not by discrimination but by the obstinate preference which James always had for his own favourites. He was not allowed to do so; and to make up to Lauzun for a disappointment which that graceless courtier could no doubt sustain with composure, James conferred on him the Order of the Garter, giving him the self-same diamond star which had belonged to Charles I. By a rather significant coincidence, the vacant knighthood of the Order was conferred at this time in England on another recipient. William gave it to General Schomberg, who was to oppose James in Ireland; and added a more material reward than James could afford—a pension of £4000 a year.

Lauzun was made a Knight of the Garter with due

form and ceremony. James went to mass at Notre Dame, and after mass a Chapel of the Order of the Garter was held : a circumstance which seems to have impressed Madame de Lafayette almost as much as the value of the diamonds on the star, or the motto of "Honi soit qui mal y pense" on the Garter. "The luck of this little Lauzun," she exclaims, "is truly extraordinary!" James then went to dine with the Papal Nuncio, the Archbishop of Paris, and other ecclesiastics; and "his friends the Jesuits" came in to bid him adieu. After dining he paid first a visit to the English Brotherhood, and touched a number of suppliants for the king's evil. A visit to Chaillot concluded the ecclesiastical part of James's leave-takings.

He paid visits also to Mademoiselle at the Luxembourg, to Monsieur at Saint-Cloud, and finally to Louis at Versailles. Next day Louis came to Saint-Germain to speed his parting guest. "Their parting," says Madame de Lafayette sentimentally, "was most tender." It was at any rate marked by a valedictory phrase on the part of "le Roi Soleil" which has deservedly passed into history. "You can never believe," said he, "that I am not grieved to see you go. None the less, the best wish I can give you is that I hope I may never see you return. Yet if by evil fortune you must, you may believe that you will ever find me as you leave me."[1]

The ceremonial visits of leave-taking having been paid, the journey began. James lost no time. He sped

[1] "Vous ne sauriez dire que je ne sois touché de voir vous partir. Cependant je vous avoue que je souhaite de ne vous revoir jamais. Mais si par malheur vous revenez, soyez persuadé que vous me retrouverez tel que vous me voyez." Nothing, adds Madame de Lafayette, was ever better said, or said more rightly.

through Brittany, says one admiring chronicler, like a meteor: though there were two accidents on the way which aroused the usual comments of the superstitious. His carriage broke down at Orleans; and when it was being taken on board at Brest again exhibited a disastrous unmanageability. The raft carrying it swung against the piers of a bridge, and James's valet was drowned. In other respects the journey, rapid as it was, had some of the aspects of a triumphal progress.

The Duc de Chaulnes, one of the plainest but one of the courtliest men of his time, did the honours of his province in the most princely manner. Madame de Sévigné recounts them with a note of admiration. He had prepared not one but two suppers for James on the way—one at Roche Bernard for ten o'clock, one at Nantes for midnight. James was extremely touched by this mark of attention, embraced the Duke, who was in waiting to receive him, and protested that he did not want anything to eat. To no avail. He was ushered by the hospitable governor into a dining-room where not merely a supper, with all the delicacies of the season, was served, but where an obsequious company of ladies and gentlemen waited to receive him. Chaulnes desired to wait on the King at table: James wished that he should sit on his right hand; and "the King ate as hearty a supper as if there were no Prince of Orange in the world." The next day he embarked at Brest.

The ceremoniousness of his departure was not very well proportioned to the meagreness of his equipment for war. Louis was not prepared to stake an army on the fortunes of his royal protégé. Ireland was to furnish that. James was only given what we may describe as the advisory staff, and a magnificent personal equipment, of which the most solid item was £112,000 in money. Otherwise "the Most Christian King gave him 6 general officers, 20 captains, 30 lieutenants, 40 cadets, 4 engineers, various artillery officers, cannons, munitions, arms to arm 20,000 men, a vessel loaded with hand grenades, 12 saddle-horses with rich harness, 3 calashes, 4 changes, a service of silver for his Majesty when eating with other people, and another service *vermeille dorée*, tents for camping out when he is at the head of his army, a bed, linen, toilette, and finally all the equipage necessary to a King when he goes on a campaign. His Majesty has also given him a cuirass, and the pistols that he carried on his saddle-bow, and prayed him to make use of them."[1]

If Louis thought it superfluous to furnish James on his expedition with the highest military talent, he and Louvois were more fastidious in the choice of the diplomatic adviser who was to counsel James and to supervise the interests of France. The Comte d'Avaux, who had taken the place on the expedition which Barillon had been expected to fill, was one of the shrewdest intellects that served Louis XIV. in his duel with William of Orange. A great-nephew of the Comte d'Avaux who had been French Minister of Finance under Mazarin, and who had received the doubtful honour of exile for having been "indiscreet, and too little respectful" to that powerful Cardinal, the younger D'Avaux shone with some of the reflected glories of his relative. If he did not belong to what may have been regarded then as the old school of diplomatists, he was at any rate a supple courtier, and

[1] Quoted from Cavelli.

he was not likely to imitate some of his great-uncle's mistakes—one of which was that of delivering a sermon to the Dutch on the superior advantages of the Roman Catholic religion. Saint-Simon is not sure if he had as great talents, but assigns to him a suave and ingratiating manner, and a perfectly cool and detached judgment. In Holland, though he was the ambassador of Louis, he achieved both the friendship and the respect of the Dutch; and he was credited at the French Court with having penetrated the designs of William on England before either Louis or Louvois had done so. "He was one of the first," says Saint-Simon, " to hear of the project of William upon England when that project was only in embryo and kept profoundly secret. He apprised the King [Louis] of it, but was laughed at. Barillon, then an ambassador in England, was listened to in preference. He, deceived by Sunderland, assured our Court that D'Avaux's reports were mere chimeras. It was not until it was impossible any longer to doubt that credit was given to them. The steps then taken, instead of disconcerting the conspirators, did not interfere with the working out of any of their plans. All liberty was left, in fact, to William to carry out his scheme. . . ." It is possible that Saint-Simon's contempt of Louvois may have led him to overestimate the penetration of D'Avaux; but it is significant that, when D'Avaux, on behalf of Louis XIV., made his famous declaration to the Dutch States General of September 9th, 1688, in which he threatened them with the intervention of Louis if they began hostilities against James, this threat merely served to convert the possibility of William's invasion into an accomplished fact.

D'Avaux, who was not of the ancient nobility, was perhaps regarded as the pushing attorney of diplomacy. He had the cleverness and the complete absence of scruple associated with that term; but he had what is not associated with it, a perfect loyalty to the master and the cause he served. His policy with regard to Ireland was perfectly definite, and it was perfectly well understood both by Louis and by Louis's minister Louvois. It was less the restoration of James to the throne of England, than the infliction of an injury on France's most pertinacious opponent, William of Orange.

It was James's belief, in which he was encouraged by the English Jacobites, that he had only to appear in England to find his subjects rally to his side. D'Avaux did not think it at all likely that William, whose resolution and ability he had had abundant opportunity of apprehending, would let go what he had won. But if that could not be hoped for, the next best thing that could happen would be the detachment of Ireland from the English crown, the possible establishment of James's son there as a king or prince of Ireland under Bourbon protection and French suzerainty. Louvois said as much in one of his letters. "The best thing that King James could do," he remarks, "would be to forget that he has been King in England, and to apply himself solely to putting Ireland into a sound condition and to attach her people solidly to himself."[1] It was un-

---

[1] Archives des Affaires Etrangères (Paris): Louvois to D'Avaux, June $\frac{3}{13}$, 1689. The frequent references to D'Avaux in the subsequent chapters are taken from D'Avaux's correspondence with Louis and Louvois, a volume of which was published by the English Foreign Office.

THE EXPEDITION TO IRELAND 151

fortunate for the success of these admirable French precepts that the difficulties of putting them into practice were not understood soon enough.

D'Avaux soon saw one of the difficulties. He perceived it on the first day he stepped aboard the French ship which floated James's royal standard at the main. It was the irresolution and want of judgment of the Prince whom he was ostensibly to serve. James has had many critics, bitter, bigoted, abusive; but none more acid than this polite ambassador, whose estimate of the King and Court in Ireland is as contemptuous as that which Saint-Simon penned of the Court of Versailles. There is an essential distinction between them. Saint-Simon's biting summaries of men and women were written for none to see, till their author should be safe from the punishment which they would have brought on his head. D'Avaux's correspondence with Louis was candid observation which was written with no basis of egotism, but which was solely intended to inform his master in the clearest possible manner of the way in which his affairs were going, and his arms and money being spent. His first letter seals a judgment which he never reversed—he speaks of James's irresolution; observes that he is always busying himself with petty things, and passing over those which are essential; and complains of his foolish want of reticence — "His Britannic Majesty speaks of everything before all the world."

The voyage was calm and pleasant; and though the King's retinue, whether of English gentlemen or French soldiers, experienced little of that strong assurance of victory which is one of the essentials of a successful adventure, there must have been some sort of curious expectancy in the expedition. With King James went Arabella Churchill's two sons, the Duke of Berwick and Henry FitzJames, Lord Dover, Lord and Lady Melfort, Lord and Lady Powis, Lord Seaforth, the Bishop of Chester, John Gordon, Bishop of Galloway, a Protestant Churchman who afterwards became a Romanist, the Hamiltons, a retinue of officers, and the King's chaplains and his confessor —a discreet cleric who is several times commended by the French ambassador for his good offices in persuading James when other means had failed.

The fleet arrived at Kinsale, in Ireland, on the 12th of March, and after the Earl of Clancarty, commanding at Kinsale, had paid his ceremonial visit to the King on board the *St Michel*, his Majesty landed, and with his sons, Berwick and FitzJames, accompanied by Lord Powis and the Bishop of Chester, went on shore and up to the Fort, glad to put his foot on land that was his own again. He wanted to press on at once, to the annoyance of the scandalised D'Avaux, without even landing the arms and ammunition, in spite of the fact that his expectant subjects had not been ready with enough horses to take the King and his escort to Cork. With difficulty some carriages were found to carry the most necessary portion of the royal equipage, the money, to Cork, and there three days later they went, to be received by MacCarty, afterwards Lord Mountcashel, in whose house James stayed. Cork, poverty-stricken little town as it was, did its best to welcome the King, and made up in heartiness what it lacked in ostentation: James, observes a Protestant leaflet sourly, " being received by the Irish in their rude and barbarous manner, by bagpipes, dancing, throwing the mantles under his horses' feet, making a garland of a cabbage stump, and such like expressions of joy." The leaflet maliciously adds that in the midst of this rejoicing the Irish rapscallions did not omit to ply their usual practices of thieving—" the Rapparees plundering, not sparing either party, insomuch that of ten oxen sent the King two of them were by these villains taken away." D'Avaux saw no humour in this state of things: he perceived only with disgust that the plundering of cattle and sheep in Ireland was a commonplace; that no one was punished for it; and that the easy-going James could hardly be persuaded to dismiss drunken officers who had been concerned in a riot.

"The King listens to everyone," says the ambassador morosely, "and it takes as much time to destroy the wrong views which he assimilates as to put good ones in their place." A letter from General Rosen to Louvois shows that the disgust of the French ambassador at the confusion and disorder, the theft and the pillage, was shared by the French soldiers. They expected too much of Ireland. Under the splendid administrative capacity of Louvois the armies and expeditions of France were organised and equipped down to the last gaiter button; and to this standard a French soldier expected other peoples to conform. But it was not so in other armies. It was not so in the army which the veteran Schomberg was to lead from England into Ireland; and when the difficulties of raising, equipping, teaching, and paying an Irish army are considered, the expectations formed by their critics in the seventeenth century seem absurd.

The deepening gloom lifted with the arrival of the

Viceroy, Richard Talbot, Earl of Tyrconnel, whose name, first immortalised by Wharton [1] in "Lilli Bulero," is still sung in the ballads of Ireland. Tyrconnel's arrival gave to the Irish reception the military glamour which Mountcashel's meagre forces in Cork had not been able to display. He came from Dublin with an escort of a hundred gallant Irish gentlemen to salute the King. The King met him, nay more, went out from his room to meet him, and embraced him as a brother. At the dinner which followed, James placed his Viceroy on his right hand, while Berwick sat on his left. The Viceroy received through D'Avaux marks of regard hardly less considerable from the French King. Louis sent him the Ordre Bleu, a sword with a jewelled hilt, together with a casket containing 12,000 louis-d'or. The anonymous chronicler of the occasion does not relate with what words the French ambassador conveyed these blushing honours, but he does add that Tyrconnel responded to D'Avaux that there were fifty gentlemen in Ireland equally worthy to receive them.

This moment, we may take it, was the proudest of Tyrconnel's life. It also marks the summit of his career. He was the most powerful adviser of the King for whom he had declared, and from whose gratitude he might expect many favours to come; he was the honoured protégé not only of James, but of

[1] "Lilli Bulero" (written when Dick Talbot was made Earl of Tyrconnel). We quote two stanzas from Wilkins's *Political Ballads*, vol. i. :—

"Dare was an old prophecy found in a bog,
Ireland shall be rul'd by an ass and a dog.

"And now dis prophecy is come to pass,
For Talbot's de dog and James is de ass."

the most powerful monarch in Europe, Louis XIV. That was no small advancement for an Irish gentleman of no very distinguished family, who had begun life as a cornet of horse, and had been obliged to earn his pay as a soldier in Flanders.

He was the youngest son of Sir William Talbot, and he was the most energetic and the most successful of a family which had little but its wits to prosecute its fortunes. Peter Talbot, the eldest, was a Jesuit who was with the Stuarts during their exile before the Restoration, and was said to have received Charles II. into the Roman Catholic Church. For the Order of Jesus, the temperamental failings of the Talbots, as exemplified in Peter, proved too strong, and they expelled him, though he remained on good terms with them. His appointment as Archbishop of Dublin was favoured by Charles; and his archbishopric is chiefly memorable for his quarrels with Archbishop Plunket of Armagh. He closed a stormy life in prison, sending for his old opponent at the last, and being absolved by him. Peter's enemies called him "lyingest villain and desperate rogue"; but it was a day when invective was the commonest form of dialectic; and much that was said of Peter was said also of Brother Tom, the Franciscan friar; or of Colonel Gilbert Talbot, who was denounced as one of Cromwell's spies; and of Dick Talbot, the soldier of fortune, duellist, gamester, and Duke of York's gentleman, who raised his family's fortunes to their highest point, but left little more than a tradition behind him at his death. This much, at the distance of more than two centuries, we may say of him —that in a day when politicians were commonly time-servers, and exceptional if they did not sell their convictions to the highest bidder, he died as he had lived, in the service of a losing cause. If he was unscrupulous, he made no secret of it; if he was venal, he carried it off with a robust humour that has its attractive side; and if he pretended, his pretences were generally made to those who did not profess to believe him. He was, as the shareholders of the East India Company complained of Governor Pitt, a "roughling immoral man";[1] but to his haughty, huffying temper he added intrepidity and an Irish carelessness of appearances.

He had been used to taking hard knocks. He fought against Cromwell at seventeen, and was wounded and left for dead in the rout of Preston's army. His boyish face served him while a prisoner, for he escaped in women's clothes, and began again as a soldier of fortune in Madrid. From Madrid he went to Flanders, and his brother Peter presented him to James, then Duke of York, and a Prince whom Condé extolled for his intrepidity. That was in 1653, and Talbot was thereafter attached to James's household and fortunes. He was in England once before the Restoration, and was arrested and examined on suspicion of being in the plot to assassinate the Protector. But he escaped, and got back to Brussels. The uncharitable said that his escape was owing to the arrangement which his brother Gilbert made for him with Cromwell to act as his spy on the Stuarts. It is not unlikely. An arrangement of that kind would never have stuck in Dick Talbot's throat—especially when its conditions could not be enforced. Cromwell would have learnt little from him that was of value. At the Restoration he came back as the Duke of York's gentleman, with the kind of

---

[1] Lord Rosebery's *Chatham*.

RICHARD TALBOT, DUKE OF TYRCONNEL.

THE EXPEDITION TO IRELAND 157

reputation that a man of thirty who had spent thirteen years of his life in camps would be likely to have. He was a duellist, and he was too successful as a gamester to be popular. He was appointed Gentleman of the Bedchamber to the Duke of York, and we need not be astonished to find that he was a boon companion in James's vices. The worst that can be said of him is that, when James was meditating a way of escape from the consequences of marrying his first wife, Anne Hyde, the Irishman allowed himself to be one of a party of four "gentlemen of honour" instructed by Lord Falmouth to give personal testimony against her reputation. The story is told by Anthony Hamilton in the *Memoirs of Gramont*, and has often been quoted. The most singular part of it is that James, after having heard the scandalous accusations of the four gentlemen of honour with as few qualms as they experienced in making them, and having indeed thanked them for their frankness, announced his marriage publicly to two of them an hour afterwards. "As you are the two men of the Court whom I most esteem," said James with serene and pleasant countenance, "I am desirous you should first have the honour of paying your compliments to the Duchess of York; there she is."[1]

One might have expected that Colonel Talbot's career would not survive an unpleasant surprise of this nature; but it seems to have made no difference in James's regard for him, though Talbot was not much at Court in Charles's reign. He lived very largely in Ireland. That, however, did not arise out of his disgrace. It was more likely due to the fact that he had

[1] *Mémoires de Comte de Gramont.*

not the means to keep his head above water in Charles's spendthrift Court: for though Anthony Hamilton says that he played deep (and was "tolerably forgetful"), the Talbots could have inherited but little from their grandfather the judge; and in Ireland, or between Ireland and England, he found a means to recruit his slender fortunes. This was as an advocate of Irish claims, an office which is a little difficult to define, but which, from the circumstances of the case, Talbot probably found lucrative.

During the Commonwealth nearly all the land of unhappy Ireland had changed hands. The lands of those who had fought for the King and had been defeated, as well as lands of the Crown and of the Church, had been confiscated. This was followed by a gigantic eviction—it amounts to that—of native Irish who had incurred the hatred of Englishmen on account of the savage atrocities during the great rising of 1641–3. All of them, except such as were needed to serve as labourers, were compelled to choose between exile and migration to Connaught or the county of Clare, where lands were to be allotted to them. Between 30,000 and 40,000 chose exile, and, like Talbot, found employ as soldiers in the wars of Europe, in France, Spain, Austria, Venice, but ever with the object of aiding the exiled Stuarts. The lost lands of the Irish went to the men who had aided in the suppression of the Irish rebellion of 1642 by advancing money, or to the soldiers who had effected the conquest. The distribution was carried out on a scientific basis, and the country was mapped out by Sir William Petty with a care which we may be sure would never have been exercised except by those who had some profit to gain by it.

THE EXPEDITION TO IRELAND 159

We need scarcely inquire whether there was jobbery, plunder, and corruption in this neat settlement. When the Restoration brought Charles back to the throne, there arose in the hearts of the exiled Irish a joyous hope of loyalty rewarded, of lands restored, of land usurpers flung out again. A disappointment more bitter than their loss awaited most of them. To most of them the Act of Settlement, which Charles's ministers evolved after long survey of a vastly complicated question, restored nothing and confirmed nothing except their discontent. Their services were acknowledged on paper in the Act of Settlement, " some as having for reasons known to us in an especial manner merited our grace and favour, others as having continued with or served faithfully under our ensigns beyond the seas." The Stuarts were incompetent to do more ; but during the years when the question was being thrashed out, and the baffling intricacies of the conflicting claims were being considered before the Irish Council in London, or the Court of Claims in Dublin, Talbot was prominent among those who pressed the claims of his fellow-countrymen. The President of the Irish Council in London was the Duke of Ormonde, who was the chief of the Protestant noblemen in Ireland, and the ablest man of affairs. It says a great deal for his sense of public duty that he was prevailed upon at this time to leave the comfort of England for the uneasy position of Viceroy in Ireland. His post as President of the Irish Council was not less thankless ; and it was during its occupancy that he came into conflict with Talbot.

Talbot was doubly engaged in the claimants' interest. He had the fierce dislike of the Irish Catholic for the Irish Protestant, and he took no doubt a commission on the claims which he prosecuted successfully.[1] His lively tongue was no respecter of Ormonde, and after some bitter repartees he threatened the Viceroy in language which would have been in place on the fields of Flanders, but was intolerable in a court. Ormonde indignantly asked the King if at this time of day he should be forced to fight a duel with Dick Talbot—and Talbot found himself, to his dismay, lodged in the Tower. It was a check from which he took some time to recover—and he recovered in Ireland.

According to Anthony Hamilton, he had another reason for going. He had been in love with the beautiful Miss Hamilton, Anthony's sister, and his quarrel with the Duke of Ormonde, who was her uncle, made the prospect of a marriage with her remote.[2] But we take it that Talbot was never the man to cry over spilt milk, and he seems to have retired to Ireland

---

[1] A petition is still preserved in the Dublin State Records of some of the officers who remained in London till 1665 to prosecute their claims. It runs:—

"The humble Petition of the Officers who served under your Majesty's Royall Ensignes beyond the Seas.

"That most of the Officers who served under your Royall Ensignes beyond the Seas have perished by famine since your Majesty's happy Restoration in solliciting for their Estates, and the few of them remaining are now like to perish of the Plague, having not any meanes to bring them out of this Towne nor knowing whither they shall goe.

"Your Petitioners humble request is that in regard that they are but few in number and their estates but small, your Majesty will be pleased to put an end to their sufferings by ordering that a proviso be inserted in this Bill to restore to the Petitioners their former estates."

[2] Miss Hamilton afterwards married the Comte de Gramont. The story goes that her brothers, Anthony and George, when the Comte de Gramont was leaving England to return to France, hastened after him, and finding him at Dover remarked politely that he had forgotten something. "Pardon me, I forgot to marry your sister, so lead on and let us finish that affair," agreed Gramont, and returned to do so.

THE EXPEDITION TO IRELAND 161

cheerfully enough, with a jest on his lips at the loss of his mistress. If his departure left Miss Hamilton unaffected, it depressed another more sentimental lady, the maid of honour whose picture Anthony Hamilton has preserved for us in the languishing Miss Boynton. Miss Boynton seems to have belonged to a later day than that of the robust shamelessness of the Restoration Court, and to have had a habit of swooning on very slight provocation. She swooned like an early Victorian heroine the first time she saw the handsome Dick Talbot, and that stalwart giant was so affected by this instance of feminine weakness that he conceived a tenderness for his admirer which at last ended in his marrying her. Not, however, by any means at once. His mobile heart was first to be disturbed by another love affair. He was one of the suitors for the beautiful but cool-headed Fanny Jennings, the sister of the greater Sarah, who married Marlborough. But she preferred George Hamilton's more settled prospects. So, not knowing why or wherefore, Talbot married his large-eyed adorer, and, we think, lived with her happily. They left England for Dublin, where she died, and where, in Christ Church Cathedral, she lies buried with her child.

But the world moved on with Talbot as with Fanny Jennings, the mother of George Hamilton's children. The "Popish Plot," the outcome of the perjuries of Titus Oates, spread out its tentacles even to Ireland, and Talbot, like James, was one of the persons implicated. He fled to France, and there once again he met Fanny Jennings, now a widow. He married her, and from this point his fortunes, just before at their lowest ebb, moved upwards again, till with the accession of James they began to soar. James had seen in Ireland a country which would be bound to him by the double bond of loyalty and religion, and which would help him to coerce England. It was a delusion born of his ignorance of the nature of Irish loyalty and of the Irish memory. But it was a delusion fostered by an Irishman whose memory contained no bitter recollection of Stuart neglect and ingratitude. Talbot encouraged James's visions partly out of self-interest, partly from an Irishman's natural enthusiasm for what he wishes to believe, and what he wishes others to believe.

James selected two instruments for his purposes. One was Clarendon, the son of the great Chancellor, and James's brother-in-law, a man of second-rate ability, of cautious temper and half-hearted resolves. The other was Talbot, a man of little judgment and no statesmanship, but of confident resolution. To Talbot was given an independent military command in Ireland, and the title of Earl of Tyrconnel. He was something more than military administrator: he made himself military dictator. The compromising Clarendon was no match for Talbot, who opposed to his cautious schemes the ready truculence of the soldier of fortune. An example of their methods—it is related by Clarendon himself—will suffice. It arose over the question of the appointment of sheriffs for the counties. "By God, my Lord," said Tyrconnel, "I must needs tell you the sheriffs you have made are generally rogues and old Cromwellians!" To which Clarendon feebly rejoined that the sheriffs were as good a set of men as any chosen for a dozen years. "By God, I believe it!" retorted the Irishman, "for there has not been an honest man sheriff for twenty years." It is extremely likely that Clarendon went down to his grave without appreciating his rival's humour. He did not long oppose his wits to it; for what he was afraid to do in Ireland, Talbot was eager to do.

Talbot set about remodelling the army and the civil authority on the plan of converting both to a weapon for James's use. He did the work thoroughly, as may be gathered from the bitter indictment penned by Archbishop King, the then Dean of St Patrick's: "This person was the true enemy of King James. He drove his Master out of his kingdom; he destroyed him by his pernicious counsels, and the kingdom of Ireland by his exorbitant and illegal management; and therefore he and such other wicked Counsellors and Ministers are alone answerable for all the mischiefs that have followed."[1] But there is another way of looking at Tyrconnel's work. "There is work to be done in Ireland," said James, on appointing him, "which no Englishman will do." The blame does not lie in the first place on Tyrconnel. But what he did was accomplished without any refinements of subtlety; it was done with the "bagonet and the butt." He disarmed the militia and the Protestants; he dismissed 300 Protestant officers from the standing army of 7000 (in 1686), and replaced them with Roman Catholics. Many of these, cashiered without compensation, went abroad to fight in Holland, and returned in after days to serve under William in Ireland. The dismissal of the men followed on that of the officers. Some 6000 of them were turned adrift. Thus far the "reform" of the army proceeded. But the civil authority was handled with the same

[1] King's *State of the Protestants in Ireland.*

mailed fist. The Privy Council, the judiciary, the sheriffs, the corporations, all were altered by Tyrconnel in the way suited to what he conceived to be the pattern desired by his master. What was gained by this policy in Ireland was, of course, lost in England; though equally fatal, perhaps more fatal, was the belief, even more firmly fixed in Ireland than in England, that the end and aim of these changes was not merely the coercion but the extinction of the Protestants. It was fear which raised rebels against James in Ireland, and which was ultimately to wrench it from his grasp.

The remainder of Tyrconnel's rule before James's arrival may be briefly told. He had hoped to preserve Ireland intact to King James when William of Orange was marching on London. Even when Protestant Ulster showed the first signs of revolting to the usurper's colours, he believed that he could keep them, and sent Lord Mountjoy to reassure them, at any rate till he was in a position to threaten them. Events seemed to be moving too quickly for him—so much too quickly that he has been suspected of wishing at this juncture to parley with William, and perhaps to betray the interests of James. We prefer to believe that he was too old a campaigner to change, and that any indecision he showed was due to a wish to gain precious time. William sent one of the Hamiltons—Richard Hamilton—to treat with him. Hamilton had turned his coat once: when he came to Dublin he changed it again, not lightheartedly perhaps, but because he must quickly have seen that Tyrconnel could not change.

It was possible, it would have been possible, by

disarming Ulster and the north, to preserve Ireland for James; or, at all events, to make its subjugation by William a task of extreme difficulty. This was the problem which Tyrconnel and Richard Hamilton took in hand. The degree of effectiveness which they had reached is described in the report which Tyrconnel gave to James when they met at Cork: "That he had sent down Lieftenant General Hamilton with about 2500 men, being as many as he could spare from Dublin to make head against the Rebells in Ulster, who were masters of all that Province except Charlemount and Caricfergus: that most of the Protestants in other partes of the Kingdom had been up: that in Munster they had possessed themselves of Castle Marter and Bandon, but were forced to surrender both places and were totally reduced in these parts by Lieftenant General Macarty (Lord Mountcashel) and were in a manner totally suppressed in the other two provinces.

"That the bare retention of an Army had done it, together with the diligence of the Catholick nobility and gentry who had raised above fifty Regiments of Foot and several troops of horse and Dragoons.

"That he had distributed among them 20,000 armes but were most so old and unserviceable that not above 1000 of the firearms were found to be of any use.

"That the old troops consisting of one Battalion of Guards together with Macarty's, Clancarty's and Newton's Regiments were pretty well armed, as also seven companies of Mountjoy's old regiment, which were with him—the other six having stayed in Derry.

"That he had three Regiments of Horse, Tyrconnel's,

Russel's and Galway's and one of Dragoons : but the Catholicks had no arms, while the Protestants had plenty and all the best horses in the Kingdom ; that for artillery he had but eight small field pieces in a condition to march, the rest not mounted—no stores in the magazines, little powder and ball, all the officers gon for England, and no mony in cash."[1]

[1] Clarke's *Life of James II*.

CHAPTER IX

JAMES'S IRISH ARMY

IT is certain that what Tyrconnel welcomed most in his master's equipage was the 500,000 crowns with which Louis had supplied him. In a letter sent from Tyrconnel in January 1688-9 to Queen Maria, which was clearly intended for James's eyes, he says that what he wants more than arms or ammunition is money, and without it the kingdom must be infallibly lost. "True it is that with arms and ammunition I may assemble a considerable body of naked men without clothes, but having no money to subsist, all the order and care I can take will not hinder the ruin of the country nor a famine before midsummer. . . . Before the middle of March at the furthest, there ought," he says, "to be sent to me 500,000 crowns in cash, which with our own industry shall serve us for a year." Tyrconnel further draws up a list of practical requirements for his army, and suggests the necessity to send him at least "6000 matchlocks and 5000 firelocks. To send me at least 12,000 swords. To send me 2000 carbines, and as many cases of pistols and holsters. To send me a good number of officers. . . ." His account of the Irish army is not unfairly descriptive of its threadbare magnificence: ". . . Four regiments of old troops and one battalion of the regiment of guards, three regiments of horse, with one troop of grenadiers on horseback. I have lately given out commissions for nearly forty regiments of dragoons and two of horse, all which amount to 40,000 men, who are all unclothed and the greater part unarmed, and are to be subsisted by their several officers until the last of February next, out of their own purses, to the ruin of most of them; but after that day I see no possibility for arming them, clothing them, or subsisting them for the future, but abandoning the country to them"[1]—that is to say, letting them live as best they can on the country.

Tyrconnel's account of his army is confirmed by his allies and by his enemies. Captain John Stevens, who took service under the Duke of Berwick, and wrote afterwards *A Journal of my Travels since the Revolution*, is a very candid critic of the army, in which he rather bitterly complains that promotion did not appear to be regulated by merit or experience. The army was over-officered, and the Irish officers were ignorant and had no experience of war. That, of course, was not true of the Irish gentlemen who, like Tyrconnel himself, had fought in the wars of the Continent; but it was true of those who had been hastily commissioned to command the raw levies of Tyrconnel's army. D'Avaux wrote to Louis that the greater number of these Irish regiments had been raised by Irish gentlemen who had never seen fighting, and the companies were captained by the butcher, the baker, the candle-

[1] Add. MSS., Brit. Mus., 28,053.

stick-maker. Another witness, a partisan one, is no less emphatic : " And as to the inferior Officers of the Army such as Captains, Lieutenants, and Ensigns, some hundreds of them had been Cowherds, Horseboys, or Footmen, and perhaps these were none of their worst men ; for by reason of their education among Protestants, they had seen and understood more than those who had lived wild on the Mountains "[1] :—such is the summary of Dr King, Archbishop of Dublin ; and though both these contemporary opinions were coloured by the prevalent attitude of contempt to all things that were native Irish, it is certain that the officers in the lower ranks were far from being " quality." The army as a whole was very raw, very undisciplined.

In the scurrilous little pamphlet on Tyrconnel, " The Popish Champion," the author remarks of his Irish army, that they had straw bands instead of hats, and were armed with ash-poles in lieu of swords, bayonets, and firearms. " Stockings and shoes were in a manner strange to them ; and as for shirts, one among three proved a miracle, . . ." with some further ribald details. But Stevens is not far from a similar estimate. Most of the troops, he said, had never fired a musket in their lives. They were as undisciplined as conceited, and followed none but their own officers, who knew no more than they did how to train them. " For want of arms most of the army were taught the little they knew with sticks, and when they came to handle pike or musket they had to begin again. Many regiments were sent upon service who had never fired a shot, ammunition being kept so choice. It is hard to guess when these men were upon action

[1] King's *State of the Protestants in Ireland.*

whether their own or their enemies' fire were more terrible to them." The French officers who came to train these raw levies were prejudiced against them; and their prejudices were not reduced by the way in which their tutorial efforts were received. The neglect of French officers was a constant source of complaint throughout the whole of James's campaign in Ireland. That James knew that such complaints were being made is evident from one of the letters of the French ambassador to Louis, in which D'Avaux narrates at length the reproaches which were levelled at him by James. One of the grievances was that D'Avaux had told Louis that James "treated the French generals ill." D'Avaux (as he coolly responded) had never been so imprudent as to put such a statement in a letter, whatever his thoughts may have been. The imputation came from other sources. D'Avaux had been restrained by no such considerations from saying from time to time that he thought very little of James's English officers; but his criticism in chief was levelled, not at the lesser grades of officers, but at the organisation of the army as a whole—at its want of discipline, at its deplorable equipment.

In a late letter to Louvois, in which D'Avaux speaks of the despatch of French regiments to the aid of Ireland, he enumerates what in his opinion should be sent with them: "A doctor, surgeons, apothecaries, a hospital director, and medicaments as well as munitions, a complete train of artillery, farriers, shoeing-smiths, carpenters. Bakers we have"; and he adds satirically, "There is no need to send butchers, for they are here in plenty. It appears to be the sole *métier* of the Irish; not a soldier but is one. But send shoemakers, for the soldiers will go barefoot as soon as they have worn out the shoes they bring with them from France; and if you could despatch a shipload of old brandy there would be something in this country for a Frenchman to drink." From which it will appear that the first impressions which D'Avaux received of Ireland were not mellowed by time. His injunctions concerning what we now call medical comforts were prompted by his acquaintance with the hospitals where the sick and wounded of James's army were lodged. It is a desolating picture. In the campaign which was to follow James's arrival in Ireland the weather was bad even for that rainy country, and the sickness in the armies of both James and his opponents was appalling. With the knowledge of what military hospitals could be like even in the nineteenth century, we may not wonder at the state of things in the seventeenth which shocked the ambassador's mind. In the hospitals between Ardagh and Drogheda hundreds of sick men lay for a day at a time on the floors of churches or empty houses, without food or drink, without light or fire, without a doctor or a surgeon. Things were little better in the face of the enemy. Maumont and Pusignan were both killed at the siege of Londonderry, one of them complaining with his last breath that he died because there was not a proper surgeon to attend him. When Louis heard of the deaths of these two officers he angrily remonstrated. General officers of this kind, he implied, did not grow on every bush. His complaint reminds one of the jest of an Irish wit two centuries later — that to lose one parent might perhaps be a misfortune, but to lose two was something suspiciously like carelessness.

D'Avaux and the French officers of the expedition were unable to perceive any good points in the Irish army. They found no health in it. To them it was an ill-disciplined mob; its superior officers venal; its lower ranks incompetent or untrustworthy. History was to prove, on the battlefields of Europe, that the sweeping condemnation levelled at the Irish was unjustified. Under adequate military guidance they proved themselves the equals of the best troops in the world; and we are not disposed to take all the French strictures at this time for granted. D'Avaux is himself not consistent. At one point he accuses the Irish colonels of stealing the regimental money and leaving their captains to shift for themselves; at another point he admits that a number of the colonels of the Irish regiments raised and kept their men together at their own expense. He protests that if the French officers complain (like himself) of the want of discipline among the soldiery they render themselves odious, and he implies that in consequence quarrels were forced on them. But he also writes in a letter a few weeks before he left Ireland that there were a good many fire-eaters among the French officers, and that they were a potent cause of disorder and brawling. It is extremely likely, having regard to the temperaments both of Irishmen and Frenchmen, that there was a good deal of friction between them. It is also probable that the exigencies and comradeship of warfare led to a better understanding and appreciation of one another. The Irishmen who were loudest in their denunciations of General Rosen, for example, were the quickest to regret his subsequent recall to France.

What the French critics did not sufficiently keep in

mind, though D'Avaux was continually aware of it, was that, as the Turkish proverb puts it, a fish begins to stink at the head. The impotence of the Irish army as a weapon of warfare was partly due to the haste with which it had been raised; it was still more due to the absence of an organiser or an iron-fisted disciplinarian. Hardly had James landed than D'Avaux has to record an instance of the King's fatal leniency. Two captains had been dismissed for cattle-stealing, and had raised a riot by way of reprisal. There was the greatest difficulty, writes D'Avaux, in persuading the King to make an example of them. "He listens to everyone," adds the ambassador querulously, "and it takes as much time to destroy the effect of the bad advice he receives, as to substitute sound views in its place."

If the King was lenient, his subordinates were incompetent. Tyrconnel had raised an army, and had done so in an incredibly short space of time; but his bolt was shot. Illness and debility were creeping on him with years, and he was in the position of some of the English generals in the Boer War, of being unable to sustain a reputation won in earlier campaigns. Lord Dover was perhaps the most incompetent commissary-general who was ever entrusted with the supplies of an army. Richard Hamilton was (almost in D'Avaux's words) too small a man for his job. Berwick, whose subsequent military reputation was to stand so high, was too young and too inexperienced; Mountcashel was a more conspicuous failure; and the discovery of born leaders and born fighters among the Irishmen had to be left to the sifting hands of time and the undeviating judgment of warfare. James had

174 THE ENGLISH COURT IN EXILE

no more ability to pick out competent officers than to select competent advisers.

Yet this disordered Irish army possessed the raw material of leadership: men sagacious of military counsel; quick to execute, able in attack and defence. The first name which leaps to the mind is one which is still preserved in Irish memory as a national hero, Colonel Patrick Sarsfield, afterwards Earl of Lucan. He is a typical figure in the double sense of combining in his person all that was attractive in the gallant Irish gentlemen who stood by the Stuarts, and in his history the career that was usually their portion. Handsome, and as brave as he was handsome, his was a form which, in the time-honoured phrase, was equally fitted to grace the camp or the court. He had been in the English Guards and had seen fighting in Flanders; and he had something of the reputation of a General De Wet among the Irish soldiers. But though his ability had attracted the observant eye of the French ambassador, there was the greatest difficulty in procuring brigadier rank for him, because James was of the sage opinion that, though he was brave enough, yet he had "no head" (Avaux's phrase is: "Le Roi disant que c'estoit un fort brave homme, mais qui n'avoit point de tête"). But it was Sarsfield who by his own exertions kept Connaught for the King, and who strove with an unabated loyalty and spirit to keep Ireland for him when the hopes of James sank into a heap of ruins after the battle of the Boyne.[1]

---

[1] In Ireland Sarsfield's abilities were continually shrouded by the blunders of others; in France, where the discriminating influence of D'Avaux would have placed him at the head of the Irish regiments which migrated there, he had a brief opportunity of revealing his martial genius. But before his reputation could be sealed with the

To most of those who fought for James in Ireland, and whose names are to be found in his army lists, the futile campaign brought as little honour as profit: their honours were to be gained on the stricken fields of the Low Countries or Spain. But in the army lists are many names of those who won a place in history, sometimes of an ill eminence, sometimes among those who sacrificed their all for an idea, sometimes as one of that company whose persistent loyalty is one of the ironies of history. One may picture among the gallant gentlemen who rode with James from Cork to Dublin, their numbers rising to two hundred as they approached the gates of the capital, many whose personalities remain distinct and striking.

Among them was Lord Galmoy, one of that great Irish Butler family which was so torn asunder by its warring scruples of loyalty and religion. Galmoy's eminence was not of the kind of which his family could be proud. Before the arrival of James he had been zealous in harrying those of the Protestants who seemed inclined to side with William of Orange, and had besieged the castle of Crom. He employed a curious device to conceal his lack of cannon. Two cannon were constructed of tin, bound with whipcord,

---

success which his ability deserved, he fell at the battle of Landen. Associated with his memory are two sayings which not unjustly sum up the attitude of the Irish Jacobites and the hopes he fought for. When, after all the hopes and useless triumphs of Limerick, the city at last surrendered, it is said that Sarsfield, on hearing some comment from an English officer concerning the Irish soldiers, said bitterly: "As low as we now are, change kings and we will fight it over again with you." The other is a nobler utterance. As he lay bleeding from the wound of which he died at Landen, a battle which his gallantry did so much to win, he exclaimed sadly: "Oh that this had been shed for Ireland!"

and covered with buckram. They were drawn by sixteen horses, as if they were real guns, and with these he threatened to batter down the castle. He was compelled to raise the siege by the arrival of Protestant reinforcements, and retreated, routed, to Belturbet. Here he stained his name by an act of gross treachery, hanging two of his prisoners, Dixie and Charlton, for treason. He had already offered to exchange Dixie for a captain of his own troops, Maguire, and Maguire had been released. "Maguire, to his honour be it said, was so indignant with Galmoy that he resigned his commission. This fruitless deed left a marked impression in Ireland, for the tale speedily went abroad. It embittered the whole contest, and made many men resolve not to give or take quarter from a Jacobite."[1] In other respects Galmoy appears to have been a competent cavalry leader, and Galmoy's Horse became the terror of the Irish Protestants, not merely because of the treachery of their namesake, but because of the degree of efficiency to which he brought them.

In Galmoy's Horse, Captain Denis O'Kelly held a commission. He was the son of the greater Colonel Charles O'Kelly, who had fought for the Stuarts since the days of Cromwell, and had taken the first Hispano-Irish regiment to Spain. Colonel Charles O'Kelly has a claim on history higher than any conferred by his ability as a soldier. He was nearly seventy when Sarsfield gave him the command of a regiment in Connaught, and he managed none too well, for he was beaten by Captain Thomas Lloyd, popularly styled "the little Cromwell." He escaped with some of his cavalry, and his name hardly again appears in the

[1] *The Revolution in Ireland*, by Dr R. H. Murray (Macmillan).

records of the campaign till after James had returned to France and the siege of Limerick heralded the end of the war. After the conclusion of the Treaty of Limerick (to the making of which it was advised that he should *not* be a party, because if he had been there would be no agreement) this obstinate old soldier retired to his residence at Aughrane, where he spent the rest of his life in writing his history of the Irish wars.

One writing, an invaluable manuscript, the *Macariæ Excidium*, has been preserved, and is the premier work of reference for any comprehension of the events of the campaign. It affects to be a history of the destruction of Cyprus, and to have been originally couched in the Syriac tongue. It therefore substitutes ingenious appellations for the men and places of the time, as, for example :—Cyprus for Ireland ; Cilicia for England ; Pamphilia for Scotland ; Syria for France ; and Egypt for Spain. Similarly, James becomes Amasis, and William is Theodore, while Louis is the famed Antiochus ; Tyrconnel is Coridon ; the Comte d'Avaux is Demetrius ; Sarsfield is Lysander, "a young Captain beloved of the soldierie" ; and Lauzun, with (we cannot but believe) malicious intent, is Asimo. O'Kelly describes himself as Philotas Philocypres. It is a very able and most trustworthy record. There is another point of interest in this family of the O'Kelly's, in that they are almost linked with our own time. Captain Denis O'Kelly, an ardent and persevering Jacobite, had little else to recommend him. He married Lady Mary Bellew, a daughter of one of Queen Maria's maids of honour, and neglected her after spending her money. One of his daughters—" Miss Kelly a very pretty girl —and the beaux showed their good taste by liking her "

—was a correspondent of Dean Swift, and is spoken of by Sir Walter Scott.

Still, as we have said, Captain Charles O'Kelly was a persevering Jacobite, and nearly lost his head in George I.'s reign, on a charge of plotting to restore the Stuarts. Nothing is more remarkable, in examining the army lists of King James's forces in Ireland, than the names which appear over and over again in the subsequent history of the Jacobite cause. For example, one finds in these lists the names of Wogan, O'Toole, Misset, and Gaydon, a nephew of Tyrconnel. There was a Wogan who was one of King James's pages when he lodged, on his landing, at Cross-Green House in Cork; another, Colonel Charles Wogan, who was killed before Derry; and Captain John Wogan, and Major James Wogan, who at last went to Saint-Germain and took service with the King of France. From these Wogans descended that daring Charles Wogan who chose Princess Clementina Sobieski of Poland as wife for the Old Pretender, the young prince whose childhood was passed at Saint-Germain. The story of how Wogan plucked her out of captivity at Innsbruck, and with his chosen comrades, the Irish soldiers Captain Misset, Major Gaydon, and Lieutenant O'Toole, brought her to Italy to marry his master, has been made the subject of romance and of melodrama. But in truth it belongs to history. Colonel Sir Charles Wogan died in Spain, more than a generation after the period of our chronicle; but we cannot refuse to quote a passage from a letter of Dr Swift to him, which is relevant. " We guessed you to have been born in this country," writes the Dean. " . . . Although I have no great regard for your trade, from the judgment I make of those who profess it in these kingdoms, yet I cannot but esteem those gentlemen of Ireland, who with all the disadvantages of being exiles and strangers have been able to distinguish themselves by their valour and conduct in so many parts of Europe, I think above all other nations."

Like the Butlers, the Hamiltons owned a divided allegiance. The head of the family, Lord Claud Hamilton, created Earl of Abercorn, accompanied James from France, and was wounded in MacCarty's (Lord Mountcashel's) expedition against Enniskillen, one of the two places which obstinately kept the Protestant flag flying. By the fortune of war it fell to Abercorn to endeavour to persuade the people of Derry, the other Protestant stronghold, to submit. Derry had been just furnished with arms and ammunition by Colonel James Hamilton, a kinsman of Abercorn and a strong Protestant Ulsterman. "This Lord Claud," says Walker in his work on the siege, "came up to our walls, making us many proposals and offering his King's pardon, protection and favour, if we would surrender the town; but these fine words had no place with the garrison."[1]

Of Richard Hamilton, who betrayed his trust, we have already spoken. He has the unhappy distinction of having received, and having deserved, one of the most stinging rebukes in history. After the battle of the Boyne he was captured, and, having been brought before William, was asked by him whether certain of the Irish horse would continue to make a stand. "On my honour," said Hamilton blithely, "I believe they will." King William turned his head—"Your honour!" he

[1] *A True Account of the Siege of Londonderry* (1689).

repeated. But in spite of a treachery which (we may perhaps admit) he had seen no way of avoiding, Hamilton was a brave and conscientious officer. D'Avaux thought, and thought correctly, that he had not enough military talent for the task of reducing Derry ; and it is rather an interesting thing that during the war he was suspected by the Jacobites of communicating with William. D'Avaux mentions a curious incident in his correspondence. A spy, who was being interrogated in the presence of the King and some of his officers, mentioned a report that Richard Hamilton was in communication with the rebel leaders. Richard Hamilton was standing at the window, and turning round said angrily: "Take care what you say, you rascal,—here I am." D'Avaux thought the incident significant ; and it is certain that, either through him or through some other correspondent with the Court of Versailles, the suspicion reached the Court of Saint-Germain. In one of Tyrconnel's letters to Queen Maria, dated April 1689, he is at pains to deny the reports of Richard Hamilton which have reached her, and to pay the highest compliment to his loyalty and good faith. As for the tale of his treachery, "the thing in itself bespeaks the ridiculousness of it." No doubt the tale was an example of what O'Kelly calls "the suspiciousness that too frequently is the sole response to Irish patriotism."

Another of the family was Count Anthony, who came over with James, and was wounded once and taken prisoner before he was able to return to the comparative peace of Saint-Germain, where he died thirty years later —no doubt a very entertaining old gentleman in his later years. Even more Hamiltons fought against

James, however, than with him. The Parliament which he convened attainted forty-six of the name.

Next to Abercorn's Horse comes Luttrell's Horse, headed by the name of Colonel Henry Luttrell, who had seen service in France, and who served James well till it became clear that his loyalty would cost him dear. He was not one of those faithful to the death. One might rather say of him that he was faithful till the Boyne. After that his preference for peace and for his own comfort steadily overbore his patriotism, and after having been nearly hanged by his infuriated colleagues at Aughrim and Limerick, he passed finally over to the English interest.

Colonel Simon Luttrell has a nobler history. He was made governor of Dublin by Tyrconnel on James's arrival; and in the general disorder of that time, he is one of the few men who earned the approbation of D'Avaux as having displayed the elements of organising ability. He made the defences of Dublin sound, and he maintained as good order as was possible in a town overrun with half-disciplined and quarrelsome troops. He may be said to have welcomed James to Dublin in his official capacity as governor; and it was his troops which covered the King's retreat thither and thence when the battle of the Boyne filled the city with fugitives.

Colonel Justin MacCarty, created Lord Mountcashel, was eminently one of those soldiers whose parts were wasted in Ireland. James had a great opinion of his judgment, and commissioned him with the arduous task of reducing Enniskillen. The expedition was a disastrous failure, owing less to MacCarty's incapacity than to the extremely inefficient character of his troops and their equipment; and MacCarty was captured. He afterwards escaped; and the incident was cited by partisans as an instance of very sharp practice, for he had been put on parole. But Mountcashel appears to have acted with what he regarded as quite fair ingenuity. Though on parole, he contrived to be arrested for some trifling breach of prisoner's etiquette; and then—being under nominal arrest—escaped. He subsequently went with the first Irish brigade to France; and the reputation he lost in the bogs of Ireland he regained brilliantly on the hills of Savoy and on the plains of Piedmont. He died four years afterwards. His old colleague O'Kelly says of him in his *Macariæ Excidium*: "He was a man of parts and courage, wanting no quality for a complete captain, if he were not somewhat short-sighted." It is perhaps characteristic of the time that this short-sighted officer was appointed inspector of ordnance and arms.

Lord Dungan, the son of the Earl of Limerick, has but a small share in history, or in the war; but his name endures because of its mention in the despatches of the time. He was the son of a house which had spent most of its goods on the Stuart cause, and which, like many others, had suffered as much pains to obtain recompense from them on the Restoration. The family were still pressing Clarendon for, at least, a post for Lord Dungan in 1687, for in two letters to England (to Lord Rochester) he alludes to it. "Pray give me leave," he says, "to put you in mind of a letter I since sent you from Lord Dungan. . . . You cannot imagine how impatient people here are who expect everything, even those who think themselves the best bred." He speaks also of Dungan's journey to England, "which makes a great discourse here, as in truth most things do, for some or other will comment on all that is done. Those officers of the army who are lately come out of England say he is gone, upon his uncle, Lord Tyrconnel's direction, to kiss the King's hand for a Troop of Horse." Clarendon adds sourly that "this young lord is a very prattling and impertinent youth, and forward enough, and is so looked upon here." D'Avaux seems to have had a better opinion of him, and speaks of sometimes "having conference with him. I know he wishes to draw a close tie between Tyrconnel and me"; and James employed him to carry despatches to Derry. He was killed at the Boyne at the very beginning of the engagement, and his body was carried from the field to be buried in the parish church of Castletown. The church fell long ago into ruins. The old Earl of Limerick followed his son's body to the grave, and when there was nothing more to fight for went with the rest to France, where he died, and lies buried in some unknown grave.

The fate of this family is the fate of scores of others, who fought for two generations of Stuarts and then vanished out of Ireland as if they had never been. The O'Donnells, the Iveaghs, the Burkes, the Galways, the O'Neills, the Dillons, the Lynchs, the O'Donovans gave their bravest and youngest to the cause, and paid for their loyalty in blood and estate—and paid again. A generation earlier the Roman Catholic Irish nobility had been wrecked on the insecure raft of Irish promises. If, as Macaulay says, they emerged from poverty in order to seek restitution, as much as to fight for a King and for their religion, yet it is not to be gainsaid that in this final throw they staked their all. They staked their all and lost, and at the last passed almost as completely from Ireland as the Irish emigrant who to-day leaves his country for the United States or the Argentine. Let not honour be begrudged those who, in the words of Ecclesiasticus, "perished as though they had never been, and their children after them. . . . Their children are within the testaments : and their glory shall not be blotted out."

Enough has been said to show that, despite all lack of comprehension on the part of those who raised this army of what an army should be, and despite an entire want of organisation or of organising ability, there was a great amount of good material in it. The ordered regiments were supplemented by a cloud of irregulars, the "Rapparees" or "Creaghts," the first a nickname derived from the weapons with which the native Irish peasants were armed. "Robbers, Tories, and wood-kernes" is the description with which the Williamite writers of the period assail them ; and they seem from Dalrymple's[1] account to have resembled, though not in equipment, some of the adversaries of the British in that Boer War of '99–'02 which took place two hundred years later—and to have caused similar inconvenience. Dalrymple has the smallest opinion of them—they were the lowest of the low ; they lived on potatoes, "and on that root alone" ; their cabins could be put up within an hour ; "the Rapparee was a part rather of the spot on which he grew than of the community to which be belonged." . . . "They rendezvoused during the night, coming to some solitary station from an hundred places at once, by paths which none else knew. There in darkness and deserts they

[1] Dalrymple's *Memoirs*.

planned their mischievous expeditions. Their way of conducting them was, sometimes to make incursions from a distance in small bodies, which as they advanced, being joined at appointed places by others, grew greater and greater every hour. And as they made these incursions at times when the moon was quite dark, it became impossible to trace their steps, except by the cries of those whom they were murdering or the flames of the houses, barn-yards, and villages which they burnt as they went along. At other times they hung about the cantonments of the troops, under pretence of asking written protections, or of complaining that they had been driven from their homes by the other army."

"It was difficult to detect or to guard against them till too late, seeing they went unarmed, and more with the appearance of being overcome with fears themselves, than of giving them to others. But they carried the locks of their muskets in their pockets, or hid them in dry holes of old walls, and they had the muskets themselves charged, and closely corked up at the muzzle and touch-hole, in ditches with which they were acquainted. So that bodies of regular troops often found themselves defeated in an instant, they knew not how or from whence. Their retreat was equally swift and safe ; . . . it became more easy to find game than the fugitives."

Change "Rapparees" into the "commandoes" of Viljoen or of Lynch, and "barn-yards" into "railway culverts," and the exploits of 1689 in Connaught and Ulster begin to resemble those of 1900 in the Transvaal and the Orange Free State. It appears probable that William's commanders attempted to utilise the Rapparees; but the guerillas were given no more quarter than they accorded. Story gives a list of 1928 Rapparees killed, and "112 killed and hanged by soldiers and others without any ceremony." On the debit side he puts: "Murdered privately by Rapparees, 800." They owned some chieftains, though more as a matter of tradition than of discipline.

Among these may be counted perhaps Balldearg O'Donnell, who was believed by the Irish to be the saviour destined by prophecy to deliver them from the English yoke. He was the heir-presumptive to the Prince of Ulster, that O'Donnell who, at the end of Elizabeth's reign, retired into Spain, where he died. Balldearg on his kinsman's death went to Spain also, and, entering the King of Spain's service, fought against France in the Spanish wars. He asked for permission to fight for James and Ireland, but, having been refused it, sailed for Kinsale without it. He seems to have been neither well received nor trusted by Tyrconnel, and James's memoirs speak very slightingly of him: "He had set up for a kind of independent commander, and having got together no less than eight regiments newly raised, with a crowd of loose men over and above, he lived in a manner at discretion, so that these troops were in effect but a rabble, that destroyed the country, ruined the inhabitants, and prevented the regular forces from drawing that subsistence they might otherwise have had from the people."[1] He was at any rate believed in by the native Irish; and although his career and conduct in Ireland were alike ineffective to the cause which he ostensibly served, it does not seem that he received at any time either assistance or even fair play.

[1] Clarke's *Life*.

The charge of plundering the country laid against the bands of wandering Irish was only too true. D'Avaux noted, on the way from Cork to Dublin, that between Kilkenny and Dublin the valleys and fields were fertile though little cultivated, and that there was abundance of pasturage. But the brief viceroyalty of Tyrconnel, which had endeavoured to divert the tenure of power and estate from Protestant to Roman Catholic hands, had also unloosed the ancient feuds between them. The balance never oscillates slowly in Ireland, but always with violence. Robbery and plunder had accompanied the transition. The Protestants had the flocks and herds; they were robbed of them and their possessions despoiled and destroyed with appalling waste. The Protestants had also the money: and it seemed not improbable that they would lose that too. But the effort to obtain their money was accompanied by a phenomenon not dissimilar from that of the destruction of the flocks. It disappeared; and James landed in a moneyless country.

In describing James's Irish army, and in recalling the careers of those who took part in it, we have overshot the chronological order of our narrative; and it now becomes necessary to retrace our steps, to take it up at the point where James first attempted to guide the difficult course of Irish affairs.

CHAPTER X

DUBLIN

BENEATH the horizon lurked the whirlwind of disappointed hopes, rising enmity, and devastated prosperity of which Tyrconnel's uncompromising policy had sown the seed; but the first days of James's progress were days of serenity and even of jubilance. If Ireland did not impress the Court he had brought with him, even D'Avaux acknowledged the warmth of the Irish welcome, and was flattered to observe that "the Irish love the French and are the irreconcilable enemies of the English." The journey to Dublin was a triumph such as must have been grateful to a King who had enjoyed little popularity at any time in his life, and had indeed been more familiar with tokens of public feeling of an opposite kind. The people came out to meet him wherever they passed, and at Carlow some "young rural maids" wildly kissed him—a tribute which he received with embarrassment and sought to avoid. His fortunes seemed to turn with his popularity. At Lismore Castle he learnt that in Scotland the Duke of Gordon was holding Edinburgh Castle for him; and good news continued to come both from Scotland and the North of Ireland.

It was news which was speciously fair, especially in regard of Enniskillen and Derry, the two Protestant strongholds, which, as a matter of subsequent history, never faltered or fell. They were in truth the rocks that were to wreck the Stuart hopes. But at this moment it was believed to be all but certain that they must yield to the pressure brought to bear on them. James wrote letters to all the Princes of Europe, informing them of his arrival in Ireland, and of his hopes, and begging their help. More especially he pressed the Pope for assistance.

Dublin welcomed him as London had never done. The narrow streets were packed, the windows thronged and, where there was neither tapestry nor velvet, bravely hung with blankets; the streets lined with the King's Irish Guards from St James's Gate to the Castle; "the Papist inhabitants shouting, the Souldiers musquets discharging, the Bells ringing, and at Night, Bonfires in all parts. . . ." The Lord Mayor, Aldermen, and Common Council met him "with their formalities"; and at the entrance to the portion of the city called the Liberties, emblematic enthusiasm had erected a stage hung with tapestries, on which two harpers were playing; and forty young ladies dressed in white joined the procession to strew flowers before the King.

In the midst of the procession of the Corporation and the Guilds in their robes, the judges in their scarlet and ermine, the peers, the gentlemen at arms, the guard of honour of Irish gentlemen, rode the King [1] "on a pad nag, in a plain cinnamon-coloured cloth suit, and black slouching hat, and a George [2] hung over his shoulder with a blue ribbon. . . ." In spite of the

[1] *Ireland's Lamentation.*   [2] The Garter jewel.

intentional baldness of the description, one cannot but see him as a kingly figure. By his side rode the Duke of Berwick, Lord Granard, Lord Powis, Lord Melfort. Tyrconnel bore the sword of state; and there was a string of coaches, in one of which was Henry FitzJames, James's second son. At the Castle gates, the heralds and coaches and horsemen were met by a cortege of a different kind, an assemblage of priests, headed by the Roman Catholic Primate. James alighted, and knelt; and it was under a canopy borne by four bishops that he entered his Castle. Over it floated a banner hung there by Tyrconnel, and bearing the inscription, "Now or Never; Now and Forever." The King and his suite went straightway to the chapel in the Castle, where the " Te Deum " was sung. Afterwards a banquet was held in the new banqueting hall which Tyrconnel had built; and thus to the strains, actual and metaphorical, of " The King enjoys his own again," James entered into his brief tenancy of a throne in Ireland.

The ceremonies were not over. The Comte d'Avaux was installed in "a house in a good quarter," Lord Clancarty's, and was next escorted to the Castle to present his formal credentials as the ambassador of Louis to King James at the Court of Dublin. Tyrconnel came to fetch him with six of the King's royal state carriages; nearly twenty carriages followed. The Mayor of Dublin's Regiment lined the streets; and D'Avaux notes with an unusual touch of approval that he was nearly as well received in Dublin as he could have been in London, and better than he should have thought possible in this country. The populace, he thought, were immensely impressed. Lord Powis as Lord Chamberlain received him at the entrance to the Long Gallery; and D'Avaux, advancing, delivered to him the autograph letters of Louis. James replied that he was beyond words grateful for the help that Louis had given to him, and that when he was re-established in his realm he hoped he might be able to give proofs of his undying friendship to his benefactor. He was grateful, he added, with a burst of feeling, not merely as a king, but as a gentleman.

At this distance of time it seems that in these brief hours James touched the highest point of his fortunes in Ireland. D'Avaux was well disposed: James had heard further good news from Scotland: he was persuaded by the enthusiasm of his new-found Irish that he had little to fear from the disloyalty of Ulster. The task of satisfying the Roman Catholics and of obtaining supplies from the Protestants without entirely alienating them had not arisen in all its magnitude. His only discomfort was that of having to make the best of material which was not of the best quality.

That difficulty might have suggested itself to him as he glanced about the castle which was to house him and his Court. It was a roomy building—too roomy for those who brought an insufficient income to keep it up, and showing in its neglect and decay the uneven but usually declining prosperity of Irish affairs. Its general construction was that of a high curtain wall embracing a large castle yard and the inner buildings, and linked by a series of towers, picturesque but crumbling. One of them had fallen down half a century before; one had been taken down—"and the rest are so crazy," said the then Lord Deputy, "as we are still in fear a part might drop down on our heads."

One tower rebuilt by Boyle, Earl of Cork, was called after its founder. His example was followed by several of his successors, of whom Henry Cromwell, son of the Protector, was the most energetic. Henry Cromwell built a new stable with granaries and stalls for sixty horses, cleared the ground about the Castle for gardens and storehouses for fuel, and removed the bakehouse which had smoked under his writing-room to a more convenient distance. Neither James nor Ireland were likely to own any debt to one of the name of Cromwell, but the Protector's son did at any rate make the Castle habitable ("whereas by my faith 'tis little better than a very prison"[1]), and did it at such cost to his own purse that he could not raise enough money to charter a ship to take him back to England.

Succeeding Lord Deputies grumbled or patched. Fires destroyed a number of the storehouses in Charles I.'s reign, and Lord Clarendon wrote that the "reparations of this old castle are very great, and it is the worst and most inconvenient lodging in the world. In good earnest, as it is now I have no convenient room: no gentleman in the Pall Mall is so ill lodged. I might add, that the keeping up—that is keeping dry—this pitiful bit of a Castle costs an immense deal. . . ." He adds more than that: the Castle moves him to pathos. "I can only tell you that it is the worst lodging a gentleman can lay in, so it will cost more to keep it in repair than any other. Never comes a shower of rain but that it breaks into this house, so that there is a perpetual glazing and tiling, but I assure you not so much as a chimney, or anything, done new upon the King's account." The Viceregal apartments

[1] Henry Cromwell's Letters.

had been rebuilt in 1684, and Tyrconnel had added a new banqueting hall; but the Court could not have been very well housed. The Castle had its own chapel; it contained also a mint, from which James proceeded to issue his new coinage, and a mill known as the King's Mill. One or other of the old towers, of which only two were standing, was used as a prison, and possibly Dr King, then Dean of St Patrick's and afterwards Archbishop of Dublin, and other prisoners were confined in what he would call the Wardrobe Tower, but which is now the tower where State records are kept. He speaks of being prisoned in a "cold nasty garret"; and he also mentions that on the old Bermingham Tower ordnance were placed on a report of a projected attack on Dublin from the sea. Nobody could have enjoyed very ample accommodation, for the rooms were very small; and in the Castle was packed an imitation on as large a scale as possible of a royal household, together with the considerable establishment of the Tyrconnels.

Lady Tyrconnel, the wife of the Viceroy, is one of the women of her time only less striking in character than her sister, Sarah Jennings, the Duchess of Marlborough. She had been one of the beauties of Charles II.'s Court, witty, gay, but with a coolness of head which preserved her reputation even from Anthony Hamilton's graceless pen. She married his brother, and perhaps the family credit may have influenced his description of her; but in an age when nobody's character was spared calumny, and when if a woman protested virtue nobody believed her, Fanny Jennings could hardly have earned her immunity from reproach unless she had deserved it. She is said by

Sir Bernard Burke to have had "the fairest and brightest complexion that ever was seen; her hair a most beauteous flaxen; her countenance extremely animated—though generally persons so exquisitely fair have an insipidity. . . ." She was slender and not tall, but "her whole air and person was fine"— exquisite compliment! Tradition has preserved the quickness of her wit; history has recorded of her at least one instance of a determination of character which resembles that of her greater sister. She inspired White, the Westmeath poet, to the enthusiastic tribute :—

> Tyrconnel, once the boast of British Isles,
> Who gained the hearts of heroes by her smiles,
> Whose wit and charm throughout all Europe rang,
> From whom so many noble peers have sprang,
> Whose virtue, courage, parts, and graceful mien
> Made her fit companie for a Queen.

She was, like James's Queen, very popular in Ireland; but, unlike Maria d'Este, she herself loved Ireland well enough to wish to die there.[1]

Among other ornaments of the Court was Lady Melfort, a handsome lady, of whom Melfort was extremely fond, and, says D'Avaux, extremely jealous. He was hardly ever out of her company, comments the ambassador, with something approaching indignation, and was constantly to be seen taking long walks in her company. One may surmise that Melfort, who

---

[1] She went to Saint-Germain after her husband's death, and a tablet to her memory was put up in the Scots College in Paris; but she returned to Dublin, and died in the Nunnery of Poor Clares which she had founded. She outlived the events we are describing by nearly half a century.

FANNY JENNINGS, LADY TYRCONNEL.

had not many friends and no confidants, found both in his wife. Lady Powis was more generally attractive, a clever, witty woman, but "très intrigante." If she were intriguing she was in the fashion with the rest of the Court, who seem, from various cross-references in the correspondence of the time, to have spent a good deal of their leisure in writing letters to Saint-Germain complaining of one another. One of Tyrconnel's despatches to the Queen contains a sentence apparently protesting against some of the scandals in "these foolish letters." Of Lady Dover, Irish history makes no mention, except to record that she was given a pass out of Ireland by William III., together with her household, "Mrs Duckett, Betty Smith, and Richard Lucas." Lady Arabella MacCarty, a daughter of Strafford, the Minister of Charles I., and Lady Seaforth were attached to the Court. There is a scandalous mention in a letter of the Duchesse d'Orléans of other ladies of no importance in whom the King was interested ; and there is no reason to suppose—rather the reverse—that the Court of Dublin was conspicuous in a licentious age for the austerity of its morals. It was, at any rate, a Court which, gaily improvident for the future, made the best of the present. Banquets and balls were given, one great levée filling the Castle yard with coaches ; one great ball, according to the surmise of the imprisoned Dean of St Patrick's, in order to celebrate the birthday of the Queen[1] ; and we can picture the Long Gallery laid out with counters on which were dishes, wine, and sweetmeats ; and a gay and brilliant company, radiating high spirits—with

[1] The Dean was, however, clearly unaware of the date of Queen Maria's birthday.

not a little horse-play—and crowding in and out the rooms lighted with flambeaux and candles.

Dublin participated in the gaiety, not in a half-hearted manner, but, let us say, with a portion of its population—the Roman Catholic portion. It was not, to adapt a phrase used by a recent Irish Secretary, a gilt-edged time for Protestants. While the Papists were thronging to acclaim the King and his French allies, the Protestants were stealing off at night by every tide. Those that remained quickly felt the burden of their unpopularity. The Dean of St Patrick's and several other Protestants, as we have noted, were apprehended and imprisoned, though there seems reasonable ground for supposing that the charge against the Dean of being in communication with James's enemies was justified. Soldiers were quartered on the Protestant inhabitants in oppressive numbers; and since the Protestants were for the most part the people who had the money which was imperatively necessary to James and the carrying out of his projects, they naturally were the persons on whom the burden of levies fell.

No one was ever placed by his allies, by his chosen servants, and by his previous policy in a more inextricable dilemma than was James in Ireland. Tyrconnel's filibustering strategy had hopelessly alienated the Protestants; yet it was from the Protestants alone that James could obtain money. For a campaign that must cost a million, France had sent a sum that would not buy powder, and D'Avaux's interpretation of France's interest and intentions might be signified by saying that he did not mind who paid so long as France did not. There was only one source of revenue—the

DUBLIN

Protestant—and if money could not be gotten it would have to be created. It is easy to overrate the amount of money in a country, for money is like a stage-army: by its circulation it always seems more ample than it is. Disturb its circulation by a destruction of confidence or credit, and it disappears like water into the earth.

In a letter written by Tyrconnel to the Queen at Saint-Germain, he says (December $\frac{12}{22}$, 1689): "There is not a farthing of silver or gold to be seen in the whole nation." In another letter he says, with courageous humour: "We are, as the old proverb says, 'heart-whole and moneyless.'" But the general tone of his letters is far from gay. He estimates the cost of carrying on the war as at least £100,000 a month; and he declares that money must be had to pay the troops. Some money came in by the sale of Irish commodities—wool, hides, tallow, beef, butter; but the export of these was naturally interrupted by the war between France and England. Moreover, the supplies of these became exhausted, for, as Tyrconnel admits, the "army have ruined and destroyed all our cattle and sheep" (February 22nd, 1690). It is easy to blame James and the Irish for their failure in the futile struggle against William and England; but if the causes of the failure be closely examined, they will be found to consist in the want of money. Dalrymple[1] speaks of the "impolitic parsimony natural to French councils," and no phrase was ever truer in regard to the attitude of those who engineered the resistance in Ireland, and would have been the chief to profit by it.

[1] Dalrymple's *Memoirs*.

The Stuarts had no money; they could only beg it, and they begged from everyone. James's first letter to the new Pope, Alexander VIII., asks for some "releif of money," and ingenuously points out that it will be of more use now than at any other time. The Queen, through Melfort, suggested a collection for the good cause in Catholic churches.

As money began to disappear, an ordinance was first made for increasing the value of the coins. Thus a guinea was to rank as twenty-five shillings, a shilling as thirteenpence, a "ducatoon" as six shillings and threepence instead of four shillings and sixpence, a "cob" as five shillings, the "louis-d'or" brought from France as nineteen shillings. But as this device effected nothing, the fatal step was taken of debasing the coinage by introducing a new one which would cost practically nothing. From the mint in Dublin Castle was issued the notorious "brass money." Its detested memory clung to Ireland for generations, and two hundred years afterwards Orangemen drank to the glorious, pious, and immortal memory of the great, good King William III., who saved us from "popery, slavery, arbitrary power, brass money, and wooden shoes." The "wooden shoes" were the French; and, rather oddly, the master coiner of the mint was a Huguenot, one of the little colony which had fled from France to Dublin, and was established there. D'Avaux, who inherited some of the proselytising zeal of his uncle, thought that a Huguenot ought not to enjoy this important office; but an attempt to supersede him proved singularly unsuccessful, for the master of the mint, an arbitrary but efficient artificer, beat the interloper and threw him out of the foundry.

From the accounts of the master of the mint it appears that no less a sum than £1,596,799 was issued in this coinage, of which £689,375 was in shillings. After the brass had run short a pewter coinage was projected, and some coins were struck but never issued. The coins for the most part had on the one side the King on horseback, and the inscription, " Jas. II. Dei Gra. Mag. Britt. Fra. et Hib. Rex," and on the other the crown with the four scutcheons of England, Scotland, France, and Ireland, the date, " Anno Dom. 1690," and the motto " Christo Victore Triumpho." On the rim of some of the coins was stamped, " Melioris Tessera Fati : Anno Regni Sexti."

" The metal of which this Mony was made," writes the Archbishop of Dublin, " was the worst kind of brass : old Guns, and the Refuse of Metals were melted down to make it : work-men rated it at threepence or a groat a pound, which being coyned into Sixpences, Shillings, or Half Crowns, one Pound weight made about Five Pounds. . . . Later the Half Crowns were called in and being stamp'd anew were made to pass for Crowns : so that for 3d. or 4d. worth of metal made £10. There was coyned in all from the first setting up of the Mint to the Rout at the *Boyne* being about twelve months £965,375.[1] In this Coyn King *James* paid all his Appointments, and all that received the King's Pay being generally Papists they forced the Protestants to part with the goods out of their shops for this mony and to receive their Debts in it. But the Protestants having only good silver or gold, and goods bought with these, when they wanted any thing from Papists they were forced to part with their gold or silver,

[1] An underestimate.

having no means of coming by the Brass Mony out of the King's Hands: so that the loss of the Brass Mony did in a manner intirely fall upon the Protestants. Brass Mony was subsequently proclaimed current in all Payments whatsoever. . . . The Governor of Dublin, the Provost Marshal and their Deputies threatened to Hang all that refused the Brass Mony: of which we have had many instances. . . ."

The Archbishop quotes the case of the widow Chapman, whom the Provost Marshal's deputy, one Kearney, "threatened with many Oaths and Execrations that he would have her burnt in the morning, and her solicitor hanged for interceding for her. . . ." The widow Chapman seems to have received these threats as mere Irish emphasis; but the deputy squeezed £4, 10s. out of her before letting her go. When the Protestants, having perforce acquired quantities of brass money, endeavoured to return it to the Papists, the way was not smoothed for them. They had to go to law about it, and found that justice was not less spurious than brass money. The resources of Protestant ingenuity were not exhausted: they tried to expend the brass money in hides, wool, tallow, corn. This endeavour was countered by the issue of a proclamation, mediæval in character, which fixed a rate at which goods should be sold.

Even the supply of metal for brass money fell short. Tyrconnel's letters to the Queen are full of requests for copper with which to coin it. "Let not copper be forgot: for we are all undone if that does not come out of hand . . . it is our meat drink and cloathes and we have none left . . . we are forced to coin our brass guns" (Louis, it may be noted, magnificently sent two old brass guns to be coined into Irish money). "Send us fifty tons of copper," Tyrconnel adds despairingly in another letter, "even if you have to pay for it."

There is a curious entry in Dr King's diary[1] on which the necessity for accumulating copper seems to throw some light :—" Mrs C—— came to see us in the afternoon and told us that Lady Tyrconnel owed her £12, of which £6 for rent and £6 for malt she had bestowed in charity on ye Nunry [nunnery]. She had frequently petitioned and spoke to her about yt : yesterday she had promised her positively her money and to give her steward order about it and had bidden her come for it to-day which she did. She met my Lady's steward who told her yt he had by order of Lady T. sent four men to bring away her copper which cost £60. This startled Mrs C—— who told him she could not believe it : that she came for £12 which being a debt of 2 years standing her Grace had positively promised it yt morning. He assured her it was true and desired her to make application to his Lady which she did and with much ado obtained of her Grace an order to stop bringing away ye copper on condition she should not call for ye £12." A more apocryphal story of Lady Tyrconnel and the brass money has a gleam of humour. A sum of £3000 being due to Colonel Roger Moore, in order to pay off a mortgage on an estate that was to be the marriage portion of Tyrconnel's daughter when she became Lady Dillon, an offer was made of £2000 in cash. Colonel Moore accepted, and being invited to Lady Tyrconnel's house to receive his money, found it

[1] The Diary of Dr King, kept during his imprisonment in Dublin Castle, 1689.

laid out on long tables which were covered "with copper and brass." Lady Condon is also mentioned, as "Condon's lady giving double the quantity of brass for so much silver."

Naturally, the prices of commodities went up. D'Avaux fills a good many of the pages of his correspondence with Louvois, and even with Louis, in complaining of it. Even the King's table was poorly supplied, and the household accounts very strictly supervised. In a manuscript account of James's household when Duke of York [1] it can be seen that everything was strictly regulated and apportioned—the number of "Flambeaux, Tallow Lights; the notches of billets; the bushells of coke and of sea-coal; the gallons of beere a day" apportioned to each department of the household and to the several members of it. A special arrangement was made for the Lady Mary and Lady Anne to "eat at dinner with the Duke when att St James's," and every member of the family and household was apportioned so much bread a day, even to the baby Lady Henrietta "for papp."

It is very likely that this strict method of supply, being superimposed on Tyrconnel's administration of the Castle, gave rise to the misapprehension that the royal household was eventually put on very short commons. That we do not think to be the case; but some colour is lent to the idea by the irritated declaration on the part of D'Avaux that his own table and that of the French embassy were better furnished than the King's. This declaration was in rejoinder to a

[1] "The Orders and Rules of Ye Rt. Hon. and Hon. the Commissioners for the Orderly Regulating of his R. H.'s Household Affairs" (1662–1678).

report which had reached D'Avaux from France that he was saving the money which he should have been spending in keeping up the magnificence of his own embassy, and is one of the many allegations and accusations which arose out of the twin facts that there was little money for anyone, and that D'Avaux was the keeper of the French purse.

In spite of the general tightness of money, Dublin comported itself with a good deal of careless and licentious gaiety. Those who were in a position to rejoice had never been wealthy; and the dissatisfaction of the Protestants troubled none but themselves. Dublin was a town which, judged by modern standards, was small, dirty, and picturesque. Its narrow streets with high gabled houses were dust-bins in dry weather and gutters when it rained. At night they were lighted only by the rushlight lantern that should have been hung out from every fifth house. In some parts of the town the old mud and wattle houses remained. But Dublin had shared in the general prosperity which had settled on Ireland during Ormonde's[1] quiet rule, when "Gentlemen's Seats were built or building everywhere, and Parks, Enclosures and other Ornaments were carefully promoted." Ormonde had improved the northern quays and developed the northern suburbs, so that what had been a waste was now becoming covered with good houses. Ormonde had built a market and had planned a series of wide and pleasant riverside streets leading to his great new park. St. Stephen's Green, reclaimed from a poor common, was neatly laid out, and lime trees planted about it; so that it had become a fashionable quarter. Even during

[1] James Butler, Duke of Ormonde.

James's brief stay it was improved, the soldiers being set to dig trenches to drain it, while the ratepayers of the day looked on indignantly at work which they were to pay for. Bridges had been built over the Liffey, one of them already known as Bloody Bridge, because of the fierce fight which had inaugurated it. Before the French and Irish soldiers of James were quartered in Dublin, the faction fight had been common enough. The leading antagonists were the butchers of Ormonde Quay and the weavers. Butchering, as D'Avaux sardonically remarked, was one of the chief Irish industries; but during his stay in Dublin weaving was almost as prosperous. Tradition ascribes the foundation of the weaving industry in Dublin to Huguenot refugees. There was a colony of Huguenots in Dublin when James arrived there; and Chamber Street, Pool Street, and Weaver Square are often now called Huguenot streets.[1] But the guild of weavers far surpassed in numbers its foreign founders. In the part of Dublin known as the Coombe, beneath the walls of the Castle, where the murky Poddle was fed by the drains, they lived and were numbered by the thousand. All through the occupation of Dublin by James's men the whirr of their shuttles was heard, as they sat at the small-paned windows weaving stockings for the army.

But the faction fights between the weavers and the butchers were not the only ones with which Dublin contributed to the gaiety of nations. When, after some months' ineffectual campaigning, French soldiers were sent to support the cause of James in Ireland, the private soldiers imitated the dissensions of their superiors.

[1] *The Story of Dublin*, by D. A. Chart (J. M. Dent).

"There happened a scuffle in Town between some Frenchmen and some Irish soldiers, two of ye Irish were killed as reported," Dr King notes in the diary of his imprisonment; and the entire absence of discipline, coupled with a disastrous weakness in neglecting to punish offenders, encouraged continual scenes of drunkenness and rioting. D'Avaux recounts several. He begins with a personal grievance. An order had been given that the soldiers were not to steal the fruit from Dublin gardens. There were fruit-trees in the garden of D'Avaux's fine house, and a sentry was on duty there to protect them. A drunken lieutenant came by, and, ignoring the order and the sentry alike, began to break down the fruit branches. The sentry interposed, and the lieutenant promptly beat him. Other soldiers and servants, roused by the outcry, came rushing out; the lieutenant, with the spirit of a Mulvaney, fought them all. The lieutenant had companions with him, and, says D'Avaux, the disturbance would have grown to a riot. But, as it chanced, Tyrconnel was dining with D'Avaux, and the two came out to see what was the matter. Tyrconnel, black with wrath, strode forward, struck the lieutenant furiously, and put him under arrest. D'Avaux, not anxious to court unpopularity, said that he had purposed to intercede for the lieutenant, but " it was not necessary, for two days later I saw him at the head of his company, at which I was rather surprised."

Quarrels between the King's bodyguards and the guards disturbed the streets. On one occasion a drunken riot, soldiers fighting, firing off their muskets, and dragging two guardsmen by the hair, passed under the very balcony where D'Avaux stood with General de

Rosen, M. de Gace, General Boisseleau, and other French officers. So little was discipline of moment that not merely was the presence of the commanding officers ignored, but it was felt that it would not only be useless but dangerous to interfere, because all the rioters were obviously drunk. "And if," says D'Avaux bitterly, "the French officers press for discipline they become odious." Even when D'Avaux's horses were stolen, the ambassador's complaints to Richard Hamilton were received coldly—the General replied "forte sèchement." But D'Avaux, in reporting other disorders and duels, has to admit that there "are Frenchmen here who foment quarrels, brawlers who bring the rest of the foreign legion into disrepute."

After all, there was little else to be expected in a town that was under martial law so far as its civilians were concerned, and under no law at all for its soldiers. The soldiers were quartered in every Protestant house; and even if it were necessary to discount the complaints of Dr King, we can well believe that the misery of the town was very great,[1] when ten, twelve, or even twenty men were quartered on a householder. There were 3000 soldiers in a town of 7000 houses, which alone would be a factor of disorder as well as of acute discomfort to those who were their hosts. The soldiers would come home if it suited them at midnight or in the small hours, shouting and singing, and turn people out of their beds. Owing to a system by which the soldiers' quartering was computed as a fixed charge, it was the ingenious device of company officers to find several quarters for their soldiers, so that they might pocket the money for the commuted charges.

[1] King, *State of the Protestants in Ireland.*

DUBLIN

In these circumstances one can believe—in fact, one can scarcely disbelieve—the stories which the Protestant victims have left of their miseries. Their churches were shut or deserted; presently their houses became empty too, as they abandoned them; the Protestant ministers were shouted at in the streets; even the Frenchmen cursed them as "diables des ministres hérétiques." The Protestant aldermen were turned out of the Town Council—even the charwoman at the old Tholsel was replaced by a Papist—and they took refuge in an obscure nook, near the belligerent weavers' quarter, called Skinner's Alley. Here they held furtive meetings and preserved the city regalia, till such time as the arrival of William enabled them to emerge.[1] One of the dispossessed aldermen was Bartholomew Vanhomrigh, the father of Swift's unhappy Vanessa.

Dublin quickly became Romanised. "The Priests and Friars multiplied in Dublin to the number of 300 or 400, well fed and well clothed: there were not more lusty plump fellows in the Town than they," says a contemporary Protestant, who adds that they were "importunate and experienced beggars." It is not

---

[1] As the anniversary of their reinstatement came round, the Protestant aldermen held a banquet, and finally formed a society called the Aldermen of Skinner's Alley. One of the verses of their charter song ran :—

"When Tyranny's detested Power
Had leagued with superstition,
And bigot James in evil hour
Began his luckless mission,
Still here survived the sacred flame,
Here Freedom's sons did rally,
And consecrate to deathless Fame
The men of Skinner's Alley."
      D. A. CHART, *The Story of Dublin.*

clear that more than a few new "chappels and convents" were founded. One convent was already in existence, the convent of "Gratia Dei," to which Lady Tyrconnel had charitably contributed. Another was founded a very short time before James left Ireland for ever; and his charter of foundation to Lady Mary Butler was followed a few weeks later by a warrant signed by King William giving Lady Mary and her nuns safe conduct beyond the seas.

Christ Church Cathedral was closed for a fortnight, after which it was opened and was converted temporarily into a Roman Catholic chapel. James went there in state to mass, and Dr Alexius Stafford, who afterwards fell in the bloody rout at Aughrim, was made its dean. Here a sermon was preached before the King by Father Hall, and a more famous but less successful one by the erudite Dr Michael Moor, who incurred the royal displeasure and was exiled from the Court for inculcating in his discourse that kings ought to consult clergymen in their temporal affairs, the clergy having a temporal as well as a spiritual right in the kingdom; but that kings had nothing to do with the management of spiritual affairs, but were to obey the orders of the Church. That was scarcely James's view of the functions of the clergy. He found a more pliant ecclesiastic in Dr John Gordon, Bishop of Galway, the soundness of whose Protestant principles at this time or any other is open to doubt. He had come over with James from Saint-Germain as a guarantee of good faith, and was made Chancellor of Dublin and Vicar-General of the diocese. Dr King, the Dean of St Patrick's, stigmatised him as an ignorant, lewd man; but Dr King's mouth was quickly closed by imprisonment, and Dr Gordon was able to go on his way sequestrating Protestant benefices without hindrance.

Other Protestant institutions suffered with their churches. The Fellows had fled from Trinity College, with the exception of four who courageously clung to their dangerous posts; the students were turned into the streets to make room for soldiers, and to secure the revenues. Dr Moor and Father MacCarthy were appointed to the vacant offices of Provost and Dean. To these two men Trinity College owes a great debt in its troublous times. They preserved the library, and they performed also the thankless task of alleviating the lot of the Protestant prisoners who were confined here.

During the summer of 1689 Dublin was, as far as we can reconstruct its conditions, a busy and uproarious town. The newcomers were making the most of their opportunities, and the motto of them all was, "Devil take the hindmost!" As the summer drew on to a rainy and cheerless autumn, an uneasy menace crept into the air, and Dublin began to feel its chill. William's general, Schomberg, had landed in Ireland; Derry and Enniskillen were still holding out; and—a more tangible source of uneasiness—the price of every kind of commodity was going up; provisions and drink were becoming more scarce; at one time a salt famine threatened, so that there was not enough salt to cure the beef.

Then there came a period of reaction. The incredible rains of autumn, which cost James 6000 men in deaths from sickness, had also rendered Schomberg impotent, and Dublin returned to its feverish gaiety. It was a riotous time of drunkenness. D'Avaux tells with cold disgust the story of a drunken quarrel in which young FitzJames, a boy of seventeen, played the leading part. Lord Dungan had been dining with some of his fellow-Irishmen, and they were sitting over their wine when Berwick and young FitzJames, in his usual spirits, joined them. One of the Irishmen reproached FitzJames, who, in spite of his years, was colonel of a regiment, for having dismissed one of his friends. FitzJames retorted angrily; and the pacific Berwick, to smooth matters over, turned the subject and said, "Let us instead drink to the health of all good Irishmen, and confusion to Lord Melfort, who has nearly lost the kingdom." FitzJames, with a foolish lad's obstinacy, rejoined that Melfort was a very honest man —one of his own friends. Dungan at this rose and said, with a laugh, that at any rate nobody wanted to drink Melfort's health. Before Dungan had finished the ironical bow with which he had accompanied this speech, FitzJames flung a glass of wine in his face. . . . The scandal was inevitable, though Dungan with admirable good temper took the blame on himself, and said that FitzJames was after all only a boy. But he was a youth, adds D'Avaux severely, who was extremely dissolute and generally too drunk to sit his horse.

With this kind of example in high quarters, not much could be expected of the army when it returned to its winter quarters in Dublin. Gaming, drinking, and worse occupied the time and thoughts of the Court and the soldiery. "The army became debauched by success. Dublin was a seminary of vice, an academy of luxury, or rather a sink of corruption, a living emblem of Sodom"[1]—and every historian of the time says the

---

[1] Stevens, Brit. Mus. Add. (36,296). We are indebted to Dr R. H. Murray's *Revolution in Ireland* (Macmillan) for this reference.

same thing plainly or indirectly. Thus on the one hand we see the representatives of the Stuart hopes, aspirations, and methods, in Dublin, disgracing their cause while they ruined it; and on the other hand we have the picture of the Protestant inhabitants of the town, who should have shared with the Roman Catholics the task of upholding the King, stealing furtively away at night, leaving their possessions, and taking with them barely enough to bribe the tide-master at Ringsend and the adventurous ship-masters to find them a passage to England and liberty.

CHAPTER XI

THE FAILURE OF THE IRISH CAMPAIGN

FRANCE, like Ireland, was at this period living on its capital. The slackening of the sinews of its finances was presently to become perceptible in its Continental wars. D'Avaux, as the representative of France, had therefore to see to it that no money was wasted on a subsidiary campaign in Ireland—regarded as a mere distraction of William's larger aims—and neither D'Avaux nor Louis perceived the mistake till too late. In D'Avaux, the penetration, which a few years before, had pierced the designs of William was either in abeyance or was dulled by his dislike of Ireland and of James. Dalrymple, an impartial historian,[1] said of his appointment to accompany King James that he was, "in his person, a sad monitor of past errors; and in his office an omen of future misfortunes." Dalrymple's antithesis was warranted. The advice of D'Avaux, good as it was—to set the affairs of Dublin in order, to organise or reorganise the army, to allow the armies of William to wear themselves out against a concentrated resistance —was a counsel of perfection to a King whose affairs were in such hopeless disorder that time would only

[1] Dalrymple's *Memoirs*.

disorder them more. James had nothing to gain by waiting. Every moment that he stayed in Ireland, the breach between Protestants and Catholics must widen, his chances of bridging it must lessen. There was something in that idea to which he so pathetically clung during life—that all was a mistake, a misunderstanding, and that if but his subjects could see him, all would once again be "glad confident morning." If by some miracle he could have been transported (with a sufficient display of force) to England, at a time when reaction had bred discontent with the Dutch and with William, one may be permitted to think that he would have been reinstated—by some form of compromise. But while he did nothing to assert himself as a King, the double fear of France and of the imposition of Popery in England was reinforced by everything that happened in Ireland.

One may therefore, as a preliminary, define the policy of D'Avaux as one that was directed to keeping James quiescent in Dublin, and consolidating his position there—at the expense of the Protestants. The policy of James was to strike a blow at William through an invasion of England, or by going to Scotland, where Claverhouse was raising his standard. The policy of Melfort was to support these ideas of James. Tyrconnel, thoroughly disliking and distrusting Melfort, was disposed to side with D'Avaux, because he very shrewdly perceived that D'Avaux held the purse-strings, and that on his advice to Louis must depend the success of any campaign in Ireland. That he trusted D'Avaux completely we do not believe—but the bluff Viceroy was soldier enough and diplomatist enough to recognise that France was James's only hope.

It was not long before the essential differences of these policies declared themselves. While Roman Catholics and Protestants were eagerly waiting with mouths open or shut for what was next to happen, the future of Ireland was being decided in the Castle. Every evening at seven o'clock a little cabinet council met—the King, D'Avaux, Tyrconnel, Melfort. One may picture them—the King restless, by turns eager and wavering, but obstinate in clinging to his purposes; Melfort speaking seldom and slowly, but always in agreement with the King; Tyrconnel downright, but concealing under his soldierly plain-speaking his distrust of D'Avaux, and making no concealment of his dislike of Melfort; D'Avaux cool, correct, with not a shred of liking for any of them, nor to be moved a hair's-breadth from his appointed policy. "As for me," he says in one of his later letters, "I go my own way": and it expresses his attitude very well. Rather oddly, the same expression occurs in one of Tyrconnel's letters to the Queen: "I go my own old road"; and we cannot but think that he pursued it well, according to his lights and to his ability. It is certain that he never betrayed himself to D'Avaux, who from first to last regarded him as an ally—as French as a Frenchman.

The first difference arose about the King's expedition to Derry. Derry, to the pained surprise of everyone, and not a little owing to a moment of indecision on the part of Tyrconnel, had boldly declared for William, and was resisting every attempt of Richard Hamilton to reduce it. It never was reduced, though Pusignan and Maumont, and Pointis the French engineer, fell in its siege; and Rosen failed to subdue it by threat or by famine. But it was James's hope and belief that if he went to show himself before it, his presence would be powerful to prevail on the inhabitants to submit. It may also have been his hope that, once he arrived there, and especially if the city submitted, he would be by that much nearer to the expedition to Scotland on which he had set his heart. D'Avaux opposed both these projects—the one that was immediate, and the one that was in the clouds. He moved Tyrconnel to oppose the expedition; he wrote to France that the Queen must be induced to write to James to discourage the hare-brained descent on Scotland. But the advice he tendered in the Council was the practical counsel that James should stop in Dublin setting in order the affairs of the army and the commissariat, no less than those of the city and of the country.

In vain. They set out (the complaints are those of D'Avaux) with no beds nor any sufficient travelling equipment—in the teeth of a wind strong enough to stop the horses. The disgust of the Frenchman lends vigour to his pen: they passed over rivers that the rain had swollen to torrents, and travelled for miles that were as long as French leagues over detestable roads and hills that were precipices. The towns were deserted. In Omagh, abandoned by the rebels, there was "ny bien ny bierre," a precious phrase easily to be rendered as "neither bite nor sup." The windows and doors had gone from the houses; the fires smoked on the floors of the hovels where the cavalcade lodged; there was no forage for the miserable nags they rode on. One can well believe that this untimely excursion soured D'Avaux's views of Ireland. He never reached Londonderry. The King's expedition, continued without him, did no good. His suspicious subjects, so far from receiving him with open arms, fired on him; and James returned to Dublin.

Here there arose new problems and new difficulties. Tyrconnel, nursing an incipient fit of gout, was growing daily more irritated with Melfort, and less capable of conducting his share of the government. He had never been a man of the cabinet; he grew lethargic as his illness gained on him. He suffered from heart attacks, the most depressing and the most alarming of symptoms, and he finally left the Castle to take to his bed. D'Avaux clearly thought he would die, and directed the whole of his energies to undermining the influence of Melfort. He scanned every pamphlet and every broadsheet published in Dublin for evidence of the Scotsman's unpopularity; he reported to Louis that Melfort was unpopular alike in Ireland, Scotland, and England; he quoted Lord Dover's saying that if James took Melfort with him to England no one would declare for the King. In response to a suggestion that he himself should try to reconcile Melfort and Tyrconnel, if only for working purposes, D'Avaux observes that their differences are not personal but fundamental. "Each wishes to have the ear of the King, each inclines to a different policy." He concludes with a scathing denunciation of the Scot—incompetent, slow, neglectful of business, and he is "always walking with his wife, by which he loses a great deal of time." D'Avaux's disapproval of the enjoyment of leisure probably extended to the King, who spent a great deal of time in driving around Dublin in the afternoons.

Then arose the overwhelming difficulties of the Irish Parliament which James summoned to meet in Dublin.

The Irish Parliament (which met on May 7th, 1689) was a Roman Catholic Parliament. Out of a total of ninety Protestant peers, only five temporal and four spiritual obeyed the summons. Ten Roman Catholic peers attended; seventeen more, by new creation or reversion of old attainders, sat in the House. Tyrconnel's policy had ensured a Roman Catholic House of Commons. Two hundred and thirty-two members were returned; only six were Protestants.[1] This Parliament, thirsting for the restoration of property which had passed from the hands of its original owners earlier in the century, was the crown and symbol of James's political failure. What could be expected from the Protestants of Ireland if their lands were confiscated; what support for King James could be expected from the Protestants of England if their sympathies were alienated and their apprehensions aroused by the robbery of their co-religionists in Ireland?

Such considerations the Parliament was determined to ignore. They began by repealing the Act of Settlement; they ended by passing the Act of Attainder. The first, by destroying James's credit in Ireland, made a successful war there impossible; the second, joined to it, extinguished every shred of sympathy with James in England. James was quite sensible of the disastrous effect of repealing the Act of Settlement. "I shall most readily consent to the making of such good wholesome laws as may be for the good of the nation, the improvement of trade, and relieving of such as have been injured by the late Acts of Settlement," he said, in the able and sincere speech with which he opened the Parliament, "so far forth as may be consistent with reason, justice

[1] *Cf.* Dr R. H. Murray, *The Revolution in Ireland.*

and the public good"—and no one knew better than he that many hard cases had gone neglected and unrecompensed under the Settlement of Charles II. Many have never to this day had justice done them, and even in the last century worthless documents with Charles's seal were preserved in decayed homesteads and cabins. But James's idea of what could be done to render partial justice was very different from that of the country gentlemen who had been smarting under deprivation and a sense of wrong for a generation. Their view was not far removed from that of D'Avaux, who suggested, as the most reasonable solution of the problem, that the lands held by Protestants should be taken from them and given to dissatisfied Roman Catholics.

James struggled, protested in vain. Popular feeling ran high; the soldiers quarrelled in the streets about it. "Alas!" said James, "I am fallen into the hands of a people who will ram that and much more down my throat." One night in desperation he called for his carriage, and would have gone down in his private dress to the House of Peers to plead with some of its members, and press them to stand by him in rejecting the Repeal. D'Avaux was told of it, and hurried into the Castle yard in time to stop him. One can imagine the cool, polite Frenchman, the representative of an authority higher than any in Ireland, interposing his barrier of diplomatic emphasis against that which the King would do. France and the popular clamour effected between them what James would not have yielded to public feeling alone; but in that moment, as it seems to us, he realised the hollowness of his position, and the instability of the Irish platform. The

FAILURE OF THE IRISH CAMPAIGN

Act was passed, though James by private generosity endeavoured to mitigate some of its injustices.

It was followed by the Act of Attainder, which nominated thousands of people who were to be adjudged traitors against James—and were to lose their lands in consequence—and which was the most stupid, ill-digested, and hasty measure passed by any Parliament. Its chief object was not vengeance but confiscation. James disapproved of this Act also, though the disapproval was ineffectual and never, either at the time or since, counted to him for righteousness. It was part of the irony of his career that those acts of popular injustice to which he was so opposed should have been put down to him and contributed to his failure.

It would have been little wonder if at this juncture—mid-July—the Protestants in Dublin should have been a source of treason and danger. Whether they were or not, it was D'Avaux's cue to say they were; and his spies told him, and the news was communicated to the King, that an uprising in the city was projected. James hastily doubled the guards of the Castle—he had the nervousness of the unpopular ruler; and he put under arrest some of the more prominent Protestants. Dr King, the Dean of St Patrick's, was, as we have already noted, confined in the Castle with other prisoners, to whom he piously preached on Sundays. The suspicions of his loyalty were not without foundation, but the chief thing alleged against him was that he was regarded by the King as a "dangerous man." Twelve other prominent Protestants were arrested on the same day, Captain Robert Fitzgerald, Sir John Davies, Sir Humphrey

Gervaise, Alderman Smith, and several councillors among them, and "were carried through the streets in the most evident manner imaginable." D'Avaux adds that three spies were arrested.

By this time, and probably by reason of some of the foregoing events, James was growing restive in his anxiety to leave Ireland and make his descent on England. Tyrconnel was ill. D'Avaux says he was still languishing but hopeful of cure, and we might suspect him of malingering in a time of extreme difficulty of counsel, but that we know he was nearing the end of his hard-lived life. At any rate Melfort's counsels were dominant with the King, and were peculiarly grateful to James because he favoured the idea of the English expedition. "The reason why Melfort's counsels prevail over Tyrconnel's and mine," explains D'Avaux sourly, "is that he humours the King. Whatever the King says, Melfort agrees. . . . Even the King's confessor, whom I have approached and who is a good man and not meddlesome, can do nothing. He has done what he could"—but evidently James had been something more than chilling.

A new complication arose for the French ambassador in the arrival from France of Mr James Porter, the Vice-Chamberlain of the Court of Saint-Germain. It is not unlikely that Porter brought letters to James from the Queen in which D'Avaux's uncomplimentary criticisms of James's methods, the defects of his policy, and the want of organisation of his army returned, like the kiss the lady returned to Rodolphe, "revus, corrigés, et considérablement augmentés." At any rate James sent for D'Avaux, and received him with an angry outburst. D'Avaux had written of him to

Louis, said James with rising indignation, as "if he had been a culprit who knew no better than a child how to behave himself." These were his own words, writes the scandalised ambassador; and goes on to say that "the Queen had wondered what kind of a black-hearted *ingrat* I must be to write so much ill of a King so well disposed towards me; that I had said the King spent Louis's money in giving it to Berwick and FitzJames; that he treated the French generals ill; and that he was managed by Berwick, Hamilton, and Dungan. . . ." D'Avaux replied with commendable coolness that, as a matter of fact, he had written to Louis nothing but what he told James every day; and as for the gifts of money to Berwick and FitzJames, this was the first he had heard of any such report. But that even if he had conceived the sentiments ascribed to him, he should have never been so imprudent as to commit them to writing, because they would have been reproved by Louis, besides being repeated at Saint-Germain and to the Queen. James said he was satisfied. D'Avaux may also have been satisfied. He thought that this ill turn had been done him by Lauzun, though he suspected Dover of a hand in it.

By way of confirming the reconciliation, D'Avaux's advice was asked on the preliminary steps for a re-organisation of Irish affairs. He recommended the formation of a small Privy Council, and a Secretary of State for Ireland. As regards the army, a number of officers should be dismissed, and the others carefully weeded. The competent petty officers should be promoted to commands, and the ammunition trains should be put in order—all sound canons. The Privy Council was formed. It included:—Sir Alexander Fytton,

Lord Chancellor, Lord Chief Justice Nugent, Chief Justice Keating, Sir Stephen Rice, Baron of the Exchequer, Tyrconnel, Lord Clanricarde, Lord Mountcashel, the Hamiltons, Richard and Anthony, Lord Galmoy, and Simon Luttrell, Lord Powis, Lord Dover, Lord Thomas Howard, Colonel Sarsfield, and William Talbot, a nephew of Tyrconnel. William Talbot was one of the suggested Secretaries of State for Ireland, but D'Avaux thought little of him. Of the other candidates, no one was quite fit for the post in his opinion. Chief Justice Herbert was faithful and loyal, but a Protestant ; Lord Thomas Howard, honest but not very capable. Of Lord Galmoy, D'Avaux opined that he might be more capable than he seemed.

Encouraged by this restored cordiality, D'Avaux reopened his campaign on Melfort. We may not say that D'Avaux was a good hater, but he was an unwearying opponent. The attack on Melfort in his letters is persistent: every incident that may tell against him is recounted. D'Avaux complained, for example, that even the King's Life Guards were ill-mounted. Dr King, looking out from his window on the Castle yard, corroborates this view. Melfort answered with a sarcastic grin that if D'Avaux really felt this to be a matter of importance, the Guards could be mounted in an hour by enlisting the Dublin coach-horses. D'Avaux, ignoring this pleasantry, pressed the point. James assented, and then asked time to think over the matter. So exasperated did the ambassador become that he went to see Tyrconnel, to take counsel as to what was to be done. Melfort's hopeless incompetence, in D'Avaux's view, was ruining the kingdom. Everything was neglected. The town of Newry was

JOHN DRUMMOND, LORD MELFORT.

FAILURE OF THE IRISH CAMPAIGN

left without powder—Melfort's fault. James gave orders that a proclamation should be issued, calling on his subjects to rally to his standard, and to send in their horses for the use of the army. The proclamation was not printed. Why? The Recorder of the Council (a zealous Protestant) excused the omission on the ground that he had no money to pay for the paper. Melfort again. And though at one time Melfort was so humble that Tyrconnel used to blush for him (so Tyrconnel said, though Tyrconnel and blushes must long have been strangers), now that Tyrconnel was ill, the Scot, like other persons, felt free to "gang his own gait." Lady Tyrconnel went to see him, and subduing a natural imperiousness of manner, begged him to consult the judges and the other councillors about the alarming state of Irish affairs. Melfort replied with studied rudeness that there was not the least necessity for anything of the kind. No one was better served than King James: an angel from heaven could not do better than he—the good Melfort—had done. Moreover, he was entirely indifferent as to what anyone in France, England, Scotland, or Ireland said or thought about him. He was not afraid of the future himself; and if anyone was less courageous, all he hoped, with all his heart, was that they should go off to some other country which suited them better. . . . Thus far the indomitable Melfort, whom the absence of any ability or any approval of his colleagues could not stir, and who continued his daily walks with his wife.

D'Avaux nullified the effect which the soundness of his own counsels might have had, by a proposition which was as shameless as it was absurd. He proposed not once but twice that a St Bartholomew's Day should be organised against recalcitrant Protestants. James seems to have been too taken aback at D'Avaux's cynicism to make a suitable rejoinder in the first instance. But when D'Avaux returned to the charge, James replied angrily, and at once, that he was not going to cut the throats of his own people. "Il m'a répondu d'un ton fort aigre qu'il ne voulut pas égorger ses sujets, que c'estoit son peuple, et qu'on ne l'obligerait jamais à les traittes de la sorte." Such loyalty to unworthy subjects astonished D'Avaux, who protested that he was proposing nothing inhuman : after all, there had been occasions in Irish history when the Protestants had cut the throats of the Catholics; the King might reserve his pity for the Catholics. James replied shortly that he would wait to defend the Catholics till the Protestants attacked them ; and when the persistent ambassador endeavoured to pursue the discussion by saying it might then be too late to save the Catholics, James closed the discussion with a dry "Tant pis, Monsieur." He may be congratulated on having for once found a way of stemming the flow of D'Avaux's discourse.

It may have been this incident which led D'Avaux to the suspicion that the King was dissatisfied no less with the situation in which he found himself than with the French ambassador. He reported James as being out of spirits, as well as out of humour, and gloomily asking whether it was of any use to struggle against the numberless difficulties of the situation. "What is the good of anything?" we almost seem to hear him asking ; and we can imagine the impatience with which he listened to D'Avaux's eternal monitions that there was nothing to be done but to set his house in order. D'Avaux thought that the King was ready at a moment to throw up everything and quit Ireland, though James had manfully said that he asked nothing better than to stay at the head of his army and strike a blow for his lost kingdom. But he had little cause for congratulation on his affairs. He prorogued his ungovernable Parliament on the 20th of July, but the mischief of its proceedings was done; and on the 1st of August the siege of Derry was raised. It had withstood hardships which make its resistance memorable in history; it had inflicted as much material injury on its assailants as it had sustained, and incomparably more moral damage. The same day that Derry was relieved, the Jacobite forces assailing Enniskillen were disastrously beaten at Newtown Butler. General MacCartny (Mountcashel) was captured; Anthony Hamilton escaped, but half their combined forces, numbering 3000, were killed or captured. Enniskillen and Derry had been the Kimberley and Ladysmith of the campaign. Ulster, now entirely in the hands of the Williamites, was as disastrous a hindrance to the success of the Jacobite arms as was the Peninsula to the Napoleonic plans. Against these reverses James had nothing to set but Dundee's Scottish victory at Killiecrankie. No wonder the King's thoughts turned to Scotland. Melfort, always supple, would have sustained his wish to leave Ireland at any rate. Tyrconnel was able to prevent it.

It was time that something was done; for England, stirred by the stories of Derry's resistance, had at length prepared and sent that army under General Schomberg of which we have already made mention.

It was an army which landed on August 13th, and which, though as ill-equipped as the Irish levies of James, was yet an army—with the force and presence of Ulster behind it—and a forerunner of the sustained effort to come. Impending events did something more than cast their shadows before them. They consolidated Irish belligerence on both sides into something more like organisation. Dublin was alive with a new and bustling activity. The proclamations were sent out; the drums were beat. Rosen, who had cursed the Irish soldiers for cowardice, now joined with James in assembling a new army in Dublin.

The most evident sign of the times, however, was the departure of Melfort, so long assailed, so tenacious of an unworthy office. He went back to Saint-Germain, ostensibly to go thence on a mission to the Pope. The King may have sped his parting servant. Tyrconnel saw him go with a curse, and sent after him the most damaging of testimonials to the Queen at Saint-Germain. "I ask with all my soull," he observes, "that he may serve you. But a man of not truth will quickly be found out in all countrys. . . . Such men doo seldom bring any great matter to pass." Melfort stopped long enough in Saint-Germain to make himself heard; for two months later evidences of his activities are found in one of D'Avaux's replies to some allegations sent on to Dublin from Versailles. "My Lord Melfort knows quite well," remarks D'Avaux, "that nothing but French arms keeps King James in Ireland. Tyrconnel is also aware that King James will quit the scene at the first check. Moreover, Melfort was the first to counsel James to do so, and if he says otherwise, he holds very different views in France from those he expressed in Ireland." D'Avaux's pen was quite capable of dealing with his adversary even at that distance, and Melfort was hurried off to Rome by Louis. He was fortunate enough to impress the new Pope less unfavourably, for, in a response to the appeals addressed to him by the Queen on behalf of her husband's cause, Alexander VIII. recommends my Lord Melfort as "a subject truly worthy of your benevolence."

The new situation in Dublin, and the town's improved order and appearance, impressed even D'Avaux, between whom and the King more cordial relations appeared to be in prospect as soon as Melfort had gone. Tyrconnel, recovering somewhat from his illness—though he writes to the Queen that his "old distemper" has not left him, and that the "palpitation of the heart daily increases on me"—began to assume more influence in affairs. But the activity was more apparent than real. Schomberg's army was a wretched one, miserably equipped, but it had a head, one of the safest among veteran soldiers. James's levies — we cannot call them an army—had no capable head, and no initiative. Thus, through a miserably rainy autumn which bred appalling disease in the two armies facing one another, nothing was done on either side. Schomberg, in addition to the losses by sickness in his army, knew its weakness too well to risk a battle: he had everything to gain by waiting. James had everything to lose by delay, and so had France, if France had but recognised it; but still James's armies rested quiescent and the French supplies tarried. That autumn was the seal of James's failure; and James knew it, and Tyrconnel knew it— though in James's letter to the Pope the situation had been glibly summed up by the representation that the "King hath obtained frequent small victories over the Rebells: they avoided a great one by obstinately declining the same."

Meanwhile Dublin, sheeted in rain, was growing despondent and hungrier. The cattle market stood almost empty of beasts on market days; provisions and clothing cost famine prices; there was "hardly any salt," and "only wine in Dublin for two months" —a depressing prospect for convivial soldiers; wood and coke were "hard to get and far to send." Discontent bred disagreements. D'Avaux had his unfailing panacea, which was to put things in order; and he records an encounter between the King and himself which would be humorous if it were not for the seriousness of the situation. General Rosen was to be recalled—rather to the dismay of those Irish officers who had begun by disliking him, but had ended by appreciating his abilities; and D'Avaux, who shrewdly suspected that his own position was being undermined, thought he might usefully supply the King with a memorandum of his remedies in writing. He politely introduced it with the remark that he had just noted a few recommendations to which the King might say "Yes" or "No" as he pleased; the Secretary of State would then execute those the King approved. Nothing new in the suggestions—they had merely been reduced to writing. James hardly waited for the ambassador to begin before angrily protesting against D'Avaux's exaggerations. "But, your Majesty," responded the ambassador imperturbably, "you do not understand. This is no manifesto, no proclamation, not even an address to you; nobody has seen it. I merely thought it most important that you should learn the truth without flattery or disguise. If your Majesty would rather not—I will read no more." James, still fuming, bade him read on. He listened to the end, and with a nonchalance equal to D'Avaux's own asked for the paper when the reading was finished. For all practical purposes it went into the kingly waste-paper basket.

That is, in effect, the last conspicuous interference of D'Avaux in Irish affairs. It was true that intrigue was on foot to recall him. D'Avaux, with less than his usual perspicacity, or with intentional blindness, ascribes his recall to Dover and Lauzun, and remarks that it is deplorable that a person like Lauzun should strive to do him an injury out of mere lightness of heart. But in truth it is not unlikely that the Irish resented the hard-fisted parsimony which he represented; and, in spite of Tyrconnel's hearty bonhomie, it is more than doubtful whether he had either as great an affection for France or as great a confidence in D'Avaux as the ambassador said that he had. Doubtless he preferred him to Lauzun, of whose substitution for D'Avaux he had no doubt heard rumours. But the shrewd Irishman once discloses to the Queen what he felt in his heart about the French alliance: "We are only destined to serve a present turne and be at last a sacrifice to our ennemis."

The wet autumn deepened into a wet winter, and the troops went into winter quarters. Nothing had been done; nothing was likely to be done. Such of the army as was quartered in Dublin poured back into the empty houses. The young officers gaily sought to make the best of it, and the licence of Dublin in these months became a byword. Each looked after himself: the colonels lived on the pay of their captains; the troops lived on what they could commandeer. The army, writes Tyrconnel to the Queen, "have ruined and destroyed all our cattle and sheep; there is no wool, hides, tallow, beef, butter, for export; and for the copper money we have much ado to make it pass."

Tyrconnel's heart was failing him. Not that he was not brave, but that he was too old to be careless. He saw, and said, that the King was but a catspaw; he was aware that whatever suggestions might be made about a descent on England to retrieve the balance of ineptitude in Ireland, they would fall on politely deaf ears. "The people of England," he wrote to the Queen in December, "were never in such a disposition to throw off the usurper, . . ." if but James could show himself there. One is doubtful whether he was as certain of this as he affects to be in the letters which he sends to Saint-Germain; but he was quite clear that the course of affairs in Ireland could never lead to anything but disaster at last. "The good God," he writes[1] to Queen Maria early in the new year, "has given you a great soul in all your afflictions; He has not thought fit to shake this confounded Prince of Orange coming over to us with such power as will sett us hard . . . that this country cannot possibly hold out longer than this year from falling into the Prince of Orange's hands is not to be in the least doubted."

In a nobler letter which we cannot forbear to quote

[1] February 22nd, 1689.

he indites a Tyrconnel such as we like best to think of him :—

"Since I have nothing more to ask of any kind of honour or riches, if the King be re-established—God knows I have more of both than I deserve or care to have. Madam, this I say from my heart—what should I have or care for more if God has so decreed it that I shall not live to see it? As long as my powers endure and are agreeable to him I will to the last moment of my life serve him the best I am able, for my integrity and loyalty shall end with my life—to him, to your Majestie, and to the Prince your son."

The prospects of a successful landing in England peep out more than once in this correspondence, and names like the Duke of Beaufort, the Duke of Newcastle, the Marquis of Worcester are mentioned as supporters. These hopes may have been due to the Irishman's love of pleasing—his wish to make the best of things. Mr Vice-Chamberlain Porter had gone back to Saint-Germain filled with forebodings. Tyrconnel begs the Queen not to allow him "to fright you with dismall stories." He adds later that he humbly begs that "Mr Porter may not see any of my letters, for I have known him many years." But whatever Tyrconnel's motive, he harps on the descent on England almost to the last; and at the beginning of spring he dilates on the advantages of the plan. He himself could occupy William's attention in Ireland, while James advanced in England. "I could keep up the bustle and give him (the Prince of Orange) work enough till the King was able to summon me from home" (to join him).

But meanwhile Rosen had gone, and D'Avaux was

following him, while Lauzun, with French troops, was coming in their place. Tyrconnel must have welcomed the French troops and their equipment, but the advantages of taking Lauzun with them were by no means so evident to his mind. Though he had long given up expectation of gaining much from D'Avaux, he much feared " him that cometh in his place will undoe all our affairs." He had heard from the French officers that Lauzun was a restless, quarrelsome intriguer —" fort malhonnest homme, fort brouillard, fort inquiet"—and he would rather have rested with the adviser they had. He also wondered what reports D'Avaux would bear back to France. Bespeak him fair, he advises the Queen, you know how to manage him, "and we have need of everyone's good word. 'Tis a dissembling age: and I confess I do not love it and care not to practise it: but nothing's lost by being civil to all." D'Avaux might possibly have been managed by the Queen; but his reports had been much too categorical and too damaging to be explained away. To the last he is to be found proffering advice—as, for example, that in the camps and garrisons wine and beer should be sold at fixed prices; and that part of the levies should be more widely distributed, and further removed from Dublin, where they ruin and despoil what is necessary to the subsistence of other troops; and the last message he left for Lauzun was that he had come " to be a sacrifice to a poor-spirited and cowardly people, whose soldiers will never fight and whose officers will never observe orders."

It is probable that D'Avaux was not sorry to go, though he had once protested in his letters at being ousted, especially by Lauzun, who, as he said, had done

FAILURE OF THE IRISH CAMPAIGN 233

him an ill turn out of pure light-heartedness. He disliked Ireland; he saw no profit or credit in his embassage; and he had private business in France which was suffering. Moreover, in his recall he was assured by Colbert that Louis was not recalling him out of any sense that he had been a failure. Colbert adds: "His Majesty is quite satisfied with your services, and it looks as if you would not want for good employment (*de meilleurs employs*) in the future." Louis himself wrote to his withdrawing ambassador, ending his letter with the polite and kingly formula: "Sur ce je prie Dieu qu'il vous ayt Monsieur le Comte d'Avaux en sa sainte garde." Thus went the able but little-liked counsellor. Berwick shortly says of him that he was not respectful.[1]

Lauzun heralded his arrival at Dublin by complaining that proper arrangements had not been made to receive him and his troops at Cork: which is likely enough. He landed with 7300 men at Kinsale; and, in exchange for the men he brought, Mountcashel sailed for France with the four regiments of Irishmen who formed the nucleus of that Irish Brigade which was to become so famous in the European wars. The exchange was an unnecessary and foolish piece of parsimony. Louvois had entrusted the new commander with instructions which were all part of the same prudent but insufficiently perspicuous French policy. He was "not to be carried away by the excitement of giving a sword-thrust or of winning a combat, but was to play a waiting game." The waiting game had been impressed on James since his arrival. Rosen had long before advised a retreat behind the line of the Shannon;

[1] *Life of the Duke of Berwick* (1738).

the burning of Dublin had even been counselled; the one thing which French strategy perceived and desired was to occupy William. It was a policy of pin-pricks. James had no wish to fall in with this view. He "would not be walked out of Ireland without at least having one blow for it"; but his courageous resolution was ever baffled by the want of co-operation on the part of his commanders, the division of counsels among his advisers, and the want of money or sufficient assistance from his allies. While they were bargaining William was advancing.

Lauzun was more to James's taste than ever D'Avaux had been; and, moreover, he was one of those careless spirits who despise orders and authority when occasion offers. Tyrconnel began by distrusting the new master more than the old one, though he assures the Queen that he will keep on good terms with him. Later he says that he is making advances to the newcomer—"I do all things to please him, even too much, as the King says"—though "Dover and he are very ill together." Later the crafty old soldier finds it unnecessary to dissemble: he began to like Lauzun. "I must doe M. de Lauzun justice to say I never saw anyone more zealous or more painfull in all things relating to the King's service"; and in the letters to Saint-Germain begins to steal a note even of hope.

"By Mid-May," he writes, "when the grass grows we shall march on Ulster and lay it in ashes unless the Prince of Orange advances on us"; and up to the very last, seven days before the battle of the Boyne, he speaks hopefully. In Tyrconnel's letters to the Queen, the record can be read of the hopes and fears in Dublin, almost till the battle of the Boyne laid

FAILURE OF THE IRISH CAMPAIGN 235

hopes aside for ever. "I go my old road," says Tyrconnel; and though he had no illusions as to whither it would lead, he kept up his spirits bravely enough. There is a curious reference in one of the letters from the camp at Ardee, in which he speaks of good news brought by "our flying lady"; but the good news seems to consist chiefly of unfounded beliefs in the weakness of the enemy. Tyrconnel knew better. "The Prince of Orange hath 40,000 men," he writes, and adds a complimentary opinion of their efficiency and experience. He knows that the Irish ill-equipped, ill-disciplined army cannot contend with them. "We cannot beat him," says he to the Queen in the letter of the 24th of June, "but whoever has time has life, as says your country's proverb, . . . and we may keep the small army from being beaten. . . ."

That was the unfortunate incertitude of the Irish plan of campaign. Over and over again it had been urged on James that he should retire behind the line of the Shannon, and fight the delaying actions which should weary and harass William's forces to the point of exhaustion. A victory could not be gained for James; but neither could it be for William, who would meanwhile be distributing those energies which he ought to be concentrating against France in Flanders.[1]

---

[1] After the battle of the Boyne, the Irish kept up a warfare against the superior Williamite forces for fifteen months, and, had Louis possessed the wit and energy of his rival, would, and should, have been enabled to keep it up much longer. The case is stated well and plainly in the contemporary *Light to the Blind*: "The King of France made a false step in the politicks by letting the Irish warr to fall: because that warr was the best medium in the world for destroying the Confederacy abroad, by reason that the Confederal Armies could not prolong the foraign warr without the arm and money of England, which were imployed in the warr of Ireland."

Lauzun had as little doubt as anyone either as to the upshot of a battle or as to the desirability of delay. "After the landing of the Prince of Orange, in the desperate state of his [King James's] affairs the choice of two resolutions remained for the King. One was a battle. This always seemed to me impossible. The other was to set fire to Dublin, and on his retreat from place to place, to devastate the land completely. This plan seemed so cruel to the King that he could not make up his mind to it. . . ." Let us at least do the King that justice. He was too proud, he had too little intelligent subtlety, too little perseverance, and too much obstinacy, to follow a plan of campaign of that character. Yet at the back of his intentions lay the advice that had been given him; and as in the campaign, so in the battle of the Boyne which decided it, he was caught in two minds. His smaller army, occupying the stronger position on the Boyne, was drawn up for defence, and with one eye to retreat.

The army and the commander opposed to it had but one thought, which was to win. The composite army of William, with its stiffening of seasoned Dutchmen, Danes, and Huguenots, had that which the Irish army had not. It had *morale*—a great confidence of right and of victory; whereas the feeling of the Irish army was comparable with that which a profound critic of war, the late Sir Charles Dilke, ascribed as the cause of the Russian defeats—a kind of melancholy fatalism summed up in the phrase, "Poor ould Ireland!" The feeling did not hinder them from making a most stubborn resistance—at points. The Irish cavalry, Parker's and Tyrconnel's troops fought brilliantly and gallantly: Berwick was wounded, Richard Hamilton was captured.

Their devotion averted a rout: it could not avert defeat. James's lack of artillery was fatal to the steadiness of his infantry; they would not stand before the fierce and sustained attack of veteran troops, and they could not be rallied behind the hedges when once they were on the run. It is not necessary to pursue the course of the battle further, or to moralise on its conduct. From the old church on Donore Hill James saw his hopes crumble with his army, and then turned his horse's head towards Dublin.

With what suspense and hopes and fears Dublin awaited the news of the battle can be imagined. On the day preceding the battle a cannon-shot grazed William just after he had mounted his horse, preparatory to riding round the lines. It was reported that he was wounded—then that he was killed; and the news travelled on the wings of rumour to Dublin and to France. In Paris, days after the battle of the Boyne, bonfires were being lighted for the death of William.

But in Dublin the ebb of hopes came quickly, sped by the presage of calamity. At daybreak the streets were crowded: no one but a Protestant was indoors: and during the forenoon the rumours of the fight that came in by that species of wireless telegraphy which reports battles, however distant—continually inclined to an Irish victory. Then a lull of no news. Then doubt; and in the afternoon, as tired horsemen straggled in with harassing fears, the truth followed with swift vehemence. All was lost. Thenceforward beaten troops came pouring into the town. Some marched sullenly, in fairly good order; some as men who are tired unto death; some in frenzied haste, flogging on cart-horses; many without arms, begrimed with dust and blood. Wounded men came in with the carts; the road to Dublin was strewn with muskets thrown away, with men wildly or despondently certain of defeat, or prophesying further disaster. Late at night, while Dublin throbbed with alarms, the cavalry came sounding through the town—with kettle-drums, hautboys, and trumpets—even as if they had been victors in the chase!

The King arrived long after dark had fallen. He made his way through the Castle gates with Sarsfield and an escort of cavalry, and was received at the Castle by Lady Tyrconnel. Tradition says that he announced to her with gloomy bitterness that the Irish had run away—which it is likely enough that he did; but her apocryphal retort that he had distanced them does not sound very probable. "After he was upstairs," says Story, "her ladyship ask't him what he would have for supper. Who then gave her an account of what breakfast he had got, which made him have little stomach for his supper. . . ."

Lauzun, in obedience to the dictates of a policy which would have been discomfited had James been made a prisoner, had counselled James's flight, and now urged him further to leave Ireland. James stood in no need of great persuasion. Of him might have been said, in a phrase less justly applied to Tyrconnel, that he was brave in danger but pusillanimous in disaster. He was bitterly disappointed in Ireland; he had no faith in it, nor liking for the part he was compelled to play in it. So he left it, and sailing from Kinsale arrived in France almost as soon as the news of his defeat, and while his allies were still taking counsel on what his future action in Ireland should be.

FAILURE OF THE IRISH CAMPAIGN

Before he left, he sent for the Lord Mayor and the Council and, with a spurt of bitterness, repeated his complaint of the Irish army which had basely fled the field, and added that thenceforward he was determined never to head an Irish army, " but to shift for himself, as they must do. . . ." That is not quite his own version of what he said, which he believed rather to have been to the effect that " he had justice on his side, but fate was against him. He therefore directed the release of the Protestants and the surrender of the city to the Prince of Orange, and obedience to his orders, for there had been blood enough spilt already. After which he went from Dublin without doing any damage, leaving untouched the plate and furniture of the house where he lay." [1]

[1] Clarke's *Life*.

Part III

The Jacobite Court

CHAPTER XII

REVIVAL OF JACOBITE HOPES

To Louis the defeat of James in Ireland, and his return to France, were a blow of which he realised the seriousness, though probably even he did not perceive the full extent of the disaster. It was doubly disappointing because the French victory off Beachy Head on June 30th, when the Count de Tourville had beaten the English fleet under Torrington,[1] and had burned Teignmouth, greatly raised Jacobite hopes. Maria had herself written to Tourville :—"After what you have lately done I consider the King [Louis XIV.] as master of the sea, and in a condition to establish the King my husband in his Kingdoms, and to free himself thereby from a great part of his enemies. If we are lucky enough to return soon to our own country, I shall always consider that you was the first to open the way to it; for it was effectually shut against us before the success of this engagement, to which your good conduct has contributed so much. But if I do not deceive myself, it appears to me now

---

[1] Admiral Herbert, Lord Torrington, the bearer of the invitation to William. His half-hearted tactics, ascribed to lukewarmness, contributed to the disastrous defeat of the combined English and Dutch fleets.

to be completely open, providing the King could gain some little time in Ireland, which I hope he will, yet I tremble with fear lest the Prince of Orange, who sees clearly that it is his interest to hinder him, should push the King and oblige him to give battle"[1]— prophetic words which can hardly have reached him for whom they were intended before James was defeated and a fugitive after the battle of the Boyne! During his flight he received a letter from Louis XIV. advising his return, and promising to land him in England with 30,000 men. James reached Brest on July 20th, and immediately sent an express off to the Queen, in which he told her "he was sensible he should be blamed for having hazarded a battle upon such inequalitys, but sayd he had no other post so advantageous to doe it in, unless he should have abandoned all without a strok, and have been driven at last into the sea." This letter shows James to have had some searchings of heart about his action, at all events to begin with, though he afterwards threw the blame on Tyrconnel for urging his departure.

"It is wonderful on what grounds my Lord Tyrconnel thought fit to press it [James's departure] with so much earnestness, unless it was out of tenderness for the Queen, who he perceived was so aprehensive of the King's person, as to be in a continual agony about it; she had frequently begged of him to have a special care of the King's safety, and tould him he must not wonder at her repeated instances on that head, for unless he saw her heart, he could not imagine the torment it suffered on that account, and must always

[1] Quoted by Macpherson from a translation. The date given by Clarke is June 27th.

REVIVAL OF JACOBITE HOPES

doe so."[1] James's conduct of the war in Ireland had shown, though he did not realise it, that he was not a person on whom men and money could be squandered with advantage, and, much to his mortification, his hopes of Louis XIV.'s further intervention were soon disappointed. The French King came to see him at Saint-Germain the day after his arrival, and welcomed him with general expressions of kindness.

But when James spoke in explicit terms of how opportune a moment the present would be for a descent upon England, with the English fleet so lately defeated, and so many troops absent in Ireland, Louis put him aside with vague excuses; and when James protested that he was certain his own sailors "would never fight against me, under whom they so often had conquered," the French King replied definitely though politely that "it was the first favour he had refused to his friend, and it should be the last." James, who was slow to take a hint, and could not realise the immensity of his disappointment, was not to be put off so easily. He attempted to press the point, "but his Most Christian Majesty by pretending indisposition waived seeing the King, till it was in effect too late to do anything."[2] "'Tis certain," comments poor James on this incident, "his [James's] patience never underwent so great a tryall in the whole course of his life." When at last he succeeded in seeing Louis, the French King would neither consent to his going aboard the fleet, nor to sending reinforcements to Ireland, saying, with great good sense, "it would be so much thrown away to send anything thither."

[1] Clarke, ii. 406, with much more to the same effect.
[2] *Ibid.*, ii. 412.

In spite of his determination to take no important step to restore James in the autumn of 1690, Louis was evidently anxious to show his guests that there was no diminution in his cordiality towards them. It is all to the French King's honour that his kindness outlasted all prospects of the Stuart restoration, and that up till James's death in 1701 Maria was writing to Caryll from the French Court that "this King is still as civil and kynd to us as he uses to be," though by that time the Stuarts diffidently avoided any mention of politics. In the October after James's ignominious return from Ireland,[1] Louis, as if to demonstrate to his guests his lively and unalterable kindness for them personally, invited them to spend some days at Fontainebleau. Here they arrived at six o'clock on Friday, and found Monseigneur in waiting for them. Louis was immediately on the spot to welcome them in person, and waving James on to take precedence of himself, he gave his hand to Maria and led her ceremoniously to the apartments of the Queen Mother, which she was to occupy. In the evening a Court was held. The Queen listened to the music that was performed in their honour, while James played at "Hombre" with Cardinal Furstenberg and Madame de Croissy. This Cardinal was one of the gay, intriguing ecclesiastics of that time; he was not above accepting a bribe from the King's mistress to secure the promotion of her son to an archbishopric. The bribe was paid through the Cardinal's own mistress and niece by marriage, the Comtesse de Furstenberg. When past middle life she was a woman who still showed the remains of great beauty, and retained her dominion over the Cardinal,

[1] July 1690.

"though tall, stout, and coarse-featured as a Swiss guard in woman's clothes." It was on behalf of Furstenberg, a creature of the Court, that Louis XIV. had quarrelled with the Pope over the election to the archbishopric of Cologne.

The next day was so wet that there could be no outdoor sports; the royal hunt had to be postponed. James and his wife looked on at a game of "paume." All the ladies attended the Queen's toilet, and accompanied her to chapel, where she knelt between the two Kings, with her husband on her right. This order was still maintained when Louis was seated with his guests. At table, Monsieur and Madame, their young son the Duc de Chartres, Monseigneur, and all the Princesses of the Blood were present. The same day Boisseleau[1] was graciously received by Louis on his return from Ireland; he had worked well for the glory of his country and himself, the King told him. The next day, Friday, was fine. James went stag-hunting with Monseigneur; Louis took the Queen to a boar-hunt. The visit was to have ended on the following Monday, but they appeared to be so much enjoying it, that Louis invited them to prolong it, to which they willingly assented. James visited all the Princesses of the Blood, and renewed his acquaintance with Madame de Montespan, who introduced to him her young daughter, Mademoiselle de Blois. After dinner on Sunday James and Maria walked by the canal, and then heard *Salut* at the Carmelite convent at Basses-

[1] Boisseleau was a captain of the French Guards, who had some knowledge, which none of the Irish had, of the defence of fortified towns. He accompanied James to Ireland, was made Governor of Cork, and afterwards conducted the defence of Limerick, during its first siege, with great skill (O'Conor's *Milit. Mem.*).

Loges, where the feast of St Theresa was being celebrated. The evening was spent as usual. On Monday James went on a wolf-hunt with Monseigneur, returning early to dine with the King. On Wednesday the Stuarts were present at another boar-hunt, and afterwards saw from the terrace of the *grand appartement* by torchlight the *curée* of a stag. James and Monseigneur had killed it in the chase that morning. It was "a very agreeable spectacle."[1] The same day Lauzun arrived in Paris.

On Wednesday James and Maria took leave early in the morning, at ten o'clock. Their host drove with them as far as the forest of Chailly. Madame and Monsieur were also there to see them off. Lady d'Almond sat facing the King and Queen of England in their carriage. Their hosts, after taking leave of them, went off to the chase, and James and Mary, stopping to dine at Plessis, got home to Saint-Germain the same evening.[2] There is no special mention made of Madame de Maintenon on this occasion, though no doubt she was much in evidence, and it appears from Maria's letters how careful she was to keep on good terms with this all-powerful lady. Madame, who hated her sister-in-law with a virulence only possible between relations, rages against the servility De Maintenon exacted towards herself, especially from the Dauphin, whose feebleness of mind and character made him an easy prey to his crafty stepmother. "The gallant," wrote Madame, "is in such fear of the great man's old muck-heap, that even if he wanted to marry again, he would not let such a thing be suspected as long as he saw that it was not agreeable to the lady. It is

---

[1] Dangeau.   [2] *Ibid.*, ii., October.

shocking how he fears her, considering his age. In her presence he is like a child trembling before its governess."

This statement is borne out by the Dauphin's own letters to Madame de Maintenon. A man of twenty-seven years and heir to the throne, he writes to her while in camp before Mons, in the Netherlands: "Tout ce que je vous dirai c'est que je m'applique le plus que je puis à devenir capable de quelque chose et que j'entre en tous les détails et me fais rendre compte de tout. Je vous pris d'être persuadée que personne n'est plus à vous que moi." And again: " Your letter has given me so much pleasure, by showing me the kindness that the King has for me, and how content he is with me, that I cannot resist writing to you, to thank you for having sent it to me. I assure you, that I count you as the best friend that I could have, and that you will give me pleasure, should I do anything which displeases you, by telling me frankly of it, in order that I may try to do better." Even Madame herself adopts a servile and conciliatory tone in addressing her. Speaking of the King, she says: "All his kindness to me proceeds from you, since it was you who brought about a better understanding between us. I beg you to believe that my sense of gratitude towards you could not be increased, and I assure you that my affection for you, Madame, will soon equal the esteem that is owed you by—Elizabeth Charlotte."

It is interesting to compare Madame's letters about her sister-in-law with those to her, though Madame de Maintenon was probably shrewd enough to know how the Duchesse d'Orléans really regarded her, especially as she was well provided with spies. "The King's old ullage[1] has wielded this terrible power for a long time," Madame writes. "She is not so mad as to have herself declared Queen; she knows the humour of her man too well. If she did that, she would soon fall into disgrace." And again, speaking still more feelingly: "I hope that she will go to hell, whither may she be conducted by the Father, the Son, and the Holy Ghost. It was with these words that a little Capucin used to conclude his sermons: 'You will go to hell, whither may you be conducted by, etc.'"

In the autumn James and Maria paid frequent visits to Louis XIV. Once more they were closeted with him for long private talks. For affairs in England were encouraging to their easily fanned hopes. Earlier in the year (1690) the English Jacobites had plucked up courage and rallied their forces. They were becoming a united party. The absence of William in Ireland had seemed to afford a favourable opportunity for some combined effort to effect James's restoration. Advices from Scotland as to the unrest there had fomented the desire to invade that country which is so evident in the letters from Tyrconnel. A letter to the King while he was in Ireland (April) from Melfort[2] is characteristic of the feelings both during and after the Irish failure:—

"Who gains time gains life, and therefore the King should show them all the kindness, all the trust, all the confidence in the world; write most affectionately to them, seem to grant even more than he intends to perform, but in the meantime, delay. A good reason of delay of such acts as we cannot grant is, to see them

[1] *Ripopée*, wine that has gone bad, drippings of casks.
[2] Macpherson's Original Papers.

penned and sent him. Such as he can grant, to assure them of them with all cheerfulness, and brag extremely of what assistance he will send them, and that they shall have all content. Naturally they are hot and unwarie, and not able to brook the present pressure of the Prince of Orange, as appears by their uneasy messenger's stories; that they can hardly be kept in,—consequently if encouraged by the King will break out."

The Quaker, William Penn, had assured James that if England were invaded from France and Ireland his supporters would rally round him.[1] All over England there was a sense of unrest and disquiet. The Jacobites were forming themselves into organised companies, especially in the northern counties; and in London grew so bold, and had paraded together in Hyde Park with so aggressive an air, that Mary noticed them as she was taking her afternoon drive, and commented on it in a letter to William in Ireland. Among the leaders of the movement in England were the Earls of Clarendon and Ailesbury, and Lord Dartmouth. Henry Hyde, Earl of Clarendon, whose sister had been James II.'s first wife, was a timorous, untrustworthy man, but he had been so far honest as to refuse to take the oath of allegiance to William III., which was made compulsory before March 1st, 1689, on pain of being ineligible to vote or sit in either House. The other two had taken the oaths, but had no scruple in violating them. Dartmouth, like so many other men of that time, though he was at heart attached to the Jacobite cause, had made himself safe with William. James had no doubt of his loyalty at the time of his enforced flight, and he says in his

[1] Avaux to Louis XIV., June 1689.

252 THE ENGLISH COURT IN EXILE

Memoirs: "There was no man in whose fidelity the King had greater confidence than this Lord's, his obligations to his Prince (if that had been any ty in those days) were infinite . . . but his loyalty was worsted in that conflict, and it was the Prince of Orange's contempt of his service rather than his want of good-will to serve him that hinder'd my Lord Dartmouth from falling in with the current as others did."

Dartmouth had accomplished a good understanding with William by December 1688, for the Prince of Orange replied on the 16th of that month: "I am glad to find you continue firm to the Protestant Religion and Liberties of England, and that you resolve to dispose the fleet under your command to those ends, to which not only the fleet, but the army, and the nation in generall concurr'd." The letter is signed "Your affectionate friend, G. Prince d'Orange." Yet Dartmouth could write to James earlier in the month: "May I never hope to see the face of God if I study any other thoughts than your Majesty's true interest. This is a time to try and search the hearts of all that pretend to be your servants, and those who have or doe prevaricate with you are the worst of men."[1] Such was the standard of honour of that time,[2] and the men who acted on such principles condoned them among themselves. Even Feversham, writing to Dartmouth on December 14th, says: "My own heart has been almost breaking. Oh God! what could make our master desert his kingdom and his friends. Certainly nobody could be so vilainous as to hurt his person; it cannot be the effect of his own thoughts, but of womanish or timorous councells. . . .

[1] *Hist. Com. Reports*, Dartmouth.   [2] *Ibid.*

God in His infinite mercy restore him to his throne with comfort again." But he concludes with the significant words: "I have taken the same measures with the Prince of Orange that you have done."[1]

Dartmouth's part in the conspiracy of 1690 was to furnish all information concerning the fleet that could be of advantage to the enemy. A more important Jacobite leader was Viscount Preston, a Scottish peer who had occupied the position of Secretary of State under James, and was regarded by all true Jacobites as holding it still.

The leaders in London were of course in constant communication with the Court of Saint-Germain, through the means of secret emissaries. Among these was a former page of Lady Melfort's, called Fuller. In the spring of 1690, when the Stuart prospects in London were at their most hopeful point, Fuller was sent to London with important letters concealed about him. He betrayed his employers by taking them straight to William. For the moment Jacobite hopes were entirely frustrated, while the disaster of Beachy Head,[2] and the fear of a French invasion, caused a reaction in favour of William. He could afford to be generous; but his leniency to those implicated by Fuller's evidence encouraged a fresh conspiracy later on. The same leaders took part in it—Preston, Clarendon, William Penn the Quaker, Turner Bishop of Ely, and Dartmouth. As they were all Protestants, they sought to make terms with James that should safeguard their civil and religious liberties. In the first place, they insisted that James must not give offence to the people, immediately

---

[1] *Hist. Com. Reports*, Dartmouth.
[2] June 30th, the English and Dutch defeated by the French.

on his arrival, by bestowing office on Catholics. "He might live a Catholic in devotion, but must reign a Protestant in government; that the utmost he could expect for Catholics was a legal liberty of conscience, and that the least he must think of for the Protestants was to put the administration into their hands, who being at least two hundred to one, had the wealth, heads and power of the nation on their side." They advised the retention of at least eight Protestant lords and gentlemen in his Council at Saint-Germain, as an earnest of his good intentions. It was essential that he should come supported by force of French arms, but "upon these conditions, that the Most Christian King would engage his word only to assist his Majesty as a friend and mediator, and not send the offended Prince back with the ungratefull character of a conqueror." They put in a plea for their co-religionists in France, that Louis "would pleas to permit the English Protestants to have chapels at their own cost"; and lastly, James was to publish a declaration that he would dismiss the forces he brought with him so soon as his aim should be accomplished. This summary of the Jacobite proposals is quoted from James's *Memoirs*; he forbears from any comment, though such guarantees would have been in the highest degree distasteful to him. Such an apt pupil of the Jesuits would, however, have found pledges like these as easy to give as to break when occasion served.

The Jacobites deputed three emissaries to convey these resolutions to Saint-Germain, and see what terms could be made with James. They were Lord Preston, John Ashton, a faithful and devoted Jacobite, who had been in Maria d'Este's service when she was on the throne, and a young man called Elliot, who was not trusted with the dangerous secret of the enterprise. The three men started on the last night of the old year 1690. They had represented themselves to the owner of a smack they had hired as smugglers, but his suspicions were aroused, and he gave information to the Government. As the smack dropped down the Thames it was pursued, overtaken, boarded, and the conspirators were arrested. At this supreme moment Preston showed himself to be far from possessing the requisite coolness and courage for the dangerous task he had undertaken. Fluttered and unnerved, he dropped on the ground the packet of incriminating letters he was bearing to Saint-Germain from James's adherents. Ashton, with ready presence of mind, hastily concealed it, but it was quickly discovered when the fugitives were searched. No greater misfortune could have befallen the Jacobite cause than the entire exposure of all their schemes, and the names of all their leaders, by the discovery of these papers; but as they referred James to Preston for fuller information on every point, it rested with him still to safeguard his master's cause to some extent. The letters were, moreover, written in cipher. Lord Preston had not, however, sufficient resolution to play the man. "When he had dined well he resolved he could die heroically, but by next morning that heat went off, and when he saw death in full view his heart failed him."[1] While Preston was fluctuating between the dictates of vanity and cowardice, his young daughter, who was about the Court, stood one day in the Queen's presence, looking long and earnestly at James's portrait in Kensington Palace. Mary asked

[1] Burnet.

her what she was doing, and the girl replied courageously: "I am reflecting how hard it is that my father should be put to death for loving your father."[1] She was to marry a man worthier than her father of her brave spirit, for long afterwards her husband, Lord Derwentwater, lost his head on Tower Hill for supporting the claims of James II.'s grandson.

Among the letters found on Ashton were a list of the English fleet supplied by Dartmouth, notes concerning the project of invasion, and a number of letters written under assumed names and in an ambiguous style, though their meaning was not far to seek. Thus the Bishop of Ely, writing to James under the name of Mr Redding, answered for the Archbishop of Canterbury as well as his brother Bishops: "I speak in the plural because I write my elder brother's sentiments as well as my own, and the rest of the family's; though lessened in number, yet, if we are not mightily mistaken, we are growing in our interest, that is in your's." A letter from Clarendon advises speedy action on James's part. "The sea will quickly grow so troublesome, that, unless you dispatch what you intend for us, you will lose a great opportunity of advantage. I hope the account he has to give of our negotiations here with the merchants that deal with us, especially those that have lately brought us their custom,[2] will both encourage a larger trade, and excite the utmost diligence."[3] In another letter James's brother-in-law was even more explicit: "Now is the

---

[1] Dalrymple.
[2] Alluding to the accession of some of the Whig party to the Jacobite cause.
[3] Dalrymple.

REVIVAL OF JACOBITE HOPES

time to make large advantages by trading; the sea being freer than it has been these two months past, or we can hope it will be two months hence. It is most earnestly hoped that this happy opportunity may not be lost. . . . Opportunities are to be used; they cannot be given by men."[1] Notes in Preston's handwriting implied the disloyalty of the sailors, and in some cases of their officers, notably of Rear-Admiral Carter at Portsmouth; they disclosed schemes of blocking the export of coal from Newcastle to London by a fleet from Scotland, while Plymouth and Portsmouth were to be commanded by the French navy.

The evidence against Preston and Ashton was irrefutable. They were tried, found guilty, and condemned to death. Ashton held his tongue and died like a gentleman. Preston wavered, cringed, and ignominiously bought his life by a confession which involved incriminating all his associates. These were treated with considerable mildness. Clarendon underwent a short and not rigorous term of imprisonment in the Tower. Penn and Turner were allowed to abscond. Dartmouth was sent to the Tower, where he died shortly afterwards of an apoplectic fit.

James felt deeply the fate of his friends, especially that of Ashton, "being the first that suffered by a court of justice for the royal cause, which was a new subject of grief to the King, for he knew not what would be the consequence when he found the law, as well as the sword, turn'd against him; and those suffer as traitors who were most distinguished for their fidelity and loyalty."[2] James adds that William forbore to take any steps with regard to

[1] Dalrymple.   [2] Clarke's *Life*.

many of those accused by Preston. "What he knew was sufficient either to be aware of them, or by forgiveness and a seeming clemency gain them to his interest, which method succeeded so well, that whatever sentiments those Lords (accused by Preston) might have had at that time, they proved in effect most bitter enemies to his Majesty's cause afterwards."

While the trials of Ashton and Preston were proceeding in England, life at Saint-Germain went on as usual. Louis XIV. had a New Year's party for James and Maria. They arrived on Twelfth Night, January 6th (1691), at six o'clock, and spent some time playing "portique" and "lansquenet." At supper there were five tables of sixteen covers each. This fête was known in France as "Le jour des rois," the festival that commemorated the coming of the Magi or the Three Kings. At each table one of the guests was "King." Louis was King at his own table, with the Queen of England on his right and James on her right. Monseigneur presided at the second table, with the Princesse de Conti as queen. Monsieur was King at his own table. Mademoiselle Dangeau was Queen at Madame's table, and the Duchesse de Noailles was Queen at the fifth table, at which Mademoiselle presided. The young Duc de Chartres was at Monseigneur's table, and six English ladies were present; while a long table for less distinguished guests, French and English, was laid in the billiard-room. The King's orchestra occupied the two tribunes, and played during supper "orgues, trompettes, timbales, et l'on criait 'Vive le roi' au musique."[1]

Intercourse was temporarily interrupted between

[1] Dangeau.

Versailles and Saint-Germain by the illness of the Queen, but later in the month she and James went severally to call on Madame la Duchesse [1] after her accouchement. She had had a daughter a few days before Christmas. She was a woman of considerable character, and in the quarrels between the Princesses took an active part. Monsieur tried to make her address her sister, Mademoiselle de Blois, as "Madame" after she had married his son, the Duc de Chartres; but Madame la Duchesse declined, and insisted on calling her "Mignonne." As her appearance was such that this pet name was obviously a sarcasm and drew ridicule upon her, Monsieur was very angry and complained to Louis, who put a stop to it. It was most likely she who instigated another escapade, in which the three sisters went out at night and let off crackers under Monsieur's window. He again complained to Louis, who was very indignant with them all, especially Madame de Chartres, who felt his anger for some time. The other two appeared to be impenitent. Madame la Duchesse was also suspected of being the author of songs upon the Duchesse de Chartres.

A fortnight later James was taken ill with an inflammation in his eyes. It was considered necessary to bleed him, a remedy which was without much effect, and he was fortunately cured by one of those home-made specifics, prepared generally from herbs, that were treasured carefully and passed on from one to another in those days when doctors knew little more than their patients. Affections of the eyes seem to

---

[1] Wife of "M. le Duc," and daughter of Louis XIV. and Madame de Montespan.

have been particularly common. Sir William Temple, writing to Henry Sidney, recommends a tobacco leaf thrust tightly up the nostrils as an excellent remedy against this kind of disease.[1] Maria does not, unfortunately, mention the ingredients of this particular prescription, though she wrote to tell her friends at Chaillot of her husband's illness:—

"To the Reverend Mother Superior
of the Visitation.[2]

"St-Germain, 11th Feb. 1691.

"It is true, my dear Mother—and I say it without compliment—that the time I have been without news of you and your dear sisters has seemed very long to me. It is also true that I don't at all like writing, but I very much like my friends to write to me, and I have less difficulty in writing to you than to the majority of people that I know. You can easily guess the reason, which is not to your disadvantage. . . . Last week the King had such violent inflammation in the eyes that he was bled, but that did not cure him. It was a 'water' of the Fathers of the Oratory that did the business in two days, and he is at present, thank God, in perfect health as well as my son. He has ordered me to give you his compliments, and to tell you that he would be indeed happy if he were such as you believe him to be, but he hopes that your prayers will aid him to attain to it. I have no need to prescribe prayer to you, my dear mother; you understand that better than I, and that

---

[1] Blencowe's *Sidney*, i. 294: "I never found any thing do mine so much good as putting a leaf of tobacco into each nostril as soon as you wake and keep it for an hour, either sitting up in your bed or dressing yourself."

[2] Translation from the Chaillot Letters published by the Roxburghe Club.

is better in your hands than in mine. . . . Next Friday is the anniversary of the late King my brother. I recommend him to your prayers and to those of your daughters, to whom you will give my compliments, but such as they may expect from a heart in which they have very good places. You cannot doubt, my dear mother, having in it one of the best. MARIA R."

CHAPTER XIII

THE HOUSEHOLD AT SAINT-GERMAIN

It was not till after the return from Ireland that James established his little Court on a permanent footing. In attempting to reconstruct the household of Saint-Germain, it will be instructive to examine first the account James caused to be written of it in his *Memoirs*, and afterwards to see how far contemporary evidence confirms that picture. The Memoir reads as follows:—

"The King submitting patiently to his fate began to think of settling himself at St Germains, and of modeling his family and his way of living suitable to the pension of six hundred thousand livres a year, which he received from the Court of France, and which he managed with that prudence and frugality as not only to keep up the form of a Court by maintaining the greatest part of those officers that usually attend upon his person in England, but relieved an infinite number of distresed people, antient or wonded, widdowes and children of such as had lost their lives in his service; so that tho' the salleries or pensions he allowed were but low, yet scarce any merit ever went without some reward, and his servants had wherewithal to make a decent appearance, so that with the help of the guards (which his Most Christian Majesty appointed to attend him, as also upon the Queen and Prince) his

Court notwithstanding his exil had still an air and dignity agreable to that of a Prince, for besides those of his family and several other loyal persons both Catholicks and Protestants, who chose to follow his fortune, there was for the most part such an appearance of officers of the armie, especially in the winter, as would have made a stranger forget the King's condition and have fancyd him and his at Whitehall. . . . There was no distinction made of persons on account of their Religion. Protestants were countenanced, cherished and imployd as much as others; indeed the laws of the country would not permit the same privileges as to public prayers, burials and the like, but the King found means of mollifying what he could not obtain a total relaxation of."

This last passage appears like a justification, and opens up a very disputed question. It is difficult to decide how much truth there is in the statement that James's Protestant adherents were neglected and abused at Saint-Germain. A contemporary writes: "The English Protestants about that Court do wish themselves at home again, for there they are respected as strangers, but hated as Protestants and looked upon as spies from England."[1] It is certain that the Protestant Lord Chancellor, Herbert, was not permitted to become a member of the Council, though representations were made to James on his behalf. And the author of the curious *View of the Court of Saint Germains from 1690 to 1695*[2] asserts that Protestants, notably Dunfermline, were denied the rite of Christian burial. But the author's tone is bitterly inimical to James, and the whole document is virulently polemical. How far

[1] *A Short and True Relation*, etc., 1694.
[2] See Macaulay, who assumes the truth of this document.

James was actually inclined to carry principles of toleration, supposing he had been restored to the throne, may be gathered from the paper drawn up by him in 1692, and left to be delivered to his son after his death.[1]

By far the most circumstantial account of the Court of Saint-Germain was written by Anthony Hamilton in the preface to *Zeneyde*. He admits to having had a fit of spleen at the time, but deducting something for exaggeration, and making every allowance for the impressionable mood of the writer, it bears the impress of truth. "The Château," he says, "has so little accommodation that with the exception of thirty or forty priests and Jesuits the rest of us have to find lodging outside. It is true," he continues, "that the view is enchanting, the works wonderful, and the air so exhilarating that one could make four meals a day, though we have not the wherewithal to provide half that amount, and we should be really better off in some marshy place, where our senses and appetites were subdued by being always enveloped in a thick fog. As for the men here, we can hardly muster enough merit to furnish the Prince of Wales's household; for the rest, those whom example has not brought to play the hypocrite, they are thought little of here whatever their reputation elsewhere.

"Our occupations have all the air of being very serious and Christian, for this is no place for those who do not either spend half the day in prayer, or pretend to do so. Common misfortune, which usually brings its victims together, seems only to have sown discord and bitterness among us; the friendship which we profess

---

[1] "For my son the Prince of Wales," Clarke, ii. 619 *et seq.*

for one another is always simulated, the hatred and envy that we conceal is always sincere. Agreeable flirtation, even love-making is severely proscribed in this melancholy Court, though in the whole of Cupid's realm there is nought more beautiful, more dangerous, more inspiring than are to be found there."

The splenetic courtier who had known Whitehall at its gayest goes on to describe a day at Saint-Germain. Lost in gloomy thoughts, he sought refuge in the gardens. But it was a fête day, and the townspeople had possessed themselves of every walk, with their horrid little children, and husbands uglier than their wives. He took flight to the terrace, and than that there is no more superb and spacious promenade in the world; but here he finds a Jesuit father, exciting himself in fervent exhortations for the conversion of two English soldiers, trying in vain to convince them in Italian of the damnation of English Protestants. At last he thinks himself safe from molestation, when he sees approaching a widow whose husband has recently died of apoplexy in the King's service, and who ever since has swept the castle corridors and the garden walks with her black serge tail, demanding a pension from everyone she meets. She was making straight for him, when Hamilton, selecting the least precipitous spot, flung himself over the terrace and sought safety below.

This, in a free and abridged translation, is the picture that Hamilton left of Saint-Germain, and we think it cannot be entirely explained away. It is true that he left much verse in praise of one and another of its inmates, for he always admits the claims of the Court ladies to distinction—"la troupe adorable de nos nymphes de

Saint-Germain," he calls them in a letter to Berwick; and elsewhere he declares that the "most difficult taste would be gratified among our ladies, in whose small circle beauty, charm, wit and wisdom shine in all their brilliancy."

There are in existence two manuscript lists of the residents at the Château in James's lifetime. The first of these is taken from among the Nairne Papers in the Bodleian Library, and was evidently made comparatively soon after James's arrival there; and the second was drawn up towards the end of his life for Matthew Prior, Secretary of Legation at Paris under the Earl of Portland when he went as ambassador to France in 1698, after the Treaty of Ryswick.[1] It was made for the information of the English Government, partly with a view to ascertaining James's resources, as is shown by the insertion of the salaries in the margin. These may look well on paper, but it appears from the Queen's letters that money was not always forthcoming to pay the royal dependents. If these two lists are compared it will be seen that for the most part the residents at the Château changed little during James's lifetime; they also dispose of Anthony Hamilton's complaint that there were forty priests under its roof. There do not appear to have been much more than half a dozen. Prior's list speaks of "a great many chaplains and servants below stairs," but these can hardly have amounted to thirty.

[1] This list is preserved in the Welbeck Archives, and is here inserted by kind permission of the Duke of Portland.

HOUSEHOLD AT SAINT-GERMAIN

A LISTE OF SUCH AS LODGE IN Y^E CASTLE[1] (NAIRNE)

One paire of Stairs

Mr Controller Skelton.
Dutchesse of Tyrconnel.
Mr Hide.
Lord Chamberlain.
Duke of Berwick.
Lady D'Almond.
Earle of Melfort.
Count Molza.

Mr Carill.
Mr Turene.
Mrs Turene.
Lady Sophia Buckly (Bulkley).
Lady Walgrave.
Mr Conquest.
S^r Jo. Sparow.
Lord Dumbarton.

Two paire of Stairs

Lady Governess. | Lady Strickland.

Three paire of Stairs

Mr Lavery and ye Kings necessary woman.
Father Warner.
Marquis D'Albeville.
Mr du Puis and the Lady Strickland's servants.

Lady Governesses Servants.
Mr Baltazar.
Mr London.
Mrs Walgrave.

(f. 287^b.)

4 paire of Stairs

Mr Brown.
Mr Graham.
Mr Jo. Stafford.
Officers of ye Guard.
Father White.
Mr Benefield.
Sr Will. Walgrave.
Count Lauzun.
Mr Biddulph.
Mr Leyburn.

Mr Vice chamberlain Strickland.
Mr Inese ye priest.
Father Gally.
Mrs de Lauter.
Mrs Chappell.
Mrs Rogé.
Lady Lucy Herbert.
Fa. Ruga.
Fa. Sabran.
Sr Edward Hales.

---

[1] In the index this list is described as follows: "List of who lodg'd in ye Castle of St G——." No date. [MS. Carte, 208: *Nairne Papers*, vol. i., 1692–1718.] (f. 287.)

268 THE ENGLISH COURT IN EXILE

5 *paire of Stairs*

Mr Buckingham.	Mr Beaulieu.
Mr Noble.	Mrs Sims.
Mr Cadrington and the princes necessary woman.	Mr du Four.
	Mess. Ronchi priests.
the Kings Barber.	Mr Ronchi Gentleman Usher.

Ground rooms

Mr Martinash.	Mr Vice Chamberlain Porter.
Mr Atkins ye Cook in a room Lent him by ye Concierge.	Cap^{ne} Macdonnel.
	Mr Labady.
Cap^{ne} Travanian.	Mr Riva.
Mr Harrison.	Mr Crane.
Mr francis Stafford.	Sr Roger Strickland.
Mr Inese ye Gentleman Usher.	Mr des Arthur.
Mr La Croix.	Mr Nevil.
Mr Gothard.	Madame Nurse.
the Kings Wardrobe.	

[*Endorsement*] A Liste of all those that Lodge in the Castle.

The following paper was given by Matthew Prior to the Earl of Portland. It is in the handwriting of Prior's secretary, Adrian Drift, who has endorsed it: "An Acc^t of ye Late King James's Household etc., *at St Germains*." [The words in italics are added by the second Duke of Portland, who went through his grandfather's papers.] To this Prior has added, "to be given to my lord."

	The Lord Chancel^r Herbert	. Chancellour.
liv.		
6000	The Lord Middleton and	} Secret^{res} of State.
6000	Mr Carrol . . .	
5000	Sr Richard Naigle . .	. Secretary of Warre.

HOUSEHOLD AT SAINT-GERMAIN 269

pist. 400	Mr James Porter . . .	Vice Chamb{n} to ye King.
pist. 400	Mr Robert Strickland . .	Vice Chamb{n} to ye Queen.
2800 each	David Floyd, Trevanion . Slingsbee, Beedle MacDonnel .	} Grooms of ye Bed Chamb{r}.
1200	Bagnel, Franc Stafford . . Mr Carney, Vivel and Hatcher	} Gent. Men Ush{rs} to ye King.
	Mr Crane and Mr Barry . .	Gent. Men Ush{rs} to ye Queen.
	Mr Conquest, Sr Willm Ellis .	Comiss{rs} of ye Green Cloth.
pist. 400	Mr John Stafford . . .	Comptroler.
	Mr Richard Hamilton . .	Master of ye Wardrobe.
	Mr Labadie, Mr Lavarie . .	Valetts de Chambre.
	My Lady Tyrconnel, The Lady Dalmont, and Lady Sophia Buckley	} Ladies of the Bed Chamb.

To the Prince—

liv. 1500	The Ld Perth, formerly Chancel of Scotland and Mr Ployden .	} Gouvern{rs}.
	Mr Leyburn and Mr Vivel .	Grooms of ye Bed Cham{r}.
	Depuis gentleman Usher . . Capt. Magimis, young Beedle .	} Queries.

and Mr Buckingham.

Mr Barkenhead and Mr Parry . Clerks of the Kitchin.

The Ld Griffen is a Volontiere sometimes there and as often at Versailles . . . . } Volontiere.

A great many Chaplains and Servants below staires.

[The sums in the margin are added by Prior.]

270 THE ENGLISH COURT IN EXILE

When James reorganised his household in 1692, the Lord Chamberlain was William Herbert, Earl of Powis, to whom James gave the title of Duke. He had been regarded as the head of the English Roman Catholic aristocracy, and was one of the four Catholics who had been made Privy Councillors in 1686.[1] He was a respectable man of moderate views, and had accompanied James to Ireland. His wife was among the most faithful of the Queen's ladies, and was greatly in her confidence. Burnet describes her as "a zealous managing Papist"; and the attribute of "managing" is confirmed by another interested observer—D'Avaux.

Colonel Porter, who had been first dispatched to Ireland, where he hardly saw James,[2] and sent on a mission to the Pope afterwards, held the office of Vice-Chamberlain.

The Earls of Dumbarton and Abercorn were Lords of the Bedchamber. Dumbarton was so much trusted by the King that he was selected to accompany him alone on one of his periodical visits to the monastery of La Trappe.

Captains MacDonald, Beadles, Stafford, and Trevanion, who had sailed the boat in which James escaped to France, were Grooms of the Bedchamber.

Fergus Graham was Privy Purse. This was probably Lord Preston's brother, who with him was concerned in the conspiracy to restore James, but succeeded in making good his escape.[3]

Edward Sheldon and Sir James Sparrow, of the Board of Green Cloth.

Robert Strickland was Vice-Chamberlain to the Queen.

---

[1] Powis, Bellayse, Arundell, Dover. [2] D'Avaux. [3] Burnet, 564-5.

HOUSEHOLD AT SAINT-GERMAIN

A sort of Cabinet Council was formed of the five following :—

Mr Brown, brother of Lord Montacute, was Secretary of State for England.

Sir Robert Neagle or Nagle was Secretary of State for Ireland. He had formerly been Attorney-General for that country, and had played an important part in James's administration there.

Father Innes, President of the Scotch College in Paris, and supposed author of part of the abridged Life of James II., was Secretary for Scotland.

John Caryll of Lady-Holt was Secretary to the Queen.[1]

John Stafford, formerly Spanish envoy, was Controller of the Court, a post that was also filled by Colonel Skelton.

Sir William Walgrave, the Prince's London physician, accompanied the Court abroad in the same capacity.

There were besides other followers of the Stuart fortunes who occupied some position at their Court :—

Sir Roger Strickland, formerly vice-admiral of the English fleet, and Lady Strickland.

Sir Edward Hales, whose unpopularity had involved James in so great difficulties during his first flight, and two others who had figured on that occasion, Labadie and Biddulph.

Leyburn, the Queen's equerry, and Dufour, her page, together with the faithful Riva, were with her at Saint-Germain.

Among the priests were Father Saunders, author of a biography of James, and an Italian, Don Giacomo

[1] See *West-Grinstead et les Caryll*, Max. de Trenqualéon.

Ronchi, who has left considerable correspondence, which is still preserved in the archives of the House of Este.

The Duchess of Powis continued to fulfil the duties of governess to the Prince of Wales after the removal of the Court to Saint-Germain, with Lady Strickland as deputy governess. She was succeeded in this office on her death by Lady Errol. When the Prince grew older, the Earl, afterwards Duke, of Perth became his governor.

About some of the persons figuring in these lists little is known; others had played important parts in public affairs before the Revolution; others, again, are interesting not so much for what they did as for what they were. Of such was John Caryll, secretary to the Queen. His letters to her have not been preserved, unless they are among the un-catalogued Stuart papers at Windsor; but sometimes letters written to a person are as much an indication of their character as letters written by them. Maria's letters to Caryll show that he must have been discreet, sympathetic, and of a chivalrous and devoted loyalty.

In some of them there is a tone of almost playful tenderness that is absent from all her other correspondence. She reproaches him for delaying to write frequently enough to her, during a few days' absence; assures him—though the intimate tone of her letters makes all such assurances superfluous—of her unalterable confidence. There is less of the nun, less of the Queen, and more of the woman in these letters of Maria's than in any other memorial preserved of her, for she writes spontaneously, and with a conviction so assured that every detail of her daily life will be of

JOHN CARYLL.
From "West Grinstead et les Carylls," by M. de Trenqualéon.

interest to her correspondent that she is unconscious of her own confidence. These invaluable letters, together with a great mass of other correspondence of all kinds, accounts and literary papers, belonging to the Carylls, were bought by Mr Charles Wentworth Dilke and rescued from destruction in circumstances the secret of which has never been divulged.[1] They were presented to the British Museum by his grandson, the late Sir Charles Dilke, and form one of the most valuable sources of information concerning the Stuart exile. John Caryll, afterwards titular Lord Caryll, was born in 1625. He came of an old Roman Catholic family who had been settled at Lady-Holt at West Harting since the sixteenth century. He was a man of literary tastes, and wrote several plays of a mediocre kind : among his papers are some translations, as well as lengthy religious essays after the fashion of the time. His plays were performed, for Pepys mentions having seen *The English Princess, or, The Death of Richard III.* acted in 1667 at the Duke of York's Theatre, and describes it as "a most sad and melancholy play, and pretty good but nothing eminent in it."

Caryll was imprisoned in the Tower during the agitation occasioned by the Popish Plot, but was released on bail. He became secretary to the Queen on his return from a mission to Rome on which he had been sent when James succeeded to the throne. He accompanied the royal family to Saint-Germain at the Revolution, dying there in 1711. He was buried in the church of the English Dominicans at Paris. His estates were not confiscated till it was discovered that he had furnished money to Barclay for his plot in

[1] *Papers of a Critic*, C. W. Dilke, vol. i., Essay on Pope.

1696. They were then sequestrated, and Caryll was attainted. His nephew redeemed the estates for £6000 from Lord Cutts, who had obtained the reversion of them. It was the nephew—not Caryll himself, as is stated by Macaulay—who was the friend of Pope,[1] and whose name appears in the *Rape of the Lock*.[2] Pope, who wrote an epitaph on Caryll and sent it to his nephew, afterwards utilised the same lines on the death of Sir William Trumbull.[3] They begin as follows:—

> " A manly form, a bold yet modest mind,
> Sincere though prudent, constant yet resigned,
> Honour unchanged, a principal profest,
> Fixed to one side but mod'rate to the rest,
> An honest courtier, and a patriot too,
> Just to his Prince and to his country true."

James Drummond, Earl of Perth, who was made governor of the Prince of Wales, was highly valued by James, and consulted both by him and Louis on current English affairs. He did not, however, take refuge at Saint-Germain till 1698, for after the Revolution he was imprisoned in Stirling Castle till 1693, and subsequently spent two years in Rome. Perth had taken a prominent part in public affairs before the Revolution, and held the office of Chancellor of Scotland. A contemporary says of him that " he was passionately proud, told a story very prettily, was of a middle

---

[1] See Elwyn's *Pope*.
[2] " What dire offence from am'rous causes springs,
What mighty contests rise from trivial things,
I sing. This verse to Caryl, muse! is due,
This ev'n Belinda may vouchsafe to view.
Slight is the subject, but not so the Praise,
If she inspire, and he approve my Lays."
[3] Secretary of State under William III.

stature with a quick look, a brown complexion";[1] and the Earl of Lauderdale, who knew him well, describes him as "busy and spiteful." Perth, together with his brother John Drummond, Lord Melfort, had become Roman Catholics. Perth had made many professions of his attachment to "the Church of England, of which I hope to live and die a member," and his apostasy, as well as his brother's, was too obviously due to interested motives. They reported themselves to have been converted to Popery by the papers said to have been found by James in Charles II.'s strong-box after his death, and were subsequently very well received at Whitehall. Perth took an active part in the complicated public affairs of Scotland, where he incurred great unpopularity. He supported James in his attempt to introduce Roman Catholicism into Scotland, an attempt which resulted in riots in Edinburgh. He was still more detested for his cruelty. The custom lingered in Scotland of extorting evidence by torture, after it had disappeared elsewhere. "When any are to be stuck in the boots it is done in the presence of the Council, and upon that occasion almost all offer to run away. The sight is so dreadful that without an order restraining such a number to stay, the Board would be forsaken." But Perth added to the boot, and invented the thumb-screw "that screwed the thumbs with so exquisite a torment" that the most recalcitrant witness succumbed to it. Yet "Lord Perth," says Burnet, ". . . for about ten years together seemed to me incapable of an immoral or cruel action ; . . . in this I saw how ambition could corrupt one of the best tempered men I had ever known."[2]

[1] Douglass's *Peerage*.   [2] *History of His Own Times*.

When the news of James's flight reached Scotland, Perth at once attempted to follow his example. He fared, however, considerably worse than his master had done, and he had not had the forethought, like James, to provide beforehand for the safety of his wife. She had been a widow, and his first cousin, and he married her within a few weeks of his wife's death. She was going to have a child at the time of their flight, but was obliged to ride twenty-four miles through deep snow over the Ochil Hills. Husband and wife succeeded in embarking, and had got safely off, when the news of their escape was noised abroad; they were overtaken, brought back, and imprisoned. Perth wrote an account of their capture from Stirling Castle, where he was confined, to his "dearest sister," Lady Errol.

His captors, he says, "came aboard like so many furies and asked for me; they searched long, and had it not been for the falsehood of one of our men they had gone off again, but one of our people betrayed me, and so they broke open the place where we were hid with hatchets; my wife would fain have got out first to have exposed herself to their fury, but I pulled her back, and then they pulled me out, threw off my hat and periwig, and clapt their bayonets to my breast, for a great while keeping me in the expectation of being murdered. I cry'd to them (for they were all clamorous at once) to save my life, which at last they said they would do, but they pulled us up out of the cabine, and so soon as my wife could get on her cloaths, (for she was in men's disguise) they forced us into the boat. By this time it was night, and we within 3 miles of the Bass, so that to have sailed two hours sooner had preserved us. They began to smoak tobacco, and speak filthy language beside my wife so soon as ever we were into the boat, and used us with all the barbarity Turks could have done, keeping my wife 5 hours without any shoes or anything on her head. And having rode 24 miles the day before, being with child, you may judge if the condition she is now in, be not bad enough." They were put ashore at Kirkcaldy and imprisoned in the tolbooth, where, says Perth, " the hole we lay into was cold, strait, and ill-aired. The bed so bad we could not lye on it." Here they were in some danger of being lynched by the mob, or Perth thought so ; and after his removal to Stirling Castle, where he was closely guarded, he says again : " The rabble arose and would tear me to pieces " ; and he tells Melfort : " A centinell stands at my door from 9 at night until the same hour in the morning, who would not the other night permitt me to call for help to my wife, though she was like to dye of a violent colique." Perth confidently expected his trial and death, and he writes with every appearance of sincerity : " Now I am under the Great Phisitian's hand, and I can say with joy to Him, Burn, cutt, administer bitter things, provided all my sufferings be here ; yet, Lord, let me dye in the agony of suffering, amidst torture and disgrace, provided it can either advance Thy honour, the great interest of Thy Holy Church or the salvation of my own soul, or that of any other."

John Drummond, first Earl and titular Duke of Melfort, Perth's brother, who after his return from his mission to Rome became James's principal adviser, was not less ambitious, indiscreet, and unscrupulous. He was also a man of great personal attractiveness : " very handsome and a fine dancer, a well-bred gentleman, very ambitious, with abundance of lively sense, understood the belle lettres, was very proud, not able to bear a rival in business, tall, black, and thin, with a stoop in the shoulders." The ineptitude of his counsels had been shown in Ireland—it had been shown before, and it was to be shown again; but in spite of the disaster which his advice always brought on the King, his influence was never sensibly diminished.

He had escaped to France at the beginning of the Revolution, and was joined there by his wife and child. His blunders in the Irish expedition have already been recounted, as well as his unpopularity, which, in D'Avaux's venomous phrase, was such that " he was afraid to show his face in Dublin, and would have to leave by night." It is perhaps worthy of passing notice that in the interval before his embassy to Rome he endeavoured to retaliate on Tyrconnel by writing to James from France : " There is one other thing if it could be effectual were of infinite use which is the getting the Duchess of Tyrconnel for her health to come into France. I did not know she had been so well known here as she is; but the terms they give her, and which for your service, I may repeat unto you is, that she has 'l'âme la plus noire qui se puisse concevoir.' I think it would help to keep that peace, so necessary for you, and prevent that caballing humour which has very ill effects." He also has a thrust at D'Avaux, having heard that M. de Lauzun is to go over, "and I am afraid that he and the ambassador will not agree long together. This will draw in my lady and consequently my Lord Tyrconnel, and then will be a war in your Court, which I fled hither to shun."

James's supporters gradually became divided into two

camps of moderates and extremists, or compounders and non-compounders, as the party opposed to all compromise were called. Melfort was naturally on the side of the latter, who were for the most part Catholics, and advocated an absolute monarchy and an unconditional restoration. The compounders had the wisdom to see that the restoration of James was only practicable on the basis of a general amnesty and the safeguarding of civil and religious liberties. The non-compounders were in the highest favour at Saint-Germain, and it was against James's own inclinations that, partly by advice from Versailles, he was eventually induced to supersede Melfort by Lord Middleton.

Charles, Earl of Middleton, was no stranger to Saint-Germain. He had been brought up at the exiled Court of Charles II., and was made Secretary of State by him after his accession. Middleton, a "black man of moderate stature and sanguine complexion," was able and popular. He was distinguished by his ability and integrity. He was besides consistently in favour of moderate counsels, and had opposed James's indiscreet religious zeal. Though he had married a Catholic wife, Lady Catharine Brudenel, the beautiful daughter of the Earl of Cardigan, he had remained steadfast to Protestantism in spite of all James's efforts to convert him. "A new light," he said, "never comes into a head but by a crack in the tiling." Burnet describes him as "a man of a generous temper, but without much religion, well learned, of a good judgement, and a lively aprehension." He was always steadfast in his loyalty to James, though his known abilities could easily have gained him office under William. He remained in England till 1692, though his wife and children had already gone to Saint-Germain, and he had been arrested and sent to the Tower, when it was believed that an invasion from France was imminent. He was at first made joint Secretary with Melfort, whom he succeeded later in ousting from James's counsels.

James's Court was not without its lighter side. It had its poets and painters. Mignard, Rigaud, and Largillière painted other portraits of the royal family besides those which figure in the inventories of Chaillot. Melfort had a fine taste in pictures, and a not inconsiderable gallery at his house in the Rue des Petits-Augustins at Paris, where Lauzun's hôtel also stood. The most brilliant of this little society was, of course, Anthony Hamilton, whose denunciation of the Court's accommodation and whose panegyrics on its ladies have already been quoted.

Lady Middleton and Lady Melfort were both famous for their beauty, and the former was declared by Saint-Simon to have "pour le moins, autant d'esprit que son mari." The beautiful Comtesse de Gramont was a frequent visitor at Saint-Germain. Of the lady who was the wife of Patrick Sarsfield, Earl of Lucan, and who, after his death in 1695, married the Duke of Berwick, the critical Saint-Simon says she was "une très aimable femme, belle, touchante, et faite à peindre, et qui réussit fort bien à la cour de Saint-Germain." She only survived the marriage three years, however, and after her death Berwick married Anne Bulkeley, a daughter of one of Maria d'Este's former maids of honour, Lady Sophia Bulkeley. Anthony Hamilton immortalised her under the name of Nanette in *Zeneyde*. Many Irish beauties came to the Court when the fall of Limerick and the treaty which followed it flung into the dust the last hopes of Ireland, and drew from her shores thousands of her bravest men to self-chosen exile. Tyrconnel died, a loyal soldier to the last, before Limerick fell. His wife, the Duchess of Tyrconnel, so hated by Melfort, came to Saint-Germain, but she returned to Ireland to die.[1]

Gradually there grew up at the melancholy old château a group of a younger generation who hardly remembered any other home than that of exile. Lady Middleton had two sons and three daughters, one of whom inherited her mother's beauty. Hamilton apostrophises her as—

> "La fraîche et brillante Middleton
> Que l'amour prenait pour l'aurore";

while the Duchess of Perth was—

> "Digne de l'amour d'un époux
> Que tout le monde honore :
> Son mérite est digne de vous
> Et sa naissance encore.
> Tant que le soleil brillera
> Dans la voûte azurée,
> Illustre Perth, on vous verra
> Parmi nous honorée."

Spies and adventurers came and went constantly, people often of small credit, to whom James was wont to lend too ready an ear.

The French harboured no delusions about James's Irish campaign. Paris was full of popular songs on

---

[1] She died a very old lady in the Convent for Poor Clares which she founded in Dublin (Walpole).

the subject. Madame reports a conversation that he had with one of her household :—

"The King of England is not very 'viff en repliques.' It is just as well sometimes that he keeps quiet, but I must all the same repeat to you the conversation that he had with my *chevalier d'honneur*. 'Sire,' said M. de la Rongère, 'what became of the Frenchmen who were with your Majesty ?' (in Ireland). 'I don't know anything about them,' replied the King. 'How is that?' said La Rongère: 'Your Majesty knows nothing about them and they were not with you!' 'Pardon me,' said the King, 'I am going to tell you. The Prince of Orange arrived with 40,000 men, I only had half that number; he had 40 cannon, I only had 16. I saw that he drew his right wing towards Dublin, and that he was going to cut me off, and I should not have been able to come back. On that I came away and am come here.' 'But,' said La Rongère, not perhaps without malice, 'they talk of some bridge that your Majesty did not guard: apparently you had no need to do so.' 'Oh, as for the bridge,' replied James innocently, 'I had them very well guarded, but they brought up men and cannon, and the cannon made the troops that I had put there retire, and the Prince of Orange passed them.'"

In another of her letters Madame mentions that she has enclosed some songs of the moment, "not precisely eulogistic for the good King of England." She regarded James with a kind of indulgent pity; writing from Saint-Cloud she says :—

"Last Thursday we had the poor King and Queen here. She was very serious, while he was very gay. I heard in the carriage a conversation which very much amused me. Monsieur, according to his custom, was

ELISABETH CHARLOTE PALATINE DVCHESSE D'ORLÉANS Fille de
Charles Louÿs Prince Palatin du Rhyn Electeur de l'Empire &c et de
Charlote Fille de Guillaume Langrave de Hesse Cette Princesse Est Née
le 17.e de Maÿ 1652, et apres avoir fait Abjuration de Son heresie à Metz
entre les mains de Monsr l'Archeues.^{q.e} d'Ambrun le 19.e de Novembre 1671. Elle
Espousa le Lendemain Son Altesse Royale Phillipe de France Duc d'Orleans, frere
Unique de Louis le Grand,:-

"Madame."

talking of his jewels and his furniture, and ended by saying to the King: "And your Majesty, who had so much money, have you built and furnished some beautiful house?' 'Money!' said the Queen, 'he hadn't any; I never saw a sou!' The King replied (sententiously): 'I had some, but I did not buy precious stones or furniture with it, nor did I have houses fitted up. I spent it all in building fine vessels, casting cannons, and making muskets.' 'Yes,' said the Queen, 'much use that has been to you, and all that is now used against you.' Here," concludes Madame, "the conversation dropped."

Madame evidently thought that James was kept in strict order by his wife in later years, for on one occasion, when he was hunting with her at Marly, Maria following in a *calèche* with Louis, she writes that the Queen "would be very glad, if her husband never saw anyone better-looking than I am; she might then have a tranquil mind, and be free from jealousy, while the good King James would not get so many boxes on the ear." She goes on to repeat some servants' gossip about James in Dublin, where "il avait deux affreux laiderons avec lesquelles il était toujours fourré, . . ." thereby fulfilling the prophecy of Charles II. which Madame de Portsmouth quoted: "You may be sure you will see my brother, when he is King, lose his crown from religious zeal, and his soul for 'villaines guenipes.'"

And she finally sums up her impressions as follows: "To tell the truth, our good King James is a brave and honest man, but the silliest I have ever seen in my life; a child of seven would not make such crass mistakes as he does. Piety makes people outrageously stupid (*l'abêtit énormément*)."

284 THE ENGLISH COURT IN EXILE

There does not exist any record among the "Archives of France" in Paris of the orders given by Louis XIV. for the furnishing and setting in order of the Château of Saint-Germain for the reception of the King and Queen of England. M. Dunoyer, the authority for the period, at the "Archives Nationale," concludes from this fact that it was furnished from other royal houses. It is to his kindness that the authors are indebted for the following list of expenditure on Saint-Germain, from original documents in his care. What follows is an exact reproduction of a page of the accounts, as they were passed by the Minister of Finance, Colbert, in whose handwriting are the successive notes of approval, "*bon*," in the margin. The second list is from a *résumé* of the whole subject published by M. Jules Guiffrey.

1689. *Menuiserie*
Janvier.
  16   Bon. A François Millot, menuisier, XV^c l, à compte des tables de cuisine et armoires qu'il a livrés au château de St Germain en Laije aux endrepreneurs occupez par le Roy et la Reyne d'Angleterre . . . . 1500 l.
  30   à luy, IIII^c l. sur le dit, cy . . . . 400 l.
Février.
  13   Bon. à luy, IIII^c l. sur le dit, cy . . . . 400 l.
  27   Bon. à luy II^c l. sur le dit, cy . . . . 200 l.
May.
  10   Bon. à luy III^c l. sur le dit, cy . . . . 300 l.
  22   à luy, II^c l. XXV^l VII^s pour avec les 2800 cy dessus faire le parfait payement de 307^l 57^s à quoy montent les dicts ouvrages 275 l. 7s.
Aoust.
  14   Bon. A luy, III^c l. sur les réparations au château, cy 300 l.
  27   Bon. A luy, II^c l. sur le dites, cy . . . . 200 l.

(*Archives Nationales, Série O^1, registre 2170, folio 449.*)

1689. *Serrurerie*
Janvier.
  30   Bon. Joseph Rouillé, serrurier V^{c}L^l, à compte du gros fer qu'il a fourni aux nouveaux bâtimens de la cour des cuisines et de la serrurerie qu'il a aussi fournis au dit château pour les appartemens occupés par le Roy et la Reyne d'Angleterre, cy 550 l.
Février.
  13   Bon. à luy, IIII^{c}L^l sur le dit, cy . . . . 450 l.
  27   Bon. à luy, CL^l sur le dit, cy . . . . 150 l.

Avril.
24   Bon.   à luy, II^{e}L^l sur le dit, cy   .   .   .   . 250 l.
Juillet.
3   Bon.   à luy, II^{cl} sur le dit, cy .   .   .   .   200 l.
17   Bon.   à luy, C^{xxl}X^s pour avec 1800^l à lui ordonnéez scavoir 200 le 26 X^{bre} . . . . 1688 et ce que dessus fera le parfait paiement de 1921^l 10^s à quoi montent les dicts ouvrages et réparations, cy .   .   . 121 l. 10s.
Aoust.
14   Bon.   A luy, III^c l. sur les gros fers et ferrures qu'il a fourni et reparées au dict   .   .   . 300 l.
28   Bon.   A luy, CL^l sur le dict, cy   .   .   . 150 l.
Octobre.
23   Bon.   A luy, II^c l. sur le dict, cy   .   .   . 200 l.
Novembre.
6   Bon.   A luy, II^c l. sur le dict, cy   .   .   . 200 l.
Décembre.
18   Bon.   A luy, II^c l. sur le dict, cy   .   .   . 200 l.

(*Archives Nationales, Série O^1, registre* 2170, *folio* 451.)

1689.   *Dépenses extraordinaires de St Germain*
Juin.
5   Bon.   Mathieu Lambert fayancier LXXVII^{l}X^s pour son payement de 31 pots de fayance de differentes grandeurs par luy fournis pour mettre des fleurs dans l'appartement de la Reyne d'Angleterre au château de St Germain, cy   .   . 77 l. 10s.
Octobre.
23   Bon.   Aux nommés Constillier jardiniers du Val, II^{c}XXV^l pour le port des fruits et fleurs qu'ils ont portéz à la reyne d'Angleterre à St Germain pendant les mois de May, Juin, Juillet, Aoust, et Septembre de la présente année, cy .   .   .   . 225 l.

(*Archives Nationales, Série O^1, registre* 2170, *folio* 467.)

Comptes des Bâtiments du Roi sous le Règne de Louis XIV., tome iii., 1688–1695, publiées par Jules Guiffrey

St Germain, 1689
Menuiserie
16 janvier–22 mai : à François Millot, menuisier, parfait payement des tables de cuisine et armoires qu'il a livrez au chasteau de

St Germain aux endroits occupez par le Roy et la Reyne d'Angleterre (6 p.). 3075H.[1] 0s. 7d.
10 avril–27 aoust : à luy, pour réparations de menuiserie dans le passage de l'appartement du Roy et autres endroits du d. chasteau (3 p.). 531H. 3s. 11d.

Serrurerie

30 janvier–17 juillet : à Joseph Rouillé, serrurier, parfait payement de 1921H. 10s. à quoy montent les gros fers qu'il a fournis aux nouveaux bastimens de la cour des cuisines et de la ferrure qu'il a aussi fourni au d. chasteau pour les appartemens occupez par le Roy et la Reyne d'Angleterre (6 p.). 1721H. 10s.
14 aoust–18 décembre : à luy, sur les gros fers et serrures qu'il a fourni et réparé au d. chasteau (5 p.). 1050H.

Plomberie

22 may : à Jaques Lucas, plombier, parfait payement de 1133H. 14s. 5d. à quoy montent 28343 livres de plomb qu'il a mis en œuvre et livré au nouveau bastiment de la cour des cuisines.
633H. 14s. 5d.

Peinture

3 juillet : à Louis Poisson, peintre, à compte des ouvrages de dorure et de peinture en blanc qu'il a fait aux oratoires de l'appartement de la Reyne, au d. chasteau de St Germain. 100H.

Dépenses extraordinaires de St Germain

5 juin : à Mathieu Lambert, fayancier, pour 31 pots de fayances de différentes grandeurs, par luy fournis pour mettre des fleurs dans l'appartement de la Reyne d'Angleterre. 77H. 10s.
23 octobre : aux nommez Constillier, jardiniers du Val, pour les fruits et fleurs qu'ils ont portez à la Reyne d'Angleterre, pendant les mois de may, juin, juillet, aoust, et septembre de la présente année.
225H.

Ouvriers à journées

16 janvier : aux ouvriers qui ont travaillé à nettoyer et mettre en couleur les planchers des appartemens occupez par le Roy et les Reyne d'Angleterre au d. chasteau de St Germain.
311H. 12s. 6d.
à ceux qui ont travaillé à remplir de glace les quatre nouvelles glacières de St Germain et celle du Val. 1227H. 14s.

St Germain

19 mars–24 septembre : à Jaques Barbier, maçon, à compte des réparations de maçonnerie qu'il a fait en la dépendance du chasteau de Saint-Germain (9 p.) (pièces). 1300H.

---

[1] " H " instead of *l* for " livres " in the accounts.

19 novembre : à luy, pour rétablissement aux potagers, astres de cheminées et au carreau de plusieurs planchers des offices et passages du chasteau. 15H.

12 février : à Jaques Mazière et Pierre Bergeron entrepreneurs, parfait payement de 619H. 5s. 1d. à quoy montent les ouvrages et réparations de maçonnerie par eux faits dans les offices du chasteau de St Germain. 19H. 5s. 1d.

21 may : à François Gobin, maçon, pour un fourneau de maçonnerie qu'il a fait au rez-de-chaussée du d. chasteau dans une cheminée de l'appartement de M. le la Feuillade, ou loge l'apoticaire de la Reyne d'Angleterre. 15H.

Vitrerie

15 janvier–17 décembre : à Claude Cosset, vitrier pour réparations de vitrerie qu'il a fait au chasteau et dépendances de Saint-Germain-en-Laye depuis le mois de décembre 1689 jusqu'à la fin novembre 1690 (12 p.). 1361H. 9s. 9d.

Dépenses extraordinaires

15 janvier : à Prudhomme, potier de terre, pour deux cents pots de terre qu'il a livrez à l'orangerie de Saint Germain pour replanter les arbrisseaux dans la d. orangerie. 30H.

10 septembre : à Mathieu Lambert, fayancier, pour 9 cuvettes, façon de porcelaine, qu'il a livrées dans les cheminées de l'appartement de la Reyne pour y mettre des fleurs. 24H.

St Germain, 1693

Labeurs

1er février : à Charles Fontaine, terrassier, pour les trous qu'il a faits dans le fonds du fossé du Château de Saint Germain, et pour y avoir mis toutes les ordures et les pierres que les Anglais y avoient jetez. 20H.

CHAPTER XIV

FRESH SCHEMES FOR AN INVASION OF ENGLAND

IN spite of the discovery of Preston's plot, and the consequent act of retributive justice of which James complained, English Jacobites were by no means deterred from further negotiations with Saint-Germain. In the early part of 1691 there was quite a surprising crop of penitents who sought to make terms with James. At the time he seems to have believed in their sincerity: he was always credulous and optimistic, and his agents were too ready to construe vague expressions of regret for the past, or discontent with the present, into assurances of unalterable fidelity to the Stuart cause. It is probable, as James had good reason to believe in the light of subsequent events, that many of the men, who had taken the oath of allegiance to William and were now in his service, felt a certain sense of uneasiness and insecurity, lest James might after all come back, and wished to provide for their own safety in such a contingency, without the slightest intention of sacrificing any present advantages. "Their seeming repentance," thought James, "had all the markes imaginable of sincerity," though "it is hard (considering what has happened since) to make a right judgement of their intentions, and whether they had any further aim in what they did, than to save themselves from the just resentment of an offended Prince, should he fortune to return by other means."[1]

James expresses himself as being specially surprised at receiving overtures from Churchill and Godolphin. Godolphin held the office of First Commissioner of the Treasury. William appeared to trust and esteem him, and thoroughly appreciated his invaluable capacity for finance. He had so little to gain by playing false to the master he was serving, that James might well wonder at receiving any assurance of his repentance. But the Jacobite agent, Captain Henry Bulkeley, was a man of tact and resource; he was besides an old acquaintance of Godolphin. So when, on a first visit, Godolphin showed himself shy in coming to the point, he called again. This time Godolphin was less guarded, and talked of resigning his office; and on a third occasion when Bulkeley met Godolphin walking with Churchill in the Park, he invited them both to dine at his lodgings, trusting by that means to ascertain whether anything might be hoped for from Churchill. But meanwhile Churchill unbosomed himself to another Jacobite agent, Colonel Sackville, giving him the fullest assurance of his repentance for the part he had played in the Revolution, and declaring that his anguish was such that he could neither eat nor sleep. The Jacobites, consulting together, could hardly believe the evidence of their senses. What might not be hoped for from the apparently sincere repentance of a man so important on the Council board and so popular with the army as Churchill. Another of James's agents,

[1] *Memoirs of James II.*

Lloyd,[1] visited him with Sackville, when he readily acquainted them both with all William's designs, as far as he knew them, together with all the strength of the army and the fleet, and the preparations that were then being made for the conduct of the war. This amazing change of front on the part of Churchill, together with further assurances from Godolphin (encouraged, as Bulkeley affirms, by the support of Halifax), was regarded by James's agents in London as of such primary importance that David Lloyd was deputed to carry the intelligence of these repentances in high places to Saint-Germain.

James was frankly surprised, but the opportunity of coming to terms with the ministers of the usurping Prince of Orange was not one to be neglected for a moment, or, as James phrases it, "The King's mercyfull disposition inclined him to forget the greatest injurys upon the least show of amendment." Churchill committed himself to writing, for James's *Memoirs* quote from letters, the first of which was received as early as January, in which he expressed himself in the most exaggerated terms. "He would give up his life with pleasure," he said, "if he could therebye recall the fault he had committed"; and "he should be ready with joy upon the least command to abandon wife and children and country to regain and preserve his [James's] esteem." James's kind replies so much encouraged him that by April, Churchill had demanded and obtained written pardons for himself and Godolphin.

From intelligence sent to James by his agents and supporters, the King had drawn up a paper showing

[1] ? Captain Lloyd of the Navy.

the disposition of parties in England. It is preserved in the Bibliothèque Nationale, and it is dated 1691. There is a certain vagueness about its tone which could not have been very reassuring to practical politicians, if, as is likely from its being written in French, it was intended for the information of Louis XIV. and his ministers. The counties of England are gone through. Gloucestershire is described as being generally well disposed towards James, from assurances given by the Duke of Beaufort and the Marquis of Worcester. The "Comte de Lindsey" says the same of Lincolnshire; the "Comte Macklesfield" answers for Cheshire and Wales; while in Somerset and Devon James can count on the great influence of the Lords Paulet and Mohun. Exeter is strongly attached to the Jacobite cause, according to the Chevalier John Trelawney, Lord Arendel, and Mr Godolphin. In Cornwall 7000 miners would rise in James's support if they had a commander; and in Northumberland, Norfolk, Lancashire, Cumberland, and Westmorland the greater number of people are well disposed (*sont affectionés*) to James. The Commons are described as being very discontented with the present government. There follows a list of the English fleet, giving the men necessary to man each ship, and the number wanting in every case to make up the full complement. Nucleus crews were an enforced necessity of the British fleet at this time. Altogether there was good reason for James's belief that his cause was prospering and his adherents on the increase in England. During the early months of this year he and Maria were as usual frequently at the French Court. On at least one occasion they were closeted for some time with Louis discussing their prospects. (The occasion noted was when they had come over to Trianon to see a performance of *Le Bourgeois Gentilhomme*"; James had already received the first of Marlborough's letters.) The time was yet to come when Louis obviously avoided being alone with them, and when they, even if an opportunity offered, tacitly and resignedly avoided any mention of the hopes they still cherished.[1]

In March, Louis XIV. determined to go in person to the siege of Mons, hoping to disconcert the plans of the allies by suddenly wresting this all-important fortress of the Spanish Netherlands from their hands. James was eager to accompany him, but Louis knew that such a colleague would prove a distracting encumbrance, and begged him to stay where he was. After farewell visits had been interchanged between Versailles and Saint-Germain, the French King set off without him. By the middle of April he was back again at Versailles, having triumphantly carried out his purpose. William III. had learned too late of his intentions, and in spite of the most strenuous exertions the fortress fell. Visits of congratulation were paid. Maria and James went over to Versailles to compliment the Most Christian King on the day of his return; all the Court were assembled to receive him, and Monseigneur left

[1] In February an event took place at Saint-Germain which caused much gossip and excitement. The two young brothers of Lord Salisbury quarrelled and fought a duel, wounding one another very seriously. They afterwards were reconciled, asking one another's pardon, and both abjured Protestantism. The elder, who was only nineteen, died of his wounds; the other, who was very ill at the time, announced his intention of entering the monastery of La Trappe, as soon as he should be sufficiently recovered. Their brother, the Earl, James Cecil, was almost half-witted, and a favourite subject for lampoons; he had already become a Catholic; he was impeached in 1690.

JAMES DRUMMOND, EARL OF PERTH.

FRESH SCHEMES FOR INVASION

off the mourning he had worn for the Dauphine on this happy occasion.

During the early summer months (1691) James and Maria paid many visits to the French King. Now it was to Marly, where they drove on the heights, walked in the gardens full of spring flowers, and after a state supper, drove back to Saint-Germain in the cool of the evening. Another time it would be a stag-hunt, which Queen Maria accompanied, driving in a *calèche* with Madame de Maintenon, the Duchess of Tyrconnel, and the Comtesse de Gramont. Towards the middle of July Louis arranged an illuminated water party for the King and Queen of England one fine evening. They came over to Versailles, where Louis spent some time in going round his stables with James, who declared he had never seen so many fine English horses together in his life before. They then went on to the canal, where there was music, the ladies of the Court following in gondolas. They landed at Trianon, which was illuminated, and, after a stroll, supped under the peristyle at five tables. Louis and the English King and Queen sat at the first as usual, while other members of the royal family—Monsieur, Madame, Monseigneur, and Mademoiselle—took the head of the other tables.

On one of the several occasions during these months when James came to Versailles, he had a long conversation with Louvois, the war minister. In spite of all the hopeful news from England, no steps had been taken by the French King to restore James; and the delay had been due to Louvois. Louvois was always hostile to any such costly and unprofitable scheme, and threw the weight of his influence in the scales against it. At this time, however, several circumstances conspired to make him give a less unwilling ear, if not to James's plans, then at any rate to some schemes for helping the Stuarts. Lauzun had returned from Ireland, but was not in good odour. Louvois hated him, and was willing, if Louis agreed, to do something more in Ireland, at any rate for the Jacobite cause, which indeed was progressing better there than had been expected.

But on the 16th of July the great war minister died. For more than twenty years he had conducted the military affairs of France with consummate address and an organising ability which touched the point of genius. Self-confident and overbearing, Louvois had more than once offended his master, and, more important still, he had incurred the hostility of De Maintenon, who never forgave him for having dissuaded Louis from publicly recognising her marriage. He had made himself additionally unpopular a few months before, when the question of the King's presence at the siege of Mons was under discussion. He sought to dissuade Louis from taking the ladies of the Court with him, on the ground of the expense it would involve. In spite of the weakening of his influence, he still further inflamed the King's irritation by obstinately opposing him in military details of the siege of Mons. After the return of the Court, the minister realised how great had been his indiscretions; he trembled for the consequences. His friends noticed that he was moody and distrait. Saint-Simon, a boy at the time, met him one afternoon as he was going in to work with the King. Later he heard that Louvois had been taken ill, that he had returned home on foot, had taken some slight remedy, and was dead. It was not long before people began to whisper that he had been poisoned. The young Saint-Simon, with the cold-blooded inquisitiveness that characterised him, hung about the Court to catch a glimpse of the King and see how he looked after learning of the loss of this faithful, highly placed, and once highly valued servant. It seemed to the boy that the King's demeanour, though dignified as always, had a certain air of relief about it; and instead of taking his afternoon walk about the grounds as usual, he paced to and fro in the orangery, looking continually towards the lodging of the war minister, in which Louvois was lying dead.

James and Maria, hearing at Saint-Germain of this important event, hastened to send an equerry to present to Louis their formal expressions of condolence; but the French King, to the consternation and amazement of the courtiers who surrounded him, replied almost gaily: "Monsieur, give my compliments to the King and Queen of England, and tell them from me, that my affairs and theirs will go on none the worse for what has occurred." The astonished equerry bowed and withdrew in silence. The next year was to prove how far Louis XIV.'s words were justified.

In August, Maria d'Este was far from well, and left Saint-Germain for a time to take the waters at Forges, from which, however, she derived no benefit. In September, she and James paid a visit to Fontainebleau which lasted some days. The Queen seemed still to be ailing. During their visit the usual shooting and hunting parties, and military reviews, took place, with portique or the performance of some comedy in the evening, at which the English King and Queen were not always present. They had many private conversations with Louis XIV. These visits, though essential from motives of policy, seem to have become less and less congenial to Maria d'Este. She had no taste for gaieties and spectacles, she disapproved of comedies, and though she appears from her letters to have had little time to herself at Saint-Germain, she could at all events arrange her life there according to her taste. She had on this occasion tried to get Madame de Maintenon to use her influence with the King on behalf of her friends at Chaillot, who were in need of funds, as is evident from the following :—

"FONTAINEBLEAU, *Oct.* 7.

"According to my promise, my very dear Mother, I send you my news from this place, which as far as regards health, are good, thank God, although the life that I lead here is very different from that at Saint-Germain. I have already been to the chase four times, and we have had very fine weather. The King overwhelms us as usual in a thousand ways with his goodness and kindness ; we are no less sensible of it because we are accustomed to it. On the contrary, that makes us more and more penetrated with a sense of gratitude (*nous en somes toujours plus pénétrés et reconoissans*). I have seen Madame de M[aintenon] twice. She has been very out of sorts. At present she is better. Yesterday I broached the subject of Chaillot to her quite naturally. I told her what I had determined on with you, and many other things besides. She said she had made the King see the condition which your house is in. However, if you do not wish to be flattered, I must say that I do not believe anything will come of this at present, for a reason that I will tell you when I see you. I am doubtful if I shall speak to him about it. I very much wish to, for indeed I am ashamed on her account as

FRESH SCHEMES FOR INVASION

well as my own to be unable to obtain anything. I believe I have nothing to reproach myself with on this point, with regard to which I have done and will always do everything I can think of to render you some little service. . . . M. R."

Shortly afterwards the King and Queen left Fontainebleau. Their visit terminated on October 11th. James went away for his annual sojourn at the monastery of La Trappe, which was to him what Chaillot was to his wife.

The day after he had gone, Maria found time to acquaint her friends at Chaillot with a piece of personal news. She was once more in hopes of having another child. The immense importance which both she and James attached to this expected event has already been the subject of remark. It would help to remove the stigma which slander had cast on the birthright of the little Prince of Wales, and if the child should prove a boy, it would carry on the Stuart line beyond the cavil even of the most ill-disposed.

It was on account of her state of health that the Queen commissioned one of her ladies to write to excuse herself from paying some promised visit to Chaillot.

"SAINT-GERMAIN, *Oct.* 20, 1691.

"As I thought to embrace you, my very dear and very honoured Mother, I find myself forced to tell you that this time one must sacrifice to the good God the pleasure of seeing one's friends. Our wholly incomparable Queen is constrained to follow the counsels of the wisest, and not to take the air at present at the risk of bringing back the inflammation in her teeth. She is at present almost quite well, but it is necessary to take all sorts of precautions in order to keep so. The King considers this necessary; he must be obeyed. The King of France is expected here to-morrow. In short, everything combines to deprive our Queen and ourselves of one of our greatest pleasures. I hope it will be compensated for by other agreeable ones. Meanwhile, let us be prepared to bear cheerfully the pain of too long an absence. I hope to have leave to pay you a little visit next week. . . . I end my letter to give place to a worthier and more perfect pen, that will console you on the other side of this sheet. . . ."

Here Maria d'Este takes the pen from the hand of her lady-in-waiting and continues the letter herself :—

"I am wholly mortified, my very dear mother, that I shall not have the pleasure of seeing you to-day, as I had proposed; but it has seemed for some time, as if God took pleasure in sending me all sorts of mortifications. It is true that I have had several very diverse ones, even since I saw you. But what is to be said about all that except, 'Dominus est : quod bonum est in oculis suis faciat'? I must explain M. de . . . .'s letter, for it is impossible to me to have any secret from you, and I must tell you, that besides my inflammation (which, however, has been very violent), and though less so than it was is not quite gone, and besides the visit from the King that I must receive to-morrow, I have still another reason which prevents my going to you, and that is some expectation of being with child; but as I am not yet at all certain about it, I do not like it talked about. In a few days, I shall be able to decide about it, and I will let you know. If it prove true, alas! my dear mother, what pain to be so many months without seeing you! But still in that and in all else God is Master, and one must wish what He wishes. I beg you not to speak of this little secret, unless to my little sister 'la Déposée,' to whom I am going to tell it. To all the others give the reasons of my inflammation and the King's visit."

FRESH SCHEMES FOR INVASION 299

This news soon became public property, and was noted by Dangeau in his memoirs on December 1st.

An important exchange of prisoners was effected during November. Lord Mountjoy, who had languished in the Bastille for some months, was exchanged for Anthony Hamilton's younger brother Richard. This step had been proposed long before, but had been rejected for reasons which were not very creditable to James's honour or good sense. Mountjoy was one of the emissaries who had been sent over to France from Ireland before James's Irish campaign, in order to acquaint James with Irish feeling. But Tyrconnel, who sent him in company with Chief Baron Rice, who was a Roman Catholic, gave instructions to Rice to tell James that Mountjoy should be arrested—ostensibly because he was a traitor, actually because his detention would deprive the Irish Protestants of a leader. It had been proposed at one time to exchange him for Mountcashel; but James was unwilling because, so D'Avaux says, he knew in what estimate the Irish Protestants held the imprisoned nobleman. Mountjoy was a cultivated man of letters, and had formed in Dublin a Royal Society modelled on that of London. He had held the colonelcy of a regiment in Ireland. After his services to James had been so requited, he not unnaturally transferred them to William, and died fighting on his behalf at the battle of Steinkirk, the same year.

In the midst of more serious business, James took part in the marriage festivities of the Duc de Maine. This was the lame child of Louis XIV. and Madame de Montespan, to whom De Maintenon had been nursery governess. Louis disapproved of his son's marrying, and tried to dissuade him from it, on the ground that it was not for such as he to make a lineage. But De Maintenon, interceding for her favourite, overruled the King's objections, and a daughter of the Prince de Condé was decided on for the bride. The Prince was greatly pleased at the prospect. He had three daughters for M. de Maine to choose from, all extremely little. An inch of height that the second had above the others procured her the preference, much to the grief of the eldest, who was beautiful and clever, and who dearly wished to escape from the slavery in which her father kept her.[1] The dignity with which she bore her disappointment was admired by everyone, but it cost her an effort that ruined her health. The marriage was celebrated on March 19th,[2] shortly after Louis and James had returned from a great review at Compiègne. James was present, and afterwards performed the ceremony of handing the chemise to the bride, as his wife was precluded from taking part in any festivities.

During the closing months of 1691 James seems to have been much occupied with the Irish regiments that were now arriving in France. For more than a year the contemned Irish had held out, fighting with a courage and determination similar to that which two centuries later was to prolong the war so long after the British forces were in possession of the capitals of the Orange Free State and the Transvaal. Unlike the Boers, however, and unwisely, the Irish elected to sustain a siege—the siege of Limerick—and to stake their all on pitched battles. The bloody rout of Aughrim and the fall of Limerick (September–October

---

[1] Saint-Simon. [2] Dangeau.

1691) extinguished the last Jacobite hopes in Ireland and sent many thousands of Irishmen into voluntary exile. They had not been without French assistance in their struggle.

Lauzun's stay in Ireland had not long survived that of James. He had reiterated loudly the French opinion that the Irish could not and would not fight, and, after the fall of Cork and Kinsale in the October of 1690, had followed James into France. He had brought Tyrconnel with him—both were to repeat that the Irish war was useless. That appears to have been what the Stuarts were willing to believe after the disaster of the Boyne and James's flight—for which the pleas of the cowardice of the Irish and the uselessness of prolonging the war would have been the only, if not the sufficient, excuse. As early as August 15th, 1690, a month after James's arrival from Kinsale at Saint-Germain, the Queen had written to Lauzun: "In the pitiable state of affairs in Ireland I ask no better than to see you safely here again, and to have your advice in all our business, which is truly in a desperate condition." She adds that Louis had told them that he believed Lauzun was on his way home with the French troops, for positive orders had been sent to him (Lauzun) to that effect; and once more she recurs to that descent on England which James would have always preferred to the expedition to Ireland, and which he desired none the less because of his failure in the task he had undertaken. "But," adds Maria sadly, "no one believes a word we say, nor will listen to our proposals for a descent into England before the Prince of Orange returns there."

Such were the reports that Lauzun and Tyrconnel,

coming over to France together, were to bring or to confirm; but Tyrconnel changed his views (or the expression of them) in France, and said that with French help the Irish cause would, so to speak, live to fight another day. Doubtless this change of front surprised Lauzun, who found himself in disgrace in consequence, and, but for the solicitations of James,[1] and probably of Maria, would have experienced one of his periodic reversals of fortune again. The Stuarts, however, never lost faith in him. "I trust," says a letter to him from Maria, "that I may yet be happy enough to repair your losses, which are as sensible to me as my own, and to recompense your services."

Tyrconnel went back to Ireland, where he had left the young Duke of Berwick commander-in-chief—not an ideal appointment at this time; and the campaign, pumped up with fresh supplies, went on briskly during the spring and summer of 1691. Tyrconnel returned from France to Ireland with supplies, and accompanied by Sir Stephen Rice (Chief Baron Rice) and Sir Richard Nagle. Berwick was recalled, and replaced by an experienced soldier in the French general, St Ruth, who was accompanied by D'Ussen and De Tessé; the defence of Ireland was reorganised and replenished. Tyrconnel and Sarsfield were not congenial allies: though the campaign did not suffer on that account. On the 12th of July St Ruth was killed at Aughrim, and his death was the direct cause of the rout. A month later Tyrconnel, masterful to the last in spite of his failing health, died of apoplexy, and the war flickered out. The English commander, William's general, De Ginkell, tried by giving good terms—better

[1] Kelly's *Macariæ Excidium*, 383-384; *cf.* 360, 361.

terms than were subsequently ratified—to induce the Irish soldiers to stay in Ireland under the new government. In vain: the Irish would not fight for William. Five thousand sailed from Limerick, four thousand from Cork. Two thousand set out afterwards. Many left their wives and children behind.

In December James went to Brest to meet the Irish exiles, nine thousand of whom had disembarked under the Comte de Château-Renaud, who had commanded the French fleet in Bantry Bay. Louis XIV. accommodated the King of England with the relays of carriages for his journey to Orleans, whence he embarked on the Loire. James wrote to Louis to say he was forming these troops into seven regiments of fourteen hundred men, which would make two battalions each, and a regiment of cavalry of six hundred horse. There were, he adds, another four or five thousand men still to come under Sarsfield. He went over to see Louis in January (1692). Maria was now keeping her room. Louis returned the visit on January 12th, when the talk was all of the new Irish regiments. Louis consented to James's proposal that they should be provided with red uniforms, but not unnaturally declined to give them a higher rate of pay than his French soldiers, as James suggested. There were now about twenty thousand Irish in the French service. Sarsfield, who had been created Lord Lucan in the spring, and the Duke of Berwick, were given the command of James's guards.[1]

In January James's cause in England had undergone a serious reverse of fortune. Marlborough, the most treacherous of all the unfaithful servants by whom William III. was surrounded, after betraying the

[1] Dangeau, iv., January-February.

master who had made his fortunes, and transferring his allegiance to the Prince of Orange, was now believed to have formed an ingenious plan for substituting the Princess Anne, a puppet in his hands, for both of them. The Jacobites, when at last they came to suspect his intentions, informed William's trusted friend, the Earl of Portland, of the plot. Marlborough was dismissed from all his offices, and subsequently sent to the Tower. Before this Marlborough had used his influence with Anne to make her write a letter to her father expressing her regret for the past. The bearer, Captain Lloyd, was long delayed, by cross winds and the strict watch that was kept on the English coasts, from delivering it into James's hands, and the letter was not received till April (1692).

On the other hand, the death of Louvois had effected an apparent improvement in James's prospects. Louis had at last consented to attempt the invasion of England, and the preparations were now being vigorously carried on. Louvois had been succeeded by his son Barbésieux, a young and inexperienced man, whose pleasure-loving, self-indulgent nature unfitted him for so important an office, in spite of his undeniable abilities. James had everything to gain by an attempted descent on England, and risked nothing. Louis, on the contrary, had everything to lose by failure; but the strong hand of his great minister, Louvois, once removed, James's insistence gained the day. That he was insistent is shown by the survival of two at least of the memorials he presented to Louis on the subject, both of which were written in January 1692. James was besides frequently admitted to long private interviews with Louis, in which he no doubt urged his cause.[1] James determined, when all should be ready, to go down to the coast and superintend operations in person.

Before James left for the coast, on his way, as he hoped, to make a triumphal return into his kingdom, he thought it well to issue an invitation to representative officials and ladies in England to attend the Queen's lying-in. He therefore wrote to Lords and others of the Privy Council as follows :—

" . . . That we may not be wanting to ourselves now it has pleased Almighty God, the Supporter of Truth, to give us the hopes of further issue, our dearest Consort the Queen, being big, and drawing near her time, we have thought fit to require such of our Privy Council as can possibly come to attend us here at St Germains to be witness at our dearest Consort the Queen her labour. We do therefore herebye signify our royal pleasure to you, that you may use all possible means to come with what convenient hast you can, the Queen looking about the middle of May next, English account,[2] and that you may have no scruple on our side, our dearest brother, the Most Christian King, has given his consent to promise you, as we herebye do, that you shall have leave to come, and (the Queen's labour over) to return with safety ; tho' the iniquity of the times, the tyrannie of strangers, and a misled partie of our own subjects have brought us under the necessity of using this unusual way, yet we hope it will convince the world of the truth and candour of our proceedings to the confusion of our enemies."

Letters to the same effect were sent to various ladies, but, needless to say, James's invitation produced no results, for, as he put it, " none durst venter to undertake such a journey."

[1] Macpherson ; Dangeau, January 27, February 18.
[2] Old Style.

306 THE ENGLISH COURT IN EXILE

As the time approached for the invasion of England, James delivered himself of a declaration, perhaps the most tactless of all he ever penned. It began with a long preamble which leads to James's flight to France, and the settlement of England after his departure, on which his comment was that "the grounds on which they are built are too vain and frivolous to deserve a confutation." After comparing William with Nero, he points out that "if it should please Almighty God, as one of the severest judgments upon this kingdom, . . . that we should not be restored during our life time; yet an indisputable title to the crown will survive in the person of our dearest son the Prince of Wales." After prohibiting William's subjects from paying any taxes, he promises pardon to his rebellious people, with the exception of a long list of nobles, divines, and other distinguished men, down to the wretched crowd of fishermen who had maltreated him at Feversham. Among this formidable list of exceptions were further included all those judges and juries who had been guilty of convicting conspirators against the Government which employed them, and all spies who had reported Jacobite counsels to William. Protection was promised to the Church of England, and liberty of conscience was to be established; but the English people knew from experience just how much might be expected of James in the matter of religious toleration, and it was noticeable that he had given no guarantee not to repeat his former illegal acts. The whole tone of the declaration was threatening. James could not have served William's cause better than by its publication.

It was calculated to offend his most zealous supporters by its wholesale vindictiveness, and was drawn up by the most unpopular of his advisers, Melfort. James had it inserted in his *Memoirs* that the "declaration was drawn up by my Lord Chancellor Herbert, who was sure to take care of the Protestant interest, a man far from a vindictive spirit, and in the opinion of some was much more indulgent than could reasonably have been expected, considering the provocations the King had received from all ranks of people."[1] The *Memoirs* also explain that Churchill was included in the list of exceptions in order not to cast suspicion upon him, although he "looked upon him as his principall agent at that very time." The declaration was considered so damning that some English Jacobites published a false one, in which James was made to appear in a spirit of clemency; while the Government reprinted and dispersed the original. James was not left in doubt of the temper in which it had been received, for he comments in the *Memoirs* that "they thought his Majesty's resentment descended too low to except the Feversham mob; that five hundred men were excluded, and no man really pardoned except he should merit it by som service, and then the pardons being to pass the seals, look't as if it were to bring money into the pocket of some favourite." One of those who most strongly expressed their disapproval was Admiral Russell, whose adherence, as commander of the English fleet, was of paramount importance to James, and, as he phrases it, "there appeared a necessity of doing all that was possible to content a person, who held the crown of England so far in his hands as that it was in his power to set it again on his Majesty's head, if he really designed it." No one was more fully alive to this than

[1] Clarke.

Russell himself. In his opinion, the important services he had rendered to William at the Revolution could not be, and had not been, highly enough rewarded.

Arrogant, avaricious, and of an ill-conditioned temper, Russell listened to James's emissaries and coquetted with Saint-Germain. In an interview with the indefatigable Lloyd at this time, Russell expressed his desire to serve James—on conditions—" if he would reign a Catholic King over a Protestant people. He must forget all past misdemeanours, and grant a general pardon, and then he would contribute what he could to his restoration." At the same time, Russell declared that if he met the French fleet " he would feight it even tho' the King himself were on board." He held out hopes, however, that he might so dispose the fleet under his command as to give James an opportunity of landing on the English coast. James had to exact what satisfaction he could from such contradictory assurances, for in his position he " was forced to seem well contented with what those men were pleas'd to promis, and make use of such instruments without urging them too much as far as they could go with ease."

James's agents, like himself, were too ready to construe vague expressions of discontent into definite promises of support. In one important instance at least they were badly hoodwinked, for Rear-Admiral Carter of the Blue, after encouraging Jacobite emissaries, informed Mary what they were doing. James was perhaps only wise after the event, when he wrote that " fear alone would make those mercenary soules his friends, and that nothing but the preparations where he was could produce that effect."

These " preparations " were well calculated to ensure

success. William had gone to the Continent at the beginning of March, in ignorance that any invasion was then intended. Mary, who knew that there was a certain amount of disaffection in the fleet, sent them assurances of her entire confidence in their fidelity and zeal; they responded with a loyal address.

There was, however, a certain proportion of loyal Jacobites, especially in the North of England, where Roman Catholics had secretly collected arms and formed themselves into regiments. This time marked, in fact, an important crisis in James's fortunes, his second great chance. An initial success would have brought over the wavering and the timorous. His army was to consist of all the Irish regiments in France, under the command of Lord Lucan, together with some ten thousand French troops under Marshal Bellefonds. These troops were to be conveyed across in transports from Ushant, convoyed by a fleet of eighty ships. All was calculated to be in readiness before the English and Dutch fleets could assemble. Nothing but a special intervention of Providence for the purpose "of sanctifying the King by continual suffrings could have ordered it in the manner it fell out." Contrary winds delayed the junction of the two divisions of the French fleet, which were at Brest and at Toulon, till the English and Dutch ships were assembled in the Channel. James set out for the coast. Before he left, he invested with the Garter his son, who was nearly four years old; the Duke of Powis; and Lord Melfort. He arrived at the camp at La Hogue, on the coast of Normandy, on the 24th of April. Here he was destined to see the wreck of his hopes.

Tourville, the victor of Beachy Head, bore down on the combined English and Dutch fleet on May 19th, and was worsted and outnumbered, "for he, counting it too great a dishonour to shew his stern to the enemie, and trusting to the strength of his own ship, the *Royal Sun*, a mighty vessel of 120 guns, resolved to stand the brunt, and lay like a castle in the sea attacked on all sides, being too well mann'd to be boarded by the enemy." Thus Tourville and the captains who stood by him "could never after get cleer of the English, but were forced to that scurvey alternative, either to be taken, or run ashore," and though part of the fleet got away to St Malo, "Tourville, with sixteen great vessels, was necessitated to run aground." Here the sailors, disheartened by the late defeat, soon abandoned their posts, "at the first approach of the English (tho' but in chalops), who, notwithstanding the continual fire of several batteries rais'd on the shore, burnt all those men of war that had run upon it." "The French mariners often went off undisturbed in their boats from one side of a French ship, while the English had entered and were destroying it upon the other, . . . the enemies making little resistance because they saw it was fruitless. Few prisoners were taken, for the officers were possessed with the idea of the seamen, that the destruction of the ships was their only object."[1]

From the shore James looked on helplessly at the disaster, at considerable personal risk:—

"This defeat was too considerable to be redeemed and too afflicting to be looked upon, nor was it even safe to do it long, for as if everything conspired to encreas the King's misfortune and hazard, his own ships, as it were with their dying groans would have

[1] Dalrymple.

endanger'd his life, had he not been timely advertised to remove from the place where he fortuned to stand; for as soon as they were burnt to the guns, which were most of them loaded, they fired on all hands, which raked the very place where the King had been, and did some small damage on shore, so little was such an accident foreseen."[1]

The fight had lasted five days, and the victorious fleet drew off on May 24th.

James was abundantly mortified by this disaster. Not only had he seen his own hopes defeated, but he had involved the prestige of his patron and protector, the King of France. His own disappointment was the least of his discomfiture. "To see the King of France who had always been happy and victorious, drawn in to be a sharer of his misfortunes, was what he had scarce constancy to support, had not the hand of God which thought fit to sanctify him by the way of afflictions given him a patience and resignation suitable to those tryalls."

[1] Clarke's *Life*.

CHAPTER XV

BIRTH OF A PRINCESS: THE ENGLISH JACOBITES

DURING James's absence in Brittany in the spring of 1692, Maria was not without visitors, though she was deprived of the companionship of her friends at Chaillot. Louis had been over hunting at the end of April, and next day it was announced that Lauzun, emerged yet again from the shadow of royal disapproval, was to be made a Duke "because the Queen of England had earnestly desired it." Whatever may be believed of the ingratitude of the Stuarts, no reproach of that kind can ever be cast at Maria of Modena, who had never forgotten what she thought she owed to Lauzun for preserving James from danger in Ireland, and who kept her promise that she would try by her actions to prove to Lauzun the gratitude which it was beyond her power to express.[1]

In May came another visitor whom James and Maria had greatly hoped to see. As early as January

---

[1] "Without seeing into my heart you could not judge of my gratitude, for it is beyond my power to express. I shall try to prove it to you and all the world by my actions, and I have only too many occasions of doing so in protecting you from enemies who seek nothing so much as your ruin.... The King and I employ ourselves daily in justifying your conduct which has been faultless."—Letter to Lauzun (B. Mus.).

there had been rumours that the Queen Dowager of England, Charles II.'s widow, who had made herself rather a thorn in the flesh to William and Mary, was returning to Spain through France. Catharine of Braganza did not propose to come to Saint-Germain at first. But at last, at the end of May, the Queen Dowager actually came and spent two hours at Versailles. Little Prince James went to meet her, in his father's absence, his mother being confined to her room. Catharine spent two hours with Maria, hours full of all the latest gossip about the doings of the interlopers in London, and who was secretly inclined to the King *de jure*, while giving lip-service perforce to the King *de facto*. Maria, on her side, must have had much to say of French fashions; the kindness of the French King; her difficulties in dealing with the needy refugees of Saint-Germain. She was at this time suffering from deep physical and mental depression.

She had written to La Mère Priolo on June 14th: "What would I say to you, my very dear Mother, or rather what would I not say to you, if I could be in your arms for one little quarter of an hour? Yet I believe the quarter of an hour would be more probably passed in tears and sighs, and that my eyes, my groans, would speak much more than my lips, for in truth what is there to be said after all that has happened, and in my present state, but 'O Altitudo! O Altitudo!' Ah, how far removed are the ways of God from our ways, and His thoughts from our thoughts! Indeed we see that in our last misfortunes, and the unforeseen and almost unnatural accidents by which God has overthrown all our designs and has seemed to declare Himself so clearly against us to overwhelm us"; and she sums up her bitter disappointment, her resignation and submission to the Divine will, in the words of Samuel: "Dominum est, quod bonum est, in oculis suis faciat." "That, my dear Mother, is what I would do and say, and in this you have encouraged me by your words, and in your letters which are always so dear to me; but I do and say all this so little and so ill, with so bad a grace and so unwillingly, that I can have no reason to hope it will be pleasing to God. Help me with your prayers, and encourage me always with your letters. . . . I have suffered much in body and mind these past days, but at present I am better both in one and the other. I am weary of the continued expectation of the hour of my lying-in. It will come when God wills. I tremble with fear at the thought of it, but I very much wish it were over, in order not to weary myself and all the rest of the world with waiting. When I began my letter yesterday I was uncertain what the King was doing, and of the time when I should have the happiness of seeing him; for he would not stir from La Hogue, although there was nothing to be done there, and the state in which I am speaks for itself to make him return to me. However, he would not decide anything—and I think he has done right, although it has cost me dear—without having the King's orders, which Milord Melfort has just brought us this morning, which are that for the present there is nothing for my King to do except to return here." She adds that Louis has written a kind and encouraging letter to her by Melfort, and concludes: "All this comforts me, and the hope of having the King near me in my confinement consoles me greatly. . . . There, my very dear Mother, is some account of what has passed and is passing in my poor heart. You know and understand it better than I do myself."

Towards the end of June James returned. Once more his hopes were deferred, and he had seen them literally turn to ashes as the tinder of the gallant vessels smouldered on the water-line. A week later, on June 28th, "the Queen was delivered of a princesse, which gave him at least some domestick comfort."[1] She was christened Louise Mary: the Most Christian King stood godfather to her, and the ceremony of baptism was performed with great magnificence and solemnity, "tho' no one came out of England according to the King's invitation." However, besides the Princesses, and chief ladies of the Court of France, the Chancellor, the first President of the Parliament of Paris, the Archbishop, "the wife of the Danish ambassador, Madame Meereroon, as a person on whose testimony the people of England might reasonably rely, was present at the Queen's labour and delivery, and notwithstanding her averseness to the King's interest could not refuse owning the rediculousness of that false and malicious insinuation which had wrought him so much mischief, she being an eye-witness of the contrary herself."[2] If James could have been persuaded to take such precautions at the birth of his son, he might have still been on the throne of England.

During June Louis XIV. was in camp, and the day after the birth of their daughter James and Maria had the satisfaction of learning by a courier of the fall of Namur. This stately fortress, which raised its head proudly above far-reaching stretches of cultivated land

[1] James's *Memoirs*. [2] *Ibid.*, 497.

watered by the Sambre and the Meuse, had never surrendered in all the many wars which had swept across the Netherlands. It was believed to be impregnable, and had recently been re-fortified. Louis had the great advantage of being first on the field. He was accompanied by all the imposing ceremonial of his Court; the ladies remained at Dinant.[1] At first the siege was conducted in still, sunny weather, and the King's tent and those of all the Court were pitched in a beautiful meadow. But on the 8th of June, the feast of St Médard, the French St Swithin, the fine weather turned to heavy rain, the trenches became canals, the camp a swamp; the soldiers sought for images of St Médard, and burnt and broke all those they could lay hands on. Even the horses of the King had to live on leaves, and the French cavalry horses never recovered the effects of their hardships before Namur. But on the 1st of July the citadel of Namur surrendered.

The besiegers themselves were exhausted. Nothing but the presence of Louis, who had continued to direct operations from his bed, to which he was confined by gout, had turned the scale. William had tried in vain to dislodge the army of Luxembourg, which covered the besiegers.[2] Before he left Namur, Louis learned of the destruction of his fleet at La Hogue; but, as always, he received both James and the defeated admiral with dignified reassurances. On July 16th, when the King of England came to Versailles, Louis said to

---

[1] "According to the old Persian luxury, he used to bring the ladies with him, with the music, poems, scenes for an opera and a ball, in which he and his actions were to be set out with the pomp of much flattery."
[2] Saint-Simon.

Tourville in his presence: "I am well content with you and with all the navy. We have been beaten, but you have won glory for yourself and the nation. It has cost you some vessels; that can be repaired next year, and surely we shall defeat our enemies."

In August, when Monseigneur came to Saint-Germain, James and Maria told him of the death of poor Lord Mountjoy at the battle of Steinkirk, in which William had again been defeated by Luxembourg, the chief of Louis's generals, though the losses had been almost equally heavy on both sides.

An accusation levelled at James about this time has never been refuted. A plot for William's assassination was committed to Grandval, a French soldier. It was hatched by Louvois' successor, Barbésieux. The scheme was discovered, and Grandval was executed; but before he died he wrote a confession in which he affirmed that before setting out for the Low Countries he was admitted to an audience by James and his Queen at Saint-Germain, and that James had "encouraged him to go on with it and promised great rewards."[1]

Meanwhile, at Saint-Germain, the pressure of financial difficulties was beginning to make itself seriously felt, and must have cast a gloom over the Court. Though it was far from being the priest-ridden abode of envy, hatred, and malice that Macaulay would have us believe, there must inevitably have been a certain amount of jealousy and dissatisfaction among a number of people who, from necessity or choice, had lost their worldly possessions and incurred exile through following the fortunes of the Stuarts. There must always be among such some who believe their sacrifices to have

[1] Burnet.

been unequally requited. James was, besides, too ready to lend an ear to newcomers to the exclusion of older, more trusted advisers. The pension of £40,000 a year which Louis put at the disposal of his guests was insufficient for the needs of the ever-increasing army of dependents. James's agents had to be paid, and paid heavily, for the risks they ran in venturing themselves in London. The Queen speaks of the economies they have been forced to make at Saint-Germain in a letter written to La Mère Priolo at a rather later date, probably early in 1693 :—

"It is a long time since I have seen the King look so well, but his kind heart and mine have suffered much for some days over this desolating reform which we expected, and for which we have tried to prepare ourselves for some months, and which has now begun to be carried out among our poor troops. I can tell you with truth that the extremity of these poor people touches us far more keenly than our own losses; but I must tell you at the same time that we are well content with the King, and we have reason to be so, for he spoke to us yesterday about this with great kindness, and has convinced us that without the consideration that he has for us, and the wish that he has to please us, he would not keep a fourth part of those that he is willing to keep for love of us. I will enter into details about all this when I have the pleasure of seeing you, which will be fifteen days from to-day, please God. Meanwhile, pray do not speak of this affair, unless someone mentions it to you; for it is not yet public, but it will be soon. . . . Pray well for us, my dear Mother, for in truth we are in extreme need of it. I do not weary in praying for you as for myself that God may give us grace to fill our hearts with His holy love. If we are so happy as to obtain it, we shall be indifferent to all the rest, and even content that all else is lacking to us, provided we possess that. . . .   M.

"Here is a prayer from the hand of my son, which seems to me well enough written to send you. I believe my dear Mother will be well pleased to have in her hand something that comes from this dear son."

During the autumn of the year James and Maria had, besides their usual visits, made some stay at Fontainebleau, where there was a larger Court than usual for the occasion. Dangeau notes that all the ladies paid assiduous court to Maria. James hunted every day, and lansquenet was played in the evening, "parceque la reine aimat ce jeu là." The early months of this year had been more than usually gay at Versailles, on account of the visit to France of the Prince Royal of Denmark, who was travelling incognito. Monsieur gave a magnificent ball for him at the Palais Royal, which was attended by the royal family, and at which the Prince appeared with his suite in Moorish dress; and one still more magnificent took place at Versailles on February 3rd, to which James and Maria were invited. They were the only guests present who did not wear masks. There was an early supper, and Louis himself left soon after midnight. Most of the guests changed their dresses and appeared in different costumes during the evening. On the 13th the Prince of Denmark visited Saint-Germain, and found James and Maria falcon-flying. The usual visits were interchanged between the two Courts till March, when Maria d'Este was ill for a few days.

In the spring of 1693 took place an important change in James's Council. The Earl of Middleton was made first minister over the head of Melfort, who, however, made no difficulties about yielding the position to him. The English Jacobites had great confidence in Middleton, and at the French Court he had a high reputation for integrity and honesty. After the battle of La Hogue,[1] communications between James and the English Jacobites had been continued, hopeless as the situation then seemed. The active intriguer Lloyd had become suspect, and James made choice of a certain Cary, a priest, to take his place, and to carry the King's instructions to Middleton in England. Cary returned in January 1693, and brought with him eight proposals which the Jacobite party in England had drawn up. Middleton himself seems to have disapproved, or wished James to think that he did not wholly approve these proposals; James regarded them as hard. The Jacobites had, they said, no doubt that they could immediately effect his restoration, when he had agreed to their terms. Middleton was to come to Saint-Germain to discuss details when they received an answer from the King. As soon as Cary returned, James deputed Melfort to convey the terms of his supporters to Louis XIV. at Versailles. Cary was sent for also and interviewed by De Croissy;[2] both Louis and his minister were of opinion that James had no choice but to agree to them.

Accordingly a declaration was drawn up and reluctantly signed by James, with many searchings of conscience and mental reservations. The compounders would have effected a settlement by the simple expedient of James's resigning his crown in favour of his son, who would then have been educated in the Protestant faith.

[1] May 1692.
[2] Secretary of State for Foreign Affairs.

But to such a suggestion James was incapable of listening for a moment. The declaration that he had to sign was sufficiently humiliating. "We cannot . . . enter into all the particulars of grace and goodness, which we shall be willing to grant, yet we do herebye assure our loving subjects, that they may depend upon every thing their own representatives shall offer, to make our kingdom happy." James promised to lay aside all thoughts of animosity and resentment for the past, which "should be buried in perpetual oblivion"; a free pardon and indemnity to all who should not oppose him by land or sea; a free Parliament was to be called and all grievances redressed; all laws passed since his abdication were to be ratified by him. He was made to promise to "protect and defend the Church of England as it is now established by law, and secure to the members of it all the churches, universities, colleges, and scools together with the immunities, rights and privileges." He promised "an impartial liberty of conscience," and that he would not dispense with religious penal laws. He gave assurances that the Most Christian King would not require any money compensation, but would be content with "the glory of having succor'd an injured Prince"; and the declaration concludes: "We only add, that we come to vindicate our own right, and to establish the liberties of our people, and may God give us grace in the prosecution of the one as we sincerely intend the prosecution of the other.—April 17th, 1693."

James's apparent submission to these terms—for it seems to have been nothing more—was sorely against the grain. In his *Memoirs* he gives a long and puzzle-headed justification of his action, which amounts to little more than that he could not help himself, and he did not mean to keep his word: "He had nothing els to do." The Jacobites in England were not in a position to take the initiative. As for France, the great and long-continued drain of the war was at last making itself acutely felt. "The country being almost ruined by the great taxes, together with the scarcity of wine and corn, occasioned by the great rains which fell the summer before, so that nothing but his Most Christian Majesty's personal vigor and friendship to the King supported it; and should the King have refused those proposals, soever hard they appeared, the clamor of the whole country would have been so great, his Most Christian Majesty could not have been able to have resisted it, and probably the King would have been sent out of the kingdom as an opiniatic bigot." But though James was coerced into acquiescence, he called in his priests to salve his conscience. Those of his own household disapproved of this declaration, but some French divines, including the famous Bossuet, lent their authority in support of James's action. Melfort received instructions from James to exonerate him with the Pope for the apparent leniency of the declaration. "Enfin celle-ci—j'entends la déclaration," he wrote, "n'est que pour rentrer et l'on peut beaucoup mieux disputer des affaires des Catholiques à Whythall [Whitehall] qu'à Saint-Germain."

When Middleton arrived at Saint-Germain, Melfort's unpopularity had reached a point which would soon have brought James's affairs to a standstill. The Scots detested him, the Irish had insisted on his dismissal, and the English, especially the Protestants, despised his abilities and disliked him personally. James never sent an emissary into England, they complained, without bringing particular instructions in his favour.[1] Melfort was not at first superseded on Middleton's arrival at Saint-Germain, and between the two a good understanding seems to be indicated in the cypher letters that Middleton wrote to his friends at home. He was graciously received at Versailles, but was quite unprepared for the high estimation in which the abilities of William III. were held there and in France generally. At Saint-Germain his reception was very cordial :—

"I was overjoyed," he writes, "to find the King and Queen fully convinced how kind and useful I had been to them. I can only tell you in general that the indenture is signed, which you may see at the place you used to go to in a morning where you have often met 540 [me] to whose letter I must likewise refer you. You will not be surprised to hear that lies have been already started at Saint-Germain concerning 78 [Middleton]. But perhaps you may too hear, that from London cautions have been given of me as a Presbyterian and Republican. Excuse my not writing to Lord Churchill. But let him know, that by the next he shall hear from 540 [Middleton] and that his affairs are in as good a posture as we could wish. Post-haste. Adieu." The letter to which he refers his correspondent gives further details of the position of affairs in France: "As to what concerns Wilson [Middleton] he has reason to be satisfied, being entertained by the good farmer [King] and his wife [the Queen], better than he could expect; nor can I omit telling you that the bold Briton [Prince of Wales] surprised me with joy, being infinitely above what has

[1] Clarke, 507.

been reported of him. But what surprised Wilson [Middleton] most was the Lord of the Manor [Louis XIV.]. He less admires his fortunes, since he was acquainted with him, and received civilities from him which he cannot modestly repeat. Both he and his trustees [ministers] seemed satisfied with the particulars and the estate, and are resolved to go on with the purchase, cost what it will, but cannot determine the time, till it appears whether this season proves more favourable than the last. The greatest rub in the matter is the high value they have for him [William III.] who keeps possession, and by the glasses they have used the leech appears to be a leviathan. But nothing has been omitted to undeceive them. It is not to be doubted, but the properest means will be used to pursuade the tenants of their interest to induce them therebye to turn to us. It will be necessary therefore that they should be informed of what is designed. But the precise time is left to the lawyers who are to manage the suit, whose merits I have represented as I ought. . . . In the maine Mr Milles [Melfort] and Wilson [Middleton] are in perfect friendship ; and indeed the first is entirely disposed as you could wish ; and I doubt not you will do him justice both here and there." [1]

This very curious instance of blind prejudice, which characterised so many of Middleton's countrymen, is in marked contrast to William's own attitude about Middleton's migration to France. Like all great men, he was generous in his estimation of the abilities of others, and he expressed to Portland his dissatisfaction with Middleton's presence at Saint-Germain. " I don't at all like M. Middleton's having gone into France,"

[1] Nairne Papers, quoted by Macpherson.

he wrote. "He is not a man who would take such a step without some important and well-schemed intention." ("Il ne me plait nullement que M. Middleton est allé en France. Ce n'est pas un homme qui voudrait faire un tel pas sans quelque chose d'importance et de bien concerté.")

This year two disasters which befell William again raised the hopes of Saint-Germain and gave great impetus to Jacobite activity in England. These were the defeat of the allied troops at the battle of Landen and the loss of the Smyrna fleet. The second of these two misfortunes took place in June. The Smyrna merchant fleet of four hundred vessels sailing for the Mediterranean with wares for the Eastern markets, was attacked and destroyed by the French navy. The English admirals, believing that their protection was no longer necessary, had drawn off their men-of-war, and left the merchant vessels in charge of a small convoy. The loss to England meant several millions, and would have been still greater but for the gallant self-sacrifice of the Dutch ships that were among the convoy. Amidst the universal indignation were murmurs that the fleet had been betrayed by treachery; its departure had been delayed, it was said, until the French were ready to put out to sea, and intelligence of the movements of the enemy had been suppressed by disaffected officials.[1] The defeat at Landen was to a great extent neutralised by William's dauntless energy in reassembling his forces. The losses of the allies were estimated at 2000 men; those of the French were much greater. On this occasion Louis XIV. again went to the front, accompanied by all the paraphernalia of his Court. He

[1] Burnet.

had greatly superior forces, and William himself believed that the situation could be saved only by a miracle.

That miracle was performed for him. The tears of Madame de Maintenon at parting from Louis, and her letters after his departure, weakened his resolution, and he announced his intention of returning to Versailles, and ordered Marshal Luxembourg to send a large detachment of the army into the Palatinate. Luxembourg besought his master on his knees to change so disastrous a resolution. The young Saint-Simon, meeting his superior officer in the camp on the morning of June 9th, was told the news by him with shouts of contemptuous laughter. The general officers were unable to conceal their indignation, while their subordinates spoke loudly with a licence that could not be restrained. Notwithstanding the depletion of his forces, Luxembourg gained a dearly bought victory, after a most bloody and hardly fought contest, in which William III. had part of his scarf carried away by a musket-ball, while another went through his hat. Patrick Sarsfield, Lord Lucan, lost his life; the Duke of Berwick was taken prisoner.

It was at the battle of Landen that the Duke of Berwick, employed with Sarsfield to force the village of Neerwinden, met William of Orange for the first and last time. The Duke, in the rout which followed an unsuccessful charge, was recognised by his uncle, one of the Churchills, and was perforce taken prisoner. After uncle and nephew had embraced one another, "he told me," writes the Duke of Berwick in his memoirs, "that he was obliged to conduct me to the Prince of Orange. We gallopped off for a long time without being able to find him: at last we met him in a hollow where neither friends nor enemies were to be seen. That Prince paid me a very polite compliment, to which I only replied by a very low bow : after having gazed on me for a moment he put on his hat, and I mine : then he ordered that I should be conducted to Lewe." The kinsmen never met again, and Berwick was afterwards exchanged. It was Berwick's fate, happier than that of Sarsfield, to win a reputation only inferior to that of his uncle, the Churchill who became the Duke of Marlborough, as a soldier. Never a great victor, he was an incomparable defensive strategist. Like Sarsfield, "he was brought up to uphold a sinking cause and to utilise in adversity every resource."

France, by gaining this victory of Landen, seemed to have a momentary advantage, but the depletion of her resources by the war was beginning to tell. Two bad harvests in succession, and a failure in the vintage, caused a terrible deficiency in bread and wine ; the misplaced efforts of the government to mitigate the general distress only aggravated it. But peace was not yet, the French demands were too high to be taken into consideration by the Allies. The immediate result of William's reverses was seen in England by a great outburst of activity on the part of the Jacobites, and a whole crop of seditious pamphlets from their unlicensed printing presses. By the spring of 1694, James was in very active communication with Admiral Russell, who was once more in command of the fleet, and with Churchill and Godolphin.

Meanwhile James and Maria went to spend their usual autumn visit at Fontainebleau. They arrived there towards the end of September. The customary routine was observed ; though on this visit Louis appears to have called for Maria every morning and accompanied her to mass, bringing her back to dinner. In the afternoon there were hunting parties, in the evening cards and music, from which Louis always retired to Madame de Maintenon's room after he had done his duty by his guests. James and Maria wore complimentary mourning during their stay, because the French Court were in mourning for the Queen of Sweden, though no notification of her death had been received at Saint-Germain. On Sunday, the 4th of October, Maria learnt news that much distressed her, of the death of Lady Errol, the Prince's governess, a lady whose place was hard to fill. On the same day she wrote to Caryll :—

"I was trewly concerned at the sad news you sent me last night of my poor Lady Erroll's death, which you will easily believe knowing how great a losse she is to me, and how difficult a matter it will be to find one to fill her place, even but near so well as she did ; but God's will must be don in all things, and i will ever submit to it with all the calmnesse that my warme temper is capable of ; i beseeche God to inspire the King and me what to do for the good of our children in this unhappy conjuncture ; i shall be at St Germains by Wednesday night, if it please God, and between you and i, i shall tell you that i long to be ther, tho it is impossible to be used with a greater regarde and kyndnesse then wee are by this King, but a little retirement and the sight of my children is a greater comfort to me than any other this world can give me ; i don't doubt but Fr. Innes will take all imaginable care of Lady Erroll's concerns, and as to the burial if any thing be wanting, you may order Conquest from me to give what money you thall think fit to make it decent, and well, i think her body might be enbalmed, so that if her friends in Scotland should desire it hereafter they might have it, in fine, I would have nothing omitted in any kynd, that may shew the esteem and kyndnesse the King and i had for her, which could not be more than she deserved. If i have time, i will write one word to my sonne, and inclose it in this for you to give him. Pray remember me kindly to Mrs Stafford and Dr Betham, i am perfectly satisfyed they do theyr parte and think it needlesse to recomend it to them. Tell Sir W. Waldgrave that i have received all his trs, and am satisfyed with his care of L^y Erroll, which is all i have to say to you till we meet, for then i shall have something to tell you that will not displease you. M. R."

A few days later the visit ended. With the New Year 1694 James entered on active and widespread negotiations with English Jacobites through his agents, and it is not surprising that the King should have been buoyed up with false hopes, when his former servants were so lavish in promises, and his agents so ready to magnify their success in obtaining them. The disaster to the Smyrna transports had induced William III. to reappoint Russell commander of the fleet, and preparations were being made for destroying the harbour of Brest, where the French fleets had been accustomed to assemble. About the middle of March Lloyd was sent from Saint-Germain to sound Russell, but he could get only vague assurances of support from him in general terms. He then approached Godolphin, who declared that James's Queen had written to the Earl of Peterborough, "assuring him that means would be found to elude what had been seemingly promised, which had so disgusted those engaged in the affair that they resolved never to move their hand for the King's service." This was indignantly denied at Saint-Germain, but the fact remains that James had expressed his intention of not adhering to the terms of his Declaration. Lord Shrewsbury, weak and vacillating as ever, had accepted the Seals; but his intriguing mother assured Lloyd that he had only done so to serve James more effectually hereafter.

Churchill was in a different position from the others. William refused to employ him; he had therefore nothing to lose by serving James, and everything to gain by ruining the only man whose abilities could compare with his own. With callous and cold-blooded cruelty Churchill laid his plans. Russell refused to disclose the destination of the fleet, but Churchill discovered it from other sources. The land forces of the expedition were entrusted to General Talmash, whose death would ensure Churchill's own return to command. He wrote to James early in May, giving all the details of the English plan of campaign. He was only too successful. The English fleet was temporarily delayed; the French hurriedly made preparations to receive them. Believing that the French were unprepared and ignorant of their intentions, Talmash entered the harbour of Brest, and was compelled to beat a hasty retreat, with the loss of a thousand men. Talmash himself was mortally wounded, so that Churchill gained his ends. The death of Talmash, by removing the only man whose abilities could rival Churchill's, obliged the King to recall him to his service. And after this year, as Churchill had nothing further to gain from continuing his intercourse with Saint-Germain, it came to an end.

CHAPTER XVI

JAMES AT LA TRAPPE

WHILE the innocent soul of Queen Maria sought a refuge from the minor mortifications of her daily life in the religious consolations of Chaillot, James strove to expiate the sordid memories of his past days at La Trappe. The Revolution has swept away even the ruins of this sanctuary, to which James retired to make peace with his uneasy conscience. As the Duke of York, he had not a savoury reputation, and even when he was on the throne James outraged the self-respect and pride of his wife by bringing to Court Catherine Sedley, the brazen daughter of a scandalous father. By creating her Countess of Dorchester, he brought on himself the public outburst from his Queen that the ambassador of France and the nuns of Chaillot have alike recorded. " Let me go away," she had exclaimed passionately. "You have made this woman a countess : very well—make her a queen ; put my crown on her head, give her my dowry : I give you up. Only allow me to go and bury myself in some cloister, where I shall not be present at such an indignity. . . . You are ready to sacrifice your life and throne to your faith ; and yet you do not hesitate to sacrifice the safety of your soul to a creature of this kind!"[1] James repented of his weakness even while he was still under the spell of his ugly enchantress: penitence alternated with self-indulgence. But even as late as his Irish campaign, gossip credited the King of England with misconduct. In his latter years James believed himself to be atoning for the sins of the flesh, by emulating the ascetic lives of the recluses of La Trappe. He paid no fewer than ten visits to the convent, staying there three or four days at a time. Engraved above its doorway was the saying of St Bernard, "O solitudo, sola beatitudo." Here the old King learnt to thank God for the loss of all his earthly possessions. "I thank Thee, oh my God, for having deprived me of three kingdoms, if it was to be the means of making me better," became his daily prayer.

The rule at La Trappe was of the severest. The brothers were vowed to silence. On meeting one another they exchanged no other greeting than the warning, "We must die, brother; we must die." They contemplated open graves and slept in winding-sheets. They are described in James's *Memoirs* as "a convent of reformed Bernardins, who living up to the rigour of that most penitential Father's rule, had appear'd of late an astonishing example; what corporal austeritys, self denyals, and eminent perfection, men, who seek the glory of God, and their own salvation with a true Christian fervour, with the assistance of His grace are capable of arriveing too: perpetual silence, except when they sing the office in the church, keeps their thoughts as continually fixed upon God, as their tongues are permitted to utter nothing but His praise;

[1] Cavelli, i. 520.

their surprising abstinence from flesh, fish, eggs, milk, wine, in fine all but herbes, roots, and cider makes a numerous community, live in a manner by their own manual labour, and out of the product of a gardin; this with their other mortifications in watching, habit, labour, could and heat, together with their obedience, abjection, constant attendance at their duty tho' almost continually sick, made the King think it a proper scoole of Christian patience . . . and tho' it seem'd impossible to rais these pious monks to a higher pitch of vertue than they were already arrived too, yet they confessed it gave them an additional fervour to see so great a Prince accomodate himself . . . to their very corporal austeritys; for unless the King was indisposed he always eat in the refectory, suffring no addition but that of eggs to the penetential diet the community lived upon." The rule had been reformed by the celebrated Abbé de Rancé, who came to have all that ascendancy over James that a man of strong character can exercise over a weak mind.

A marginal note in James II.'s *Memoirs* for the year 1695 observes that this year "the King applys himself wholly to devotion." In proportion as James's earthly prospects paled, his mind turned to the compensations of a future life; but as early as the defeat of the French fleet at La Hogue in May 1692, his inclinations would have led him to forgo the unequal struggle of fanaticism and incompetence against genius. In December of that year he wrote to the Abbé de la Trappe: "You have left the world to work out your salvation; happy are those who can do it, those are the only people I envy." And his biographer adds: "The continual contradictions the King met with had so weaned him from all thoughts of present happyness, as made him in a manner now attend solely to the business of gaining a future one, to which he perceived Providence might lead him by the paths of affliction and suffring, the surest road for all, but especially such, who are penetrated with a grief and detestation of their former disorders; which the King was too humble not to acknowlidg himself guilty of, and too just not to think a punishment due too; which made him embrace even with chearfullness and alacrity such as it pleased God to send, and even ad many of his own, which, had not the discretion of his Director restrained him in, might have gon to excess."[1]

It was the first year after his return from Ireland that James began his practice of retiring to La Trappe, notwithstanding the private derision to which he was sensible that it exposed him; but the spiritual profit he reaped from it made him continue it every year, and "overlook the censures of worldly men, whose judgements are seldom true, generally ill grounded and always to be despised in such cases as these." It was always James's custom to write notes of current affairs, but in these later years he spent much time in putting on paper spiritual reflections and prayers, in which, says Mr Secretary Nairne, the King "describes what passed within his own soul, filled with the sentiments of repentance and devotion. It may truly be said, that his own picture is to be seen in them, drawn to the life, as he was in his latter days: for he practised himself all that he hath here writ." He sought in some sense to approximate his life at Saint-Germain to that of the devout monks of La Trappe.

[1] Clarke's *Life*, ii. 496.

"Although I am a great admirer of La Trappe and of the holy and exemplary lives of the monks in that convent, and am overjoyed, when I hear that any has left the world to retire thither, and though I have great reason to praise the Divine Goodness, for having put it into my thoughts to visit that holy place, as I have derived so great advantages from it; yet I cannot be so partial as to think that a man cannot work out his salvation in the world without retiring to La Trappe or some other strict order . . . for our obligations to live in the world and to discharge the duties of the station to which God has called us do by no means hinder us from leading a Christian life. . . . We are all of us, as well as the monks of La Trappe, obliged to take up our cross and follow our Saviour; and although the duty of our station does not permit us to practise so austere a silence as they do, yet we are not less obliged than they are to govern our tongues in such a manner, as not to offend our neighbour. Likewise although we have not made vows to govern our eyes in the same manner as they have, we are as much obliged as they are, to set a watch upon our eyes, so as that we may avoid to look on the dangerous objects which have caused the ruin of so many souls; and although we are not under an obligation to practise so much abstinence, nor to apply to manual labour as they do, yet we are obliged to observe temperance and sobriety in our eating, and not to allow ourselves to go to any excess in that way; and if we cannot work with our hands, we ought always to avoid idleness, to apply, with attention to our own business and to assist our neighbour as much as we can. Lastly we should have the same Christian spirit with the monks of La Trappe and allow ourselves to be guided by the same maxims, and each in his own station and manner should endeavour to work out his own salvation with the same care and the same fear and trembling, as they do."

It was with such pious if undistinguished compositions that the King sustained his leisure hours at Saint-Germain. The prayers that he composed are more characteristic :—

"*His Majesty's thanksgiving to God for the particular benefit bestowed upon him.*

"I thank Thee, oh God, for all the favours which Thou hast done me ; and particularly, for having saved me from the hands of the rebellious paricides who put to death the King my father. For having protected me, in all combats sieges and battles, in which I have been, by sea and by land, and for having delivered me from so many other dangers to which I have been exposed. For having given me such good health and patience to suffer so many injuries, and for having preserved me till now from all the snares of my enemies. For having touched my heart with a true sense of my past sins, and a regret for them ; a favour, which I beseech God to continue to me ; and to augment in me day by day, a detestation of my faults. And above all l thank God for having opened my eyes, and converted me to the true Church."

It was perhaps in 1695, when, as he says, the "constant ill success of all the King's endeavours had long convinced him that Providence had marked out no other way for his sanctification than that of suffring," that he drew up the following questions to his confessor, the Abbé de Rancé. They were preserved in Nairne's handwriting,[1] and show the state of abject self-abasement at which James had arrived :—

"*Qu.* 1. Whether considering the life I have led, and that my age, as well as the station I am in, does hinder me from using those penances and mortifications, which

[1] Macpherson's Original Papers.

would be requisite to shew the abhorrence and detestation I have of my past offences against so good and gracious a God, I ought not to be content, as a greater penance than can be inflicted on me in this world, not to make use of the prayers of the Church, to endeavour by them to shorten my time of being in purgatory ? And whether, what I have designed for that use may not be better employed in charities and praying for all the faithful departed ?

"*Qu.* 2. Whether it is not more meritorious and better to lay aside, whilst one is alive, for such charities and other pious uses, as one designs, than to leave the burden on one's heirs and successors ? And whether it is not deceiving one's self to expect any merit from such gifts, as one leaves to be paid by his heirs, after his decease, since it is a burden upon them, and that one does not feel the inconveniency of it one's self ?"

James's religion was a craven and a fearful thing. The sense of God's mercy and lovingkindness, or of the peace that passeth all understanding, were far from his confused and troubled soul. Priest-ridden and timorous, he looked up to Heaven much as Caliban regarded his Setebos :—

> "Lo! Lieth flat and loveth Setebos!
> Maketh his teeth meet through his upper lip,
> Will let those quails fly, will not eat this month
> One little mess of whelks, so he may 'scape."

"He sought rather than avoided," wrote Innes, "those humiliations which affected his own person, and was not content with that abjection the malice of his enemies had reduced him too ; but by contemplating his own former failings as to his morral life, more than the indignities he had suffered in respect of his character, he was much more intent to do penance for the one, then to be deliver'd from the other; this made him turn St Germains into a sort of solitude, and not content with that went to seek it at certain times where it was to be found in its greatest perfection."[1] Yet, in spite of all the honest endeavours after a religious life which his priestly scribe admiringly records, James never attained to the spirit of forgiveness. He could single out for punishment the poor crowd of ignorant fishermen who had handled him roughly at Feversham. He was far from attaining to the spirit of "the truly patient man" who "minds not by whom he is exercised, whether by his superiors, by one of his equals, or by an inferior; . . . but indifferently from every creature, how much soever, or how often soever anything adverse befall him, he takes it all thankfully as from the hand of God, and esteems it great gain."[2]

Perhaps it was in a sense of humanity that poor James was primarily lacking, and it is that which makes him appear so unlovable. It was his own soul which he sought so assiduously to save; as he says of La Trappe, "it gave me a true sence of the vanitie of all worldly greatness and that nothing was to be covited but the love of God, and to endeavour to live up to his law, and to mortify one's self by all lawful means, and to be sencible (at least such a miserable creature as I that have lived so many years almost in a continual cours of sin till God out of his infinite mercy call'd me by his chastisement to him) how necessary it is to continue visiting such a holy place to gain strength, who have so much need of it."

---

[1] Clarke, ii. 528. Supposed to have been written by Innes.
[2] The *Imitatio Christi*.

The Abbey of La Trappe,[1] which was founded when St Bernard was Abbot of Clairvaux, lay in a deep valley on the western edge of a wild and isolated forest, alternating with wide stretches of water. At the time James visited it, it contained about forty-eight inhabitants. The rule, which had fallen into disuse, was restored by the Abbé de Rancé. In doing so while still young himself, he had to struggle against monks whose advanced years gave to their resistance, as to their bad habits, the sanction of experience, and the authority of old age. Although he wished to bring them back to the ancient practice of their discipline, he had against him the appearance of making innovations; he incurred the reproach of changeability, inconstancy, exaggeration. In order to succeed in his desired end, he employed the only means which ensure success—gentleness, firmness, and perseverance. His attempt provoked bitter animosity and revolt. The indignant monks reproached him with the notorious shortcomings of his own youth, and then opposed to him the more impregnable resistance of inertia. So high ran the feeling against him, that he was in danger of personal violence. But De Rancé's patience and firmness triumphed. In 1663, with the exception of a few old men, who were pensioned off, the monastery reverted to the strict observance of the Rule of St Bernard. The studies of the monks were limited by De Rancé to the Bible and some treatises on asceticism; their occupations, to prayer and agricultural labour.

The desolate neighbourhood he rendered even more lonely by diverting a road which led near the convent to some distance from it. The soil was poor and sterile,

[1] Du Bois' *Histoire de La Trappe*.

the climate unhealthy from the abundance of stagnant water; the only inhabitants, miserable beggars who inhabited huts on the stony slopes. The convent itself was planned with a view to the exercise of that charity and hospitality which in bygone days rendered these institutions so great a boon to the poor, and to those who journeyed through unpopulated neighbourhoods. The first court contained a hospice for travellers of both sexes; it was separated by a high palisade and a thick hedge from the court of the monks. Beyond was a large court-yard planted with fruit trees; here stood the dove-cot till 1674, when it was pulled down, as flesh food was forbidden to the monks. On the left were the storehouses and outhouses necessary for the agricultural labours on which the monks were always engaged. The mill was beyond this lower court. It was worked by a stream which separated the great court and the garden of the monks from the church. At the door of the convent one of the monks fulfilled the office of porter. The visitor entered a little hall with the reception room for strangers or guests on the right, and the dining-room on the left. While waiting in the reception room he read the following rules :—

"On supplie très humblement ceux que la divine providence conduira dans ce monastère, de trouver bon qu'on les avertisse des choses qui suivent.

"On gardera dans le cloître un perpétual silence. Lorsque l'on parle dans les lieux destinés pour cela, ou même dans les jardins, on le fait d'un ton de voix le moins élevé que l'on peut.

"On évite la rencontre des religieux autant qu'il est possible, en tout temps dans celui du travail manuel.

"On s'adresse au portier si l'on a besoin de quelque chose dans le monastère parceque les religieux qui sont étroitement obligés au silence ne donnent nulle réponse à ceux qui leur parlent. On ne se promène dans les jardins entre onze heures et midi."

Visitors were allowed a slightly less restricted diet than that of the monks. They dined on soup, two or three dishes of vegetables, and a plate of eggs. They had wine, cider, and beer to drink. The guests' chambers were kept scrupulously clean. Women were not allowed in the church; they attended a little chapel in the court.

James's first visit to La Trappe was paid in November 1690.[1] He arrived there towards evening, and as soon as the Abbot heard of his arrival he hastened to receive him at the door of the monastery. When the King alighted, De Rancé prostrated himself before him. "It is the custom among these solitaries to behave thus towards all those from outside who come to visit them, but the Abbot performed this action, with so profound a humility and such a lively expression of it on his features, and in his manners, that it was easy to judge, that in respecting the sacred dignity of the King's person, one could add nothing to the veneration that he had for virtue."

James was distressed at seeing the holy man thus abase himself, and hastened to raise him, on which the Abbot exclaimed: "Sire, God visits us in your person; it is a grace and an honour of which we are not worthy, but it is at the same time an inexpressible consolation. What happiness for us to see in this desert this great prince on whose behalf we have for so long continually

[1] This account is taken from "The Materials for the Life of James by Johnston, Prior of the Benedictines in Paris," Add. MSS., British Museum.

offered prayers to God! Yes, sire, we do nothing more frequently or more ardently than ask God that He will accord to your sacred person all the strength and all the protection necessary to it, that He may pour forth His grace upon you, and that He will finally give you the immortal crown that He has prepared for all those who have had the happiness, like your Majesty, to follow Jesus Christ, and to prefer Him before all things." James replied to this exordium in suitable terms, and was then conducted to the church to pray. The Abbot afterwards brought him back to the hall, where they talked together till it was time for complines, which the King attended.

James was entreated to retire immediately after service, because the church was very cold and damp; but he insisted on remaining for the quarter of an hour's meditation which completed the religious exercises of the day. Supper was then served to him by the monks and others. It consisted of roots, eggs, and vegetables, which he ate with a good appetite, in spite of the simplicity of the repast. A cleanly poverty reigned everywhere, and took the place of the magnificence with which kings are accustomed to be served. The Abbé remained near the King, who, turning continually to talk to him, questioned him about the solitary life. . . . He admired the framed rules of conduct, and gave orders that copies should be made for Saint-Germain. When he retired for the night, Abbé de Rancé accompanied him, and remained in talk for half an hour in his room.

The next day the King rose early, and attended Tierce and High Mass, sitting in the first chair to the right of the altar. While he made his confession and

JAMES AT LA TRAPPE

communion, the choir sang Psalm 118, which occurred in the office for the day, the feast of St Cecilia. All present were struck by its appropriateness. James remained to Low Mass, and then went to watch the monks at work. He "admired the order, the modesty, the silence of these holy solitaries." But he found the work very rough for people not intended by Providence for manual labour, who were moreover weakened by fasting and by the austerity of their rule. He commented on this to the Abbé. De Rancé replied: "That might be so if one were working for pleasure, but when one worked as an act of penitence one did not count the cost, and found strength sufficient for it." James insisted on sitting at the Abbot's table, with De Rancé on his right, Bellefonds on the left. He also used the service of copper and faience that was in use in the convent, and shared the ordinary food of the monks. During the meal, which lasted an hour, silence was preserved while one read aloud. An elaborate code of signs was practised by the monks as a means of communication when it was necessary.

Lord Bellefonds having told James about a hermit who lived at some distance in the woods, the King was anxious to visit him, and did so accompanied by Bellefonds and Dumbarton. Bellefonds inquired of the recluse how he managed to attend mass every morning in winter when there were no roads and snow was lying. The solitary replied that what he had done for an earthly king when he was a soldier, he could do for a heavenly King. "But what do you do all day? aren't you bored?" persisted the flippant inquirer. The hermit replied that, when one's thoughts were continually directed towards eternity, time seemed a thing of small moment. He went on to tell them of his military life and experiences. "You gave up all that," exclaimed Dumbarton, "to retire into this desert?" "By the grace of God," replied the hermit, "I make little account of all worldly fortunes." On taking leave of him James regarded the solitary long and earnestly, almost with envy, it seemed to the bystanders. "À bien, monsieur," he said at last, "pray God for me, for the Queen, and for my son." The anchorite replied by a profound reverence, and the King retraced his steps to La Trappe, passing with indifference over the rough road and through wet fields which lay between him and it. On his return he attended vespers and complines.

Next day he heard mass at 5.30, and listened to the prayers for those about to set out on a journey. While he was waiting for his carriage in the guest-room, it was noted that he read attentively the rules of conduct for the forgiveness of enemies, as if he would commit them to memory. On bidding farewell to the Abbé, he said, with that kindly air which characterised him : "One must come here to learn how God ought to be prayed to and served. I shall try to imitate you as far as it is possible in my position, and I hope, God willing, that this will not be my last journey here." So far from its being the King's last visit, it became his annual practice, and on at least one occasion he was accompanied by the Queen. There are two letters of hers relating to her journey to La Trappe and her experience there. The first of these was written to Chaillot in May 1696 : "I believe my dear Mother will not be vexed to learn that I am at last resolved to give myself the pleasure of visiting La Trappe. I shall begin my journey on Saturday, please God, and shall sleep that night at Chartres, where I shall remain all Sunday, to perform my devotions in the Church of Notre Dame, and I shall find also a few minutes to go and see our sisters who are in the town. Monday I shall sleep at La Trappe, where I shall stay two whole days, leaving on Thursday morning. I shall be back here [Saint-Germain] Friday evening. For my journey I shall want the costume which is at Chaillot, which please send me."

Besides his intercourse with La Trappe, James was assiduous in visiting convents and churches in Paris and the neighbourhood which were famous for their piety. He practised penances regularly in his own house, adding "many bodily mortifications to his long and assiduous prayers, as fasting, discipline, and wearing at certain times an iron chain, with little sharp points which pierced his skin."[1] He fasted on Saturdays from Christmas to Candlemas, though it was not the custom, and the Queen attempted to dissuade him from it, pointing to Mr Innes, the almoner in attendance, whom she instanced as an example of a good man who did not fast on these days. "Upon which the King whispered the Queen in the ear, 'Had I lived in my youth as Mr Innes has done, I would now doe as he does.'"[2] He was sensitive about concealing his acts of self-chastisement, and "haveing once accidentally left his discipline where the Queen fortuned to see it, her Majesty never perceived him, (she said), in greater confusion." On the same principle, James "shun'd not the diversions of the French Court; till the end of his life he hunted, and accepted the Most Christian

[1] Clarke.   [2] *Ibid.*

King's invitations to Versailles, though "he was for takeing away, if possible, by publick authority all such dangerous diversions as gameing, operas, plays and the like." In his last years "he was far from saying any harsh or bitter things of those who had used him with the greatest indignity, . . . looking upon them as instruments of God's justice to exercise his patience, . . . and therefore blessed God for his misfortunes, which brought him into the occasion of knowing the truth in his youth, and of following its prescriptions in his old age."

CHAPTER XVII

FURTHER JACOBITE NEGOTIATIONS—THE ASSASSINATION PLOT

THE year 1694 passed uneventfully for Maria d'Este. Like the other five of her exile, it had been one of frustrated hopes. She seems to have recovered from the painful illness of which she complains to her friends at Chaillot in the closing days of December 1693, for she and James were much at Versailles, staying there till one o'clock to play lansquenet with Monseigneur on January 5th. A hard frost put a stop to all hunting and outdoor sports, and made the roads impassable. But in February James and his wife went to Versailles to celebrate Mardi Gras, which fell on February 23rd. A masked ball of great magnificence took place; the young Duchesse de Chartres and her sisters led the dancing, and James and Maria stayed till one o'clock, though Monseigneur kept up the dancing till four.

In May the cabal against Melfort was at last successful in effecting his dismissal,[1] for he was besides accused of infidelity to James by English Jacobites. James himself parted from him very reluctantly. When Louis

[1] "Il y avait à Saint-Germain une cabale fort opposée à lui" (Dangeau).

went over to Saint-Germain a few days later, on June 2nd, the English King told him that Melfort would be given some new title in recompense for his dismissal, and in token of his own and the Queen's unalterable regard. Middleton remained at the head of James's advisers, an arrangement much more pleasing to Versailles; but Melfort was obviously a more congenial adviser to James, whose arbitrary nature resented all suggestions of compromise urged by Middleton [1] and the party he represented. That Melfort was neither in favour with Middleton nor Louis XIV.'s ministers appears clearly enough from a letter written by Middleton to John Caryll from Fontainebleau, when James and Maria were staying there later in this year: "I wish the Lord Melfort does not come to spit in our potage; for if the ministers believe that he will be acquainted with what hath been proposed, we need think no more about it." [2]

From Maria's letters to Chaillot and to John Caryll at this time, she seems to have taken little pleasure in the numerous visits they were paying to Fontainebleau and to Versailles—in spite of the efforts which Louis made to amuse and interest her in his fountains and in his new contrivance of moving mechanical bridges on one of the artificial lakes. None the less they may have served as a distraction from the sordid anxiety about money which seems to have pressed more heavily than usual on the Court of Saint-Germain at this time, when the claims of their pensioners were outrunning their means of supporting them.

[1] Melfort succeeds with the King by humouring him and always telling him that he is right, said Tyrconnel (Avaux).
[2] Macpherson, October 3rd, 1694.

Middleton wrote in June to an English member of Parliament :—

"I have received yours of the 23rd of May. It is most certainly true that the merchant who owns the goods, 368 [King James] stands in great need of money, and indeed it is not to be wondered at, considering his great losses and his numerous family; and would therefore be glad if any of his friends or old customers would advance him what they can spare, which shall be punctually repaid with interest as soon as he is in a condition to appear on the exchange. In the mean time he might be put in a condition to maintain his poor workmen, who are in great misery."[1]

In August Louis commissioned the artist Mignard to paint James and Maria's portraits. They came to Versailles to sit to him, because "Le bonhomme Mignard" who was over eighty, declined to go to Saint-Germain on the score of its being unhealthy.[2]

A gloom was cast over the visit of the English royal family to Fontainebleau this year by the news of the death of Maria d'Este's brother, the Duc de Modena, who was succeeded by her uncle, the Cardinal Rinaldo d'Este. The Queen learned of her brother's death on Sunday, September 26th. She was overcome with grief and spent the next day in bed, where all the courtiers came to condole with her in the evening. All amusements were suspended. The next day Louis was ill with gout and unable to leave his room, and he was still an invalid when James and Maria's visit came to an end next day, so that Monseigneur and Madame saw them off. Louis's next visit to Saint-Germain, at

---

[1] Nairne Papers in Macpherson.
[2] "Qu'il y a de maladies" (Dangeau).

the beginning of December, was for the purpose of inquiring into an untoward incident that had recently taken place there between some of James's and his own men, in which two Englishmen, the Governor of the Bass and his brother, had been killed in a scuffle. The accused had taken flight, so that justice could not be done; but James was much distressed at the loss of his adherents.

So the year slipped away without having materially altered the position of the exiles at Saint-Germain for better or for worse. In 1695 James, to quote his *Memoirs*, "applied himself wholly to devotion." He inaugurated this access of piety by turning one of his illegitimate daughters out of the house. She was Henrietta, the widow of Lord Waldegrave, the former English ambassador at the French Court, who had died some time before, and, like the Duke of Berwick, was the daughter of Arabella Churchill, Marlborough's sister. But "its having been discovered," as Dangeau discreetly puts it, "that she was *dans un état où une femme veuve ne doit pas être*," she was banished to a Paris convent. The affair appears to have been conducted with considerable publicity, and James and Maria evidently thought the scandal aggravated by Lady Waldegrave's refusing to give any clue to the author of her disgrace. This sordid little tragedy had a sequel two months later, when she married Lord Galmoy, James and Maria still declining to see her again. She went subsequently to live in England. Lord Galmoy already had a record in Ireland of cruelty and treachery, though he was a capable cavalry leader. The murder of Captain Dixie, to which allusion has been made, left an indelible stain on his character, and was directly responsible for the bloody and ruthless character of some of the fighting—at Newtown Butler, Enniskillen, and elsewhere—which afterwards took place. Galmoy had stayed in Ireland till the last, fighting under St Ruth, and being present in the last stand before Limerick. William gave permission to Lady Galmoy to return to England in November of the same year. Her mother, Arabella Churchill, had married some time before James left England, and cherished a violent hostility towards her former lover, although he had recognised all her children, in opposition to the wishes of Maria. James must, or should, have felt at this time that the sins of his youth were being visited upon him, for both he and his wife were much opposed to the marriage which the Duke of Berwick contracted on March 26th with Lady Lucan, Sarsfield's widow. It was a love-match, and took place at Montmartre. James had gone over to Versailles the Sunday before to tell Louis privately about it.

If James was disappointed in the marriages of his natural children, he learned with indifference of the death of his eldest legitimate daughter. The news of Mary's death from small-pox, which had taken place at the end of the year (December 28th, 1694), was not confirmed at Saint-Germain till January 15th following. Her father comments on "so favourable an occasion for engaging in some new attempt," but adds that "all the King got by it was an additional affliction to those he already underwent, by seeing a child he loved so tenderly persever to her death in such a signal state of disobedience and disloyalty." He stooped to the pettiness of requesting Louis XIV. that the French Court might not wear mourning.

The hopes of Saint-Germain were raised by the news

of the complete mental and physical prostration of William III. after his wife's death. In England a scheme for the King's assassination was set on foot in the spring of 1695, by the lowest class of adventurers among the Jacobites. Sir John Fenwick, a notòrious and swaggering malcontent, had cognisance of it, but afterwards denied that he had approved of their design ; and while the conspirators were awaiting James's authorisation of the scheme, William had sufficiently recovered himself to go into Flanders.

In the Flanders campaign of the coming year the tide of success turned in William's favour. The fortunes of France, and with them those of James, underwent a heavy and irreparable loss in the death of the distinguished general who had defeated the Allies at Steinkirk and Landen. " M. de Luxembourg est mort ce matin," wrote Maria to Chaillot on January 4th. " Le roy y fait une grande perte, et par conséquent nous aussi."

Louis replaced Luxembourg in the command of his troops by the Duc de Villeroy, a man to whom he was personally attached, but who had small qualifications for the post. The young Duc de Maine was to accompany him to the Netherlands. Meanwhile William III., leaving an army in Flanders under Vaudemont, proceeded to invest the fortress of Namur, which he had determined to retake. Villeroy wrote to Versailles that he would compel William to retire after he had defeated Vaudemont. But he had formed his plans without estimating the character of the Duc de Maine in the capacity of subordinate officer. This young man now proved himself an apt pupil of Madame de Maintenon. When he received orders to

FURTHER JACOBITE NEGOTIATIONS 353

charge, he insisted on first confessing to a priest; thus invaluable time was lost, and Vaudemont was able to effect a retreat. The general officers saw in desperation an easy victory slipping from their grasp. One of them came to the Duc de Maine and implored him with tears to obey orders; but, stammering and nerveless, he refused to stir. No one dared tell Louis the truth: the Duc de Maine—Madame de Maintenon's nurse-child—was the dearest of all his children, legitimate or illegitimate. To learn what had really taken place, he sent for a valet called Lavienne, "an honest, but coarse, rough, and outspoken man."[1] From him he learned the humiliating truth. Studiously composed as Louis XIV. was in all emergencies of life, his self-control was not proof against this blow to his pride. Shortly afterwards, as he was leaving the dinner table, he saw a servant, in the act of clearing away the dessert, put a small biscuit in his pocket, whereupon the King, rushing upon the terrified man, broke his cane across his shoulders, while the courtiers, who could form no conjecture as to the real cause of the King's anger, looked on fearful and bewildered. Meanwhile William had achieved his purpose; the fortress of Namur had surrendered, and Boufflers, the general commanding it, had been arrested in response to Louis XIV.'s breach of faith over the garrisons of Dixmuyde and Deyne, who had been carried as prisoners into France. This was the great military event of the year.

Meanwhile life at Saint-Germain had run on its usual course. Maria d'Este had been ailing again early in the year, for, writing to Sister Marie Constance at Saint-Cyr on the Tuesday in Easter week, she says: " I

[1] Saint-Simon.

passed the three holy days at Chaillot in good health, thank God, but since Easter Day I have not been very well. It is not a serious illness, but it is tiresome for me, since it prevents my going to Versailles to pay my court to the King, whom I have not had the honour of seeing for a long time."

In April James and Maria may have been present at the wedding festivities of their friend Lauzun. This intrepid adventurer now settled down in life. On May 28th he married Mademoiselle de Lorges, sister-in-law of the Duc de Saint-Simon, a little girl of fifteen, who had attracted the elderly attentions of Lauzun (he was then sixty-three) at the wedding reception of Madame de Saint-Simon. "You are a bold man," said Louis to the bride's father, "to take Lauzun into your family." The wedding was private, but the bride afterwards "received company in bed." Lauzun had not asked a dowry with his wife, and she was to remain under her father's roof; but he very soon had a violent rupture with her family and took her away.

With the graceful kindliness that always characterised Louis XIV. in his dealings with Maria, he had a party at Trianon for the celebration of little Prince James's seventh birthday, on June 20th. They arrived in the evening for lansquenet, and saw a performance of Lully's last opera, *Acis and Galatea*, returning home after supper. Another little instance of the French King's consideration for her is noted by Dangeau in the following August, when Louis had arranged to meet Maria in the Forest of Marly for a stag-hunt. The weather was atrocious, but he persisted in keeping his appointment because he "had promised this little diversion to the Queen of England," and he thought that in any case they would be able to go for a drive together, "being always very careful to give to the Queen every consolation great or small that was in his power." In July James had spent some days at La Trappe, and in October he and his wife paid their annual visit to Fontainebleau. They left home on September 28th, early in the morning, and dined at Frémont, where Louis's servants attended on them, arriving at Fontainebleau at eight in the evening. Maria was accompanied by the Duchess of Tyrconnel, the Comtesse d'Almond, and the Duchess of Berwick. The visit was much the same as former ones. The usual "appartements" took place in the evening, from which Maria absented herself on Saturday in order to make her confession for the Sunday communion. The days passed in music, cards, and hunting parties. Louis always spent some time with his guests every evening, and saw that the Queen's card-party was made up before he withdrew to Madame de Maintenon's rooms. Maria gave some account of this visit in a letter from Fontainebleau to Mère Priolo, the ex-mother superior at Chaillot, "La Déposée":—

"For the last six days I have been trying in vain to find a moment in which to write to you, my very dear Mother. Yesterday evening I thought myself sure of one before supper, but M. de Pontchartrain[1] came into my room, as I was finishing the letter to our Mother, and prevented me. It was not any more possible to do it before leaving Saint-Germain, but you are sure of my heart, my dear Mother, and for that reason I know well that you will not stand on ceremony over my letter. . . . I try here to do my best towards God and man, but alas! I fail greatly in my duty

[1] Minister of Finances.

towards both. There is a great deal of dissipation here, but it is true besides, that I am never so convinced of the littleness and vanity of the world, as when I am in the midst of its greatness and its highest magnificence. To-morrow I shall complete my thirty-seventh year; pray God, my dear Mother, that I do not pass another without serving and loving Him with my whole heart. I entreat Him to fill yours with His Divine consolation, or with strength to forgo it. . . . I am as usual here always very well treated by the King and everyone else."

The visit of the King and Queen ended on October 11th.

They paid other visits during the last months of the year; but from this time on, when James and Maria went over to spend an evening at Marly or Versailles, the Queen adopted the discomposing habit of leaving the card-table during the evening for an hour or so, in order to say her prayers—a practice that must have savoured rather of ostentation. Later she returned and played again till supper-time. The visits that the French royal family paid to Saint-Germain seem to have been merely in the nature of afternoon calls. They were always of frequent occurrence. Monseigneur and La Princesse de Conti sometimes came over together, and James often joined royal hunting parties. The year 1695 had been uneventful, but 1696 dawned with fresh hopes for the exiles of Saint-Germain. James, "awaked again about the beginning of 1696 by fresh solicitations from his friends in England, was prevailed upon to try his fortunes once more." The King of France lent his support to the scheme. This was James's last chance, and the last serious menace which beset William from Jacobite animosity.

During the winter the English Jacobites had been

FURTHER JACOBITE NEGOTIATIONS

boldly displaying their sentiments, aggressively drinking their symbolic toasts to King James, and announcing their expectations of a revolution in his favour in the near future. The Jacobite scheme was twofold. James's English supporters were to rise in arms, while an army of ten or twelve thousand men was to be assembled at Calais and invade England, with James at its head. But to make things doubly secure a secret plot was formed, known only to a few conspirators, for the assassination of William. The scheme of invasion was doomed to failure from the first, owing to James's inveterate disingenuousness. Just as a debtor can never prevail upon himself to give a complete statement of his liabilities to the well-wisher who is seeking to clear him from them, so James was guilty at this crucial moment of a duplicity towards the man to whom he already owed so much, which ruined the last chance of his ever seeing England again.

At the outset James seems to have conveyed to Louis a wrong impression of the intentions of his supporters quite honestly. A certain Mr Powell, deputed by the leading Jacobites to acquaint James with their intentions about the beginning of February, had a rather hurried audience with the King and Queen at Saint-Germain, and, carried away by zeal, gave them the impression that "the Jacobits offered to rise out of hand, if the King were but ready to pass." James told him to put the messages from his supporters in writing, but immediately after gave verbal information to Louis that England was ready to rise whenever required.

On this understanding the French King prepared for an invasion. It was not till James received Powell's written note of his instructions that he realised that his Jacobite supporters were prepared to declare themselves only when he was landed at the head of a French army. James then dishonestly determined to leave Louis under the false impression he had given him. He "thought not fit to unsay what had been already tould his Most Christian Majesty, or alarme the French Ministers, which would certainly retard the preparations, if not make them be quite laid aside." Thus the preparations went on. Berwick was deputed to go to England to make all arrangements with the English Jacobites for their rising, and to tell them that French troops were being assembled in readiness for embarkation at Calais as soon as the news arrived that their insurrection had begun.

Another point of interest concerning this scheme of invasion is its bearing on the question of how much James knew about the Assassination Plot. His *Memoirs* protest that he "was no ways privy to the design, neither commissioned the persons nor approved the thing"; but Sir George Barclay, the leader and instigator of the plot, relates how the King "called me into his closet" for a private audience, before he left Saint-Germain, and gave a written commission authorising "such . . . acts against the P^ce of Orange and his adherents as may conduce most to our service."

On February 28th James left Saint-Germain for Calais, after many interviews with Louis XIV., being "hasten'd away from the Court of France sooner than otherwise he intended, . . . which giveing too early an alarme, hinder'd his friends in England from performing their part, and in the end ruined the whole designe."

FURTHER JACOBITE NEGOTIATIONS 359

Louis had hurried James off because he thought the secret of the proposed invasion could no longer be kept, giving him parting injunctions "not to let the men embarke till he was sure the Jacobits were up in England." On the way to Calais, where he arrived on the 2nd of March, James met Berwick returning with the unwelcome news that the English would not rise till the invasion was accomplished. Berwick was well aware of the details of the Assassination Plot. James, however, went on "after having heard the relation and what condition he had left things in in England," as "he still hoped something might happen, on which he could rais a request to let the troops embarke first." There can be little doubt that this "something" was William's assassination, for Berwick had gone on to Versailles to acquaint Louis with its probable accomplishment.

Berwick's own account of his visit to England is quite without ambiguity on this point. "I went to London," he says, "where I had general conversations with some of the principal Lords, but it was in vain that I told them all the strongest reasons that I could imagine to impress on them the necessity of not letting slip so favourable an opportunity; they remained firm in their desire that before they rose, the King of England should land with an army." Berwick admits that they were wise in this decision, because, if a revolt had taken place in England, William would have instantly blockaded the French ports, while the raw levies of the insurgents would have been opposed by disciplined and seasoned troops. On learning of the Assassination Plot, Berwick immediately returned to France, "in order not to find myself confounded with the conspirators, whose design appeared to me difficult of accomplishment." On reaching France he met James, who had, he thought, been "too precipitately" despatched by the French Court. He informed Louis XIV. of the Assassination Plot, and it was decided that all should go on as arranged if anything happened. Berwick then returned to Calais to await events, while James was waiting at Calais or at Boulogne, whither he went later.

The Queen was in her usual state of anxious disquietude in his absence. She had been ill in the early part of February. Monseigneur, coming over to call, had found her in bed; but she was sufficiently recovered to take refuge with her friends at Chaillot the day her husband left. She was not, however, in good health, for she writes from Saint-Germain in March to "La Déposée": "If you could imagine, my dear Mother, to what point I have been overwhelmed by pain and business since I left you, your good heart would have pity on mine, which is more oppressed and discouraged than it has ever been.... The King remains at Calais, or perhaps is now at Boulogne. As long as he remains there, there is some hope." Louis was more than usually assiduous in paying the Queen visits of consolation during these weeks of waiting, but she did not recover either her health or spirits. At a review at Gressillon in April, at which Louis attended the door of her carriage on horseback, those present commented on the great change in her appearance since her illness, which was accentuated by the fact that, as a pious tribute to her husband, Maria never rouged in his absence.

She had, though, other occupations besides saying her

prayers and being entertained by Louis. She evidently took an active part in whatever business was being transacted. There had been much discussion as to what form of Declaration James ought to draw up : he seems to have intended to please all parties by confining himself to amiable generalities, and only dispersing his Declaration on landing. It is evidently to this fact that Maria alludes in the following letter to Caryll :—

"I have sent my tre to Paris as you desired to go by the post. Col. Dorington goes to-morrow morning post to the King. if ther be any mor declarations don, you might send them by him ; i have to-day a tre from the King from Montreuille, wher he lay a thursday night ; . . . the King sends me no news at all, he was to be yesterday at noon at Calais ; M. de Croissi is sick and could not com hither, he has sent me l'Abbé Renaudaux[1] to whom i have given the declaration, to give to Croissi from me.   M. R."

Another letter follows closely on the above. Caryll seems to have been the only person outside Chaillot upon whose sympathy and understanding the Queen felt she could rely, and in the next few years the tone of her letters to him becomes more and more intimate and affectionate, and even gay. She was now again at Chaillot :—

"CHAILLOT, *Sunday night, Ap.* 1696.

"I kept the groom in hopes to have sent you word that i had heard of the King's being at Calais, but ther was no tre for me at the post-house this day, which i believe was caused by the King's not coming to Calais a Friday till the post was gon, but to-morrow I shall certainly heare, and send you hear enclosed the news

[1] The Abbé Renaudot was a political agent, and a friend to the Jacobite cause. The Renaudot Papers in the Bibliothèque Nationale are a valuable source of information on the Stuarts at this period.

that the King of France was pleased to send me this afternoon, which you will see by his owne tre was all he had. O pray God send us som to better purpose, however i take it very kindly of him to send me what he has. The news you may shew to Mr Stafford, but the tre is only for yourself. Pray send me both back tomorrow, your tre came to me this morning just as i was writing to the King, so that i sent the great paquet with my letter. There is no doubt but Lord Middleton intends you should open his closet, for els, how should you send him what he asks. I believe you may safely do it. M. R."

Though James remained at Boulogne till the end of April, all chances of the hoped-for invasion had long since dwindled away. Soon after his arrival at Calais he learned that the Assassination Plot had been discovered. The plan had been to lie in ambush on Turnham Green, and fall on William as he was returning from hunting in Richmond Park. To ensure its success the conspirators found it necessary to increase their number to forty, and thus, unfortunately for themselves, accidentally included among them one honest man.[1] As soon as he fully understood that he was to be one of eight men who were to stab the King to death in his coach, this man, a certain Catholic gentleman, whose name was Pendergrass, gave immediate information to Portland. The royal hunt was postponed; the conspirators were arrested, tried, and executed, though Sir George Barclay, with remarkable prescience where the safety of his own skin was concerned, made good his escape to France.

Meanwhile the French fleet was detained in port by

[1] There were in all three informers, but the character of the other two would not have entitled them to credence.

contrary winds. The English fleet put out to sea, and every preparation was made to resist the proposed invasion. James's last chance was gone, and this attempt in two ways ruined his prospects. In the first place, the discovery of the proposed scheme of assassination and foreign invasion produced an immense wave of loyalty towards William throughout the length and breadth of England ; in the second, the conspirators on trial accused many public men of being in communication with Saint-Germain. This was no news to William, but Godolphin, Churchill, Russell, and others were indignant that James had kept their secret so ill that it should be common talk, " so ever afterwards gave that for a reason why they should correspond no more." Even Anne, who " had all along kept up a fair correspondence with the King full of assurances of duty and repentance," now wrote asking his consent to her acceptance of the Crown should it be offered to her, in the event of William's death.

At the end of April, James realising that any further stay at Boulogne was now futile, wrote to Caryll :—

"BOULOGNE, *Ap*. 29, 1696.

"I received this morning yours of the 27th, and send you back here enclosed the bill you sent me and signed so that you have but to send to Parry to receve the summe mentioned in it, and lett him keep it in his hand till further orders, believing I shall now stay so little here as not to have need of it, since I see no manner of reason for my staying here any longer now that the world must find the descent is layd aside for the present, but before I stir from hence must expect an answer to E. Mid ; letter went yesterday to M. de Ponchartrain which is all I have to say at present. J. R."

On May 5th he was back at Saint-Germain. Maria met him at Saint-Denis. The next day, Sunday, Louis came over to visit them, but James was deeply dejected. "He was more and more convinced that afflictions were necessary for him ; . . . his present concern was to reap a Christian frute from these seeds of affliction which Providence had sent." To the end that he might obtain a more abundant harvest of this nature, he set out for La Trappe on June 2nd, taking Maria with him; but they were hardly arrived when they were followed by the news that little Prince James had an attack of small-pox. Maria wrote to Caryll the same day :—

"*June* 5, 1696.

"You know me to well not to believe that i was very much allarmed yesterday morning, at the news you sent the King of my son's being ill, i had once a mind to have gon back, but having no horses upon this road, and the King hoping my son would do well persuaded me to com on, we had a terrible journey of it, and did not get hither till almost 10 o'clock, tho' wee left Chartres at half an hour past nine this morning. Parry came by eight, and i thank God, your letter and Sir William Waldgrave's has put me at ease, pray tell Sir William that i do not at all doubt of his great care, and that i have charged my son to obey him exactly till i get to him, which will be on Friday night if no accident happens to hinder it, of which we have had good store since we left you, the worst has been this last night, that by the carelessness of one of my grooms, one of these stables was sett on fire, all burnt with 4 of my horses, but we shall make a shift to go back for all that on Thursday morning, as i intended. It was great comfort the whole convent was not burnt, and that 'scape comforts me for that other losse, pray tell Mr Plowden, whom I think is in waiting this week,

JAMES II., HIS WIFE MARIA, AND THEIR TWO CHILDREN.

and also to Mr Perkins that i am pursuaded of theyr care, and that I am sure they will not leave my son without one of them night nor day, if his illness lasts any time i think it necessary he should have some woman to look after him as I sent word by Mr Wyburn yesterday, not having time to write. They cannot have a better than Mrs Stafford near my child. . . . I thought to have written two words to her but I fear I shall not have time : pray bid her embrace my poor girl for me and the King . . . and keep her from her brother till he is quite well. i thank God i am so, ever since i had been a few hours in the coach the first day of my journey, we are hear in a terestial Paradise, yett, i dont at all forget my friends, at the head of which without wronging any, i putt Mr Secretary Caryll. MARIA R."

CHAPTER XVIII

TREATY OF RYSWICK—END OF JAMES'S HOPES

WHILE James was, as he phrased it, "turning his whole attention to gaining a heavenly crown," to his great surprise an earthly one was offered him. This was none other than the crown of Poland. The late King, John Sobieski, died "under general contempt." His wife was a Frenchwoman who intrigued continually with Versailles, and his government was consequently so vacillating and feeble that latterly hardly any business had been transacted. The King had devoted himself to amassing sufficient money to secure the election of his son to the throne after his death. When this took place there was a considerable party in favour of the young Sobieski, notwithstanding his mother's unpopularity. The Polish nobility, however, "plainly set the crown up for sale," and encouraged all candidates that would bid for it. The crown was eventually given to the Elector of Saxony, who abjured his religion, distributed eight million florins among the Poles, and was supported by all the other candidates, who united in opposition to the French party.[1] It does not appear that James would have had much chance of sitting on

[1] Burnet's *History of His Own Time*.

the throne of Poland even if he had entertained any idea of it. But the offer, which took the form of a message sent through the French ambassador in Poland, the Abbé Poliniac, was immediately declined by James on the ground that "it would amount to an abdication indeed of what was really his due, and therefore he was resolved to remain as he was, tho' he had less hopes of being restored than ever."

The summer passed uneventfully at Saint-Germain; the only domestic event of importance was the appointment of Perth as governor of the Prince of Wales. The selection of the child's tutor had been made with many prayers and searchings of heart by his mother. She writes to "La Déposée" at Chaillot on July 25th: "I have another kind of news to send you, which is that the King has this morning named Milord Perth governor of my son; we have just put him into his hands. It is a great business settled for me, and I hope that God will bless this choice that we have made after having prayed more than a year, in order that God may inspire us to do well. Tell this to our dear Mother from me, for I have not time to write to her. Her prayers and yours, with those of all our dear sisters, have had a great part in this election, which I believe to be pleasing to God; for he is a holy man, of distinguished merit, as well as of great ability (*grande qualité*). I am content to have my son in his hands, not knowing any better; but I have put him above all, and in the first place, into the hands of God, who by His mercy will take care of him, and will give us grace to bring him up in His fear and love." The Queen adds—giving a little glimpse of their daily occupations—that yesterday and the day before the

368 THE ENGLISH COURT IN EXILE

King of France and Madame de Maintenon had been to Saint-Germain, and that the next day they were to visit Saint-Cloud, to be present at the baptism of the Orleans grandchild, Mademoiselle de Chartres.

It is Madame who, in one of her letters, written about this time, gives a picture of little James. This poor child, brought up in an enervating, priestly atmosphere, showed early promise of intelligence :—

"20 *Sept.* 1696.

"The Prince of Wales is the prettiest child it is possible to see. He understands French now, and talks readily. He is not like his father or mother, but greatly resembles the portraits of the late King of England his uncle, and I am persuaded that if the English saw this child they could not doubt that it was of the royal family."

Writing a year later, the kind-hearted Madame says :—

"15 *Sept.* 1697.

"I love this child with all my heart. It is impossible to see him without loving him. He has a very good nature. I believe that in time he will become a great King, for although he is only nine years old, I am persuaded that from now he would govern better than his father."

In October James and Maria went to stay at Fontainebleau, arriving there on the 10th. It must have been a melancholy visit, for the Queen was ill at the time, and was obliged to stay indoors, while Louis was suffering from an attack of gout, and had himself carried in to see her in a chair. The visit was prolonged till the 26th on account of her illness, which continued so as to cause James some alarm. Sir William Waldgrave was sent for from Saint-Germain to attend on her. The King wrote himself to Caryll, asking that her own physician should come at once, and at the same time reassuring their faithful friend and servant. After telling Caryll that the Queen's "cholick" continues, James asks him to send Sir William Waldgrave, "he knowing her constitution, while those of his profession here do not, it not being good to lett such an ailment continue upon her; besides there is a reason at this time, which has hindered those here from giving those remedys she can take proper for her distemper; you need not be allarmed at my sending for Sr Will. for I hope by that tyme he can gett hither she will be quite well. However there will be no harm in his coming hither, therefore lett him know from me, he should immediately come away in a post chaise, so that if this letter gets to you to-morrow morning, he may be easily here to-morrow night.—J. R."

Maria had already written to Caryll two days earlier, telling him of her illness, and replying to some request of his on a family matter. The niece alluded to in the following letter was most likely one of the daughters of Philip Caryll, about whom John wrote later to his sister, Mary Caryll, Abbess of the Benedictine monastery at Dunkirk. She was thought to have a religious vocation, and John Caryll promised to settle an annual sum upon his sister's monastery on behalf of this niece, if she made her profession there. This letter was written by Maria on October 15th, 1696 :—

"FONTAINEBLEAU.

"I approve intirely all that you have done concerning your niece, you may at all times with all safety make use of my name, when it is to do you or yours any good, for you may be sure i shall always be ready to do that. i shall take care to have Mrs Rutter remooved when i com back to St Germains which i hope will be in eight or nine days at furthest ; wee shall speak of it to-morrow to this King who is very civil and kynd to us, as he used to be, but doe not care to enter into busenesse with us. You will have heard that the Emperor and King of Spain have accepted the neutrality in Italy, so the peace is quite made of that syde, and i have reason to beleeve it will soon be made everywher, God's will be don, he knows what is best for us, and for all the world, and will certainly turne all to his greater glory. . . . i cannot brag of my health for i have not been well these three days, i have the cholick. 　　　　　　　　　　　　　　　Maria R."

Two other points touched on in the letter call for elucidation. Louis's determined avoidance of business with the King and Queen of England had a definite reason. In spite of the exhausted state of his treasury, he had laid up stores and provisions for the year's campaign at Givet ; but the town had been taken by surprise and all its provisions totally destroyed. He was not then in a position to take the offensive. England, meanwhile, was passing through an acute commercial crisis during the restoration of the currency. William was at his wits' end for the means of feeding his army in Flanders. In August, Portland had gone over to London to bring back supplies ; his mission had been successful, but there was a general feeling of uneasiness among the Allies that England was reaching the end of her resources. France was nevertheless reduced to opening secret peace negotiations, in which Louis consented to recognise the Prince of Orange as William III. of England. But meanwhile an important

PRINCE JAMES STUART (THE OLD PRETENDER) AND HIS SISTER,
THE PRINCESS LOUISE.

defection took place among the Allies. The Duke of Savoy joined France, and insisted that Spain and the Emperor should recognise thenceforward the neutrality of Italy. They consented in spite of William's remonstrances. It is to this that Maria alludes in her letter. The peace was to be consummated by the marriage of the Duke of Savoy's daughter to Louis XIV.'s grandson, Monseigneur's eldest boy, the Duc de Bourgogne. This had already been much talked of, and had even reached the ears of the little Princess Louise at Saint-Germain. It is again Madame who tells us of it in one of these delightful letters of hers :—

"26 *July* 1696.

"The other day they were saying at Saint-Germain before the little Princess of England that the Duc de Bourgogne was going to marry the Princess of Savoy. The dear child began to cry violently, and said that she thought the Duc de Bourgogne would never marry anyone but herself, but from the moment he married the Princess of Savoy she would go into a convent and would never marry all her life. They cannot console her ; she is quite sad since she has heard the news."

As the Princess Louise was at this time just four years old, she must have been as precocious as Madame declares all French children to have been.

In the following November the Princess of Savoy arrived. Louis went to meet her at Montargis. The little girl, with a preternatural shrewdness, at once ingratiated herself both with Louis and Madame de Maintenon, the only two people who really counted. Louis wrote to De Maintenon as soon as he had seen the Princess : "She has the most grace and the most beautiful figure that I have ever seen, dressed like a picture, with very bright and beautiful eyes, and regular complexion, red and white just as it should be; the most beautiful black hair, quantities of it. She is thin, as is proper at her age. Very red thick lips, white but very irregular teeth, well-made hands, but of the colour of her age." The King found her rather awkward but pleasing, and just what he could have wished. Onlookers noticed that as he led her up the steps the little girl frequently kissed the King's hand. Writing to De Maintenon, Louis expresses a kindly wish that he will be able to maintain the ease of manner that he has assumed till they reach Fontainebleau. Soon after her arrival, James and Maria came over to Versailles to make the Princess's acquaintance. As prospective Queen of France, she was given a fauteuil. She returned the visit, calling at Saint-Germain on November 16th. She was afterwards taken by De Maintenon to Saint-Cyr, where she was to continue her education, as she was then only eleven years old.

The year 1697 was to be fraught with humiliation for James and Maria. The tentative peace negotiations which had come to nothing in 1696 were resumed and concluded. Maria had foreseen this, but James seems to have been hurt and surprised that the faithful friend and benefactor, who for the last eight years had sacrificed men and money in his interest, should at last be forced to consider the condition of his own exhausted country. As he wrote to the Abbé de La Trappe, "The world was indeed no less astonished than the King that when his Most Christian Majesty seem'd to have got a perfect superiority over his enemies by so many victories, and now a separate peace with Savoy, he should however grasp so greedely at a general one, as to abandon for the sake of it, the cause of a Prince, his near relation, his friend and ally, whose protection as it gave lustre to his actions, so the glory of his restoration seem'd to be what was only wanting to complete his character. . . ."

James did not acquiesce in the proposed negotiations. He made a futile appeal to the Emperor, representing to him, through a private agent whom he despatched to Vienna, "what he had suffered and how unjustly he had been oppressed, . . . how shocking and misterious it appeared to the Christian world, that his Imperial Majesty, and other Princes of the House of Austria, so famed for their piety and religious zeal, should contribute to the dethroning a Catholic Prince." He suggested that his own restoration would fitly consummate a European peace, and hinted that his Most Christian Majesty was open to concluding a separate peace with the Empire on advantageous terms. His agent was refused an audience, and told that the Emperor, as it was, had very recently received a letter "full of deep resentment from the Prince of Orange," because he had admitted an emissary from Saint-Germain. The Imperial confessor, Father Millingatti, told James's agent that his master "had done nothing but what was both conscientious and allowed by the common practice of Christian princes." That in entering into an alliance against France he had merely sought to defend his own State from an unjust aggressor, and that he always looked upon William III.'s invasion "as unjust and impious, and heartily prayed for King James's restoration"—a piece of mysterious casuistry which James compared with "Charles V. makeing public prayer for the Pope's delivery, whilst he himself kept him prisoner in the Castle of St Angelo."

Disappointed in this direction, James then sought at least to be represented by a minister in the Peace negotiations; this, of course, was refused, and he was forced to derive what satisfaction he might, from drawing up a manifesto setting forth his hard case, hoping thereby at least to obtain some reparation; but this too the confederate Princes ignored. "By certain rules of policy he was totally neglected."

The King and Queen had besides at this time to suffer an access of anxiety as to their ability to meet their household expenses. A nun of Maubuisson, Marie de Brinon, writing in February 1697 of recent events, says: "Our good King James regards everything in a spirit of constancy and virtue. He endures not only as a saint, but as a King removed from all baseness, the loss of three crowns that God will restore to him in heaven, if He does not do so on earth. . . . The Queen of England is no less saintly, and in truth, it is a great happiness to be so in the midst of so great misfortunes. I have heard a lady of her Court say that she despoils herself of everything that she has to support the poor English who have followed them, and that she sells even her diamond sleeve-links, and tells her as she performs these charitable actions that she is overjoyed to deprive herself of things to keep others."

The peace negotiations which were opened by Louis XIV. early in the spring dragged on because Spain and the Emperor wished to continue the war. Spain, with an imbecile and moribund King, had always been an obstructive influence in the coalition. Both Louis XIV. and the Emperor had claims on the Spanish throne when Charles II. should die; this event was now believed to be imminent, and it was obviously to the advantage of the Emperor that the coalition should still be in arms to support his claim when the throne fell vacant. The plenipotentiaries met in March at a house belonging to William III. at Ryswick, between Delft and The Hague. William, having decided that the conditions offered by Louis were advantageous, decided to put a stop to these discussions. The terms of the treaty had been privately decided by Bentinck, Earl of Portland, on behalf of William, and by Marshal Boufflers on behalf of France, and committed to writing in July. By September a treaty was concluded between England, Holland, France, and Spain.

The following month the Emperor also made terms. His delay involved the loss of Strasburg, which Louis was at first prepared to resign. By the terms of peace, France gave up all conquests made since the Peace of Nimeguen in 1678. Louis consented to recognise William as King of England, and Anne as his successor. William asked that James and Maria should no longer be permitted to reside at Saint-Germain, to which the King of France replied that he could not withdraw his hospitality from his luckless guests, or suggest their resigning their asylum at Saint-Germain. Boufflers, however, gave Portland to understand that the matter might be arranged by the English royal family's removing to Avignon, where they would be too far off to stir up malcontents in England. Louis, on his side, asked that William should grant a general amnesty to Jacobites in England, and that Maria should receive the jointure of £50,000 a year that had been settled on her as Queen of England. All these

376 THE ENGLISH COURT IN EXILE

matters were arranged by compromise. William, while declining to entertain any suggestions as to his course of conduct towards his own subjects, gave assurances that Maria should receive whatever sum she was legally entitled to, as soon as the Stuarts should have retired to Avignon or Italy. There was nothing left for James but dignified acquiescence, a course of conduct always incompatible with his temperament. The opportunity for another manifesto was too tempting to be resisted. He was so ill advised as to issue a most futile protest, which could only make him look ridiculous. The preamble was as follows:—

"James, by the Grace of God, King of England, etc., to all Princes, Potentates, etc. After so long and ruinous a war to Christendom, being convinced that all the contending parties are disposed to peace, and even on the point of concluding it, without our participation, we think it requisite in this conjuncture to make use of the only means remaining in our power to assert our undoubted right, by a solemne protestation against whatever may be done to our prejudice."

After citing the manifold injustices from which he held himself to be suffering, the King continues:—

"We therefore sollemly protest (and in the strongest manner we are able) against all what-soever may be treated of, regulated, or stipulated with the usurper of our Kingdoms, as being null by default of a lawfull authority.

"We protest in particular against all Treatys of Allyance, confederation and commerce, made with England since the usurpation, as being null by the same want of authority, and consequently incapable of binding us, our lawful heirs, successors or subjects. We further protest in general, against all Acts whatsoever that pretend to confirme, autherise, or approuve directly or indirectly the Usurpation of the Prince of Orange, against all the proceedings of his pretended Parliaments and whatever tends to the subvertion of the fundamental laws of our Kingdom, particularly those relating to the succession to our crowns."

This monumental act of folly was perpetrated by James in June. The student of history can only contemplate its vast futility with compassion, and hope that, while it provoked sneers and laughter among his contemporaries, its author derived some gratification to his pride from this ill-timed act of self-assertion.

Through the summer visits were interchanged between Saint-Germain and the French Court, as if there were no epoch-making decisions pending at Versailles. But as the time for the annual autumn visit of James and Maria to Fontainebleau drew near, they had need of all their fortitude to support it, for it unfortunately coincided with the conclusion of peace. James and Maria do not seem to have appreciated these visits very highly at the best of times—such, at least, was current gossip, to which Madame de Sévigné gives expression: "The English Court is at Fontainebleau, where they are having comedies and fêtes and being bored (according to what they say), and so much the worse for them." How much the worse for them at this moment an entry in the King's *Memoirs* records: "One would have thought the King had now gon through all the stages of contradiction, yet one remained which nothing but an absolute dominion over himself, could have made him bear with so good a grace, this Peace fortuned to be concluded about that time of the year his Most Christian Majesty was used to go to Fontainebleau, and whither he was always accustomed to invite the King and Queen for ten or fifteen days, which invitations his Majesty receiving as formerly, arrived there the very day the news was brought this Peace was being signed" (September 24th). James seems to have behaved very creditably, and merely sympathised with Louis on the disagreeable necessity of having had to conclude it; while Louis—so James told the Abbé de La Trappe—" was more mortify'd in telling it me than I in heering it, he say'd indeed he would do all he could to sweeten the bitter draught."

Neither James nor Maria was present at the "appartement" that was held on the evening of their arrival. For the rest, the visit passed as usual with hunting and card parties. At one of the former the little Princess of Savoy was accidentally present at the death of a wolf, while out driving. The visit ended on October 6th, and a few days after her return to Saint-Germain, Maria wrote an account of it to her friend, Mère Priolo, "La Déposée," at Chaillot:—

". . . I will be content with telling you that notwithstanding all that has happened, we are satisfied from the bottom of our hearts, with our great King. He was beside himself with vexation at seeing us arrive at Fontainebleau at the same time as the courier who brought news of the peace. He showed for us much kindness, pity, and even pain over what he was unable to avoid doing; for the rest, no change will take place in our residence at Saint-Germain. It appears quite decided by what he has told us; I say 'appears,' for truly, after all we have seen happen, how can one believe oneself sure of anything in this world? They have promised the King to give me my dowry. I have begged him to be so kind as to let it be paid to him for me, for I do not wish to ask or receive anything except from him, to whom alone I wish to be under any obligation. But I am letting myself be carried away, without wishing to enter into the matter. I don't know what I've said, but in any case pray burn my letter."

There were great festivities this autumn, in which James and Maria took part at Versailles, and which, one hopes, served as some distraction after all they had been through. People said that his humiliations had impressed James but little—"in so much that as the most shining virtues are not exempt from censure, so the King's patience and seeming easiness was term'd an insencibility and he in some measure despised, for what merited the highest praises; but he was no less apprised of that than of the rest, and upon occasion speaking of it, to a person of great piety sayd he was glad that haveing lost everything else he had such frequent occasions given him, of making a sacrifice of his reputation too."

In November of this year the marriage of the Princess of Savoy and the Duke of Burgundy was celebrated with great magnificence, with gorgeous and prolonged festivities. James and Maria arrived after the actual marriage service, which took place on the morning of November 23rd, when the two children, accompanied by Monseigneur and all the Princesses, proceeded to the chapel, where the marriage was celebrated and the register signed. Dangeau helped to carry the bride's train, which, he observes, was very heavy, in the passage to and from the chapel. After mass there was a grand banquet of the royal family at a horseshoe table, the King in his arm-chair in the middle, with all the Princes and Princesses of the Blood to right and left. The little Duchess was discreetly carried off by Madame de Maintenon to her own apartments, to rest there during the afternoon.

The day passed wearily. At seven o'clock James and Maria arrived, and were at once set to play portique, till eight, when a magnificent display of fireworks took place, in spite of heavy rain. Supper was served immediately afterwards, at which those present sat in the same order as at dinner, except that Maria sat, as always, between Louis and her husband. After supper, which was on the most magnificent scale, they repaired to the little Duchesse de Bourgogne's bedroom, where, after the King had dismissed the men present, there was conducted the legal and elaborate ceremony, customary in those days, which are in some ways so akin to ours, in others so infinitely remote, of putting the newly married couple to bed. The little Duke undressed in an anteroom with his tutor, the Duc de Beauvilliers, where James presented him with the nightshirt; the little Princess was undressed by her ladies, and presented with her nightgown by the Queen of England. The two children were then put to bed on either side of the great old heavily draped four-post bed of the period, with all its curtains looped back; and Louis and everyone else went away, except Monseigneur and his son's tutor [1] and the Duchesse de Lude, and some other of her ladies who were in charge of the Princess. Monseigneur chatted for about a quarter of an hour with the newly married couple, and then, as the Duc de Beauvilliers was taking his son away, he told him he

[1] They sat in the "ruelle," the space between the bed and the wall, which, in times when it was the fashion to conduct business and receive guests in bed, played an important part.

might kiss the Princess, against which the Duchesse de Lude indignantly protested. Louis had said that his grandson was not so much as to kiss the tip of the Princess's finger till they became man and wife in more than name, which did not take place till two years later. The bride returned next day to her ordinary life and her lessons at Saint-Cyr.

One would like to know what Maria d'Este wore at this marriage. She cannot have hoped to vie with the ladies of the French Court, for on this occasion a sort of madness of extravagance seized everyone. Louis himself said he wondered men could be such fools as to ruin themselves in dresses for their wives. Even Saint-Simon, while sneering at the folly of his neighbours, spent 20,000 francs on dresses for himself and his wife; and there was such a demand for workpeople that Madame la Duchesse, truculent as usual, sent her servants to take away those of the Duc de Rohan by force, of which the King hearing, sent them back immediately, with his usual good sense, though he very much disliked De Rohan. On the 11th James and Maria came over again to a Court ball, the finest, thinks that experienced courtier, Dangeau, that he had ever seen. It began at the early hour of half-past six, directly the party from Saint-Germain arrived. About forty ladies, all magnificently dressed, took part in the dancing, young and old, from the dowager Princesse de Conti to the little bride. But the arrangements had been made so badly that there was frightful overcrowding. Even Louis himself was inconvenienced, and Monsieur was hustled in the crowd. James and Maria were at another ball on the following Saturday, December 14th, at which things were better arranged.

They arrived half an hour late, for the roads were slippery with hoar-frost, and their horses had been delayed. After midnight the guests supped at seventeen tables, and Louis found time for some talk with James and Maria. The wedding festivities came to an end with a performance of Destouches' opera, *Issé*, at Trianon, at which the King and Queen of England were again present.

CHAPTER XIX

JAMES II'S FORLORN HOPES FROM THE PAPACY AND
SCOTLAND—PORTLAND'S MISSION

THOUGH James's hopes of seeing his wrongs redressed through the intervention of the Papacy had ended in a succession of disappointments, he still cherished expectations from that ineffectual potentate. Of the three men who had occupied the Chair of St Peter since James's accession, Innocent XI. was the greatest. Beneath an outward bearing of studious gentleness and extreme humility he concealed a dauntless courage and unyielding integrity. No one of his predecessors had ever shown a more unflinching determination to uphold the rights and dignity of the Papacy. He had abolished the nepotism which was threatening to produce a public bankruptcy, and he had defied at all hazards the pretensions of Louis XIV. He was encouraged in his attitude of resistance by the universal opposition that the King of France had aroused in Europe, and by the formation of the League of Augsburg, which he had secretly joined. Innocent had never approved or encouraged James's course of action when he was on the English throne. He disliked the Jesuits, and, as Ranke points out, " saw in everything which was done in France and in England contrary to his wish and will, the work—not indeed of the whole order of the Jesuits, for their General in Rome stood rather on the side of the Pope—but of a section of it which had attached itself to the policy of Louis XIV., and on its side did not recoil with horror from a breach with the Pope."[1]

Innocent XI., moreover, induced the General of the Jesuits to rebuke James's Jesuit adviser, Father Petre, for his ambition. James had not, therefore, much to hope from the Pope when he took refuge with the Most Christian King. Innocent's successor, Alexander VIII., who ascended the Papal chair in 1689, maintained the spiritual claims of the Papacy. The unsuccessful attempts to interest him on James's behalf have been recorded in a previous chapter.[2] Alexander died in 1691, and was succeeded by Innocent XII., a member of the ducal family of Montelione in Naples. He modelled his policy and conduct on those of Innocent XI., by whom he had been promoted to the cardinalate, and he patched up the quarrel with France and received the submission of the French clergy. James sent Sir John Lytcott on a mission to him to ask for financial assistance for his proposed descent on England before the battle of La Hogue in 1692. Innocent promised to furnish twenty thousand crowns, after an interview in which Lytcott urged his master's claims with extreme importunity.

Lytcott, in his report of the audience, says: "The truth is, I find on the whole he has been so teized and threatened by the House of Austria, that he is in a

[1] Ranke, *History of England in the Seventeenth Century*.
[2] Chap. vii.

manner forced to trim, even *contre-cœur*, nay so far that even the money mentioned is, he said, to pass as subsistence for the poor Catholics and Churchmen. Further he has given a kind of promise, he will still use all efforts as soon as the news comes of the descent." The Pope was as good as his word about the money promised, which he sent to Lytcott next day—rather more even than had been promised. But the envoy lingered on through the summer months of 1692, and in the meantime the victory of La Hogue had cooled the zeal of James's friends at Rome, including the Pope himself. At the end of July Lytcott wrote an account of his farewell audience. On this occasion his Holiness "reiterated his promises that he would in *ogne Punto* do whatever he could. Quickly after" (to prevent, perhaps, a further address) "he rang his bell, and called for a little plate, on which was a chaplet, two gold and two silver medals of his own *impresa*, which he was pleased to give me out of his own hand, with 200 indulgences, and a gracious kind of embrace, whilst I did *inginochiarmi* to receive his last blessing; after which and returning humble thanks for all, and leaving him to his own piety, I retired in form; and truly, whatever comes from him seems to proceed perfectly from the bottom of a most sincere heart."

After Lytcott's return James had no representative at Rome, though Cardinal Howard looked after his interests unofficially and reported on them. Later on Perth was sent to Rome. He gives a very instructive and full account of the feeling with regard to the claims of James and William III., whose respective abilities were fully realised there. "All here," he says, "are very cold in our concerns. Press them with the injustice the King meets with, you get a cold—' Yes, he is ill dealt by, but what shall we do to get a peace? For the Prince, if he lives, will reign no doubt; but how turn out the Prince of Orange? He is in possession. He is brave and wise, and has got the way of managing England. He is master of Holland; he is the cement, that glues together the different interests of the confederacy. If at last the *collegati* should fail him; if England should grow uneasy, he has money laid up, an army at his devotion, and will trouble Europe, if he get not leave to live out his usurped possession.' This is the common talk, and even some we look on as our firm friends believe this to be reasonable."[1] A little later, in June 1695, Perth sent a full account of his audience with the Pope.

He appeared fully sensible of James's sufferings, and " said he was a saint. 'But what can we do?' cried the old man bitterly. . . . 'Catholic Princes will not hearken to me, they have lost the respect that used to be paid to Popes: religion is gone and a wicked policy set up in its place.' . . . 'God knows,' he said, 'to restore the King I would give my blood; but Christians have lost all respect, even to us, to us!' said he. 'But can it be believed,' continued his Holiness, 'that I should ever consent to any peace, that excludes that good King from his just right. God forbid! God forbid! But what will become of all this? The Prince of Orange is master: he is arbiter of Europe. The Europeans and King of Spain are slaves and worse than subjects to him. They neither dare nor will venture to displease him'—and here he struck twice with his hand upon the table and sighed. 'If God'

[1] Macpherson's Original Papers.

(said he) 'by some stroke of omnipotence do it not, we are undone.'"

To all these letters Caryll wrote sympathetic and encouraging replies. He compares a European peace that shall exclude James with that between Herod and Pilate, and truly he exclaims : " It requires a virtue no less consummated and try'd than our master's ; and give me leave also to add, your lordship's, not to be scandalised, at so much of the scribe and pharisee so near the chair of Moses. In the meantime it is no small comfort to every true Christian to find that his Holiness himself, of all the Court of Rome, is the least tainted with that corrupt policy which makes a sacrifice of justice and even of religion to worldly interest."

James sent a memorial to the Papal nuncio when the terms of peace were being discussed, entirely dissociating himself from any agreement with the proposals, and especially from the suggestion that the Prince of Wales should succeed to the throne of England on William's death, to which "his Most Christian Majesty had underhand prevailed with the Prince of Orange to consent."[1] James seems to have immediately repudiated this suggestion without giving any consideration to it. His reasons for doing so he set forth explicitly in his letter to the nuncio. The Roman Catholic Princes, he affirmed, were in a league to strengthen the enemies of their Holy Religion ; and he continued : " But if to punish them God abandons them to their blindness and that the state to which Europe is reduced will oblige it to conclude a peace, without doing justice to his Britanic Majesty, he hopes

[1] Clarke, 574.

that his Holiness will not allow himself to be surprised by the artful expedients which the mediators may propose; as his Britanic Majesty will never consent that his incontestible right shall be called in question. For instance, it cannot be denied but by receiving a pension from the Prince of Orange, though there were never so much cause for it, his Britanic Majesty would tacitly renounce his right, and if he consented that the Prince of Wales should reign that would be a formal renunciation, because the Prince of Orange could only promise a thing he could not perform because of the reversion to Anne. The Prince of Wales by succeeding the Prince of Orange yields his sole right which is that of his father, and being obliged to the people for his elevation would not reign except during their pleasure, and therefore if his Britanic Majesty was capable of consenting to so disgraceful a proposal he might be justly reproached with ruining the monarchy, which has always been hereditary, by making it elective." Thus James obtained little from the Papacy but sympathy, and that was practically all that the successive Popes had either inclination or ability to give him.

At the beginning of the year 1698 he had to undergo a new humiliation. William III.'s great friend and confidant, William Bentinck, Earl of Portland, was sent on a confidential mission to Versailles. Among other instructions confided to Bentinck was that of inducing Louis to consent to the removal of James and his family from Saint-Germain, and to refuse shelter in France to conspirators against the life of the King of England. The question of the Spanish Succession, which was also to be discussed, did not directly concern James.

His *Memoirs* only make brief mention of this embarrassing occurrence. "His [James's] enemies could not so easily lay aside their malice, as he the remembrance of it, for immediately after the peace, the Prince of Orange sending his great favorit Bentinck in quality of ambassador into France, made use of that occasion to press further hardships against the King . . . the guilty conscience of his master, and those of his party could not bear so near a sight of what obraided them continually with their injustice and infidelity, and hovered over their heads like a cloud that still threatened a storm."

For obvious and practical reasons, it was a serious inconvenience for William to have a father-in-law at his gates who was unwearied in fomenting sedition, and would have condoned his assassination. The pangs of a guilty conscience did not appear in the demeanour of his ambassador. England had never been so splendidly represented. Portland was accompanied by his son, Lord Woodstock, and twelve gentlemen, each of whom had a numerous retinue. Crowds lined the streets to see his entry into Paris in a state coach drawn by eight grey horses; he, whose stiff bearing and uningratiating manners had rendered him generally unappreciated among the English, with whose language he was unfamiliar, became the man of the moment in Paris.

The ambassador was fêted, courted, admired as a model of all that was elegant and courtly. "The Earl of Portland," says Saint-Simon, "came over with a numerous and superb suite. He kept up a magnificent table, and had horses, liveries, furniture, and dresses of the most tasteful and costly kind." Portland had his first audience of the King on the 4th of February, and remained four months in France. His politeness, his courtly and gallant manners, and the good cheer he gave charmed everybody, and made him universally popular. It became the fashion to give fêtes in his honour; and the astonishing fact is, that Louis XIV. who at heart was more offended than ever with the Prince of Orange, treated this ambassador with the most marked distinction. One evening he even gave Portland his bedroom candlestick, a favour only accorded to the most considerable persons, and always regarded as a special mark of the King's favour.

Portland kept William III. fully informed of his interviews with Louis XIV. and his minister. Writing from Paris on February 16th, he says:—

"This morning I went to Versailles and saw the King. . . . After I had finished speaking, he said that he could not imagine why I asked that he should remove King James; that he was so near a relation, that he was grieved for his misfortune, that he had liked him for so long, and that in honour he could not send him away, that Mar[l] de Bouflers had told me the same thing positively at our interviews, and that upon this I had desisted from my request, and that it ought to be sufficient, that he gave his word that he would not help him, and that he would sincerely maintain the peace. I told him that there was no need to feel compassion for his withdrawal, since your Majesty had engaged to give him or the Queen his wife about £50,000 sterling annually to live elsewhere, that if he refused to withdraw on these terms it could only be in the hope of using this money to raise commotions or something worse, that your Majesty expected this withdrawal as a thing agreed, since my only reason for not continuing to insist upon having this inserted in an article of peace was the regard which was felt for his Most Christian Majesty, and that your Majesty did not wish to exact a thing which might be disagreeable to him, but that I had positively declared to him that without this withdrawal the peace could not last, and that he had immediately afterwards in the conversation asked me where it was wished that he should retire, that I had mentioned Rome or Modena, as to which he had asked if Avignon would not be a suitable place, to which I had consented, that what confidence your Majesty had in the word of his Most Christian Majesty could not extend to what did not depend upon him, as, for example, to what the seditious in England might attempt, otherwise the English nation would be in a perpetual mistrust as to the continuance of peace, and that from the constitution of the Government, Parliament would not be induced to do what was necessary to make it lasting, and that the principal means to that end was to cause his withdrawal, as to which he answered that absolutely he could never be prevailed upon to make him do it. After this I reminded his Majesty that he had said nothing as to the second point which I had had the honour to mention to him, which was that of the assassins. He said that he was not acquainted with them, and did not know that there were any of them here, and that his knowledge of the affair was imperfect. I said that I could well believe that his Majesty was not acquainted with men of that sort, or at least not as such, and that if it were his pleasure to be informed of the persons and the fact, he had only to let me know in what authentic form he wished me to do it, and that I would charge myself with the duty of doing it to his satisfaction before any steps were taken against these men. I named to him the principal people in the proclamation; he answered that the D. of Barwick could only have been in England for the landing (*pour la descente*), that Sr George Barckle was cashiered (*cassé*) with the company, and that he did not know where he was, that of Harrisson he had never heard speak, although I told him that he had been made prior of an English convent here, and as to Berkenhead, his Majesty said that he had never been employed except to carry letters, and after a short silence he said that it was useless to speak further on the subject, since he could give no other answer as to the one point or the other; upon which I withdrew. I can tell your Majesty that the Most Christian King spoke this time in a much drier tone than on the former occasion."

Writing later on this same subject of those concerned in the plot to assassinate William, Portland says :—

"The D. of Berwick expresses himself everywhere with extreme resentment because when, in conformity with your Majesty's orders, I have spoken of all those who took part in that horrible plot to assassinate your Majesty, he finds himself named amongst them, and does not consider that his name is first in the Proclamation. All the officers who are his creatures do the same. If they continue to do this indecently against one who is vested with the honorable character of your Majesty's ambassador, I think that I shall be obliged to take notice of it and to complain to his Most Christian Majesty."

Portland was naturally anxious to avoid coming into contact with the late King of England. Not so James, who, with characteristic lack of tact, rather sought him out: "On the 27th [of May] there being a Review of the troops of the Household in the Plain of Arches, where the King and the Dauphin, the young Princes of France, and divers persons of quality were present, his Excellency went thither also; but would perhaps have forborne coming if he had known that King James and the titular Prince of Wales had likewise been there. The Prince of Wales, by his Father's directions, endeavoured to join in conversation with the Lord Woodstock, but the Lord Portland, his Father, knowing the young Prince's design, order'd his son to avoid him ; as he did himself all those that belong'd to the Court of Saint-Germain, tho', it was reported, King James had caused it to be insinuated to his Excellency, that he never pretended to make his Lordship answerable for the ill usage he received from him he represented. At this Review King James did all he could to engage the attention of Lord Cavendish, and the other English noblemen to accost him, but all imitated the Earl of Portland."

This was after Louis had given James a very definite hint to avoid the English ambassador and his suite ; he sent him a message through Lord Middleton, soon after Portland's arrival in France, requesting him to keep his household out of the way when the Earl was at Versailles.[1] Dangeau, who mentions this fact, says, apropos of Portland's visit, that James, who bore this new reverse of fortune with admirable modesty and constancy, lost nothing of Louis's attention to himself, and was some cause of inconvenience to Portland, who twice had to retire, once from Marly, once from Meudon, when he intended to be present at the royal hunt, because James was in the field. The ambassador, he adds, received a rebuff from De la Rochefoucauld, to whom he applied for permission to hunt the royal hounds, receiving for answer that De la Rochefoucauld was unable to put them at his disposal, as he always held himself ready to receive the King of England's orders. Louis himself was puncti-

[1] Dangeau, February 17, 1698.

liously careful not to intermit his usual visits to Saint-Germain, or his entertainments to Maria and James, while the English ambassador was in France.

Portland comments in his letters to William on the embarrassment caused him by coming into contact with James and his court :—

E. of P. to K. W.

"22 *Feb.* 1698 (N.S.), PARIS.

"I have reason to think that for the future they will not allow Englishmen of the suite of King James to come where I am, and the care which they take in this regard will perhaps be all that I may expect."

"7 *Mar.* 1698, PARIS.

"Your Majesty's refusal to permit the English, Irish or others to remain in England contrary to the Act of Parliament angers them against King James, and disquiets them greatly because they are poor and have difficulty in living here. The Duc de Lauzun who is the principal counsellor of King James seems to affect to pay me civilities to a degree that surprises everyone. I do not know what his intention may be, if he has one as I think. As King James often goes hunting with the Dauphin, this often hinders my going, as I do not wish to find myself with him. From the way in which everyone tells me he speaks in my favour it is thought that he would make no difficulty about meeting me."

In June Portland took his leave.

The Act of Parliament alluded to by Portland was another result of the peace which caused serious inconvenience and a fresh burden to James. This law made it high treason to hold any correspondence with the exiled royal family, and obliged all those who had been in James's service since the Revolution, or even in

France, unless they had had a pass from the Government, to quit the British Isles, or be held guilty of high treason. "This his Majesty sayd, afflicted him more than all the rest, he was sencible what he had suffered himself was nothing comparatively to what his past disorders might justly deserve, but to see his Loyal Subjects so used for their fidelity to him, was what made him stand in need of a more than ordinary grace to support." As a matter of fact, by far the greater number of those who had incurred this penalty obtained leave from William to remain in England, on giving a guarantee of good conduct.

An additional cause of distress to James was the influx of Irish priests into France, in consequence of the banishment of the regular clergy after the peace. "So that they came flocking over into France, and above four hundred arrived there in some months after: the relief of these distressed persons, together with such numbers of other Catholicks as these bills of banishment forced out of the kingdoms, brought a new burden as was sayd, upon the King, who had the mortification even after having distributed amongst them what was necessary for his own support to see great numbers perish for want, without his being able to relieve them." The law enforcing this, to which William had always been opposed, was found necessary, as its preamble states, because the Popish priests "do not only endeavour to withdraw his Majesty's subjects from their obedience, but do daily stir up, and move sedition and rebellion to the great hazard of the ruin and desolation of this kingdom." All bishops, vicars-general, and regular priests were to leave Ireland before May 1698, or incur the penalties of high treason.

A solemn procession and intercession was held at Rome for the persecuted Catholics of the three kingdoms. Maria, writing to Chaillot in February 1698, says:—

"From Rome they send us news that the Pope has had public prayers for our persecuted Catholics in the three kingdoms. There has been one of the most solemn processions that has ever been seen in Rome. All the secular and regular clergy took part in it, all the Sacred College of Cardinals except three, two of whom were ill. Our Holy Father intended to go to it himself, if the weather had not been very bad. It took place on Sunday, the day of the Conversion of St Paul. I am sure they will be very glad to hear this news at Chaillot, and I hope that God will hearken to the prayers of so many of the faithful united together for the conversion of sinners, and the perseverance of the persecuted; for this was the intention of these prayers. The King, my husband, was not mentioned by name, but as he is the chief of those persecuted, he is prayed for in the first place, and I hope I am also included, as I am among the number."

In this letter also Maria gives some details of their life at Saint-Germain. She has been very well herself, but the King has had slight fever for about a week, though not sufficient to prevent his hunting and going to Marly, where "we were the day before yesterday till one o'clock, watching youth and age dance. I take very little pleasure in all that, and even after it is over I am greatly fatigued." She goes on to send news of her children: "The Prince of Wales has had two big teeth pulled out, and bore it with much fortitude. They had been very painful and prevented him from sleeping. They were decayed," adds his fond mother, to whom all such details are precious, "and were the last two in his mouth. . . . My daughter's nose is still a little black from her fall; for the rest, both of them are well. Here is an exact account of the health of all those who are dear to me, and to you as well, for my sake." During this summer the Queen was ill with fever, which left her very weak; but she was well enough to attend the baptism of the Chartres baby, Madame's grandchild, at Saint-Cloud in August. Louis was present. The Duchesse de Bourgogne was godmother to the child, who was christened Adelaide, while Monseigneur stood godfather. After the ceremony was over, the guests drove in the grounds in *calèches*. James and Maria returned to Saint-Germain without waiting for the "collation" that subsequently took place.

In September James attended the magnificent review which, at De Maintenon's instigation, Louis was holding at Compiègne for the military instruction of the young Duc de Bourgogne. It was so costly that, coming after so long and exhausting a war, it amazed Europe, and ruined individuals as well as whole regiments.[1] All the Court were present. Marshal Boufflers entertained James and Maria to lunch, together with Monseigneur and his children, waiting on them himself. The review seems to have resembled in some respects modern manœuvres. James was present at several mimic engagements, and made a round of the trenches to see the "improvements in modern warfare."

In October James and Maria paid their annual autumn visit to Fontainebleau, coming *via* Paris. Louis and the Court received them between their lodgings and the chapel. The visit this year was diversified by the marriage of Mademoiselle, Madame's daughter,

[1] Dangeau.

with the Duke of Lorraine. His father had been deprived of his dominions by Louis XIV., and died on his way to Vienna, where he was to receive the command of an army that might have restored to him his birthright. On his deathbed he wrote to the Emperor: "I departed from Inspruck to come and receive your orders. Our God calls me hence, and I am going to render Him an account of a life which I had devoted to you. I humbly beseech your Majesty to remember my wife, who is nearly related to you, my children, whom I leave without any fortune, and my subjects, who are oppressed."[1] Lorraine was restored to the young Duke Leopold by the terms of the Peace of Ryswick.

James and Maria spent the second day after their arrival in calling on members of the royal family. The Princesses, who never seem to have lost an opportunity of annoying Monsieur, announced their intention of wearing mourning at the forthcoming marriage of his daughter "Mademoiselle" with the Duc de Lorraine. As usual, he could never settle their quarrels for himself, and complained to Louis, who ordered them to send at once to Paris or Versailles for suitable clothes.

The *fiançailles* of Mademoiselle took place at six o'clock on the evening of Sunday, October 12th. Louis went to see Mademoiselle beforehand, but she burst into tears and cried so that he was quite affected by it himself; as for the Duchesse de Bourgogne, who also went to see her, she cried so that conversation was impossible. At the *fiançailles* the dresses were superb, especially that of Monsieur, who had decked himself out in cloth-of-gold, with black satin trimmings and

[1] Dalrymple.

diamonds. A magnificent diamond shone in his hat, which was trimmed with black plumes; he also wore black silk stockings. Mademoiselle's dress was black embroidered with gold, over a petticoat of silver cloth embroidered with gold, and a veil of *point d'Espagne*. The whole sounds heavy for her years, but the weight of their clothes cannot have been heavier than the hearts of the sad little reluctant brides of those days. The marriage was by proxy, the Duc d'Elbœuf representing Leopold Duc de Lorraine. After the wedding the Duchess of Lorraine was taken to Paris by her father.

Kind as Louis was to his guests, and considerate as ever in all that concerned their comfort, they could not help feeling that their relations towards him were not what they had been. Writing to the faithful Caryll on October 14th, the Queen says: " . . . i thank God the King is quite well, and i have been so ever since i came hither, wee have seen this King in private but once, and i sayd nothing of my concerns, i keep it for the last visite, which will be to-morrow or next day, and on Wednesday i hope to find my children and friends at St Germains in good health. . . ." James also wrote to the Secretary the day after, a letter which suggests that he was something of a hypochondriac in his later years. This letter is inscribed to " Mr Secretary Caryll from J. R." It is written in a clear and large hand, but the writing is slightly tremulous :—

"This morning I recevd yours of yesterday, with the enclosd, wch I send back to you, the Queene and I read it this after diner and are much satisfyd with the exact account he gives of all things under his care, you did very well to give those directions you did to

Mr Poore, but I hope Ld Chancelor will recover by what you say of him. Should he miscarry, 'twould be a very great losse to me; I left my will with Sr R. Nagle. I had in the night a little heat and unequalnesse in my puls wch did not hinder my sleeping, all Mon. Faggon asked me was to drinke some thé, and ly some tyme in my bed, wch I did till ten in the morning, dined with the King, and have not found further inconveniance, only did not go out with the Queene to the Salut at the Lady, it being somewhat cold, hoping in God to heare no more of this little distemper, and to be able to go ahunting to-morrow, two days since a courrier came from Spaine who confirms the [news of] that King's continuing in good health."[1]

On October 22nd the King and Queen returned to Saint-Germain.

Towards the end of his life, James, disappointed alike of substantial aid from the Pope and a restoration at the hands of his English subjects, seems to have looked towards Scotland as the goal of his hopes. With the Revolution in Scotland James had been only indirectly concerned, since his expectation of making a triumphal entry into that country from Ireland had been disappointed. The change of government there had been accompanied by great disorder. The religious question was more embittered, the dividing line between parties more complicated, than in England.[2] Though actual warfare ended soon after the death of the Jacobite leader, Dundee, Scotland in 1691 was, in Dalrymple's phrase, "ripe for any mischief." The un-

[1] Caryll Papers.
[2] In the reign of the last two Stuarts, Episcopacy had been established with much persecution, and Catholics had been put in the principal offices.

fortunate Massacre of Glencoe in 1692 embittered the Highlanders against the Government,[1] and subsequently the failure of the Darien scheme profoundly irritated the whole Scottish nation against the English Court. This scheme of colonising the Isthmus of Darien (Panama), which the Scots had hoped to make the great market for Eastern trade, had ended in disastrous failure and the death of nearly all the colonists. The scheme was impracticable from the first, but the Scots attributed its failure to English national jealousy, and William's fear of rivalry to Dutch trade.

Thus it came about that James had many adherents in Scotland. Among the most picturesque and affecting scenes that can ever have taken place at Saint-Germain, was the King's farewell review of the followers of Dundee, who, being forced to fly to France, took service as privates in the French army, that they might avoid being a charge upon their King.[2] " They consisted of 150 officers, all of honourable birth, attached to their chieftains, and to each other. . . . Finding themselves a load upon the late King, whose finances could scarcely suffice for himself, they petitioned that Prince for leave to form themselves into a Company of Private Centinels asking no other favour than that they might be permitted to chuse their own officers." James assented. They repaired to Saint-Germain to be reviewed by him, before they were "modelled in the French army." A few days after they came, they posted themselves, in accoutrements borrowed from a French regiment, and drawn up in order, in a

---

[1] History has exonerated William from all blame for this savage act of tribal vengeance, to which he gave his assent under a misapprehension.
[2] Dalrymple, vol. i. p. 358, and vol. ii., App.

place through which he was to pass as he went to the chase. "He asked who they were, and was surprised to find they were the same men with whom, in garb better suited to their rank, he had the day before conversed at his levée. Struck with the levity of his own amusement contrasted with the misery of those who were suffering for him, he returned pensive to the palace. The day he reviewed them, he passed along the ranks, wrote in his pocket-book with his own hand every gentleman's name, and gave him his thanks in particular; and then removing to the front, bowed to the body with his hat off. After he had gone away, thinking honour enough was not done them, he returned, bowed again, but burst into tears. The body kneeled, bent their heads and eyes steadfast upon the ground, then passed by him with the usual honours of war."

The King's speech on this occasion rises to an eloquence foreign to him. "My own misfortunes," he exclaimed, "are not so nigh my heart as yours. It grieves me beyond what I can express to see many brave and worthy gentlemen, who had once the prospect of being the chief officers in my army, reduced to the stations of private centinels. Nothing but your loyalty, and that of a few of my subjects in Britain, who are forced from their allegiance by the Prince of Orange, and who I know will be ready on all occasions to serve me and my distressed family, could make me willing to live. The sense of what all of you have done and undergone for your loyalty, hath made so deep an impression in my heart, that if ever it please God to restore me, it is impossible I can be forgetfull of your services and sufferings. Neither can there be any posts in the armies of my dominions, but what you have just pretensions to. As for my son, and your Prince, he is your own blood, a child capable of any impressions ; and as his education will be from you, it is not supposable he can forget your merits. At your own desires, you are now going a long march, far distant from me. I have taken care to provide you with money, shoes, stockings and other necessarys. Fear God, and love one another. Write your wants particularly to me, and depend upon it always to find me your parent and King."

Perhaps James never felt the humiliation of his position more keenly than when bidding farewell to this little band of gallant gentlemen, who, after having sacrificed their families and fortunes in a lost cause, took service as common soldiers under an alien rule, rather than burden with their support the man for whose sake they were beggared. It may be that some of these men returned to their homes in 1696. For the *Memoirs* note that at the time of the Assassination Plot, when Berwick had gone over to England, "several gentlemen of the guards who were weary of serving as common men, . . . desired leave to go over into England and Scotland upon their private concerns."

It was thus towards Scotland that James's hopes were directed in the closing years of his life. This appears clearly from the letters of the Earl of Manchester, who came to Versailles as English ambassador in the autumn of 1699, just at the time when James and Maria were at Fontainebleau, so that he had to defer his audience with Louis XIV. "I shall obey his Majesty's orders," he writes, "in making the compliments, when I shall have a convenient opportunity, for at present it is not proper for me to go to Fontainebleau if I were in a condition, the Court of St Germains being there; and they are like to continue so long, that I imagine the Court will return to Versailles in less than a fortnight after they leave that plaçe."[1] Manchester took care to receive constant intelligence of the going and coming of Jacobite agents at Saint-Germain, which he immediately communicated to the English Government; they seem to have been for the most part obscure persons of little account. "The state of affairs at St Germains continues much the same as it was," Manchester wrote at the end of September; "they are still pleasing themselves with hopes the nation will recall them at last," though their best chance at present, he adds, is that the death of the King of Spain may plunge Europe into a War of Succession. He is informed that "K. J. has certainly a considerable sum of money, and it is said to be two hundred thousand English pounds. He is in a very good humour, and his emissaries here, do all they can to get the English to St Germains. I am apt to think they prevail mostly with the Scotch." On this point he is very explicit. "One Berkeley, a short thick brown fellow, aged about twenty-eight, with a large mouth, came about a fortnight past to St Germains and brought a letter from Lord Drummond and some other noblemen of Scotland, to Lord and Lady Perth. The chief matter he came about was to communicate a design they had formed of debauching the Army there, and that they had already begun by some dragoons. They have invented a sort of Button, which every one that engages for King James wears on his Coat; that they have a small Roll of Parchment in each

[1] *Memoirs of Affairs of State*, Christian Cole, 47.

Button, on which are written the first letters of these words: 'God bless King James and prosper his interest,' which will appear out of the Button, if it be turned round by an Instrument like a screw, made on purpose. Berkeley is gone to St Amand to receive Orders of my Lord Melfort."

These letters of Manchester are specially valuable, even coming from a hostile witness, as they lift the veil from Saint-Germain, about which there is little intelligence obtainable at this time. As he becomes better informed of the condition of affairs there, he writes on November 4th: "I am now assured that the only Hopes they have at St Germains is in the present conjunction of affairs in Scotland by the disappointment of Darien, etc. It is certain they are under debate, whether they shall not send some person of Note with Proposals to the most considerable men there."

Both James and Maria had been ailing from time to time during this year 1699, and towards the end of it the King's health gave cause for considerable anxiety. Maria was taken ill again with violent colic during their visit to Fontainebleau, and was unable to attend mass, or take her meals in public. Writing to Caryll on September 21st, she says :—

"i have been ill two or three days, but thank God i am quite well again, this is the first day i have been so, have been but once a hunting, and not played at all, so that i have don nothing extraordinary since i came hither; the King hunted three days together, but i thank God he is very well, we have sayd nothing yet of going away but i hope it shall be next weeke without faile. hear is not one word of news, i am sure it is non to tell you that you have all my esteem and friendship. M. R."

James also wrote to Caryll from Fontainebleau :—

"Fountainbleau, 1699.

"Parry gave me your letter with the Seale in it you sent me, wch it seems I droped, lett him that found it have a Louis-d'or, yesterday was a day of rest for we only took the aire by the cannal side in Coaches, this day we began to hunt, had a short chase, so that to-morrow I am to go out againe, pray lose no tyme in sending to me those letters I expect for no tyme is to be lost. J. R."

Nothing else of moment happened during their visit, except that James's son, Henry FitzJames, the Duke of Berwick's brother, whom he had created Duke of Albemarle, was thrown from his horse while out hunting, and picked up unconscious. It had been said of him when he was in Ireland that he was generally too drunk to sit a horse. The King and Queen left Fontainebleau on October 1st. Dangeau declares them to have been "plus contents que jamais de la bonne réception qu'on leur a faite ici et de tous les honneurs qu'on leur a rendus. On a été fort contents d'eux aussi, rien n'est égal à la vertu, à la politesse et à l'honnêteté de la reine," which Maria expresses in other words to "La Déposée" at Chaillot : "We are here treated by the King and by all the Court as we have been in other years, and that is to say all, for it could not be improved upon. You know how I have always spoken of it to you."

In November James was taken ill: he had been troubled by gout earlier in the autumn. Maria hurried back from a visit she was paying to Chaillot to nurse him. "He was surprised and very glad to see me arrive," she wrote to her friends there. "He has had very bad nights, and has suffered much for three or four days, but thank God, since yesterday, that is much better." She is sleeping in a little bed in his room, she says—"and you may believe, my dear Mothèr, that I have suffered not a little in seeing the King suffer so much." After thanking her sisters for their prayers, she continues : " My own health is good. God does not send all sorts of afflictions at the same time. He knows my weakness and He deals gently with it. . . . I recommend my son to your prayers, who will make his first communion at Christmas, if it please God."

CHAPTER XX

JAMES'S LAST DAYS AND DEATH

THE year 1700, the last that James and Maria were destined to spend together, did not dawn auspiciously for them. The kindness of the French King could not conceal from them the alteration in their position. "On vit encore poliment avec la famille royale," writes Madame, alluding to Saint-Germain, " mais on fait tout ce que veut le roi Guillaume." Manchester speaks of the Court there being in high spirits, and having large sums of money ; but in so far as the Queen's letters to Chaillot reflect their condition, they reveal failing health and financial anxiety. A letter written in August by the Queen leaves no doubt of the straits in which the Stuarts were at this time for money. It appears from a very guarded passage that Maria had made some application to De Maintenon for pecuniary help ; it is difficult to see to whom else she can be alluding by "la personne à qui j'ouvris mon cœur." Her representations were disregarded, and she describes herself as "astonished and humiliated," and continues : "However, I do not believe I am sufficiently humble to speak to her of it a second time whatever inconvenience I suffer. No more is there any order from Rome with regard to our poor. On the contrary, the Pope is very ill, and I think he will die before giving way, so that yesterday we formed the resolution of selling some jewellery to pay the pension due in the month of September, and subsequently it will be necessary to do the same thing every month, unless help comes from elsewhere, of which I see no prospect."

The discontent in Scotland, the rumours of William III.'s failing health, the possibility that Charles of Spain's death without a direct heir would plunge Europe into a War of Succession—all these chances indeed might suggest vague hopes to Jacobite exiles; but this sentence of Madame's, "We still live civilly with the royal family," shows how illusory such hopes were in reality.

In the midst of an approaching crisis which might at any moment convulse Europe, the event of most moment to Maria was the first communion of her son, the Prince of Wales, "who, thank God, has appeared to make his first communion in a very good spirit," she writes to Chaillot. "I was unable to contain my tears at seeing him communicate, and it seems to me that I have given him to God with my whole heart, entreating Him to let him live only that he may serve, honour, and love Him. The child appears to me to be well resolved to do so, and he has assured me that he would rather die than offend God mortally." Poor little boy of twelve years old brought up in this nun-like atmosphere, how could he ever hope to bear his part in the world like a man? The Queen writes again a little later of the Prince's serious illness, which has evidently caused her acute anxiety: "For myself

I have been more frightened than ill, and my illness has never been anything more than a severe cold with half a day's fever. I still have a little cold, but nothing that matters. What frightened me was the serious illness of my son, for during thirteen or fourteen days the fever never left him, and he was hardly a little recovered when the King fell ill with it. I own to you that I thought this would overwhelm me with distress, but, thank God, he only had one attack, and a very severe cold from which he is not yet free. This attack alone has very much reduced and weakened him, and he still can go no further than the little Chapel of the Children. This is why I was unwilling to leave him alone here to go to Chaillot; but for the last two days his cold has been better, and he is recovering his strength so well that I hope to see him quite recovered before the end of this week. My son is also much pulled down and is very weak, but he is also recovering these last two days, and went to mass for the first time the day before yesterday. My poor daughter also had a violent feverish attack for two days, but she has been going out for some days, and is entirely recovered, so much so, that, thank God, we are now all out of hospital, and this morning the King and I communicated together in the little chapel."

A little later, in March, the Queen writes again to "La Déposée" about her own health in the intimate way in which people of those days delighted in medical details concerning which a modern correspondent would prefer to be reticent. The poor Queen had sufficient cause for anxiety, but two hundred years ago physical ills of a serious nature were only to be met by resignation, though people sometimes called in some obscure monk with a reputation for skill in simples, much as the adventurous to-day call in a bone-setter after the legitimate practitioner has failed. Maria had at least had many opportunities of practising resignation. "I know not how God will deal with me," she writes, "in this or in aught else. I try to resign myself unreservedly into His hands, so that He may do with and through me all that He pleases. . . . The King is wonderfully well, thank God, in soul and body. My son has a very bad cold. My daughter often has toothache."

During the ensuing spring and summer, things went on as usual. There were two marriages in the English royal family. The Duke of Berwick, a widower of two years, married a daughter of Colonel Bulkeley, on April 18th; and in July Henry FitzJames married a Mademoiselle de Lussan. She was the daughter of a maid of honour to Madame la Princesse, and the marriage had been arranged with Maria through the intervention of the Duchesse de Maine, who was fond of Mademoiselle de Lussan. His bride brought FitzJames a dowry. He had, says Dangeau,[1] only 9000 livres, an allowance from James, and 6000 francs as "chef d'escadre." Manchester gives a slightly different version of this occurrence. "Mr FitzJames," he says, "who is lately married, is to be made Duke of France. I suppose she is not willing to trust to his dukedom in England (Albemarle). The King gives him a pension of 20,000 livres, and he is to have an apartment and a table from the Duke of Maine, both at Versailles and at Paris. All this is done by Madame de Maintenon, who is very fond of the

[1] Vol. iii., July 8, 1700.

young lady."[1] Maria was ill in July, but at the end of September the usual Fontainebleau visit took place. Dangeau mentions the fact that each journey they made there cost Louis 20,000 écus. The visit, which lasted a fortnight, was without incident, except that the Duchess of Albemarle, FitzJames's wife, having taken a tabouret in the presence of the Duchesse de Bourgogne, was requested to pay the usual fee of 100 pistoles due on such an occasion from duchesses. The lady, who seems to have had plenty of pretension, declined to pay it on the ground that she had a right to a tabouret as a daughter-in-law of a king, and not as a duchess. Louis upheld this wholly illegitimate claim, out of consideration for James and Maria, and instructed the Duchesse de Lude to forbid the valets de chambre to demand the fee in future.

A letter of Madame to her aunt, the Electress Sophia, gives a vivid glimpse of James at this time—becoming rather senile, and foolishly good-natured: "The King and Queen of England talked of nothing but you. The good King had tears in his eyes, he is so fond of you. He said, raising his two hands, 'Ooo pou—pour cela, ell—ell—ell me—ma toujours aimée'; for he stammers more than ever."[2] The Queen describes the visit, after her return to Saint-Germain, in a letter to Chaillot : " Thank God, I have never had such good health at Fontainebleau as this year. The King my husband, too, has been perfectly well. He hunted nearly every day and has grown fat. We had the finest weather in the world ; and the King of France, as usual, has overwhelmed us with a thousand marks of

[1] C. Cole.
[2] October 6, 1700. Correspondance de Madame.

his kindness, and of a cordial friendship, which gives us the greatest pleasure. All the royal family has followed his example, and all the Court."

To Caryll she wrote more unreservedly. Speaking of Louis's kindness, she says: "This King has been but once in privat with us, and i find that he thinks the P. of Orange is not well, he is as civil and kynd to us, as he uses to be, and wee as modest and as silent, as to any thing of businesse." In another letter she tells him that "Lord Manchester [the Earl of Manchester, English ambassador] at last is to be hear next friday to give notice of the death of the young prince of Denmark; i wish after staying so long that he had stayd three days longer, and we should have been gon, for tho we have not yet named the day for our going away, wee intend it the 11 or 12 of this month; i beleive i shall have no mor to say to you betwixt this, and that time, without you furnish me with som new matter, i shall have a real estime, and sincere friendship for you, as indeed i owe you upon a thousand accounts. —M. R., *October* 3."

Manchester, who thought Saint-Germain was giving itself too great airs, took the opportunity of paying a visit to Fontainebleau while James and Maria were there, in order to humiliate them. Writing to Lord Jersey, who was then Lord Chamberlain, on October 11th, he says:[1] "I have reason to think that my going to Fontainebleau, whilst the Court of Saint Germains was still there, may have a good effect; for of late, all about them are grown to so great a heighth as is not to be imagined, and I fear they have gained upon too many of the English that are here. They heard of

[1] Christian Cole.

my coming for some time, and yet would not believe it. I find it has humbled them mightily. I did not avoid anything that was necessary to my character (as ambassador). My coach came to the great stairs, which is under the apartment of the late King (James). I saw several faces I knew in England, but I hope never to see them there again."

The intelligence from Saint-Germain that Manchester was able to glean for his English despatches does not amount to very much, yet such little scraps of news make up the mosaic of history. Several Scottish gentlemen had come over in July to see what James was disposed to do and to raise funds; but "those of Saint Germains seem not disposed to part with money"—for the best of reasons. Manchester describes them a little later as being in "extraordinary joy" owing to the very disquieting reports of the King of England's state of health, and says "how pleased they are, and confident of being soon in England." When news came of the death of the little Duke of Gloucester, Anne's child, the Court went into mourning, and a hunting party that had been arranged for the Prince of Wales was put off out of respect for his nephew. The ambassador also conveys sinister rumours of a design for William's assassination by one William Davison, in which he was associated with William Grimes. There was apparently a family of this name at Saint-Germain. A Peter Grimes and his cousin, Colonel William Grimes, had been among Dundee's officers. He had been in receipt of a pension from James in Edinburgh, according to Manchester. But every kind of obscure adventurer seems to have had the entrée to Saint-Germain latterly. "They see every day new faces, who come

JAMES'S LAST DAYS AND DEATH 415

to make their court there," but "there are few of note that go."[1]

In November took place the death of Charles II. of Spain, an event that had long been anxiously anticipated by every European State. The question was one of the preservation of the balance of power in Europe. France and the Empire both had claims to the Spanish dominions, which comprised Spain, the Netherlands, the Kingdom of Naples and Sicily, the Duchy of Milan, besides the New World colonies, such as Mexico, Peru, Chili, and Cuba. Charles II. having no direct heir, his dominions passed to his aunt Maria, or to one or other of his sisters, Louis XIV.'s wife, Maria Theresa, or Leopold's wife, Margaret. In this very general statement of the position, the merits of their respective claims, which had now passed to their descendants, need not be discussed; but Louis XIV. claimed the throne of Spain for his grandson, the Duke of Anjou. The Emperor claimed it for his son, the Archduke Charles of Austria.

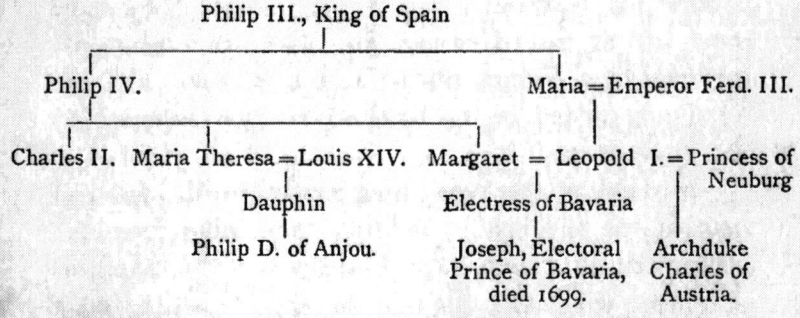

```
              Philip III., King of Spain
                       |
        ┌──────────────┴──────────────┐
     Philip IV.                   Maria = Emperor Ferd. III.
        |                              |
 ┌──────┼──────────────┐                |
Charles II. Maria Theresa = Louis XIV. Margaret = Leopold I. = Princess of
                    |                      |                    Neuburg
                 Dauphin              Electress of Bavaria       |
                    |                      |
          Philip D. of Anjou.    Joseph, Electoral        Archduke
                                 Prince of Bavaria,      Charles of
                                 died 1699.              Austria.
```

The matter, it was believed, had been arranged by a compromise. By the Second Partition Treaty of 1700, it was provided that Spain, the Netherlands, and the colonies were to go to Austria. When, however,

[1] The Earl of Manchester (Christian Cole).

Charles II. died, it was found that he had made a will leaving the whole of his dominions to the Duke of Anjou. The will was immediately accepted by Louis XIV. on behalf of his grandson.

This enormous accession to the power of France at once raised the hopes of Saint-Germain. "I do assure you," writes Manchester, "there is great joy at Saint-Germain. The late King goes this day to wait on the Duke of Anjou. I was last night at Monsieur's, who is at Paris, where I found Lord Melfort, who gives himself other airs than he used to." The ambassador adds later, that James believes he (Manchester) will be forbidden to come to Versailles. By the same letter he sends warning that a Captain Robert Maxwell has just left Saint-Germain with letters for Scotland; that he knows the whole secret affairs of that country; and may be identified as "he wants two teeth before." Early in 1701 he reports that Middleton has had an interview with the French ministers to ask for troops for Scotland. "The only hopes they have now left at Saint-Germain are, that they are to be restored by a French power in a short time, and the intrigues carried on in Scotland are too apparent to be doubted on."

In March of this year James was taken ill. He had two fits of apoplexy. Writing to Chaillot from his sick-room on March 13th, Maria says: "I take this moment, while the King is sleeping, to write you a word by his bedside. I read him your letter, and he has charged me to heartily thank our Mother, yourself ("La Déposée") and all our sisters for your prayers and for the interest that you take in his illness, which is not painful, but I fear dangerous, for he has an extreme weakness in the right hand and leg which threatens paralysis. His brain is quite free, thank God, but he trembles for fear that it may mount to the head."

Manchester gives a less favourable account of the old King's health, and his projected journey to Bourbon, to take the waters there. "He is far from being well, and is very much broke of late, so that none think he can last long. His stay at Bourbon will be of three weeks. He is to be eleven days agoing, and as long coming back. They intend to pump [douche] his right arm, which he has lost the use of, and he is to bathe and drink the waters. They desired but thirty thousand livres of the French Court for this journey, which was immediately sent them in gold. I don't know how they may advise him after that to a hotter climate, which may be convenient enough on several accounts. In short his senses and his memory are very much decayed, and I believe a few months will carry him off."

The Bourbon journey, which the Queen undertook with her dying husband, hoping against hope for his recovery, can fortunately be reconstructed step by step. For some months past, stray allusions in contemporary letters do no more than tear little rifts, as it were, in the mists of time, through which the life of the Court at Saint-Germain can be seen in evanescent glimpses; but now a fuller record survives to illumine the stages by which the King and Queen travelled with toil and trouble in their slow, lumbering carriages over bad roads. James had been taken ill while he and the Queen were at mass in the chapel of Saint-Germain on March 4th. Maria, kneeling beside him, her head bent down in prayer, did not observe it, as her coif concealed her husband from her; but the officiating priests, noticing the King's pallor, signed to some of those present to come forward, and James was lifted into a seat, where he remained unconscious and apparently dead for some time, while the Queen was beside herself with anxiety. At last, opening his eyes, and evidently believing himself to be dying, he said to her: "I pity you from my heart; for myself I am content." His wife said afterwards that there never was a more patient, obedient, and contented invalid, for he did all that was required of him, accepted submissively every remedy that was given him by his doctors, and cheerfully awaited the death that he desired.

On the 11th James had an attack of paralysis which affected his right side. He expressed satisfaction at his sufferings, saying: "Is it not just that I should do penance in my own body? for till now I have never suffered anything physically, having always had good health, and I have been a great offender before God." From this attack James gradually rallied so far that Fagon, Louis XIV.'s physician, recommended a visit to Bourbon. It was arranged that they should leave Saint-Germain on April 4th. Louis, who had been throughout James's illness assiduous in his attentions, came to bid them farewell. He was allowing them 100,000 francs a month for their travelling expenses, and had provided twenty-six carriage-horses and all the necessaries of the journey. Indeed, Maria could not speak feelingly enough of his goodness to them at this time. She was deeply touched by it. "For my part," she said to the nuns of Chaillot, "I owe him everything that I am," and after recounting his past kindness she added: "After all that, I own that I did not know him, and that I should never have believed him capable of the tenderness that he has shown for us, thinking of everything for our journey—men, money, horses in abundance; and when he came to say good-bye to us two days ago he said: 'I come to tell you on behalf of M. Fagon that it is time to start. He made you put off your journey, but at present he hastens your departure."

On the first day of their journey, James and Maria made a short stay at Chaillot, where they arrived towards evening. The King looked better than they expected; he showed the good nuns, with childish pleasure, how he could now move his hand without difficulty, but they noticed that he still dragged his right leg a little. He assured them that he believed he owed his recovery to their prayers, and begged for a continuance of them. After seeing the King off to Paris, where she was to join him the next day at the Duc de Lauzun's, Maria spent a long time talking with her friends, telling them all the details of her husband's illness, his piety, and the goodness of the French King. On leaving she gave them a purse of a hundred louis-d'or, saying that she hoped some day to be able to repay her debt to them, and, taking leave early on the morning of the 5th, joined James in Paris. The next day the King and Queen continued their journey by very easy stages of seven leagues a day, starting after dinner in order not to exhaust James's feeble energies. They went by way of Essone, Fontainebleau, Nemours, and arrived on Saturday the 9th at Montargis. From here the Mother Superior of the Convent of the Visitation sent a full account of the royal visitors to Chaillot.[1] The Queen had come to vespers and admired the singing; accompanied by only one or two ladies, she went over the monastery, winning all by her gentle and modest bearing, and holding out hopes that the King too might visit the nuns, if he were sufficiently recovered, on his return journey. She had added that her greatest ambition was to become one of the least of the daughters of the Visitation. A Protestant follower of James was left behind here ill, and abjured his religion on his death-bed, "a marvellous conversion," for which a Te Deum was sung in the parish church.

After leaving Montargis, the King and Queen slept at Briare on April 11th, arriving at Cosne on the 12th. Here Lady d'Almond takes up the pen. "We must hope," she says, "that the King will be so well from the waters for which he is making this journey that we need not complain of the fatigues that we undergo, which for the Queen are not light, or of the cold that there has been since last Tuesday, and to-day we perish of heat, of the dirt of everything except what we brought with us." On the 13th La Charité was reached, and there James was obliged to rest to recover from a slight attack of gout. They arrived at Nevers on the 19th. Here they stayed at the episcopal palace. The nuns of the convent there were assembled by the bishop to see their arrival at his house, and Maria, catching sight of them, clapped her hands and exclaimed how glad she was to see them, and that she would come to the convent that evening—

[1] The nuns of Chaillot fortunately preserved the letters and accounts of this journey of James and Maria, and collected them into a sort of journal.

a visit she was obliged to defer till next day, owing to the long addresses of welcome from the officials of the little town; for Louis had given orders as to their reception at the places visited on their route. The Mother Superior of Nevers described the splendour of their entertainment by the archbishop.

One little incident greatly annoyed the good mother on the occasion of Maria's visit to the convent. "Mme. la Marquise des Poisses, our benefactress, eighty-four years old, ill for a month, and afflicted in mind and body, bethought herself of paying us a surprise visit, as is her right, came here, and with her a number of people crowded in too. The Queen looked surprised at seeing such a crowd in our house." The mother begs that Madame Priolo, "La Déposée" of Chaillot, to whom she is writing, will assure the Queen that this shall be avoided on her return. Poor Lady d'Almond, who speaks so feelingly of the discomforts of the journey, was left behind ill, with a feverish cold, which took away her voice. She rejoined the Queen later. On the 18th the royal party arrived at Bourbon, and Lady d'Almond wrote to Madame Priolo, to say that the King was better, and the Queen was well. They have everywhere been received as if it were the King of France himself, she says. "It is indeed admirable and astonishing to see the sincere and deep kindness of the great monarch for our King and Queen. He has thought of everything that could contribute to make their journey less fatiguing and more pleasant and convenient. He has sent here furniture for their room and their house, forgetting nothing. I exclaimed in public, 'Oh! what a good thing it is for your Majesty to have such a King for a friend!'"

A medical consultation was held on the King's arrival, and " on résolu de purger le Roy samedi, et de comencer à luy donner des eaux en petite quantité dimanche." A little room opening off the Queen's was fitted up as a chapel, where the King could hear mass when it was cold, or when he was taking the waters. James and Maria were well lodged—a good room for the King, one for the Queen, an ante-chamber, a good room for the *baquets* (tubs). Their attendants were equally well cared for. The day after her arrival the Queen wrote herself to Caryll :—

"Tho' i have had no tre from you since my last, yet i will give you the satisfaction to hear from myself that wee gott safe to this place, last night at seven aclock, i thank God the King grows better every day then other, his goute is quitt gone, he eats well sleeps well, and his hand and knee are much stronger, then they were, if the waters do but never so little good, he must go back quitt well ; wee shall know this night, after having consulted the phicitians of this place, when he may begin to drink, but every body agrees, he must take som days rest after so long a iourney, it has indeed been very troublesom, but for my part i ought not to complaine, for i never was better in my life, and ther is few of the whole traine that have kept so well as myself ; it has cost poor Berkenhead[1] very dear, or to say beter, he has purchased heaven very cheap, for i hope in God's mercy he will have it ; being dead with all the sentiments of a true Christian, and a good Catholic, God almighty has been very good to him, and shewd him a particular providence in his sicknesse and death, the King and i are realy concerned for his death, but wee can not but be overioyed at the manner of it ; the King bids me tell you, that he would have

[1] The death-bed convert.

you send Hirne to take what papers he might have in his chamber, and particularly look for those that are mentioned in the enclosed note, if they be worth it, send them to me, if not keep them with the rest, that you shall find worth your keeping; i must writt to Me de Maintenon from whom i had a very kynd long tre last night, therefor i can not writt to Ld Perth, nor Lady Middleton, for i have writt to my daughter and am weary already, pray tell them so, and that i will do it the next post, by which i hope i shall hear from yourself, for i think it long since i did; (we had last night the english tres)."

James began to recover while he was at Bourbon. On fine days he walked on the terrace of the Capucins, whose church adjoined the house in which he was staying. The Queen attended mass in the little parish church. It was the season at Bourbon, so that many visitors were there, and went to pay their court to the English royal family, among them members of religious houses, whom Maria thought should have remained in their monasteries. Meanwhile James bathed and had douches and took the waters, and walked in a little garden. Madame de Maintenon wrote regularly, sending any news that could amuse and interest her correspondents. In May Lady d'Almond sends a bulletin to Chaillot. The doctors are agreed, she says, that their Majesties' health is very good, and the King is to discontinue all remedies; the douche of the day before had produced a hæmorrhage, which was not considered serious. James thought it came from his head; he had had it before at Saint-Germain, and again at La Charité, but attached no importance to it. Only it was necessary to avoid irritating him. On their return journey, which was to take place shortly, they would make some stay at Moulins, where the Queen wished to visit a convent of the Visitation.

Before leaving Bourbon Maria wrote again to Caryll :—

"I have putt off writing to you in hopes still every post to receive a tre from you, but i find what i thought impossible, that you hate writting yet mor, then i do, since you can hold out longer without writting to me, then i can to you, for without any manner of compliment i may tell you, that it has realy been uneasy to me, to be so long without hearing from you, and even without writting to you ; but having engaged myself to my children to write to them every post, and beeing often obliged to write to Lord Perth and L^y Middleton for what concerned them, besides the Duchesse of ———, and once a week constantly to Me de Maintenon as she has don to me, i realy was comonly so weary every post day, that i still putt it off, not doubting but that Ld Middleton and Mr Innesse gave you an account of all that was worth it hear, which is only the King's health, which also i gave an exact account to my children, and when ther has been any thing extraordinary i have made Mr Constable give an account to Sir William to impart it to you ; you need not be frighted at the last account, for God be thanked the King is very well, and i dont doubt but you will find him much altered for the better, when you see him, we shall go from hence on munday if it please God, but you must not expect us in a fortnight after that, you shall have our roote, and i desire to hear from my children upon the road as often as i have don hear, tho i do not promise them to writt them so often, the King would have had me som time ago have writt on purpose to you, to putt you in mind of his memoirs, but Mr Inesse has assured us, that you are hard at worke about them, so that now wee only owe you thanks, and wee give them to you most heartily, begging of you to go on till you perfect the worke, i hope in God the King will perfect that of his health for all the Doctors hear assure us, that he will find yett mor benefit by these waters a month hence, then he does at present, tho he finds a great deel; i hope you have kept your health as well as i have don mine, and that wee shall find one another when wee meet, as well, as when we parted, and as good friends, mor of me you can not desire, for it is impossible to augment either the esteem, or kindnesse i have had for you ever since i knew you well. M. R."

The visit of the King and Queen to Moulins on their return journey must have exhausted James's feeble energies. They arrived on Monday, May 24th. He was tired, and rested the most of the day. On Tuesday they went to hear mass at the Jesuits, and in the afternoon received congratulatory addresses from all the officials of the place. In the evening Maria went over the convent of the Visitation, spending some time in edifying conversation with the nuns, and kneeling before the relics of the convent, the heart and eyes of Mère Chantal of blessed memory, which were preserved in crystal. The next day they both heard mass at the Visitation, and received the holy communion from Monseigneur d'Autun. From thence they proceeded to the parish church, where they listened to an address from the bishop at the head of his clergy, and afterwards high mass. After this James was allowed a short respite; he sat on his balcony to watch a religious procession from Notre Dame, which was followed by the Queen on foot. In the evening they both went to Notre Dame for the sermon and *Salut*.

On the 7th of June the King and Queen arrived home again, and the next day Louis went to Saint-Germain to visit them, as well as most other members of the family. James was much better for his journey, but, as Dangeau phrases it, "ce n'est pas une santé sur laquelle on puisse conter." He was well enough to visit Marly in August, but in September he became rapidly worse. Madame, who went to visit him, wrote afterwards :—

"*Sept.* 8, 1701.

"I found King James in a piteous state. His voice, it is true, was still as strong as usual, and he recognised people; but he looks very bad, and has a beard like a Capucin. Last Sunday, after having received the sacraments, he summoned his children and household, gave them his blessing—after which he preached a long sermon to the Prince of Wales and the servants."

At times he rallied, but it was obvious that the end was near, and in these last days the old King sought to impress his little son with the vanity of earthly honour. However dazzling a crown might appear, there came a time, his father told the boy, when it seemed a thing of no moment: God alone was to be loved, and eternity to be desired. He must remember always to show respect to his mother, and affection and gratitude to that King from whom he had received so great benefits.

On one of Louis's last visits James expressed a wish to be buried without any ostentation or ceremony in the parish church, with no monument, and for epitaph the words, "Ci git Jacques second roi d'Angleterre." During these last days Louis and other members of the royal family came to visit him. Louis was so touched by the sufferings and piety of this old friend, kinsman, and pensioner of nearly twelve years, that, carried away by emotion, in defiance of all his treaties, in violation of all the duty he owed to his exhausted country, he gave rein to sentiment, and, by declaring that he would recognise the Prince of Wales as King of England, once more plunged Europe into war. This scene, so momentous and dramatic, took place on Tuesday, September 13th, on the occasion of Louis's last visit to James.

James had already taken the last sacrament, and was fallen into a kind of lethargy. The Queen was so overcome by grief that he had asked those present to lead her into her room. On Louis's arrival, he first went to the Queen and acquainted her with his resolution, "which was some comfort to her in the deep affliction she was in"; he then sent for the Prince of Wales and told him, that if it pleased God to call for the King his father, he would be a father to him, on which the boy replied that he should find him as dutiful and respectful as if he were his son. The King then went to James's sick-room, and asked him how he was, but the sick man appeared unconscious of his presence, till those present rousing him, and telling him that the King of France was there, James began feebly to thank him for all his past kindness, upon which Louis intercepting him said:[1] "'Sir, that is but a small matter. I have something to acquaint you with of greater consequence'; upon which the King's servants imagining he would be private (the room being full of people), began to retire, which his Most Christian Majesty perceiving, sayd out aloud, 'Let nobody withdraw,' and then went on: 'I am come, sir, to acquaint you, that whenever it shall pleas God to call your Majesty out of this world, I will take your family

[1] Clarke's *Life*.

into my protection, and will treat your son the Prince of Wales in the same manner I have treated you, and acknowlidg him as he then will be King of England'; upon which all that were present, as well French as English, burst into tears, not being able any other way to express that mixture of joy and grief with which they were so surprisingly seized; some indeed threw themselves at his Most Christian Majesty's feet, others by their gestures and countenances (much more expressive on such occasions than words and speeches) declar'd their gratitude for so generous an action, with which his Most Christian Majesty was so moved, that he could not refrain weeping himself. The King all this while was endeavouring to say something to him upon it, but the confused noise being too great, and he too weak to make himself heard, his Most Christian Majesty took his leave and went away."[1]

During the next two days James had some moments of consciousness, in one of which he sent for his son and urged him never to forget what he owed to Louis, and to remember that he ought always to prefer God and religion to all temporal interests. For the most part he remained in a stupor, from which he could not be roused, and so died towards three o'clock in the afternoon of Friday, September 16th, the day of the week on which he had often expressed a wish to die. He had almost completed his sixty-eighth year.

[1] In Clarke's *Life of James II.* it is affirmed that Louis called a council in order to discuss so weighty a resolution, that his advisers were all averse to it, but the Dauphin, and other members of the royal family, thought it "unbecoming the dignitie of the crown of France to abandon a Prince of their own Blood." Neither Dangeau nor Saint-Simon mentions a council, but only that Louis announced what he had done to his Court on his return, and that reflections were at once exchanged, privately, on the danger and difficulties it involved.

The same evening Maria retired to Chaillot. The dead King lay in state for four-and-twenty hours, while the office of the dead was said during the night, and masses during the day, at the altars which had been erected in his room. His last wishes with regard to his burial were disregarded by Louis's orders. His reputation for sanctity had been such that his mortal remains were distributed as precious relics. In the evening he was embalmed, and part of his entrails were sent to the parish church, part to the English College of St Omer. "The braines and fleshy part of the head" were sent to the Scotch College at Paris, "where at the charge of the Duke of Perth was errected a fair monument, as a due acknowlidgment of their being honnoured with those precious Reliques."

This being done, about seven o'clock, the evening after he died, they set out with his body to deposit it in the Church of the English Benedictines in Paris, till such time as his repentant subjects should seek to "repair what wrongs Earth's journey did" by paying the last honours after death to him whom they rejected in life. The funeral procession was accompanied by the Duke of Berwick, the Earl of Middleton, his Majesty's chaplains, and others of his servants. At midnight they reached Chaillot, where James's heart was to be deposited, and they strove to make no sound by which Maria should know of their coming; but she, "having a sort of presentiment of what was intended," was overwhelmed with anguish and sorrow all the while. When they were arrived in Paris, Dr Ingleton, Almoner to the Queen, delivered his body to the Prior with an "elegant Latin oration."

The subsequent fate of James's mortal remains was

investigated by an indefatigable student in Stuart history, the Marquise Campana de Cavelli, whose monumental work was unhappily never completed in print. When she visited Paris, before 1870, she was able to identify the spot where James's body had been deposited. At that date, what was left of the church and college had become a private school, and she quotes a curious document written in 1840 by an octogenarian Irishman, who had, like many others, been imprisoned in the Convent of the Benedictines in Paris. He affirmed that in one of the chapels of the church the body of James II. remained exposed to view, and in a perfect state of preservation. The "sans-culottes" had broken open and taken away the leaden coffin in which it was enclosed to make bullets. The body was afterwards removed and all traces of it lost. The same fate overtook the fragments of his remains with the destruction of the places to which they had been confided.

The parish church of Saint-Germain-en-Laye was the only exception. During the rebuilding of the church in 1824, workmen came upon three leaden boxes, lying close together, on one of which was inscribed upon a copper plate : "Ici est une portion de la chair, et des parties nobles du corps, du très-haut, très-puissant, très-excellent prince Jacques Stuart, second du nom, Roy de la Grande-Bretagne, né le XXII Octobre MDCXXXIII, décédé en France à Saint-Germain-en-Laye le XVI Septembre MDCCI." The two other boxes were identified from the archives of the Mairie as those containing remains of the Queen and the Princess Louise ; and all three were placed in the treasury of the sacristy. A tomb was afterwards constructed to receive them by order of George IV., but it subsequently fell into decay, and the present unostentatious but dignified monument on the right of the main entrance was erected by command of the late Queen Victoria. Thus, after all, James II.'s last wishes were fulfilled; and it is in the parish church of Saint-Germain-en-Laye that his mortal remains rest, beneath a monument so modest that the visitor may easily overlook it. It bears the following inscription :—

Regio Cineri, Pietas Regia

Ferale quisquis hoc monumentum suspicis,
Rerum humanarum vices meditare.
Magnus in prosperis, in adversis major,
    Jacobus II. Anglorum Rex
Insignes ærumnas dolendaque fata
Pio placidoque obitu exsolvit
    In hac urbe,
Die xvi Septembris Anno MDCCI.
Et nobiliores quædam corporis ejus partes
    Hic reconditæ asservantur.

To the Ashes of a King, the Affection of a Queen

You who look upon this monument of the dead
Ponder the mutability of human life.
Great in prosperity, in adversity greater still,
    James II. King of England
Was set free from signal calamities and grievous fortunes
By a religious and tranquil death
    In this city,
On the 16th day of September 1701.
Of his body the nobler parts
    Are here out of sight preserved.

The following description of the King, while he lived, may be from the pen of Caryll :—

"He was something above the middle stature, well-shaped, very nervous and strong; his face was rather long, his complexion fair and his countenance engaging; his outward carriage was a little stiff and constrained, which made it not so gracious, as it was courteous and obliging. He was affable and easy of access, for he affected not formalitie ; . . . and having something of a hesitation in his speech his discourse was not so gracious as it was judicious and solid. . . . He was a great lover of exercise, especially walking and hunting. . . . He was a kind husband, notwithstanding his infirmities during his youth, but especially in his later days, when he repair'd his former infidelities by a most tender affection, mixed with a respect and defference to the incomparable merit and virtue of the Queen."

To conclude in the stately periods of Sir John Dalrymple : "Whoever perceives not in the events of the period to which these memoirs relate the hand of an Almighty Providence, which, upon the ruins of an illustrious but misguided family, raised up a mighty nation to show mankind the sublime heights to which liberty may conduct them, must be blind indeed ! May that Providence which conferred liberty upon our ancestors at the Revolution, grant that their posterity may never either lose the love of it upon the one hand, or abuse the enjoyment of it upon the other."

INDEX

Abercorn, Duke of, 270.
Adda, Papal Nuncio, 6, 110, 146.
Ailesbury, Earl of, 251.
Albeville, Marquis d', 7, 267.
Alexander VIII., Pope, 132, 198, 227, 247, 384.
Almond, Comtesse d' (Vittoria Davia), 21, 57, 77, 92, 108, 115, 248, 267, 355, 420.
Angélique Claire, La Mère, 119.
Anjou, Duc d', 79, 128, 415.
Anne, Princess, 36, 304, 363, 375, 388, 414.
Arundell, Lord, 270, 291.
Ashton, John, 254.
Assassination Plot, 317, 352, 356, 358, 362, 392.
Atkins, Mr, 268.
Attainder, Act of, 217.
Aughrim, battle at, 300.
Augsburg, League of, 105, 383.
Aumont, Duc d', 46, 52, 62.
Austria, Anne of, 60.
  Charles, Archduke of, 415.
  Leopold, Emperor of, 104, 371, 373.
Autun, Monseigneur d', 425.
Avaux, Comte d', 7, 148, 168, 180, 188, 196, 203, 212.

Bagnel, 269.
Baltazar, Mr, 267.
Barbésieux, 304, 317.
Barclay, Sir George, 273, 358, 362.
  Miss, 108.
Barillon, 7, 148.
Barkenhead, Mr, 269.
Barry, Mr, 269.
Bassompierre, Maréchal de, 115.
Bavaria, Elector of, 105.
Beachy Head, French victory of, 243, 253.
Beaufort, Duke of, 231, 291.
Beaulieu, Mr, 268.
Beaumelle, La, 102, 124.
Beauvilliers, Duc de, 380.
Beedle, 269.
Bellayse, 270.
Bellefonds, Marshal, 309, 343.
Bellew, Lady Mary, 177.
Benefield, Mr, 267.
Beringhen, M., 52.
Berkeley, 404.
Berry, Duc de, 79, 128.
Berwick, Duchess of, 355.
  Duke of, 15, 42, 62, 152, 168, 173, 190, 210, 221, 236, 267, 273, 302, 326, 350, 359, 391, 411, 429.
Biddulph, Mr, 42, 267.
Bishops, Seven, trial of, 5.
Blois, Mademoiselle de, 73, 94, 247, 259.
Boisseleau, 145, 206, 247.
Bonrepaux, 7.
Bossuet, 322.
Boufflers, General, 353, 375, 390, 397.

Boyne, Battle of the, 174, 179, 234.
Boynton, Miss, 161.
Braganza, Catharine of, 313.
"Brass money," issue of, 198.
Brest, French victory at, 330.
Brinon, Marie de, 374.
Brown, Mr, 267.
Brun, Le, 118.
Bruyère, La, 16, 53. 111.
Buckingham, Mr, 268.
Bulkeley, Anne, 280.
  Captain Henry, 289.
Bulkeley, Lady Sophia, 267.
Burgundy, Duchess of, 379, 397, 412.
  Duke of, 79, 128, 371, 379.
Burkes, the, 183.
Burnet, 109.
Bussy-Rabutin, Comte de, 103, 111, 144.
Butler, Lady Mary, 208.

Cadrington, Mr, 268.
Canterbury, Archbishop of, 256.
Carlinford, Earl of, 106.
Carney, Mr, 269.
Carrol, Mr, 268.
Carter, Rear-Admiral, 257, 308.
Cary, 320.
Caryll, 14, 19, 246, 267, 272, 328, 348, 361, 363, 369, 387, 399, 405, 413, 422, 432.
  Mary, 369.
Castlemaine, 130.
Cavendish, Lord, 393.
Caylus, Madame de, 102.
Chaise, Père de la, 89, 101.
Chapman, widow, 200.
Chappell, Mrs, 267.
Charlton, 176.
Charost, Duc de, 44, 48.
Chartres, Duc de, 63, 73, 247, 258.
  Duchesse de, 131, 347.
Château-Renaud, Comte de, 303.
Chaulnes, Duc de, 147.
Chester, Bishop, 152.
Choisy, Abbé de, 102.
Churchill, Arabella, 38, 136, 152, 350.
  Lord, 62, 289, 303, 307, 323, 327, 330, 363.
Clancarty, Earl of, 152, 165.
Clanricarde, Lord, 222.
Clare, Lord, 81.
Clarendon, Lord, 162, 182, 192, 251, 256.
Claverhouse, 213.
Clement X., Pope, 11.
Cleveland, Duchess of, 81.
Colbert, 233, 284.
Condé, Prince de, 300.
Condon, Lady, 202.
Conquest, Mr, 267, 269.
Conspiracies, Jacobite, 253, 320, 327, 356.
Conti, Princesse de, 94, 119, 258.
Cork, Earl of, 192.
Cork, fall of, 201.

433   28

Coronation of William and Mary, 126.
Crane, Mr, 268.
Craven, Lord, 36.
Croissy, Madame de, 246.
　Monsieur de, 320.
Croix, Mr La, 268.
Crom, siege of Castle of, 175.
Cromwell, Henry, 192.
Cutts, Lord, 274.

Dalmont, Lady, 269.
Dalrymple, 184, 197, 212, 432.
Dangeau, 53, 68, 74, 94, 108, 131, 319, 393.
　Mademoiselle, 258.
Darien Scheme, 401.
Dartmouth, Lord, 15, 84, 130, 251, 256.
Dauphin, the (Monseigneur), 56, 59, 63, 69, 82, 87, 94, 109, 119, 246, 258, 293, 347, 371, 379, 394.
Dauphine, the, 53, 67, 74, 78, 83, 95, 126, 137.
Davies, Sir John, 219.
Davison, William, 414.
Declaration, formal, of States General, 9.
Declaration of James II., 306.
Delamere, Lord, 37.
Denmark, Prince Royal of, 319, 413.
Derwentwater, Lord, 256.
Dillon, Lady, 201.
Dillons, the, 183.
Dixie, Captain, 176, 350.
Dover, Lady, 195.
　Lord, 129, 152, 173, 216, 222, 229, 270.
Drummond, Lord, 404.
Dublin, surrender of, 239.
Dumbarton, Lord, 267, 270, 343.
Dundee, 225, 400.
Dungan, Lord, 182, 210, 221.

Elliot, 255.
Ellis, Sir William, 269.
Ely, Turner, Bishop of, 256.
Enniskillen, siege of, 179, 181, 209, 225.
Epinay, Madame d', 103.
Errol, Lady, 272, 276, 328.
Este, Cardinal Rinaldo d', 95, 111, 120, 349.
L'Estrade, 145.

Fagon, 418.
Fenwick, Sir John, 352.
Feversham, Lewis Duras, Earl of, 24, 34, 41, 252.
Fitzgerald, Captain Robert, 219.
FitzJames, Henry, 54, 152, 190, 210, 221, 406, 411.
Flanders campaign, 352.
Floyd, David, 269.
Fuller, 253.
Furstenburg, Cardinal, 246.
　Comtesse de, 246.
Fytton, Sir Alexander, 221.

Gace, M. de, 206.
Galloway, Bishop of, 152.
Gally, Father, 267.
Galmoy, Lord, 175, 222, 350.
Galway, 166.
Galways, the, 183.
Gaydon, 178.
Gervaise, Sir Humphrey, 219.
Ginkell, De, 302.
Glencoe, Massacre of, 401.
Gloucester, Duke of, 414.
Gobert, 118.
Godolphin, Lord, 289, 327, 363.
Gordon, John, 152, 208.

Gordon, Duke of, 188.
Gothard, Mr, 268.
Grafton, Duke of, 90.
Graham, Fergus, 267, 270.
Gramont, Comte de, 6, 157, 160.
　Comtesse de, 280, 292.
Granard, Lord, 190.
Grand, Monsieur Le, 53.
Grandval, 317.
Griffen, Lord, 269.
Grimes, William, 414.

Hales, Sir Edward, 25, 267.
Halifax, Lord, 37, 290.
Hall, Father, 208.
Hamilton, Anthony, 152, 157, 180, 193, 222, 264, 280.
　Lord Claude, 179.
　George, 161.
　Colonel James, 179.
　John, 152.
　Miss, 160.
　Richard, 164, 173, 179, 214, 221, 236, 269, 299.
Harcourt, Princesse d', 108.
Harrison, Mr, 268.
Hatcher, 269.
Henrietta Maria, 116.
Herbert, Admiral, 90.
　Lady Lucy, 267.
Hide, Mr, 267.
Howard, Cardinal, 385.
　Lord Thomas, 222.
Hyde, Anne, 157.

Inese, Mr, 267, 345, 424.
Ingleton, Dr, 429.
Innes, Father, 267, 328, 337.
Innocent XI., Pope, 94, 104, 112, 120, 132, 189, 383.
　XII., Pope, 384, 409.
Invasion, Jacobite, 304.
Invitation to Prince of Orange, 6.
Ireland, defeat of James in, 139.
　departure of James to, 119, 144.
　flight of James from, 238.
　renewal of campaign in, 302.
"Irish Night," the, 32.
Irish Priests, banishment of, 396.
　Parliament, 216.
　Privy Council, 221.
Iveaghs, the, 183.

James II., flight of, 23.
　arrest of, 28, 51.
　burial of, 429.
　death of, 428.
　illness of, 416.
Jennings, Fanny. See Tyrconnel, Lady.
Jersey, Lord, 413.
Johnston, Prior of Benedictines, 341, 429.

Kaunits, Count of, 107.
Keating, Chief Justice, 222.
Killiecrankie, battle of, 225.
King, Archbishop, 163, 169, 193, 201, 205, 208, 219.
Kinsale, arrival at, 152.
　fall of, 301.

La Hogue, battle off, 309, 320, 384.
Labadie, 54, 268, 269.
Lafayette, Madame de, 65, 71, 100, 124, 144.
Landen, battle of, 175, 325.
Largillière, 280.
Lauter, Mrs de, 267.

INDEX

Lauzun, Comte de, 16, 44, 61, 73, 81, 102, 130, 145, 221, 229, 232, 238, 248, 267, 294, 301, 312, 354, 394, 419.
Lavery, Mr, 267.
Lery-Giradin, 145.
Leyburn, 55, 267.
Limerick, Earl of, 182.
Limerick, siege of, 175, 177, 247, 281, 300.
Lloyd, Captain, 290, 304, 308, 320, 329.
London, Mr, 267.
Londonderry, siege of, 129, 171, 179, 209, 214, 225.
Lorges, Mademoiselle de, 354.
Lorraine, Duke of, 398.
Louis XIV., 7, 9, 55, 60, 61, 63, 65, 70, 90, 98, 118.
Louise-Marie, Princess, 117, 315, 371, 430.
Louvois, 44, 50, 81, 89, 148, 153, 170, 233, 293, 304.
Lucan, Lady, 357.
Lude, Duchesse de, 380, 412.
Lussan, Mademoiselle de, 411.
Luttrell, Colonel Henry, 181.
    Colonel Simon, 181, 222.
Luxembourg, Marshal, 317, 326, 352.
Lynchs, the, 183.
Lytcott, Sir John, 384.

MacCarthy, Father, 209.
Macdonnel, Captain, 268.
Magimis, Captain, 269.
Maguire, 176.
Maine, Duc de, 18, 59, 73, 87, 299, 352.
    Duchesse de, 259.
Maintenon, Madame de, 53, 72, 83, 86, 99, 122, 248, 293, 296, 299, 326, 352, 371, 397, 408, 424.
Manchester, Earl of, 403, 408, 413, 416.
Maria d'Este, flight of, 19.
    retirement to Chaillot, 115.
Marlborough, Duchess of, 161, 193.
Martinash, Mr, 268.
Mary, Queen, death of, 351.
Maumont, 145, 171, 214.
Maxwell, Captain Robert, 416.
Meereroon, Madame, 315.
Melani, Abbé, 13, 54, 80, 109.
Melfort, Lord, 97, 130, 152, 190, 210, 213, 222, 226, 250, 267, 277, 307, 320, 347, 405.
    Lady, 152, 194, 280.
Middleton, Earl of, 31, 40, 84, 268, 279, 319, 322, 348, 416, 424, 429.
    Lady, 279.
Mignard, 118, 280, 349.
Misset, 178.
Modena, Duke of, 50, 77, 92, 108, 349.
Mohun, Lord, 291.
Molza, Count, 267.
Mons, siege of, 292.
Montespan, Madame de, 18, 61, 86, 98, 247, 299.
Montpensier, Mademoiselle de, 47, 81, 319.
Moor, Dr Michael, 208.
Moore, Colonel Roger, 201.
Mountcashel, Lord, 152, 165, 173, 181, 222, 225, 233.
    Lady Arabella, 195.
Mountjoy, Lord, 164, 299, 317.
Mulgrave, Earl of, 36.

Nagle, Sir Richard, 268, 302, 400.
Nairne, Secretary, 334.
Namur, siege of, 315, 352.
Nantes, Edict of, 105.
Neagle, Sir Robert, 271.

Nevil, Mr, 268.
Newcastle, Duke of, 231.
Newton, 165.
Newton Butler, battle of, 225, 351.
Noailles, Duchesse de, 258.
Noble, Mr, 268.
Northumberland, George Fitzroy, Duke of, 25.
Nottingham, Daniel Finch, Earl of, 30.
Nugent, Lord Chief Justice, 222.

Oates, Titus, 161.
O'Brien, Miss, 81.
O'Donnell, Balldearg, 186.
O'Donnells, the, 183.
O'Donovans, the, 183.
O'Kelly, Captain Denis, 176, 182.
O'Neills, the, 183.
Orange, Mary of, 115, 127, 251, 255.
    William of, 2, 6, 31, 84, 94, 104, 115, 138, 143, 179, 198, 207, 213, 230, 234, 250, 257, 282, 303, 306, 317, 323, 363, 370, 375, 385, 409.
Orléans, Duc d' (Monsieur), 56, 63, 68, 119, 247, 258.
    Duchesse d' (Madame), 72, 94, 195, 247, 256, 282, 368, 371, 408, 412, 426.
Ormonde, James Butler, Duke of, 159, 203.
O'Toole, 178.

Palmer, Anne, 81.
Paris, Archbishop of, 146.
Parker, 236.
Parliament, Act of, 394.
Parry, 269, 363.
Paulet, Lord, 291.
Pendergrass, 362.
Penn, William, 251, 257.
Perth, Duchess of, 281.
    Earl of, 132, 269, 274, 367, 385, 404, 424.
Peterborough, Earl of, 10, 329.
Petre, Father, 83, 384.
Petty, Sir William, 158.
Ployden, Mr, 269, 364.
Pointis, 214.
Ponton, M., 45.
Pope, 274.
"Popish Plot," the, 161.
Porter, James, 96, 129, 220, 231, 268.
Portland, Earl of, 266, 268, 304, 362, 370, 375, 388.
Portsmouth, Louise de Querouaille, Duchess of, 66, 75, 135, 283.
Powell, Mr, 357.
Powis, Lady, 16, 21, 57, 79, 108, 152, 195, 267.
    Herbert, Lord, 16, 67, 152, 190, 222, 263, 268, 307, 309.
Preston, Viscount, 31, 253.
Priolo, La Mère, 122, 135, 260, 296, 313, 318, 344, 355, 360, 367, 378, 406, 410, 416, 419.
Prior, Matthew, 266, 268.
Puis, Mr du, 267.
Pusignan, 145, 171, 214.

Racine, 100.
Rancé, Abbé de, 333, 339, 378.
Rangoni, Marchese, 78.
Rénaudaux, Abbé, 361.
Rheims, Archbishop of, 80.
Rice, Baron, 299, 302.
    Sir Stephen, 222.
Richmond, Duke of, 66, 135.
Rigaud, 118, 280.
Riva, Francesco, 20, 51, 268.
Rizzini, Abbé, 14, 78, 90, 108.

Rochefoucauld, De la, 393.
Rogé, Mrs, 267.
Rohan, Duc de, 381.
Ronchi, Messrs, 268.
Rongère, M. de la, 282.
Rosen, General, 145, 172, 206, 226, 231.
Ruga, Father, 267.
Russell, Admiral, 166, 307, 327, 363.
Ryswick, Treaty of, 375.

Sabrian, Father, 267.
Sackville, Colonel, 289.
Saint-Simon, 17, 56, 68, 110, 131, 149, 151, 294, 326, 354, 381, 389.
Saint-Victor, 22.
Sarsfield, Captain Patrick, 174, 222, 238, 280, 302, 309, 326.
Saunders, Father, 271.
Savoy, Duke of, 371.
  Princess of, 371, 379.
Saxony, Elector of, 105, 366.
Scarron, 86.
Schomberg, 135, 153, 209, 225.
Seaforth, Lady, 195.
  Lord, 152.
Sedley, Catharine, 331.
Settlement, Repeal of Act of, 217.
Sévigné, Madame de, 49, 66, 72, 80, 95, 144, 377.
Sheldon, Ralph, 25, 84.
Shrewsbury, Lord, 37, 330.
Sidney, Henry, 260.
Sims, Mrs, 268.
Skelton, Colonel Bevil, 7, 15, 31, 113.
  Charles, 81, 267.
Slingsbee, 269.
Smith, Alderman, 220.
Smyrna fleet, loss of, 325.
Sobieski, Clementina, Princess, 178.
  John, 366.
Solmes, Count de, 36.
Sophia, Electress, 412.
Spain, King of, 371, 374, 386, 404, 409.
  death of, 415.
Sparrow, Sir Joseph, 267.
St George, Chevalier de, 19.
St Ruth, General, 302, 351.
Stafford, Dr Alexius, 208.
  Francis, 268.
  John, 267.
  Mrs, 329, 365.
Steinkirk, battle of, 317.
Stevens, Captain John, 168.
Strafford, Lord, 195.
Strickland, Vice-Admiral, 52.
  Vice-Chamberlain, 267.
  Lady, 21, 267.
  Sir Roger, 268.

Strickland, Mr Robert, 267.
Sunderland, Earl of, 6, 62, 149.
Sussex, Countess of, 81, 103.
Swift, Dean, 178.

Talbot, Dick, 155.
  Peter, 155.
  Sir William, 155, 222.
Talmash, General, 330.
Temple, Sir William, 260.
Terriesi, 18, 62.
Tessé, de, 302.
Torrington, Lord, 243.
Tourville, Count de, 243, 309, 317.
Travanion, Captain, 268.
Treaty, Second Partition, 415.
Tree, de la, 84.
Trelawney, John, 291.
Trémouille, M. de, 67.
Trevanion, 269.
  Captain, 42.
Turene, Mr and Mrs, 267.
Turnbull, Sir William, 274.
Turner, Bishop, 253.
Tuscany, Grand Duke of, 18, 62, 81, 93.
Tyrconnel, Lady, 193, 201, 208, 238, 267, 281, 293, 355.
  Lord, 111, 138, 154, 167, 173, 187, 190, 196, 213, 222, 244, 281, 301.

Ulster, Prince of, 186.
Ussen, d', 302.

Vallière, Mademoiselle de la, 61, 95, 117.
Van Citters, 8.
Vanhomrigh, Bartholomew, 207.
Vaudemont, 352.
Ventadour, Madame de, 103.
Villeroy, Duc de, 352.
Vivel, 269.

Waldegrave, Lord, 136, 350.
  Henrietta, 350.
  Sir William, 267, 329, 364, 368, 424.
Wales, James, Prince of, 6, 13, 24, 41, 44, 64, 92, 118, 129, 178, 262, 297, 306, 309, 321, 323, 354, 364, 367, 387, 392, 403, 409, 426.
Walgrave, Lady, 267.
Walgrave, Mrs, 267.
Warner, Father, 267.
White, 194, 267.
Winchelsea, Lord, 29.
Wogan, Sir Charles, 178.
Woodstock, Lord, 389.
Worcester, Marquis of, 231, 291.

Zulestein, 34.

CPSIA information can be obtained at www.ICGtesting.com
Printed in the USA
LVOW12*1432080114

368610LV00006B/74/P